Builders of Ohio

Donated to Ohio Governors
Residence by Mary Alice
Mavrose - August 25, 2004

Builders of Ohio

A Biographical History

Edited by
WARREN VAN TINE AND
MICHAEL PIERCE

The Ohio State University Press
Columbus

Copyright © 2003 by The Ohio State University.
All rights reserved.

Library of Congress Cataloging-in-Publication Data

Builders of Ohio : a biographical history / edited by Warren Van Tine and Michael
Pierce.
    p. cm.
Includes bibliographical references and index.
  ISBN 0-8142-0951-3 (hardcover : alk. paper) — ISBN 0-8142-5121-8 (pbk. : alk.
paper) — ISBN 0-8142-9024-8 (CD-ROM) 1. Ohio—History—Miscellanea. 2.
Ohio—Biography. 3. Pioneers—Ohio—Biography. 4. Politicians—Ohio—Biography.
5. Social reformers—Ohio—Biography. 6. Businessmen—Ohio—Biography. I. Van
Tine, Warren R. II. Pierce, Michael D. (Michael Dale)
F491.6.B85 2003
977.1'009'9—dc22

2003017391

Text and jacket design by The Former Factory Design Company.
Type set in Adobe Galliard.
Printed by Thomson-Shore, Inc.

The paper used in this publication meets the minimum requirements of the American
National Standard for Information Sciences—Permanence of Paper for Printed
Library Materials. ANSI Z39.48–1992.

9 8 7 6 5 4 3 2 1

Contents

Introduction

WARREN VAN TINE AND MICHAEL PIERCE

N EAR THE end of his fourth and final term as governor of Ohio, James A. Rhodes was the guest of honor at the unveiling of a statue of him—one that the governor had convinced the General Assembly to erect—on the statehouse lawn. There, his likeness joined statues of William McKinley, James Garfield, and others the state had deemed fit to memorialize, although few passersby can recite their deeds or accomplishments. By installing an idealized piece of bronze to symbolize his historical legacy, Rhodes assured that he would be remembered even if his historical role was not understood. The purpose of this book is to take the states' history beyond the homage of statues. That is, it seeks to humanize rather than memorialize Ohioans who have played important roles in the state's past.

Unlike the statehouse statues, this work is not an uncritical celebration of the state's past. There are certainly events recounted here that most Ohioans will deem worthy of praise, such as John Parker's escape from slavery, Tom Johnson's rise from poverty, and the efforts of Philander Chase and William Oxley Thompson to create a system of higher education that met the needs of the state. But there are also things in the state's past and in this book that most Ohioans will find uncomfortable, such as the mistreatment of Native Americans, the persecution of African Americans, and the inequities that accompanied industrialization. This volume contains both the positive and negative; the editors believe that an honest portrayal of Ohio's past is the best way to celebrate it.

The twenty-four essays in this volume use biography to explore Ohio's history. They are not intended to provide a narrative history offering encyclopedic coverage or describing events in chronological order. Nonetheless, they do provide a historical overview of the state's development from George Croghan's search for fame and fortune on the eighteenth-century frontier through Dave Thomas's creation of a fast food empire in the late twentieth century. Each chapter also addresses important events and transformations in the state's history such as European settlement, Native American resistance, the creation of territorial and state governments, the development of the state's educational and economic institutions, the disruptions created by the Civil War, the struggle of African Americans and women to participate in Ohio's public life, efforts to ameliorate the pernicious effects of industrialization, the negotiation of the state's role in a nation increasingly dominated by the federal government, and the ramifications of deindustrialization and rise of a service economy.

The editors chose the biographical approach for three reasons. First, the volume seeks to bring the work of academic historians to a wider audience. With its strong narrative structure and attention to the personal, biography can do just that. Second, the biographical approach underscores the contingent nature of history and the agency of individuals. In other words, history is not simply the interplay of impersonal social and economic forces; it is how individual actors responded to these forces to create the worlds in which they lived. Third, as historian David Brion Davis has observed, "By showing how cultural tensions and contradictions may be internalized, struggled with, and resolved within actual individuals, biography offers the most promising synthesis of culture and history."

These biographies are not necessarily of the most famous Ohioans. In fact, few of the twenty-five individuals are household names. Ohioans such as Pete Rose and Neil Armstrong will certainly always be better known than the likes of Benjamin Arnett or Frances Dana Gage or John Campbell. This is not to suggest that Rose and Armstrong are unworthy of scholarly attention. Certainly, Rose's career could be used to illuminate the role of celebrity in late-twentieth-century America and Armstrong's the race for technological superiority during the Cold War, but they tell us little about the state's development or what distinguished Ohio from other states or the nation as a whole. Likewise, the editors have not included essays examining Ohioans whose primary area of influence was on the national stage. Hence, there are no essays surveying the lives of William McKinley, Ulysses S. Grant, and numerous other Ohioans who have played important roles in national affairs. These individuals also tell us less about Ohio than they do about the United States as a whole.

The essays emphasize political and economic developments because that is what makes the state distinctive. Ohio is foremost a

political entity. The state was created by an act of Congress, its boundaries established as much by political intrigue as geography, and it is
only through their common citizenship that Ohioans are bound
together as Ohioans. The state's people are not united by some loosely
defined common culture or social system that terminates at the state's
borders. This in no way suggests that the state's cultural or literary figures should not be studied but that the likes of William Dean Howells,
Paul Lawrence Dunbar, and Sherwood Anderson tell us more about
regional, ethnic, or American cultures than they do about what is distinct about Ohio. If Anderson had entitled his famous novel *Winesburg, Indiana* or *Winesburg, Michigan* would that have changed the
work or how people perceived it in any substantive way?

Besides offering insight into specific periods and events, the essays
as a whole paint a picture of Ohio as a state that has struggled to come
to terms with opportunity. The earliest white settlers came to Ohio in
pursuit of economic success. Since that time, the state has continued
to attract newcomers seeking economic opportunity, from those
already with comfortable means, such as Thomas Worthington, to
those on the edge of poverty, such as African American women Jane
Edna Hunter sought to assist. In fact, only ten of the twenty-five individuals examined in this volume were born within the state. The rest
migrated either from within the United States or from Europe. Five
came from the southern United States, six from the East Coast north
of the Mason-Dixon line, one from the western United States, and
three from the other side of the Atlantic Ocean.

While roughly one-third of the individuals covered in this volume
could honestly claim humble origins, the majority climbed from economic comfort and social acceptance to affluence and prominence. Yet
the search for opportunity in Ohio did not guarantee sustained success. The last great land proprietor, John Cleves Symmes, died in
poverty as did Indian trader George Croghan; Florence Allen never
gained the seat she coveted on the U.S. Supreme Court; and Benjamin
Arnett fell from grace in the eyes of both the Republican Party and the
African American community. The industrial and moral values that
brought John Campbell early success were unable to sustain Ironton's
future. Similarly, John Bricker's aggressive advocacy of Old Guard
Republicanism brought him a successful political career that ended
ignominiously.

No matter what their origins or their individual successes and failures, the people covered in this volume insisted that it was the government's responsibility to protect their prospects. Symmes campaigned to

have Congress recognize his land claims; George H. Pendleton promoted both the Pendleton Plan and civil service reform; George
DeNucci used law and political pressure to advance workers' interests;
and James A. Rhodes dedicated state government to providing
Ohioans with "Jobs and Progress." In each case, Ohioans turned to
the political system to protect and advance their opportunities.

Still, throughout the state's history, Ohioans have debated the
limits of this opportunity: Who should be given the opportunity to
participate in civic life? Who should be allowed to attend public
schools? How much should the government use its power to ensure
economic and political opportunity? To some degree or another,
every subject of this volume wrestled with at least one of these questions. For the framers of Ohio's first constitution, the answers were
obvious. In keeping with their times, they extended the franchise only
to white, male taxpayers and created a government so weak that it
could not possibly impinge upon individual liberty. The first generation of the state's leaders also evicted Native Americans, erected barriers to keep African Americans—both slave and free—out, and
denied women the right to vote and, in some cases, to hold property.
The strength and endurance of this vision is reflected in the selection
of individuals to be profiled in this volume; seventeen of twenty-five
are white males. Today, few Ohioans favor restricting full citizenship
on account of gender, race, or financial status, and, although they
might debate particular policies, most feel that the state government
has a positive responsibility to promote the general welfare.

The volume's essays collectively document the transformations
that changed Ohio into a more egalitarian and activist state. These
changes resulted from long and contested processes, as the struggles
for African American rights demonstrates. The struggles began in the
years before the Civil War as abolitionists such as Frances Dana Gage
and John Parker pressed for the end of slavery, arguing not only that
slavery was inhumane but that it also robbed African Americans of
their natural rights. Other Ohioans, including Clement Vallandigham
and George Pendleton, opposed both the abolition of slavery and the
granting of citizenship rights to African Americans, arguing that such
actions would threaten the rights and opportunities of white males.
During Reconstruction and the Gilded Age, African Americans such
as Benjamin Arnett worked within the Republican Party to secure the
rights of citizenship (including voting), support for African American
higher education, and integrated schools. Many of these gains, however, were temporary. After the turn of the century, men like William

Oxley Thompson led efforts to resegregate public schools and limit African American access to higher education. He expressed the opinion of many white Ohioans when he stated, "our fathers in the North thought that the ballot was essential to the freedom of the colored race . . . [but] most of their sons regard that as a mistaken theory." As the twentieth century progressed, black migration to Ohio increased, and African Americans, such as Jane Edna Hunter and Carl Stokes, demanded equal access to jobs, educational opportunities, housing, and political institutions.

In the interest of readability and brevity, the authors have omitted footnotes and formal bibliographies. Those seeking additional information should consult the suggestions for further readings at the end of each essay.

1

George Croghan and the Emergence of British Influence on the Ohio Frontier

ALFRED A. CAVE

T HE MAN whose skills as an Indian trader and negotiator were instrumental in opening the Ohio country to British influence and later to white occupation was an immigrant of origins so obscure and lowly that we do not know the date of his birth. Despite his later prominence, no painter preserved his likeness, and no writer described his appearance. His life, colorful and turbulent, deserved but did not command the talents of a contemporary chronicler. Born in poverty in Ireland sometime during the second decade of the eighteenth century, George Croghan was driven from his native land by the potato famine of 1741. Settling in Pennsylvania, he quickly emerged as one of the most resourceful, successful, and prosperous of the colony's frontier Indian traders and land speculators.

Few of his colleagues or competitors could match Croghan's rare capacity to understand the hopes, fears, and expectations of Indian clients and use that understanding to his advantage. Hard drinking, flamboyant, generous, cunning (sometimes ruthless), and poorly educated, George Croghan was the quintessential frontier entrepreneur. His relationships with Native Americans, with colonial officials, and with his business partners were seldom simple and often less than straightforward. A complex man of driving ambition and great ability, he made—and squandered—several fortunes. But his most substantial achievements were in the public arena, where he excelled as a frontier diplomat and peacemaker. While misgivings about his character were rampant, there is not doubt about his impact on Ohio history. The story of Anglo-American Ohio begins with George Croghan.

Prior to 1763, France claimed the Old Northwest as part of Canada. Groghan, one of several hundred British traders who challenged that claim, established in the fall of 1744 a trading post at a Seneca village at the mouth of the Cuyahoga River, the future site of the city of Cleveland. French efforts to incite the Ottawa and the Miami to attack Croghan and his associates were unavailing. French pretensions notwithstanding, English trade goods were greatly in demand among the Indians of the region, as they cost less than French offerings and were of higher quality. Moreover, a British naval blockade soon left French traders short of supplies. Croghan, conversant in several Native American languages, made the most of those advantages. In 1747, he instigated an Indian uprising against the French, sending the scalp of a French trader with his report to the governor of Pennsylvania. With help from the Iroquois on the shores of Lake Erie, Croghan extended his trading activities to the west and south. Given his exceptional rapport with his Indian clients, the Iroquois in 1746 admitted him to the governing council of their league at Onondaga.

Croghan joined the veteran Indian agent Conrad Weiser in advocating an aggressive British diplomatic initiative to open trade and win allies in the Ohio country. Both realized that Pennsylvania's long established policy of conducting Indian diplomacy through the League of the Iroquois could no longer provide security. The westward migration of Delaware and Shawnee Indians displaced by British colonial expansion had undermined the influence of the Iroquois, their nominal overlords. Concurrently, French traders in the region actively threatened British interests. After much prodding, Pennsylvania authorities authorized direct negotiations with the western Indians. In the spring of 1748, the colony dispatched Croghan and a pack train loaded with gifts to Logstown, an Indian trading village near modern-day Pittsburgh, where he met with Iroquois and Shawnee leaders and with representatives of the Miami, a western Ohio tribe hostile to the French.

Croghan's mission paved the way for an alliance between the Miami and the British. In 1749, he established a substantial trading post on the Great Miami River at the Miami village called Pickawillany. Although France was now technically at peace with Great Britain, a French official at Detroit placed a price on Croghan's scalp. Alarmed by British incursions, Quebec authorities dispatched a military expedition of several hundred men under the command of Captain Pierre Joseph de Céloron de Blainville to the Ohio Valley to reassert French military and commercial power. Throughout the West, after warning Indian village leaders not to deal with the British intruders, Céloron planted lead plates that proclaimed French sovereignty. Everywhere, Céloron reported, he encountered resistance to his demand that Indians refuse to buy from British traders, around one hundred of whom worked directly for Croghan and his partners. Their pack trains laden with goods reached far to the south and west of Pickawillany. Soon, their presence was reported in the Illinois country and in Kentucky.

Despite his early success in detaching Ohio Indians from the French commercial orbit, Croghan's enterprise went bankrupt by 1753. A renewed French offensive, beginning with the massacre of Miami Indians at Pickawillany and leading to the building of Fort Duquesne at the forks of the Ohio River, intimidated his Indian associates and drove his traders from the interior. As Croghan recalled some years later, "We had trusted great quantities of Goods to the traders, the Chief of them were ruined by Robberies committed on them by the French and their Indians." He added that "those which were not quite ruined when the French army came down" were bankrupted "by Indians being prevented from hunting, from which means we lost all." Fifty-two of Croghan's agents had been either killed or imprisoned by the French by 1754. The flow of furs from the interior into Croghan's warehouses dried up.

Despite bankruptcy and allegations that he had fabricated an Indian request for the establishment of a British fort at the head of the Ohio Valley, Croghan nonetheless remained in demand as an Indian negotiator. In 1752, he assisted the Ohio Company, a land venture chartered by the Virginia Colony, in its efforts to secure Iroquois support for the establishment of a company trading post and settlement at the forks of the Allegheny and Monongahela Rivers. Although Virginia's claims in the area were bitterly opposed by Pennsylvania authorities, Croghan in 1749 had obtained from the Iroquois a 200,000-acre land grant near the lands the Ohio Company planned to occupy. He hoped to profit from the company's promotion of British settlement in the area.

When French military occupation threatened to terminate all British activity in the West, Croghan worked hard under adverse circumstances to neutralize French influence among the Indians of the region. The results were mixed, but Croghan saw possibilities in war as well as in peace. He contracted to supply flour to the ill-fated Virginia military expedition dispatched in 1754 under the command of

Colonel George Washington to dislodge the French from the forks of
the Ohio. He also promised the colonel that he would recruit a substantial number of Indian allies. Croghan's inability to fulfill those
commitments further damaged his reputation. Washington declared
him the least trustworthy of the Indian traders.

Pennsylvania authorities shared Washington's distrust of George
Croghan. But with the coming of the French and Indian War, they
could ill afford to dispense with his services. He was too well regarded
by the Indians of the Ohio Valley. In recognition of the colony's need
of Croghan's assistance, the Pennsylvania Assembly passed a bill
granting him a ten-year reprieve from the claims of his creditors. After
Washington's defeat, Croghan was engaged to survey two wilderness
roads for General Edward Braddock's army. When Delaware and
Shawnee leaders, offended by the high-handed manner of Braddock
and his officers, failed to supply warriors for the campaign against the
French, Croghan recruited nearly one hundred Mingo who had gathered at his estate at Aughwick on the Pennsylvania frontier. All but
eight of those warriors deserted soon after their arrival in Braddock's
camp. Croghan's friend and Oneida chief Scarouady later explained
that Braddock was "a bad man" who would not listen to Indians but
treated them "like dogs." Croghan and the eight remaining Indian
scouts were with Braddock at his defeat and death near the forks of
the Ohio on July 9, 1755.

In October, the Delaware and Shawnee, emboldened by the
French victory, attacked Pennsylvania frontier settlements. Receiving
the rank of captain in December 1755 from the colony's War Commission, Croghan raised a small, private militia to protect his exposed
and vulnerable plantation at Aughwick. Ordered to build and garrison a chain of frontier forts, Captain Croghan returned to western
Pennsylvania at the head of a force of 180 men. Establishing his headquarters at the newly constructed Fort Shirley, he soon recruited several hundred more. However, disputes with the commissioners over
his expenditures combined with criticism of his informal and friendly
relationships with his men, impelled the headstrong Irish trader to
resign his captaincy in March 1756. His shaky reputation in the east,
diminished by his refusal to continue military service, was further
damaged by rumors that he was secretly a Roman Catholic disloyal to
England. The rumors were false and may well have been the work of
one of Croghan's many disaffected creditors.

Disheartened by his poor relationship with colonial authorities
and with Philadelphia merchants, Croghan in the late spring of 1756

moved to New York, where he attached himself to Sir William Johnson, England's newly appointed superintendent of Indian affairs for the northern colonies. Johnson valued Croghan's exceptional command of several Native American languages and his uncommon understanding of Indian customs and values. After Croghan assisted Johnson in a round of negotiations with the Iroquois, Delaware, and Shawnee, he won a salaried appointment as Johnson's deputy superintendent.

Although Croghan and Indian auxiliaries he recruited fought some engagements in New York in the summer and fall of 1756, Croghan's most important contributions to the British victory in the French and Indian War were made not on the battlefield but at council fires. The British lacked the military capacity to defeat France's Native American allies and secure the West, but a diplomatic offensive might well secure, at minimum, Indian neutrality. France's difficulties in resupplying its Indian supporters hurt its cause. However, suspicion of British intentions kept Indian belligerency alive. The Indians remained mindful of General Braddock's earlier declaration that "no savage should inherit land." It fell to frontier diplomats to provide the assurances needed to allay Native American anxieties.

Late in 1756, Pennsylvania initiated peace talks with the Delaware. The British military commander in North America, Lord Loudon, was appalled by the prospect of colonial governments dealing independently with Indian belligerents, and Sir William Johnson dispatched George Croghan to Philadelphia to take charge of the negotiations on behalf of the Crown. After listening to Indians and weighing their grievances, Croghan recommended that the colony invite both Teedyuscung, "king" of the eastern Delaware, and leaders of the tribes that had resettled in the Ohio Valley to a treaty conference as soon as possible. Overcoming their prejudice against Croghan, indeed swayed by his charm and eloquence, the Pennsylvania authorities agreed to cooperate.

Even so, continual bickering between the Quakers and the Proprietors (descendents of William Penn who had inherited his proprietary rights) greatly complicated Croghan's task, already made difficult by Indian distrust of the English. Teedyuscung, with the encouragement of the Quaker faction, demanded restitution for losses suffered in the notorious "Walking Treaty" of 1737, wherein the Proprietors had invoked an old deed of questionable authenticity to divest the Delaware of much of their land in eastern Pennsylvania. Western Delaware and Shawnee, previously driven west by land hungry whites, feared British occupation of their new homelands in the Ohio Valley. Croghan presided over treaty proceedings at Lancaster, Pennsylvania, in May. With the help of the Quakers and of a large gift provided by the colonial assembly, he made much progress in winning over the western Indians. But Teedyuscung remained disaffected. After a brief diplomatic mission to the Cherokee, Croghan conducted new negotiations with the eastern Delaware at Easton in July. The Quakers, agreeing that the 1737 treaty was fraudulent, urged the Delaware not to compromise. But the Proprietors' representatives opposed consideration of Teedyuscung's land grievances. Croghan, steering a course between the two English factions, antagonized both but did succeed in obtaining a peace treaty with the eastern Delaware. The Pennsylvania frontier was now relatively secure, but Croghan warned Johnson that the Proprietors' eagerness to acquire more western land could well lead to new hostilities. Proprietor Thomas Penn responded by advising Johnson that Croghan was "a bad man," not to be trusted.

Knowing that his deputy had kept the Crown's interests foremost in his dealings, Johnson disregarded Penn's complaint. He dispatched the Irish trader to Fort Herkimer, a strategically critical and exposed frontier post on the Mohawk River. There Croghan, accompanied by his Indian spouse, traded with the Iroquois and gathered intelligence on French activities. After providing support to an unsuccessful offensive against Fort Ticonderoga in 1758, Croghan returned to Pennsylvania to conduct a new round of treaty negotiations at Easton. In addition to winning over the Seneca, an Iroquois nation whose ranks included many French sympathizers, he endeavored to resolve a power struggle between Teedyuscung, by now a drunken megalomaniac who claimed to be king of all Indians, and the representatives of the League of the Iroquois, who demanded restoration of their previous preeminence in Pennsylvania Indian matters. Croghan won over the Iroquois by securing revocation of a controversial 1754 land purchase and by marginalizing the troublesome Teedyuscung who fared poorly in the proceedings. Maligned by the Quakers for failing to support the Delaware chief's demand for immediate settlement of the Walking Treaty claim, Croghan retaliated by circulating, with Johnson's help, an outrageous rumor that Quakers had been encouraging the Indians to massacre non-Quaker white settlers. While his conduct in that instance, and on other occasions, left much to be desired from an ethical point of view, his skill as an Indian negotiator had once again helped pacify the frontier for Great Britain.

The Easton Treaty of 1758, partially neutralized France's Indian allies and paved the way for General John Forbes's successful occupation of the forks of the Ohio in the fall of that year. Although Pennsylvania leaders still expressed doubts about Croghan's character and integrity, particularly in financial matters, they generally conceded that no one else could have dealt as successfully with the Iroquois. To guard against a renewal of Delaware belligerency, Croghan accompanied Forbes's army, assisting Colonel Henry Bouquet in offering Delaware leaders appropriate assurances regarding the British resolve to respect their rights. His dealings with the Delaware were, however, somewhat controversial, and to some extent created unnecessary tensions. The Delaware chiefs denied Croghan's claim that they had asked for the establishment of a permanent English fort at the head of the Ohio Valley. In addition to playing his role as an agent of the British Indian service, Croghan apparently reasoned that British occupation would enhance the value of his land holdings. A friend of the Indian, Croghan was also a land speculator, and throughout most of his career he juggled his private interests and public responsibilities.

In the spring of 1759, Croghan, after a sojourn to Philadelphia, returned to the Ohio country, where he sought through diplomacy to counter renewed French influence among the Delaware and the Shawnee. Holding several peace conferences that summer, Croghan, through verbal persuasion and astute gift giving, won over several hundred warriors formerly committed to France. In the last year of the French and Indian War, the Irishman provided invaluable service both as a leader of Indian forces now allied to England and as a negotiator with those who remained hostile. His mission to Detroit, as part of a force led by Robert Rogers, secured a peaceful transfer of power at that crucial outpost.

Paradoxically, the defeat of France led to renewed frontier warfare. Over the objections of Croghan, Johnson, and other experienced Indian agents, the British commander in North America, Lord Jeffrey Amherst, believing that Indians were lazy parasites who no longer needed to be won over through "bribes," terminated the long-standing practice of gift giving. Ignoring those who warned that such practices in Native American cultures secured peace, by confirming alliances based on fictive kinship, Amherst compounded the offense by restricting trade, raising prices, and seizing some Iroquois lands as prizes for his officers. Amherst's restrictions on the supply of ammunition to Indian hunters led to both deep resentment and real hardship. Croghan dipped into his own diminished resources to help out his Indian friends. Soon his distaste for Amherst's methods impelled him to make plans to leave the Indian service altogether.

After conducting treaty negotiations at Lancaster (a task made difficult by the continued involvement of his Quaker enemies), in the spring of 1762 Croghan began exploring ways of rebuilding his fortune through private involvement in trade and land speculation. Croghan used his position to secure access to choice properties now made available by the Pennsylvania land office. He soon held title to vast sections of western Pennsylvania. But the outbreak of the series of frontier uprisings, later erroneously named "the Conspiracy of Pontiac," would force Croghan to delay plans to end his official service. In October 1762, he had warned Amherst that an Indian uprising was likely if the new, restrictive policies on gifts and trade were not modified. Amherst dismissed his concern, writing of the Indians "it is not in their power to hurt us." Croghan then appealed to Sir William Johnson, saying of the war he now felt was inevitable "how itt [sic] may end the Lord knows." But Johnson also lacked influence with Amherst.

In May 1763, warriors led by the Ottawa chief Pontiac besieged Detroit. In the same year, and in 1764, local war parties struck British forts and settlements from the Great Lakes to the Ohio Valley. Although Pontiac, contrary to later myth, was not the leader of a vast "conspiracy," the belligerents shared common grievances and anxieties. Amherst's policies exacerbated perennial fears of British expansionism. Rumors were rampant that the British would kill all Indians and take their land in punishment for their earlier support of France. Many of the insurgents hoped for the return of the French, who were esteemed for their respect for Indian territorial rights. Some, including Pontiac, were also influenced by the teachings of nativist prophets such as the Delaware holy man Neolin, who proclaimed that the Great Spirit was angered by Indian toleration of European invaders on lands meant for Indians. These prophets declared that Indians who resisted European territorial aggression and ceased their emulation of European ways would enjoy supernatural aid. Although the insurgents were unable to take the British forts at Detroit and Pittsburgh, they destroyed smaller British posts throughout the frontier and put numerous small white settlements to the torch. Pontiac and other leaders of the northwest nativist uprisings of 1763–64 were not able to attain their objectives, but they were not defeated either. Despite Amherst's insistence that there be no compromise and that all insurgents be put to death, the fighting was finally terminated after Amherst's departure, not by decisive British victories on the battlefield and summary executions but by a negotiated peace.

George Croghan would play a major role in these negotiations. Shortly after the outbreak of hostilities, Croghan had resigned from the Indian service. Declining a military command, he sailed for England to seek restitution for his financial losses and pursue various business opportunities. During his stay in London, he presented to the Board of Trade a plan for the future management of Indian affairs drawn up, with his help, by Sir William Johnson. The plan essentially called for the repudiation of Amherst's policies. Croghan urged the Board of Trade to give the superintendents of Indian affairs greater power. His remarks were well received and led to measures to reduce colonial and military interference with the work of the Department of Indian Affairs. He was so frustrated, however, in his hopes for personal financial restitution and so disgusted by the arrogance and sloth of imperial officials that he left London. In a comment prophetic of troubles to come, Croghan wrote, "the cheefe study of the pople in power here att present is to lay heavy taxes on the coloneys." As to their understanding of real conditions in America, he declared the members of the Board of Trade "imensly ignerant."

Returning to New York in the late summer of 1764, Croghan called on Johnson to report on his accomplishments in London. He discovered that his resignation from the Indian service had never been processed. Armed with the new authority granted to the Department of Indian Affairs, Croghan resumed his old role. His reappearance angered Colonel Henry Bouquet who complained to General Gage, "one can not but regret that powers of so great importance to this country should in this instance have been trusted to a man so illiterate, imprudent, and ill bred."

Others had a better appreciation of Croghan's talents. When the time came to negotiate peace, Croghan presided over a congress of Indian nations of the Ohio Valley at Fort Pitt in May 1765. He then undertook an arduous and risky expedition westward to seek peace with the tribes of the Wabash region and to secure acceptance of British authority from the Illinois Indians. On June 8, a party of Kickapoos attacked his expedition near the Wabash, wounding most of the whites and killing three of his Shawnee associates. Croghan later wrote: "I got the stroke of a hatchett on the head, but my scull being pretty thick, the hatchet would not enter, so you may see a thick scull is of some service on some occasions." Despite that setback, Croghan

persevered and finally secured an apology from the Kickapoo and a
peace agreement. In July, he met with the Illinois and brought them
into the British orbit. Pontiac had settled among the Illinois after the
collapse of the siege of Detroit. Realizing that the time had come to
make peace, Pontiac now assisted Croghan in his dealings with the
Illinois and then accompanied the Irishman to Detroit where he
helped in negotiations with representatives of a number of tribes
there. The Indian rebellion was over. The commander at Detroit,
Colonel John Campbell, not only praised Croghan's "great care &
attention" in Indian diplomacy but informed General Thomas Gage
that the Indians of the region "prefer him to any other person."

Croghan's participation in the peace negotiations, invaluable to
the Crown, was not disinterested. With several business partners,
Croghan had entered into an ambitious scheme to circumvent
wartime restrictions on trade with the western Indians by disguising
private trade goods, including scalping knives, as part of the Crown's
peacemaking gifts. A road accident in Pennsylvania had exposed the
knives and triggered a public outcry against Croghan, who unsuccessfully tried to deny his involvement. In a letter to Sir William Johnson, General Gage wrote that he was disturbed to learn that Croghan
had entered into "leagues with traders to carry goods in a clandestine
manner. . . . Mr. Croghan thought to take advantage of his employment to be first in the market." Croghan had broken the law that forbade Indian agents engaging in the Indian trade. For that, the general reprimanded him.

Croghan's private interests were not, however, limited to trade.
He was also promoting a visionary scheme to establish a British
colony in Illinois. He hoped to use his negotiations with the Illinois
Indians to lay the groundwork for later land grants, a plan that
Croghan had promoted while in England. After his return, he settled
in Philadelphia, bought an opulent estate called Monckton Hall, and
touted his Illinois venture to any person of influence and means who
would listen. To Benjamin Franklin, he wrote, "The Illinois country
far exceeds any other part of America that I have seen." Franklin
became one of Croghan's most ardent supporters.

Those who invested in Croghan's western schemes lost money.
The efforts to persuade London to establish a colonial government in
the Illinois country failed. The ample land grants in the West that
Croghan dreamed of did not materialize. Croghan's attempts to convince the British of the need to establish a substantial military presence on the Mississippi in order to dislodge French traders and take

control of the Indian trade were unsuccessful. The Board of Trade did not share Croghan's interest in western expansion but instead called for retrenchment. Merchants who entrusted trade goods to Croghan under the promise that they would be purchased by the Crown for presents to the Illinois tribes received only partial payment.

Croghan, summoned in 1766 to pacify Ohio Valley Indians angered by the gratuitous killing of their kinsmen by white intruders, once again demonstrated his brilliance as a diplomat. He would repeat that performance several more times, in the next few years, as white incursions on Indian land threatened to destroy the fragile peace. Croghan well understood the nature of Indian grievances and deplored the spirit of "mobb rule" that prevailed in white settlements in the West. He urged punishment of whites who invaded Indian territory. He deplored the atrocities that were a commonplace aspect of Indian-white interaction on the frontier. He lobbied for a new, enforceable boundary line between the colonies and the Indian nations allied to Great Britain, envisioning that some regions would be permanently closed to white settlement. Croghan was frequently at odds with the Black Boys, a vigilante-style group of Pennsylvania frontier ruffians who threatened to kill him if he continued to negotiate with "savages." He often traveled to treaty conferences with an armed escort. But while Croghan championed Indian rights in many ways, he also sought to persuade London that the line of demarcation should be extended westward, with appropriate compensation to the Indians displaced in the process. His motives were mixed. In part, he hoped to remove his Indian friends from harm's way. But he also expected to profit personally from the sale of western land. Croghan thus anticipated the next century's advocates of Indian removal. His own economic interests were now best served by removal. In the latter part of his business career, Croghan's hopes for the renewal of his fortune were vested in land speculation not in the fur trade of his youth.

Croghan's investments in land companies were extensive and, because of his official position, generally secret. His exploitation of opportunities afforded by the Treaty of Fort Stanwix of 1768 offers a telling example of his mode of operation. That agreement with the Iroquois opened vast tracts of western land to white settlement. Croghan purchased some 127,000 acres from the Iroquois *before* the treaty was negotiated, then lobbied for confirmation of his title. Protection of Croghan's interests was written into the treaty itself. The British government, however, balked at ratification of that clause. Lord Hillsborough, president of the Board of Trade, declared "private agreements with the Indians" illegal, a violation of the Proclamation of 1763. Croghan desperately sought to secure reversal of that judgment but failed. Pursued by creditors, ill with the gout and other infirmities, he abandoned an estate he had established in Iroquois country in western New York and took refuge at Croghan Hall near Fort Pitt in the summer of 1770.

Resuming his work as a negotiator, he was instrumental in preventing an Indian uprising in the Ohio Valley early in the decade but failed to prevent Lord Dunmore's war, a bloodletting triggered by the slaughter, by frontier ruffians, of the family of the Mingo Chief Logan in 1774. Engaged now primarily in private pursuits, Croghan's most promising speculation involved the proposed establishment of an inland colony to be called Vandalia. His efforts to satisfy creditors through sale of various other lands and properties were only partially successful. He remained at Fort Pitt to avoid imprisonment for debt in Pennsylvania or New York. A royal charter for Vandalia would have made Croghan a fabulously wealthy man, for his land holdings there, some acquired in secret negotiations with Indians, were vast. But that charter, although once promised by prominent officers of the Crown, never materialized.

The outbreak of the American Revolution destroyed his hopes for Vandalia. Although he supported the patriot cause, Croghan's enemies circulated unfounded rumors of his disloyalty. Arrested on a trumped-up charge of collusion with the British, he was forced to leave Croghan Hall and take refuge at his estate near Philadelphia, which was subsequently burned by the British army. Although finally exonerated by a Pennsylvania court, Croghan found no place in the new order. His health broken, his fortune gone, George Croghan died in poverty in 1782. He did not live to see his dreams for the West fulfilled. The future would bring the realization of his vision of white settlers building new states beyond the Allegheny Mountains. It would not, however, fulfill his hope that his Indian friends there would be treated with kindness and generosity.

Further Reading

Downes, Randolph C. *Council Fires on the Upper Ohio.* Pittsburgh: University of Pittsburgh Press, 1940.

McConnell, Michael N. *A Country Between: The Upper Ohio Valley and Its People, 1724–1774.* Lincoln: University of Nebraska Press, 1992.

Merrell, James H. *Into the American Woods: Negotiators on the Pennsylvania Frontier.* New York: W. W. Norton, 1999.

Volwiler, Albert T. *George Croghan and the Westward Movement, 1741–1782.* Cleveland: Arthur H. Clark Co., 1926.

Wainwright, Nicholas B. *George Croghan, Wilderness Diplomat.* Chapel Hill: University of North Carolina Press, 1959.

White, Richard. *The Middle Ground: Indians, Empires, and Republics in the Great Lakes Region, 1650–1815.* New York: Cambridge University Press, 1991.

2

John Cleves Symmes and the Miami Purchase

R. DOUGLAS HURT

J OHN CLEVES Symmes, who opened the Miami River country to
settlement, became the last great proprietor in name, if not in
fact, in U.S. history. In 1785, Symmes became interested in western
lands as a member of Congress from New Jersey. During May 1787,
at the age of forty-four, this Long Island–born Revolutionary War
veteran traveled west to the Wabash country in present-day Indiana
to investigate lands for colonization. Symmes liked the Wabash River
valley, and he soon informed Kentuckians in a circular that he would
solicit a land grant from Congress "not merely for himself, but on
behalf of all those who will signify to him their wishes to become
adventurers." Symmes proposed to meet interested settlers at
Louisville after he received confirmation of his grant. Then, they
would travel to Post St. Vincennes where the women and children
would remain "until a lodgment be effected and a town fortified at
the first eligible tract of country above that place." Symmes, however,
soon decided the Wabash country was too remote from suppliers and
adequate military protection to warrant the acquisition. Instead, he
cast his eyes on the Miami country, the lands between the Great and
Little Miami Rivers in present-day southwestern Ohio. Symmes chose
the Miami country sight unseen for a land grant based on the favorable reports of his friend Benjamin Stites, who had visited that area
about the time Symmes had traveled to the Wabash country.

The acquisition of a large land grant in the Miami country
appealed to Symmes not only because the region lay closer to major
suppliers in Pittsburgh, but also because the army had established in
1785 a presence at Fort Harmar at the mouth of the Muskingum
River, where the Ohio Company of Associates soon founded the

FIG. 1 Portrait of John Cleves Symmes by Charles Willson Peale,
1793 oil on canvas. Courtesy of the Miami University Art Museum.

town of Marietta. Indeed, after the Ohio Company applied for a grant
of 1.5 million acres west of the Ohio River on May 9, 1787, Symmes
petitioned Congress on August 29 for a grant of 2 million acres on
the same terms. Symmes asked Congress to begin the grant at the
mouth of the Great Miami River then run the southern boundary
eastward along the Ohio River to the mouth of the Little Miami
River. From there, the grant would run northward up the Little
Miami to a point where it intersected with a line that continued from
the northern boundary of the Ohio Company's purchase. The northern boundary would run west to the Great Miami River then downstream to the Ohio River.

Congress favorably received Symmes's petition and, on October 3,
1787, authorized the Board of Treasury to prepare a contract for the
two million acres that he requested. Symmes planned to pay for his
lands with military land warrants that Congress had authorized to pay
soldiers, in lieu of hard money, for their services during the American
Revolution. Like other speculators, Symmes planned to purchase
those warrants at less than face value from the holders who did not

want to move west and exchange their warrants for land. Symmes could then use those warrants at full face value to pay for lands that he acquired from the national government.

The Board of Treasury, in turn, authorized the geographer of the United States, Israel Ludlow, to survey the east and west boundaries of the grant. It also required Symmes, at his own expense, to survey and divide his tract into townships six miles square and sections one mile square according to the provisions of the Land Ordinance of 1785. This requirement included reserving specific tracts for Congress and the support of education and religion "unless the frequency of the Indian irruptions may render the same in a measure impracticable." The Board of Treasury required Symmes to pay one dollar per acre in either specie, certificates of debt to the United States (then worth about five shillings on the pound), or military land bounty warrants, provided the latter did not exceed one-seventh the value of the whole.

Congress, however, reduced the price per acre by one-third to compensate for poor lands. As a result, Symmes prepared to contract for the purchase of two million acres at 66⅔ cents per acre. Symmes had to pay $200,000 when he signed the contract for the land grant and a similar amount when the geographer completed his survey of the east and west boundaries of the tract. The Board of Treasury required Symmes to pay the remaining sum, including interest in six semiannual installments, that is, over three years, beginning six months after his second payment. Upon receipt of the first $200,000, Symmes would receive the right to claim 300,000 acres and another 600,000 acres after the second payment, with additional lands deeded thereafter upon receipt of the semiannual installments.

Symmes intended to sell his lands for 66⅔ cents per acre until May 1, 1788. Then, the price would increase to one dollar per acre, but still half the price of federal lands. He also intended to sell tracts as small as 160 acres as opposed to the minimum government purchase of 640 acres in order to attract settlers with less capital who would be small-scale farmers rather than speculators and thereby help settle the Miami country as rapidly as possible.

After receiving his grant Symmes moved quickly to promote what would become known as the Miami Purchase. In November 1787 and January 1788, he advertised the Miami country in the *Trenton Circular* and the *Brunswick Gazette and Weekly Monitor* respectively. Symmes told his readers that he had acquired the "most excellent tract of land on the northwest bank of the Ohio," and he called the land between the two rivers the "best tract in the federal country." The level land was, he wrote, "generally free from stone," and it consisted of a "rich easy soil for tillage." Cattle, horses, and hogs could forage in the woods, where food remained abundant through the winter. With a bit of hyperbole based as much on a lack of knowledge about the Miami River country as on his desire to sell land for a profit, Symmes also claimed that "Every kind of grain and vegetable raised in the middle states grows here, with the addition of cotton and indigo, which may be raised in sufficient quantities for family use." He contended, "The farmers profits here must be great, as horses and oxen may be raised free of expense, save a little salt which is cheap; and they may be drove to Philadelphia for less than four dollars a head." The moderate climate and nearness to the Ohio River for shipment of agricultural produce to New Orleans and the markets beyond, he believed beckoned men and women who wanted security and independence that only land ownership could bring. Symmes expected thousands, especially young men who had little or no land, to emigrate to the Miami River country. He promised to help those in need by providing a six-month supply of corn for meal until they could harvest their own crop. This advance would be reimbursable in full, plus interest, payable in money, grain, or labor at a mutually agreed upon price within two years, at which time it could be replaced with "great ease from the produce of the sale" of the settler's first crops.

Symmes also reserved a township the mouth of the Great Miami River for himself, where, in 1788, he planned to survey the lots and streets for a "considerable town" that he intended to call Symmes. He planned to encourage settlement of his city by giving away every alternate lot to individuals who would build a house within two years and lived there for three years. Cincinnati, which emerged from the village of Losantiville under the protection of Fort Washington near the mouth of the Little Miami River, however, soon put an end to Symmes's dream of founding a city named for himself. Nevertheless, Symmes offered opportunity for anyone who wanted to own land, and he promised that those who purchased from him would receive titles "clear and certain."

Symmes, however, had trouble from the start. His first payment was due by July 1788, but he did not have sufficient funds. With only $83,330 in certificates and military warrants, Symmes could not close the contract. Consequently, on June 11 he asked his agent Jonathan Dayton to seek a new land contract from the Board of Treasury that would reduce his grant by half and permit him to use the funds in hand as a down payment. The Board of Treasury quickly agreed to Symmes's request but refused to grant him the entire frontage of lands along the Ohio River between the mouths of the Little and Great Miami Rivers. The board pointed to legislation of October 1787 that provided no tract could have frontage of more than one-third of its depth along the Ohio and Mississippi Rivers. Instead, the Board of Treasury granted Symmes only a twenty-mile frontage on the Ohio River running east from the mouth of the Great Miami River. By so doing, the board changed the eastern boundary of Symmes's original two-million-acre grant. Simply put, the land along the Little Miami River that Symmes coveted and claimed now lay beyond his new grant. This change of the eastern boundary of Symmes's Miami Purchase contributed to the most disorganized, illegal, and contentious land acquisition and settlement process in Ohio and U.S. history.

Ultimately, after considerable contention, Symmes and the Board of Treasury reached an agreement on October 15, 1788, in which he received 123,297 acres for his first payment of $83,330. When he made a second payment of $82,198 within a month after the survey of the boundary had been completed, he would receive title to an additional 246,594 acres for which he could legally issue deeds to buyers. The remainder was due in six semiannual payments for a total of $571,438. Unfortunately, Symmes in his haste to raise funds from the sale of his lands in order to claim even more acreage, had already sold a tract to Benjamin Stites east of the new boundary, based on his original contract for two million acres. Stites, in turn, sold portions at the mouth of the Little Miami River to other settlers. Essentially, Symmes sold lands that he did not own, and he continued to do so, contending that the Little Miami River was the correct eastern boundary of his tract. He also operated with the belief that the more land that he sold the more difficult it would be for the Board of Treasury to deny him his original request for a tract between the two Miamis. Arthur St. Clair, governor of the Northwest Territory, however, considered these settlers "outsiders" who squatted on national lands and subject to removal.

Symmes disagreed about the technicalities of his land sales and contended that he did nothing wrong. On January 9, 1790, he wrote, "The insidious reports which have been spread abroad of my selling the same lands several times over . . . are really vexing to me." Symmes contended that applications submitted to him for land did not entitle a prospective buyer to a deed or title until they paid for it. Symmes told Jonathan Dayton that "no man had a right to locate one foot after my arrival in this country unless he produ[c]ed a warrant to cover the same." The problem was, he argued, "the promises of the applicant 'that if he could have such or such piece of land, he would take measures to pay for it' by a given time agreed on between us." When these applicants settled on Symmes's land but did not pay for it at 6 percent interest within the allotted time, he often sold the tract to another buyer. Symmes made additional trouble for himself because he sold the right to acreage that was not surveyed and mapped, that is, platted, so more than one person could end up claiming the same tract of land. Even so, in 1791, he wrote, "my business is not to buy lands, but to sell it."

To make matters worse, the geographer Ludlow did not officially complete the survey and mapping of Symmes's boundaries until he presented a plat map to the Board of Treasury on January 10, 1794. Ludlow certified that the tract contained 543,950 acres. Symmes now had to survey the interior of his purchase according to the provisions of the Land Ordinance of 1785. The surveyors who Symmes hired to lay out the townships and sections, however, made many mistakes and the corner stakes of one surveying party seldom matched with those of another when they came together. Symmes, nonetheless, began to sell lands in his tract, only to have the buyers frequently contest the boundaries of their property. Symmes attempted to remedy the situation by surveying a new north-south line from which buyers could then survey their own east and west lines to box-in their property. Still, conflicting surveys created a chaotic, haphazard process in contrast to the systematic and orderly method of survey and sale of lands by the Ohio Company.

With a host of settlers now living illegally on public (government) land that they had purchased from Symmes, Governor St. Clair made the situation worse by threatening to evict anyone who squatted on public domain without paying for their land. Symmes quickly became annoyed with the arrogant posturing of St. Clair, who Symmes thought meddled in this matter "with all the fervor and zeal which he might do if the lands had been taken possession of by a colony from Detroit, under the auspices of the British Government." Their relationship quickly deteriorated, and when St. Clair warned settlers near the mouth of the Little Miami that the government intended to appropriate public domain for the use of the garrison at Fort Washington, those who had purchased these lands from

Symmes felt betrayed. Symmes contended that "every person must admit that the governor has treated me and the settlers in a most cruel manner."

At the same time, the Shawnees, Miamis, and Delawares discouraged white settlement on public or private lands north of the Ohio River, and Symmes had little income from the sale of his tract to meet his obligations to the Board of Treasury. As a result, on April 11, 1792, Symmes petitioned Congress to grant him title to the lands for which he had already paid, because he could not meet his contractual obligations for the purchase of one million acres. The government, however, did not provide Symmes with a patent, that is, deed, to these lands until September 30, 1794. At the same time, it also expanded his grant to 311,682 acres of which he purchased 248,540 acres with $165,963 in military land warrants and other certificates after Congress waived the rule that only one-seventh of those lands could be purchased by that means.

Ultimately, Symmes probably paid for this land with warrants that he had purchased for about 22½ cents per acre and about 15 cents per acre in specie. Congress now required Symmes to locate the northern boundary of his grant within five years or lose it. It did not, however, determine or specify the northern boundary. This legislation also terminated Symmes's grant for one million acres negotiated in 1788.

Yet, Symmes continued to operate on the premise that he had the right to one million acres and that payment would follow in due time. On February 9, 1797, however, Secretary of the Treasury Albert Gallatin told Congress that Symmes's contract for one million acres, signed in 1788, was null and void. Congress also asked the attorney general to sue Symmes for the lands that he claimed but had not paid or to force him to vacate them, but nothing came of this directive. The congressional effort to sort out Symmes's land purchases and claims failed to clarify the situation. Eventually, on March 2, 1799, Congress attempted to give some relief to settlers who had purchased lands from Symmes beyond the tract to which he had title by granting them preemption rights, that is, the first right to purchase their lands at two dollars per acre from the federal government. Similar legislation followed annually from 1801 to 1804 to cover those buyers to whom Symmes continued illegally to sell federal lands. For settlers, however, who thought they had purchased lands with a clear title, preemption proved a hardship, because they had to repurchase their lands from the federal government.

In July 1799, Governor St. Clair wrote to Secretary of State Thomas Jefferson, "The law for the selling the lands claimed by Judge Symmes under his contract with the Board of Treasury, but beyond the northern boundary of his patent, has given a very great alarm to the people settled thereupon, and they are very numerous." St. Clair observed that many settlers had written or oral contracts with Symmes for land north of his congressional grant. "From almost all of them," St. Clair told Jefferson, "he has received money in part payment, which, notwithstanding the law, he positively refuses to return and from that circumstance many, who are, or at least appear to be, very willing to take the lands on the terms held out to them by the law, are unable to make the just payment at the time required, and are much agitated by fear of losing their right of pre-emption." Many of these settlers were prepared to fight to hold the lands that they had purchased from Symmes but who now found the federal government pressing them for payment. "There are others," St. Clair wrote, "I am informed, who talk plainly of holding their possessions by force of arms, and it has been hinted to me that they are stimulated to it by [Symmes]." Many settlers also sued Symmes for the return of their money, and the courts began to seize his property to satisfy judgments against him. Symmes, in turn, offered to pay for lands that he had sold outside his patent or to exchange other lands that he held for the disputed tracts, but his buyers who located on federal land wanted immediate compensation.

On January 26, 1803, Attorney General Levi Lincoln, who had studied Symmes's problems and petitions for relief, found Symmes's claims for land and relief without merit, and Lincoln issued a scathing report in which he contended that Symmes held no claim against the government based on either law or equity. "Generally," Lincoln wrote, "the establishment of a settlement in a large, new, and wilderness country, is attended with trouble, expense, hardships, and danger, to the first settlers, and with profit and various advantages to the proprietors of the country, by increasing its population, the value and sale of their lands, and, as the case has been, the security of the frontier." Then, Lincoln held, "On these grounds, [Symmes] is pathetic in the statement of his claims. They are at least specious, and perhaps deserve more attention, as his disappointment and suffering appear to have resulted, in part, from an opinion of the extent of his contract, although differing from the Government's, yet at least colorable, and supported by some official reports on the subject." Lincoln then suggested that the Senate decide whether Symmes had benefited

financially from the change of his contract, that is, the eastern boundary of his one-million-acre tract, as well as whether he had sufficiently
profited from the use of military land warrants, which he used to purchase a considerable acreage, and whether he had the right to the one
million acres that he claimed. The Senate referred Lincoln's report to
a committee and ignored it.

Without congressional relief from his problems, Symmes continued to lose his lands to pay judgments against him for selling acreage
that he did not own. Symmes always believed that he had not done
anything intentionally wrong, and he contended the government
should honor his original request for lands that would then solve his
legal problems in the disputed purchase area. He also considered the
litigation against him as nothing less than persecution. Symmes
believed the suits "unjust" and perpetrated by the "deepest conspiracy,
fraud, and perjury" to destroy the "earnings of a long, industrious,
frugal and adventurous life." He denounced the federal government
and his enemies for treating him with the "blackest ingratitude." Still,
Symmes proclaimed that he intended to pay his debts. In his will of
December 31, 1813, he directed that his "few fragments of land" be
used to settle all claims against him. Symmes died in bitterness and
poverty on February 26, 1814, at Cincinnati, burial followed at
North Bend, Indiana.

In retrospect, Symmes differed from the other land speculators in
Ohio, such as Nathaniel Massie in the Virginia Military District,
Lucas Sullivant in the U.S. Military District, or Zalmon Wildman in
the Firelands, not only because he initially had the right to a larger
tract of land, but also because he essentially served as the sole proprietor for the Miami Purchase. Unlike the proprietary system of the
colonial period when individuals, such as William Penn in Pennsylvania and Cecil Calvert in Maryland, controlled large tracts of land,
Symmes had the rights to the land but not to the government that
would be established by the settlers who purchased it. At the same
time, as the proprietor, Symmes did not owe feudal-like restrictive
obligations to Congress, nor did individuals who purchased his lands
owe fealty to him. Rather, he held his acres with a fee simple title, that
is, he had a clear title or deed to the acres that Congress granted him
and for which he paid.

Symmes also differed from other land speculators in Ohio by combining the New England survey system, given legitimacy in the new
nation with the Land Ordinance of 1785, which provided for the regular survey of lands into townships and sections with specific sections

reserved to support education and religion, with the southern tradition of irregular surveys by individuals. In contrast to the Ohio Company, which had a systematic process for land sales and settlement, as well as to small-scale speculators who surveyed and sold their lands, Symmes did not have the organizational structure to monitor the survey, sales, and management of his 311,000 acres, let alone his intended one-million-acre purchase. The Ohio Company did not permit land buyers to settle where they pleased. They could only purchase lands that were closely situated to a town or village. Others, such as Thomas Worthington, also surveyed and mapped their tracts before sale and provided terms of payment in both cash or kind, the latter of which involved a settler paying for land by clearing a certain number of acres over a specific amount of time for the speculator. These small-scale speculators primarily had acquired their lands with little capital over time by purchasing and exchanging military warrants for acreage and by surveying for which they were paid in land. In contrast, Symmes had to pay the Board of Treasury a considerable amount in advance for his lands before he received title, but he did not have the money to claim his entire grant.

Moreover, Symmes did not provide for the accurate survey, platting, sale, and registry of his lands. For example, he sold tracts not less than 160 acres for which the buyer paid with military warrants or some other form of paper certificate or money. Symmes, however, did not sell specific tracts of land as provided by the Land Ordinance of 1785. Rather, he provided buyers with land warrants that entitled them to select a township, section, or quarter section of land on their own within the Miami Purchase, provided no other person had settled on or registered that land as their tract. Then, the buyer had to survey his own property.

Symmes also sold lands on credit but never bothered to ensure payment, although he complained about Kentuckians who agreed to purchase land but then deserted before payment became due, even transferring their claim to others with advice to pay Symmes for the land. Although Symmes regretted not getting the money, he was glad to see the Kentuckians leave, contending that they were "very ungovernable and seditious." He hoped for better clientele. But, until Symmes received a patent, that is, title, from the federal government, the deeds that he issued to his buyers upon payment had no legal validity. Still, he attempted to give some semblance of order to the settlement process in the Miami Purchase by requiring those who purchased land to settle within two years and make improvements, such as clearing trees, plowing fields, and building a houses. If buyers did not meet this requirement, unless prevented by hostile Indians, the owner forfeited one-sixth of his holding located at the northeast corner of his township, section, or quarter section. Another settler could then live on it and make improvements for seven years after which time he would receive a deed to that land.

In the end, Symmes primarily differed from other land speculators in Ohio because he played fast and loose. The Ohio Company of Associates, the only other purchaser in Ohio besides the defunct Scioto Company to control extensive lands, operated systematically as a joint stock company. Investors purchased shares in the Ohio Company for $1,000 in Continental currency or $10 in hard money. No investor could own more than five nor less than one share in the company. When Congress granted the Ohio Company 1.5 million acres on October 27, 1787, the Ohio Company's agents had the grant surveyed according to the Land Ordinance of 1785 and began the orderly, documented sale of those lands. In contrast, settlers or other land speculators purchased unsurveyed land from Symmes or his agents in New Jersey, New York, or Philadelphia. Symmes, however, did not have a systematic method to record which tracts had been sold. He did not hire a registrar to oversee his land sales and keep accurate records that showed who bought and settled which specific lands. To make matters worse, Symmes permitted individuals who could not raise sufficient money or military land warrants to pool their capital with others in order to purchase a township, section, or quarter section and then divided it among themselves.

Symmes final patent of 1794 eventually permitted the establishment of his northern boundary in present-day Warren County, a few miles north of Lebanon and south of the continuation of the line that marked the northern boundary of the Ohio Company's purchase. When he failed to make good his claim to lands farther north, but after selling considerable federal lands as his own, Congress required those settlers to purchase their land again. Congress provided, however, that settlers, who had purchased land from Symmes that he did not own, had the first right to repurchase it from the federal government at two dollars per acre. Little wonder, then, that Symmes had more enemies than friends in the Miami Purchase.

As the bickering about the extent of his land grant dragged out with Congress, Symmes believed he could hold his claimed but as yet unpurchased lands by scattering settlers across his desired million acres. By so doing, he would gain some funds to pay for more lands and make it politically difficult for Congress to evict them and even easier for it to comply with his requested grant. In May 1789, Symmes wrote that in contrast to the Ohio Company's purchase, "The different method adopted for settling Miami, put it in the power of every purchaser to chuse his ground, and convert the same into a station, village, or town at pleasure: and nothing controuls him but fear of Indians." Speedy rather than orderly settlement meant the most to Symmes. Still, one individual could not conduct the entire organizational task required to acquire, survey, and sell such a great tract of land. Thereafter, the federal government, land companies, and small-scale speculators would sell land in Ohio. After the disaster of Symmes's Miami Purchase, the federal government never again contracted with private speculators for the sale of Ohio land, and it confirmed the need for the federal government to accurately survey public lands before those lands were sold in a systematic manner to private individuals. The Ohio frontier offered remarkable opportunities to gain personal wealth in land speculation, but success was determined and limited by personal ability.

Further Reading

Beaver, R. Pierce. "The Miami Purchase of John Cleves Symmes." *Ohio Archaeological and Historical Quarterly* 40 (January 1931): 284–342.

Blum, Carol Jean. "'A Devotion to the West': The Settlement of Cincinnati, 1788–1810." *Queen City Heritage* 48, no. 1 (1900): 3–19.

Hudson, John C. *Making the Corn Belt: A Geographical History of Middle-Western Agriculture*. Bloomington: Indiana University Press, 1994.

Hurt, R. Douglas. *The Ohio Frontier: Crucible of the Old Northwest, 1720–1830*. Bloomington: Indiana University Press, 1996.

Smith, Dwight L. "John Cleves Symmes." *Timeline* 5 (April–May 1988): 20–23.

3

Arthur St. Clair and the Establishment of U.S. Authority in the Old Northwest

JEFFREY P. BROWN

A RTHUR ST. CLAIR, the first governor of the Northwest Territory, played a significant role in the development of the early U.S. frontier and helped shape the state of Ohio's early political system. In the process, St. Clair aroused much controversy during his long service as an army officer and frontier administrator.

St. Clair rose to prominence from a relatively middle-class background through military service and an advantageous marriage. Born in Thurso, Scotland, in 1734 or 1736, he was probably the son of a merchant who died when Arthur was young. St. Clair attended the University of Edinburgh, evidence that his family had some money or connections, and in 1756 became an apprentice to a respected London physician. St. Clair decided that he did not want a medical career, however, and when his mother died in 1757, he apparently used his inheritance to buy his apprentice time and purchase a commission as an ensign in the Royal American Regiment of Foot. St. Clair came to North America during the French and Indian War with the regiment and never returned to Europe.

Later in his career, St. Clair would be described as a gallant, polished man with a knack for setting people at ease. He probably made a good impression as a young officer, and in 1760 he courted and married Phoebe Bayard, the niece of wealthy Governor James Bayard of Massachusetts. Her dowry, reported to be 14,000£, made St. Clair one of the wealthier citizens of Boston. In 1762, however, he resigned his military commission and with his wife moved to the western Pennsylvania frontier. It is not clear why he made this move, although he had apparently toured the area on behalf of his kinsman,

26

FIG. 2 Arthur St. Clair. Engraved by E. Wellmore from a drawing by J. B. Longacre after original portrait by C. W. Peale. From William Henry Smith, ed., *The St. Clair Papers*, vol. 2 (Cincinnati: Robert Clarke & Co., 1882).

General Thomas Gage. While perhaps overextending his finances, St. Clair developed a four-thousand-acre estate at Ligonier and portrayed himself during the late 1760s as the wealthiest man on the Pennsylvania frontier. Although other major landowners in the region, as well as many ordinary settlers, accepted Virginia's sovereignty over the area, St. Clair accepted Pennsylvania rule. He was appointed one of Pennsylvania's judges in its new Westmoreland County in 1773.

St. Clair opposed the mobs that supported Virginia rule in 1774 and was forced to flee after he ordered the arrest of an individual trying to organize Virginia's militia in the area. This affair contributed to St. Clair's skepticism of the Revolutionary groups who met in 1775 to proclaim their support for Massachusetts' militiamen. He ignored an invitation to help choose the Pennsylvania delegation to the First Continental Congress and proudly wrote to John Penn that he had persuaded the local citizens' association to adopt a resolution calling only for the restoration of pre–Stamp Act conditions. In a private letter, he observed that the people were "all mad." St. Clair clearly believed that ordinary people should defer to their established leaders, and relished his own status as a community leader. He served on the local Committee of Safety, and when the Westmoreland County militia elected him their colonel, he accepted.

St. Clair, although rising to the rank of major general during the Revolutionary War, had a mixed military record. He received considerable criticism when he led an American retreat from Fort Ticonderoga, even though the fort could not have been defended. Anthony Wayne hated him, seeing him as a stodgy rival for attention. But St. Clair's steadfast service throughout the war won him George Washington's friendship. He consistently opposed attempts to form officers' committees of grievance, seeing them as destructive to discipline, and in many ways he exemplified the type of officer who found comradeship, social status, and confirmation of patriotic devotion in his military service. St. Clair was a natural choice after the war to be president of Pennsylvania's chapter of the Society of the Cincinnati, an hereditary organization for veteran officers.

After the war, St. Clair fell into serious economic trouble. Wartime destruction in the Ligonier area had brought him close to bankruptcy. He moved to Philadelphia, where he won election to the state Council of Censors, a body that oversaw tax collections and reviewed the constitutionality of state laws. He was also elected to Congress, where he won the largely titular role of president of Congress. When Manasseh Cutler, William Duer, and others began to negotiate the land sales that helped produce the Northwest Ordinance, St. Clair appeared to them to be a good choice for governor of the Northwest Territory, and Congress selected him for this position. St. Clair, in turn, happily accepted this opportunity to build an estate and return to frontier prominence. He may well have planned to spend only a few years in the Northwest, since his family stayed in Pennsylvania.

St. Clair arrived in the Northwest Territory in July 1788. By then, New England veterans had begun a planned community at Marietta, and other pioneers had begun to move into a speculative grant owned by John Cleves Symmes at Losantiville (the future Cincinnati). A number of squatter families had also scattered through the upper Ohio Valley, although threats of Indian violence and campaigns by the U.S. Army to burn squatters' homes had reduced their numbers. To the west, French-speaking villagers and Americans in communities such as Vincennes and Kaskaskia acknowledged the central government's authority to some degree, while Great Britain continued to control Detroit and the Great Lakes region. Most of the Northwest Territory was, in fact, ruled by resident Indian nations, but the United States neither accepted their sovereignty nor regarded them as Americans.

St. Clair's first priority was to adopt territorial laws, and immediately thereafter he appointed officials and established local governments that would accept U.S. authority. Since the central government was far away and had commanded little respect during the Articles of Confederation period, and since many frontier people were convinced that seacoast investors and politicians were hostile to their interests, establishing any U.S. authority was no small task.

The Northwest Ordinance of 1787 directed the territory's governor and three appointed judges to produce a legal code by adopting laws already in force in other states. It left vague whether the governor had only one vote in this process or could veto laws favored by a majority of the judges. St. Clair insisted that he had a veto power, and at their first meeting he denounced Judges Samuel H. Parsons and James M. Varnum for writing their own laws rather than adopting existing state statutes. After a short power struggle, the men worked out a compromise. The judges accepted St. Clair's veto power, and in turn he supported loose versions of state laws, particularly in creating a militia system, and appointed one of their favorites as the court clerk. The incident showed that St. Clair had a strong sense of his own prerogatives and was willing to fight for them but also that he could work out sensible agreements when he had to compromise.

St. Clair and the judges adopted laws creating county courts and establishing officers such as county sheriffs. Their code emphasized moral and orderly behavior. It forbade drunkenness, profanity, and Sabbath violations as well as crimes such as robbery and arson. Children or servants could be jailed for disobedience. The governor argued that fourteen should be the minimum age for female marriage, maintaining that this rule would produce both moral behavior and rapid population growth. Although territorial secretary Winthrop Sargent mishandled a legislative gathering early in 1790, St. Clair worked well enough with new Judges George Turner and John Cleves Symmes in adopting another set of laws later that year.

St. Clair also established local governments in the far-flung Northwest under the ultimate authority of the U.S. government. During 1790, he organized county governments in both the Losantiville area, which he renamed Cincinnati, and at the French settlements in Illinois, while Secretary Winthrop Sargent extended government to the Vincennes area in southern Indiana. By appointing existing leaders of these communities to new offices, St. Clair and Sargent ensured the acceptance of the authority of the United States. St. Clair also worked to recognize official land titles in the Illinois region. On the whole, he and Sargent appointed capable men to local offices. St. Clair, though, worked too quickly in trying to unravel complex land claims in the Illinois country, and a number of fraudulent claims slipped past him.

The governor placed a particularly high priority on winning the allegiance of French villagers in Vincennes and Kaskaskia, fearing that they might be influenced by the Spanish government in St. Louis or move to land under Spain's control. After Judge George Turner ordered Vincennes slaves freed in 1794, St. Clair ruled that the Northwest Ordinance did not apply to slaves who had lived in the Northwest before 1787. Many of the early slave owners in the western part of the Northwest Territory were French, and St. Clair may have taken this step to help ensure their loyalty, although his sporadic quarrels with Judge Turner may have also played a role in his decision. In general, St. Clair worked well with local officials in the Illinois/Indiana area, and the area's French and Anglo-American inhabitants seemed content with American rule.

While St. Clair succeeded in two major tasks, he met disaster in conducting a war that developed against the Northwest's Indians. The central government wanted to win the allegiance of frontier settlers and felt that it had to demonstrate that it would support them in their on-going conflicts with Indian nations. It wanted Indians to allow more American settlement north of the Ohio River, since this would both please settlers and help persuade eastern investors to buy federal land and bring revenues to a government that had few resources. Finally, President Washington wanted to reduce British influence over the Indians, end British control of the Great Lakes fur trade, and pressure Britain to abandon outposts such as Detroit. However, the government had to rely on a small standing army and on militiamen if it wanted to force a military solution in the Northwest. St. Clair, who also held the position of superintendent of Indian affairs, tried to get the Indians to peacefully accept some degree of American settlement in their lands but only angered Indian leaders when he sought to over-awe them in negotiations. The government then turned to a military solution. After an expedition under General Josiah Harmar in the fall of 1790 suffered significant casualties, Washington appointed St. Clair a major general and instructed him to organize an expedition that would advance northwest against the Indians.

St. Clair's ponderous army left Cincinnati in the fall of 1791. Along the way, scores of Kentucky militiamen deserted, and St. Clair had to detach hundreds of soldiers to guard his supply train against the deserters. His quartermaster was so inefficient that many supplies never reached the army, and more soldiers began deserting. St. Clair himself became very ill. On November 4, 1791, the Indians attacked St. Clair's sleeping camp, and as panicked soldiers fled into a clearing, the Indians poured in a murderous crossfire. St. Clair and hundreds of men survived and fled the battle after suffering the most one-sided defeat in the history of the U.S. Army. General St. Clair clearly bore much of the responsibility for the disaster—for poor planning, for quarreling with other officers, and for a poor response during the battle itself. His own bad health offered little excuse.

St. Clair's defeat greatly damaged his ability to govern the Northwest Territory, since few pioneers now respected him. Although President Washington gave him a public letter of support, he convinced St. Clair to resign his commission. St. Clair offered as an excuse for leaving the Army his need to stay in Philadelphia for an inquiry by the House of Representatives. He continued to serve as governor and superintendent of Indian affairs, but for the remainder of the Indian war neither the president nor General Anthony Wayne consulted him.

St. Clair's loss of influence was evident everywhere. When he had first tried in 1791 to stop fraudulent land sales by Judge John Cleves Symmes, Symmes could only counter that St. Clair was dictatorial. After the defeat, Symmes began to lobby for St. Clair's outright removal from office, and by 1794 Symmes convinced Congress to sell him the land that he had already marketed to settlers. St. Clair remained governor in name, but he seemed virtually irrelevant to national leaders.

Arthur St. Clair soon lost interest in his isolated and meaningless post. He had probably always felt out of touch with national politics when he was on the frontier, and during the first years of his governorship he remained active in Pennsylvania and national politics. St. Clair left the Northwest in 1789 to attend Washington's inaugural. In 1790, conservative Philadelphians put him forward for governor, but he was defeated by Thomas Mifflin 27,725 to 2,802. St. Clair spent much of 1790 going to war conferences in the capital. After his military defeat, he spent all of 1792 and most of 1793 in Philadelphia, giving testimony, sending out memoranda, and pursuing reimbursement claims for money he had spent during the campaign. He also tried to win support in 1793 from the Pennsylvania Assembly for a seat in the U.S. Senate but got only one of eighty-three votes.

The governor returned only sporadically to the Northwest during the next five years. From August 1, 1789, until May 11, 1795, he was present in the territory only 35 percent of the time. Although he went to the Illinois country in 1795 and spent a brief period thereafter in Cincinnati, St. Clair was out of the Northwest during the summer of 1796 and again from September 1796 to May 1798. When he was in the Northwest, St. Clair hated his isolation. He felt that his career was over and described himself as "a poor Devil banished to another Planet." St. Clair told President Washington at some point before 1797 that he did not wish to serve another term as governor.

Territorial Secretary Winthrop Sargent served as acting governor during St. Clair's long absences. St. Clair seemed to resent this, as if he felt that any successes by Sargent would reflect his own failures. During a three-year period up to January 1795, Sargent reported that he received only one letter from St. Clair. While Sargent succeeded in establishing U.S. authority in Detroit, he was generally ineffective as an acting governor. Sargent was also absent from the Northwest for about two years, including periods when St. Clair was gone. He quarreled with the judges and alienated most pioneers in Cincinnati by trying to protect friendly Indians and enforce wartime discipline. Although St. Clair defended Sargent from politically motivated indictments in 1795, he also denounced the secretary on fairly trivial grounds and described as usurpation actions that Sargent had taken when (unbeknownst to him) St. Clair had reentered the Northwest. Sargent responded to this by complaining to Secretary of State Timothy Pickering, who had disliked St. Clair since the Revolution, when Pickering felt that the Scottish general had claimed too much credit for military victories. Pickering commiserated with Sargent and worked to remove St. Clair and replace him with Sargent.

Although Sargent and Pickering expected St. Clair to retire, he surprised them in 1798 by seeking another term. St. Clair wrote to President John Adams, arguing that he deserved the position because he had ruined his health and fortune in his country's service. Adams, who generally paid little attention to northwestern affairs, found these to be reasonable arguments and nominated St. Clair for another term. Friends warned St. Clair that this was probably his last chance to redeem his reputation, and he moved his family to the Northwest this time. St. Clair expressed strong support for the Adams administration's policies during the Quasi-War with France and paid enough attention to his duties to regained the administration's support. Pickering persuaded Adams to nominate Sargent to be governor of Mississippi Territory, and Sargent left the Northwest.

St. Clair learned that the Northwest had grown much more populous during his long absences. After the Treaty of Greenville in 1795, the Indians ceded control of the southern part of what would become Ohio and more American settlers began to move to the territory. Virginians in particular moved into the Virginia Military District along the Scioto River, while other frontier families settled near Cincinnati, Marietta, and Steubenville. The absorption of Detroit added several thousand French-speaking residents to the Northwest's population. This population growth meant that there were now more counties, more positions to which a governor could make patronage appointments, and more official fees that would flow to the governor. Although he did not succeed in persuading the president to appoint his son, Arthur Jr., as the new secretary to replace Sargent, St. Clair may well have found that being governor could bring him both a good income and personal prestige. He even bought some land from Symmes near modern Dayton. In short, his position was much more desirable than before.

As newer areas were settled and the earlier communities grew more populous, ambitious men competed for wealth and for social and political prominence. Merchants, speculators, and surveyors who had been prominent in their home states resented the orderly system of appointments that St. Clair, Sargent, and some of the judges had established over the years. They preferred elections, not appointments, and were confident that local voters would choose them. Most were also Jeffersonian in their political sympathies, holding a low opinion of the Adams administration. Like many Northwest pioneers, they wanted to develop a territorial assembly and move into statehood as quickly as possible. When Acting Governor Sargent fought efforts by Nathaniel and Henry Massie to make their town of Manchester a county seat in the lower Scioto Valley, and when he tried to enforce moral and orderly behavior in Cincinnati, his actions were widely resented. Even before St. Clair returned to active duties, leaders in Cincinnati and the Scioto Valley had begun to seek both the establishment of an elected territorial assembly and the rapid development of statehood. Only Federalist Marietta seemed content to remain under administrative rule.

Governor St. Clair inherited this troubled situation in 1798. He quickly made two decisions. Like Sargent, he fought the Massie brothers' efforts to make Manchester a county seat. St. Clair had long found open land speculation distasteful, and he genuinely thought

that Manchester was a poor site for a county seat. St. Clair recognized
a different town, and when Nathaniel Massie and Benjamin Gooden
insisted on holding winter courts in Manchester, St. Clair discharged
them as justices of the peace. St. Clair's Manchester decisions alienated most leaders in the quickly growing Scioto Valley communities.
At the same time, he launched another futile campaign against
Symmes's land machinations in Cincinnati. Symmes tried to work
with the Massie brothers and lobby President Adams for St. Clair's
removal, but since Cincinnati's pioneers were becoming increasingly
upset with Symmes, his enmity did St. Clair little political harm.

More important, the governor tried to delay movement towards a
territorial assembly and statehood. St. Clair was convinced that the
Northwest did not have enough able, educated citizens to govern
itself. He believed that he was one of the few men there who had the
wisdom, experience, and personal honesty to handle the duties of
government. St. Clair fully agreed with eastern leaders who feared
that frontier self-rule would lead to chaos and to defiance of central
authority. The governor also recognized that local elections would
probably elevate other men to power and reduce his own role. Since
he linked his own status with the maintenance of civilized order, St.
Clair almost automatically tried to stop the very popular assembly and
statehood movements.

Although Cincinnati's pro-statehood leaders had fought with
Winthrop Sargent before St. Clair's return to the Northwest, they
hoped that they could win the governor's support for creating a territorial assembly, which they saw as the first step towards statehood.
However, St. Clair challenged their claims that they represented the
public and did not attend a pro-assembly banquet in June 1798. A
Cincinnati committee then decided to hold censuses throughout the
Northwest Territory. The Northwest Ordinance specified that an
assembly could be created as soon as the territory held five thousand
adult free males, and these men were convinced that the recent
increase in settlement had brought it well above this level. A census
in Hamilton County (the Cincinnati region) found 456 adult free
men in mid-1798, and after the committee began steps to invite other
counties to hold censuses, St. Clair gave way. He officially announced
in October 1798, that the Northwest now held more than five thousand free adult males and directed township officials to begin collecting an authorized census.

St. Clair set the first territorial elections for December 1798, when
voters would elect fourteen men for the House of Representatives,

the lower house of the territorial assembly. They were to meet in a "pre-session" in Cincinnati on January 22, 1799, to nominate ten men for the upper house (the Council); President Adams would then choose five men from this list. St. Clair allotted seats to each county and specified that delegates had to be American citizens for three years and residents of the counties that elected them. He also announced that voters must be freehold owners of at least fifty acres and that assembly members had to own at least two hundred acres. St. Clair restricted voting to the county seats, often a considerable distance from voters' homes. In all probability, he felt that the relatively prosperous townspeople would be the most likely to vote and that they would generally select men he could work with. Since under the Northwest Ordinance St. Clair could dismiss assemblies and veto their laws, he would actually have more power under this system than when he had to meet with the judges to adopt laws.

St. Clair soon found opportunities to use his formal veto power. The first assembly included a number of his supporters but also opponents from Hamilton County and the Scioto Valley. St. Clair failed to win a majority vote to appoint his son the Northwest's non-voting delegate to Congress, a new position that came to the territory when it moved into the assembly phase of government. Instead, the assembly chose Secretary William Henry Harrison. It also created several new counties and named their seats. This reflected the spread of settlement and a widespread desire for local, accessible government but also pleased speculators such as the Massie brothers. The assembly passed a bill removing the governor's right to collect official fees for marriage, ferry, tavern, and other licenses. St. Clair vetoed eleven bills, including those creating the new counties and removing his fees. The vetoes were particularly controversial because many settlers did not believe that an appointed official should overrule an elected assembly. While St. Clair vetoed the fee removal bill, he signed a bill that gave him $500 "for services extraordinary" that was designed to compensate him for ending his ability to collect fees, thereby keeping both the fees and the $500. Many members accused him of outright greed, and even supporters who accepted his power to veto bills wondered why they had gathered for the assembly.

Although the governor angered many assemblymen, he soon took steps to strengthen his own position. He proposed dividing the Northwest into three smaller territories. The division would delay statehood for any individual area, since even a growing population would be spread over multiple jurisdictions. Delaying statehood might lengthen his tenure and give the frontier more time to acquire the kind of prosperous and educated citizens who might support a conservative government.

St. Clair also thought that if the boundaries were well drawn, it might be possible for a Federalist state to develop in at least one jurisdiction. He urged that the Northwest be split along the Scioto River, with two of the new territories centering on Marietta and Cincinnati. Since the majority of early settlers in the Scioto Valley lived west of that river, they would be placed in the Cincinnati-based region, a step that would leave Marietta the center of a potentially Federalist state. St. Clair recommended that the outlying French communities, so different from the rest of the Northwest, be placed in the third new jurisdiction.

Territorial Delegate William Henry Harrison was willing to seek a territorial division but on his own terms. Harrison persuaded President Adams and a Federalist Congress to split the Northwest into two territories, with Cincinnati at the western edge of the reduced Northwest. The territory included modern Ohio and lower Michigan and centered on the Scioto Valley. Congress established a new jurisdiction named Indiana Territory for the Indiana-Illinois region, and Harrison was appointed its first governor. Adams was apparently not concerned about the Northwest's long-term political development, since creating Indiana Territory removed only a few thousand residents from the Northwest Territory and would not greatly delay what seemed likely to become a Jeffersonian state from joining the Union.

Governor St. Clair quickly capitalized on the fears of Cincinnati's leaders that Chillicothe would now dominate the state. He built a coalition to support a second territorial division along the Scioto River, with Cincinnati and Marietta as the two new territorial capitals. If that division could not be achieved, his plan was for these two towns to alternate as the territory's capital. St. Clair cemented this alliance by backing Cincinnati's foremost Jeffersonian leader, William McMillan, for Harrison's vacant office as territorial delegate. McMillan had supported statehood for a number of years. Since Marietta also had a candidate interested in the office of delegate, Federalist attorney Paul Fearing, McMillan and Fearing worked out an agreement. The coalition passed a bill in the 1800 assembly that elected both men as delegates, with McMillan completing Harrison's term and Fearing preselected to serve for the following two years. After St. Clair created a new county for Connecticut settlers along Lake Erie by executive decree and promised to establish other new counties, some of the resentment against him began to wane. At the same time, mistrust between the Marietta and Cincinnati assemblymen led to a narrow defeat for a bill to rotate the capital between them or to move it to Cincinnati. The assembly rejected a bill to call a statehood convention but narrowly supported the desirability of statehood and passed a bill allowing rural voting places that in the long run would reduce the relative power of town voters. St. Clair finally prorogued the legislature on December 9, 1800, the date his current term expired.

During this struggle, St. Clair's foes wrote to President Adams, charging the governor with being incompetent, alcoholic, and dictatorial and urging the president to not reappoint him. St. Clair defended his record, attributing the Northwest's growth to his steady administration and arguing that he was too poor to be an alcoholic. Adams ended up sending all correspondence to the Senate, and with strong support from Senator John Brown of Kentucky and from the popular Territorial Delegate William McMillan, St. Clair received another term. However, when Thomas Jefferson was chosen president in 1801, and a Jeffersonian majority prepared to take their seats in Congress later that year, the Northwest's Jeffersonians suddenly acquired powerful allies.

St. Clair's coalition dominated the assembly that met late in 1801. He won this support by creating more new counties by executive decree and cementing the alliance between Marietta and Cincinnati. The assembly that met in Chillicothe passed a bill to move the capital to Cincinnati, and it petitioned the central government for a new territorial division along the Scioto River. This sparked angry riots in Chillicothe, with populist attorney Michael Baldwin leading a mob that threatened some of St. Clair's supporters. St. Clair and Thomas Worthington, a much more restrained Republican leader, faced Baldwin down, and the potential for violence faded. Before it adjourned, the assembly defeated a proposal for instant statehood, although it passed a bill calling for a census. While the assembly's actions seemed to augur well for a new division of the Northwest, Chillicothe's leaders soon launched their own response, sending Worthington and Baldwin to Washington to lobby against division and for the removal of St. Clair.

The Chillicothe delegation presented a major challenge to the Marietta-Cincinnati coalition, which responded with great apathy. Supporters of another division proposed sending a counter delegation to Washington but never raised the money to cover the costs. It seems that the supporters had simply assumed that proposing a new division would be the only step that would be needed. That might have been the case under the Adams administration, but when coalition members realized that President Jefferson and a Republican Congress would soon meet a Republican delegation from the Virginia-settled Scioto Valley, they lost all hope of getting a new territorial division.

Territorial Delegate Paul Fearing, the only lobbyist in Washington in 1802 seeking support for another division, proved ineffective, but he probably could not have won in any case. Even the majority of Federalists in the U.S. House voted against his proposal to divide the Northwest along the Scioto River, which was defeated 81 to 5. Congress went on to pass a bill summoning a statehood convention for the Northwest. Since members of the territorial assembly from Detroit had supported St. Clair, and therefore given Wayne County (lower Michigan) a reputation for Federalism, Congress removed this area from the proposed state, thus guaranteeing that Ohio would be strongly Jeffersonian.

While Baldwin and Worthington managed the defeat of the Federalists' division plan, they failed to remove St. Clair from office. The governor made a personal visit to Jefferson, and after a private conversation, the president decided to keep him. Although Jefferson did not discuss this decision, he probably wanted to avoid controversy and felt that rapid statehood would end St. Clair's tenure quickly enough. There were also several Republicans who hoped to succeed St. Clair, and retaining him in office was one way to avoid having to choose among them.

St. Clair may have felt that he had little to lose at this point. After he returned to the Northwest, he got into a series of petty quarrels with Secretary Charles Willing Byrd, so that if Jefferson had hoped to achieve harmony by allowing him to stay in office, this was clearly not happening. More important, St. Clair joined other Northwest Federalists in trying to elect anti-statehood delegates to the potential state's Constitutional Convention. The governor clearly misread the situation. When the convention began in November 1802, St. Clair tried to take it over. He appeared on opening day, named a secretary, and told the members to give him their election certificates. They ignored him. Two days later, however, they accepted his request to make a speech. Nathaniel Massie accurately predicted that St. Clair would speak intemperately. The governor charged that only Chillicotheans supported statehood and that their goal was to introduce black slav-

ery on a massive scale. He denied that Congress had any right to force
a convention or statehood upon the Northwest, noted that Vermont
had governed itself for eight years, and concluded that "We have the
means in our hands to bring Congress to reason, if we should be
forced to use them. If we submit to the degradation, we should be
trodden upon, and what is worse, we should deserve to be trodden
upon." St. Clair's enemies immediately sent a copy of this address to
President Jefferson, who promptly fired him. St. Clair declared upon
hearing of his removal that he could now escape from a position that
he did not want.

St. Clair remained with his sons in Cincinnati for a few years after
his removal from office. He returned to Pennsylvania to run an iron
furnace, and tried to get $9,000 from Congress to compensate for
money he had spent during the 1791 campaign. Since a fire had
destroyed War Department records, Congress would not approve the
funds. St. Clair's business failed in 1810, and he thereafter eked out
a living running a tavern and horse relay station. Pennsylvania voted
him a $200 annuity in 1813, and increased it to $600 in 1817. St.
Clair died in 1818.

Arthur St. Clair enjoyed both success and failure in his long tenure
as governor of the Northwest Territory. He extended U.S. authority
to distant regions and built up a chain of appointed officials loyal to
him and the central government. He also made a strong stand against
excessive land speculation. Although he had little real chance to delay
statehood, St. Clair developed the one possible coalition that might
have produced a Federalist state. At the same time, he quarreled with
judges, legislators, and others over matters both serious and minor.
He did not hesitate to collect fees despite approving an assembly bill
that was to compensate him for giving them up. He was a poor general in the 1791 campaign against the Indians, and when he fell into
a deep depression about his ruined career, he became an absentee
governor for more than six years. Like many eastern leaders, he sincerely doubted that frontier settlers could govern themselves and
never understood their deep desire for self-government. His efforts to
delay the assembly process and statehood, and to retain a system that
included top-down political appointments and the creation of local
government units by decree, were doomed to fail. St. Clair represented a form of paternalism that might have worked in the 1750s but
was clearly no longer viable in the post-Revolutionary frontier. He
was in many respects a tragic figure, elevated somewhat above his
talents and placed in authority during an era when his political

philosophy was outdated. Given his flaws, he accomplished perhaps as much as the nation could have hoped for.

Further Reading

Brown, Jeffrey P. "Arthur St. Clair and the Northwest Territory." *Northwest Ohio Quarterly* (Summer 1987): 75–90.

Bond, Beverley W., Jr. *The Foundations of Ohio.* Columbus: Ohio State Archaeological and Historical Society, 1941.

Cayton, Andrew R. L. *The Frontier Republic: Ideology and Politics in the Ohio Country, 1780–1825.* Kent, Ohio: Kent State University Press, 1986.

Onuf, Peter S. *Statehood and Union: A History of the Northwest Ordinance.* Bloomington: Indiana University Press, 1987.

Sword, Wiley. *President Washington's Indian War: The Struggle for the Old Northwest, 1790–1795.* Norman: University of Oklahoma Press, 1985.

4

Little Turtle, Blue Jacket, and the Second Tribal Confederation, 1783–1795

ALLAN R. MILLETT

AFTER CONGRESSIONAL passage of the Land Ordinance of 1785, which provided for the survey and sale of federal lands north of the Ohio River, promised to unleash a stream of white migration into the region, outraged representatives of the area's eleven Indian nations met along the Detroit River in late 1786 to coordinate their response. Mohawk leader Joseph Brant opened the meeting by reminding those assembled that "the interests of any one nation should be the welfare of all others," but divisions soon developed. The Shawnee and the Miami, whose lands were among the most vulnerable to white encroachment, demanded united action to hold the Ohio River boundary against the Americans. Tribes that had already ceded land north of the Ohio to the United States—the Delaware and Wyandot—and tribes whose land was not immediately threatened—Ottawa and Potawatomi—urged reconciliation with the Americans. In the end, the noncompromisers prevailed as the tribes agreed that without some sort of coordinated resistance, the Americans would continue their western movement by negotiating land cessions with individual chiefs. The assembled representatives sent to Congress the Huron Town Declaration, which invalidated all previous treaties and declared the Ohio River as the boundary between their tribes and the United States. The tribes also agreed to hold all of their land in common and make no further cessions without the approval of all the other tribes. In effect, the tribes at Huron Town declared war on the United States.

This Native American alliance became the Second Tribal Confederation. The First Confederation occurred in 1763 as tribes united behind the Ottawa war chief Pontiac to fight the British and their American colonists. The Third Confederation, led by the Shawnee chief Tecumseh and his brother the Prophet, began in the first decade of the nineteenth century and ended in defeat during the War of 1812. Fittingly, the hard liners took the lead in the Second Tribal Confederation. Miami war chief Mesekinnoquah ("Little Turtle") and a Shawnee counterpart Waweyapiersenwaw ("Whirlpool," known to Europeans as Blue Jacket) emerged as the two most important leaders of the Native American alliance that would defeat two of the three expeditions sent to destroy it and block the white settlement of Ohio until the middle of the 1790s.

The Miami and Shawnee nations—themselves confederations of clans—arrived in the lands north of the Ohio River in the early eighteenth century. Although the Miami and Shawnee shared a common linguistic and cultural heritage, they came from different directions, both fleeing hostile tribal confederations. The Miami arrived after being pushed south and east from the lands around Lake Michigan and Lake Huron by the Chippewa, Ojibwa, and Potawatomi. Their eastward movement was stopped by other refugee tribes—the Wyandot, Delaware, Ottawa, and Shawnee—who had been displaced by the Iroquois Confederation. Numbering four thousand men, women, and children in the 1780s, the Miami occupied the lands near where the St. Joseph and St. Mary's Rivers join to form the Maumee and where the Eel River meets the Wabash (now northwest Ohio and northeast Indiana). The Miami hunted as far south as the Ohio River. The Shawnee (Saanwanwa or "southern people") had been wanderers from the southern Appalachians until they were driven from western Pennsylvania by the Mohawk, the westernmost member of the Iroquois Confederacy. Unable to migrate south due to the presence of the Creek and the Cherokee, the Shawnee settled in villages along the Muskingum, Licking, Scioto, the Little Miami, and the Great Miami Rivers (now central and southern Ohio) and hunted south of the Ohio River.

Both tribes were integrated into the frontier trading network. Indians hunted for meat for themselves and hides and fur, which could be sold to English or French traders for European goods. The hunts required men to be away from their villages for months at a time and to range over large areas looking for game. Consequently, women engaged in maize-bean-squash agriculture, a staple diet for many of the Miami and Shawnee. While the Shawnee traded with both European powers and their colonists, the Miami favored French traders operating out of Fort Detroit.

Little is known about the early life of either Little Turtle or Blue Jacket, who were both born in the mid-1740s. Legend has it that Blue Jacket was actually a white captive named Marmaduke von Swearingen who adopted Shawnee ways, but there is no evidence to support this myth. Like most Shawnee youth, Blue Jacket's father taught him how to hunt and fight as a warrior. These skills were necessary as Blue Jacket came of age during the French and Indian War (1754–1763). Although the Shawnee sided with the French, they fought to keep their land free of European control. The young Blue Jacket probably joined the raiding parties that ranged along the Pennsylvania and Virginia frontiers.

Compared to Blue Jacket, Little Turtle's early life was relatively peaceful. With their villages west of the main theaters of the French and Indian War, the Miami managed to avoid the conflicts. The son of Turtle, a Miami war chief, and his Delaware wife, Little Turtle grew up in the Miami village of Turtletown in present-day northeastern Indiana. His first opportunity to lead a war party came in 1780 when he and a Turtletown war band ambushed a French-American party intent on looting the Miami village of Kekionaga in the name of the American Revolution. Little Turtle's plan worked to perfection. The Miami band lost just five of its thirty warriors, while killing over half of the sixty raiders. Little Turtle had established himself as a sagacious and courageous war chief.

In the years after the victory, Little Turtle forged a special relationship with a white youth, William Wells, with whom he would remain close until their deaths in 1812. Captured in a 1784 raid on Kentucky, the red-headed Wells had been orphaned during an earlier raid by the Shawnee. Wells took quickly to tribal life, and from 1784 until 1792 he lived a full and dangerous warrior's life, even luring settlers to their death. Known as "the Carrot," he married one of Little Turtle's daughters, Sweet Breeze, and became a trusted counselor and negotiator for Little Turtle's dealings with the hated Kentuckians. As a champion of the Miami and a foe of the Shawnee, who had killed his father, Wells's life became entwined with those of Little Turtle and Blue Jacket.

The Second Confederation had roots in the aftermath of the French and Indian War. With the defeat of the French in 1763, the British took control of the former French posts around the Great Lakes and in trans-Appalachia. As guardians of the frontier, British troops faced conflicting land claims and commercial interests. White settlers from the coastal colonies claimed trans-Appalachian lands as

their reward for their service against the French. However, Native
Americans who had been British allies, especially the Iroquois Confederacy in the north and the Cherokee in the south, expected the
Crown to help protect their lands. British agents also had to deal with
hostile Great Lakes tribes that had fought alongside the French. After
the French surrender, these tribes, led by Pontiac, joined together in
the First Confederation and attacked British posts on the Great Lakes
and the Ohio Valley. Although the British defeated Pontiac's Rebellion at a great cost of men and money, they realized that the Great
Lakes tribes had to be appeased or cowed if the area was to remain
peaceful and British expenses kept at a minimum.

Initially, the British tried to solve these problems with the Proclamation of 1763, which forbade white settlement west of the fall line
of the Appalachian Mountains. This ruling infuriated the colonists,
many of whom were also upset by British efforts to tax the colonies
to pay for the entire French and Indian War. Trying to appease the
colonists while not alienating the Iroquois or the Cherokee, the British
negotiated the Treaty of Fort Stanwix (New York) in 1768. This
treaty with the Iroquois permitted white settlement south of the
Ohio River in what is now West Virginia and eastern Kentucky, an
area occupied or hunted by relatively weak and patronless tribes—the
Delaware, Mingo, Wyandot, and, especially, the Shawnee. Later, the
British allowed white migration as far west as the Kentucky River near
the border of Miami lands.

As settlers moved into the Ohio Valley, hostilities between
the whites and the tribes increased. Raids, massacres, retaliatory
expeditions, and outright murders of innocents and peacemakers
culminated in Lord Dunmore's War (1774), which ended with the
settlers' Pyrrhic victory over the Shawnee at the Battle of Point
Pleasant (West Virginia). The battle marked Blue Jacket's first major
fight with the Virginia "big knives" and taught him the value of surprise and firepower under traumatic conditions. The outbreak of the
American Revolution in 1775 ensured that frontier warfare would
intensify and spread westward since the colonists sent expeditions
against British positions as far west as the Mississippi River. In these
battles with the Virginians and Kentuckians, Blue Jacket emerged as
one of the most effective and successful of the Shawnee war chiefs.

The frontier fighting between 1776–1783 cemented the alliance
between the Shawnee, most area tribes, the British, and their Loyalist sympathizers. Using posts at Detroit and Niagara as bases, the
British organized several expeditions against American positions on

the frontier and aided Indian efforts to drive off the American settlers. Loyalists such as William Bulter, John and Walter Butler, Alexander McKee, Matthew Elliot, and the Girty brothers (James, George, and Simon) fought alongside the Indians. Often the Loyalist-tribal relationship was strengthened by marriages with Shawnee or Wyandot women. To get closer to their allies and away from white settlers, the Shawnee relocated their villages westward to the banks of the Mad River and later to areas near the confluence of the Auglaize and Maumee Rivers.

The Miami tried to remain isolated from the war, but George Rogers Clark's seizure of Kaskaskia and Vincennes put the Americans on the Miami's beloved Wabash River. Little Turtle's victory over an expedition attacking the Miami village of Kekionaga constituted the only notable Miami contribution to the fight against the Americans. Although Little Turtle did not refuse British aid, he never fully trusted his allies, preferring to depend upon French traders for food, supplies, weapons, and military advice. Nevertheless, he watched with alarm as Kentucky settlements spread west along the Ohio River.

Victories by the Delaware, Wyandot, and Shawnee in 1781 and 1782 stopped American expeditions into the Ohio country, but the British defeat at Yorktown signaled a new phase in the conflict. When the British told their tribal allies that the Great King's war with the Americans had ended, they did not explain that their lands were now a "national domain" under the jurisdiction of the U.S. Congress. Instead, the British officers and traders promised that they would still do business with the tribes. If the warriors continued to fight, the British would do nothing to discourage them. Under the leadership of Joseph Brant, tribal delegations met in July 1783 and again in the fall of 1784 to discuss a coordinated strategy to stop settlement at the Ohio River, the boundary agreed upon in the Fort Stanwix Treaty of 1768. But while the tribes debated, the Americans were negotiating with the Iroquois a second Treaty of Fort Stanwix (1784) that gave them entree into the area north of the Ohio River. Even with this provocation, tribal unity did not come until the chiefs met in late 1786 and issued the Huron Town Declaration.

American movement into the Ohio country increased in 1787 with the passage of the Northwest Ordinance, which provided for a territorial government, prohibited slavery, protected the rights of individual landowners, required a system of public education, and established the process to transform the territory into as many as five states. Within two years more than twenty thousand settlers flooded

into the area, mostly along the Ohio River. Arthur St. Clair, a
mediocre general in the Continental Army and a powerful Pennsylvania politician, became territorial governor. He established his meager
office at the army post at the mouth of the Muskingum. With only
five hundred men commanded by Colonel Josiah Harmar at his dis-
posal, St. Clair recognized the need to avoid conflict with the Indians. In late 1788, St. Clair enticed some curious or defeatist Ottawa,
Delaware, and Wyandot to a conference to receive money and gifts
for lands ceded east of the Miami River. Delegates from the Sauk,
Chippewa, and Potawatomi appeared for the handouts since none of
the lands were theirs anyway. No Shawnee or Miami attended.

After St. Clair played out the limited peace talks of late 1788, a
new national government headed by President George Washington
took control of frontier affairs. Secretary of War Henry Knox wanted
St. Clair and Harmar to march on the Second Confederation's heartland, the Miami and Shawnee towns along the Maumee and Wabash
Rivers. The mission would have two purposes: to disrupt the Second
Confederation and to pressure the British to live up to their treaty
obligation to hand over Fort Detroit to the Americans. Since the
Americans regarded the Shawnee leaders—Black Hoof, Black Snake,
Blue Jacket, and even the young Tecumseh—as dangerous adver-
saries, they decided to attack the Miami villages first. This would be
the first test for Little Turtle and the nineteen-year-old William Wells.

By September 1790, Harmar had assembled 1,400 officers and
men for the expedition against the Miami villages. Although this constituted the largest military force yet assembled by Americans on the
frontier, the numbers did not translate into military effectiveness.
Regular troops numbered only 320 with the rest coming from militia
units composed of inexperienced and undisciplined settlers and border riffraff. Leaving Fort Washington (now Cincinnati) in late September, Harmar's army moved cautiously northwards for two weeks
without any contact with Miami or Shawnee scouts. Unknown to
Harmar, the size of his army had demoralized the tribes, who had
fled, allowing the Americans to burn thousands of bushels of corn
and the five southernmost Miami villages. Harmar then ordered his
army northwestward toward the heart of the Miami territory. By this
time, intelligence from scouts directed by William Wells had convinced Little Turtle that the American force was less fearsome than its
size suggested and that Harmar was too concerned with his supply
lines to devote all of his force to battle. Little Turtle reasoned that the
key to defeating the American expedition was to destroy the U.S.

Army regulars and a unit of mounted Kentucky riflemen, which together composed about one-third of Harmar's force. With only two hundred Miami and a handful of Shawnee, Little Turtle began a battle of attrition with the hope that any victory would draw more warriors into the fray.

Little Turtle got the needed victory on October 19 when he surprised a mounted reconnaissance patrol. Harmar sent the 180 regulars and militiamen under the command of John Hardin to reconnoiter the area around Turtletown. A mile outside, Hardin sent mounted riflemen into the village. The riflemen reported that a handful of warriors were retreating and that the village was open to swift attack. Hardin ordered his force to attack the village, but not all of his men received the word. With the Americans strung out for a mile along a forested trail, Little Turtle's warriors struck. The battle quickly became a rout with Hardin losing about half of his force and Little Turtle losing less than ten warriors.

Stunned by Hardin's disaster, Harmar concluded that the campaign must end soon because of dwindling supplies and the militia's unreliability. Before leaving, though, Harmar decided to launch one last raid on the Miami village of Kekionga, hoping to catch Little Turtle's two hundred warriors by surprise. To ensure success, Harmar picked four hundred of his best soldiers who would lead the attack and placed them under the command of Major John Wyllys. Wyllys and Hardin devised a clever but risky plan to encircle Kekionga and annihilate Little Turtle's force. The Americans divided their force into three columns. One group would attack from the south, while the other two would march on the village from the east and west. The plan depended on speed, surprise, good tactical judgment, decisive numerical superiority, discipline, timing, and luck.

Although his scouts detected the movement of the Americans, Little Turtle had little inkling of the American plan when he prepared his men for battle. He set fires in nearby villages and cornfields to give the illusion of Miami defeat and deployed about half of his men along the steep north bank of the Maumee River with orders to ambush the Americans from concealed positions. After the initial encounter the men were to fall back until they reached a second ambush site in the woods where Little Turtle and the rest of his men waited.

The battle did not go as either side envisioned. The timing of the American plan went awry when one of the three columns engaged a solitary Miami scout. Hearing the gunfire, Wyllys believed that the plan had been compromised and prematurely ordered his column

into action. His column crossed the Maumee into the Miami ambush.
Wyllys's force suffered heavy casualties and would have been wiped
out if Major James McMillan's Kentucky militia had not arrived on
the scene and flanked the Miami ambush party. McMillan's men
routed the Miami, who fled so quickly that Little Turtle could not
spring the second ambush in time to catch the Kentucky militia.
Wyllys's infantry, however, now following behind McMillan's horse-
men, stumbled into Little Turtle's ambush with devastating results.
Wyllys and all but ten of his soldiers were cut down before McMillan's
men came to the rescue yet again. Seeing that the Americans had con-
solidated what was left of their forces, Little Turtle concluded that the
Miami could not win an open battle against a numerically superior
force and ordered a withdrawal. The defeat further demoralized the
Americans, who lost nearly two hundred men to the Miami's forty.

A freak of nature probably saved Harmar's expedition from a
much worse defeat. Little Turtle learned from prisoners that Harmar's force was low on moral, food, and manpower. At the same
time, Blue Jacket arrived with seven hundred Shawnee and Ottawa
warriors. With Blue Jacket's arrival, the two men began their military
collaboration, devising a plan to attack Harmar while the Americans
were stretched thin on a march through a forest. That night, however, a lunar eclipse blotted out the full moon, and the Ottawa and
other new arrivals decided that the omens were not propitious and
departed before daybreak. With only the battered Miami and too few
Shawnee, Blue Jacket and Little Turtle called off the attack. They
had, however, seen an outnumbered and determined tribal force
defeat the largest U.S. army sent to the frontier.

Little Turtle's unexpected victory over the Harmar expedition
steeled the determination of both sides. The Shawnee, Delaware,
Wyandot, and Ottawa had homelands to recover, not just defend,
and they sent small raiding parties as far as the Ohio River in the winter of 1790–91 and put more settlers into early graves. Blue Jacket
himself took one successful war party within twenty miles of Fort
Washington. British agents in Detroit kept up the flow of weapons
and handled the business of selling loot and ransoming prisoners.
Although Little Turtle remained wary of the British, reflecting the
counsel of his family and William Wells, Blue Jacket and the Shawnee
strengthened their ties to Loyalists such as Matthew Elliot and
Alexander McKee. During the that winter, President Washington
and Secretary of War Knox held tutorials on frontier warfare for St.
Clair, now reappointed to his Revolutionary War rank of major gen-

eral. The three decided that St. Clair should take an expedition north to establish a fort near the Miami villages. They wanted St. Clair to assemble three thousand troops, one-third regulars and two-thirds volunteers from Ohio and Kentucky, but mustered into federal service for six months and paid and supplied by the national government. Raising federal volunteers made sense since the strategy demanded administrative skill, patience, and discipline, attributes that most militias lacked. Like Julius Caesar in Gaul—and Washington and Knox knew the *Commentaries*—St. Clair would establish a line of forts along his route from Fort Washington to where the St. Mary's River met the St. Joseph to form the Maumee (now Fort Wayne, Indiana). Washington advised St. Clair to assume all tribesmen were hostile and to make short daily marches and fortify his camps nightly.

While he was assembling his expedition, St. Clair encouraged Kentucky to send raiding parties against the Miami tribes. A party of 750 mounted riflemen destroyed four villages along the Wabash and took fifty-three Miami women and children hostage. A second party burned Turtletown and took thirty-four hostages, including the wives of Little Turtle and William Wells.

St. Clair's expedition left its encampment more or less as planned in early September 1791. Unfortunately, that fall proved to be much wetter and colder than normal, making marching and fort construction arduous and time consuming. The expedition's biggest problem, though, was St. Clair. He proved unable to master the complicated logistics of moving three thousand troops (and several hundred women and children who accompanied the expedition as dependents and laborers), disregarded the advice of capable deputies, ignored Knox's suggestion to take additional mounted troops, and became so obsessed with supply problems that he reduced his troops' rations by half even before they had encountered the enemy. By the middle of October, morale was low and desertions were high.

From their lodges along the Wabash and Maumee Rivers, Little Turtle and Blue Jacket watched St. Clair's ordeal with some amusement. While scouting parties, often led by Wells and Tecumseh, kept track of St. Clair's every move, more than one thousand warriors were gathering along the Maumee. Since more than half of the warriors were Shawnee or Miami, Little Turtle and Blue Jacket dominated the discussions of tactical planning, but the war chiefs of the Ottawa, Chippewa, Wyandot, Potawatomi, and Delaware no doubt spoke their turn. Given his earlier success against Harmar, Little Turtle probably emerged as the de facto general of the Confederation. The chiefs decided to surprise St. Clair's army as it crossed the Wabash, the place where it would be most disorganized. The warriors broke camp on October 28 and headed south to meet the Americans, who were fifty miles away and unaware of the force that awaited them.

On November 3, the main body of St. Clair's army reached the Wabash River near the present site of Greenville, Ohio. Cold, wet, and exhausted, the army set up its camp in a rectangle, seventy yards east-west and four hundred yards north-south. That night St. Clair met with his officers and announced that the army would wait for the return of the U.S. First Regiment, which he had dispatched to round up about sixty deserters. St. Clair, though, ordered no entrenchments or special efforts to fortify the camp.

As the Americans slept, the tribal army deployed for an early morning attack designed to trap and annihilate St. Clair's army, which had a slight numerical advantage and light artillery. The plan was simple and reflected the fact that no tribal war party could be redirected once engaged. Blue Jacket and Little Turtle would lead the Miami and the Shawnee in the main attack along the long western perimeter, while the other tribes would attack from other directions. Blue Jacket and Little Turtle hoped that with pressure on the entire perimeter that St. Clair would have difficulty moving reinforcements to meet a breakthrough.

The battle began around 5:00 A.M. on November 4 and ended before noon in the worst defeat of an American army in the history of Continental expansion. The Blue Jacket–Little Turtle main attack began well, but it was unable to break through as the Americans reinforced the western line. The attacks on the other three lines did lead to some breakthroughs, especially on the southern line where the tribesmen easily overwhelmed the lone mounted company and massacred many of the camp's women, children, and stragglers. Only through the effort of Lt. Col. William Darke and the U.S. Second Regiment were the Americans able to seal the breaches in the lines, but they remained surrounded. The tribes continued their fire. Around 10:00 A.M., St. Clair, who had been unhorsed several times and had too few staff members to influence the battle, ordered a breakout. The Americans stormed the eastern line and began pouring through the Wyandot position, but the Shawnee and Miami closed from the rear, wiping out the regulars holding open the breach. Groups of tribesmen prowled the road and woods, killing and scalping those who could not make their escape. The corpses of more than six hundred American soldiers and two hundred civilians littered the battlefield. One survivor remembered clouds of hot pink fog hanging over freshly scalped soldiers. Little Turtle did not organize any real pursuit of the Americans, who managed to escape. Only about six hundred Americans survived battle, more than half of them wounded. When Washington received word of the disaster, he railed against St. Clair's stupidity: "Oh God! Oh God! He is worse than a murderer."

St. Clair's Defeat, as the Americans called it, brought the tribes a brief respite from American military pressure while the Washington administration formed another army. Blue Jacket and Little Turtle now pursued different strategies to protect their people. Little Turtle and his son-in-law William Wells tried to use the victory to reach an accommodation with the Americans. Little Turtle and most of the Miami did not give up their insistence that there be no American settlement north of the Ohio, but they did open negotiations for the return of hostages, including Little Turtle's wife and daughter. A few minor chiefs, however, signed nonaggression pacts with the Americans. Perhaps trying to drive a wedge in the Confederation, the American commissioner, General Rufus Putnam, secured the release of the Miami hostages and showered the Miami with gifts and pledges of friendship and peace. These activities did not stop Little Turtle from launching attacks on American military targets in an attempt to force the army to abandon its outposts north of the Ohio.

At this time, Wells decided to leave his life as a Miami warrior and return to his brother's family in Kentucky for what he said would be a quiet farmer's life with his wife. Wells, however, remained in touch with the Miami and agreed to serve as one of Putnam's negotiators in peace talks with the Delaware, Potawatomi, and other Miami clans. Wells clearly retained Little Turtle's trust and protection as he was the only one of six American negotiators to return alive from their missions. The Shawnee, Wyandot, and Ottawa as well as the British did not trust Wells, whom they considered to be interested only in the welfare of the Miami and the Kentuckians, but they allowed him to live for the sake of the Confederation.

As the Miami sought some sort of accommodation with the Americans, the other tribes that had participated in St. Clair's Defeat remained inflamed with "victory disease," an absolute conviction of military invincibility. This lessened the influence of Little Turtle over the Confederation and increased the influence of the bellicose Blue Jacket, who became the most dominant figure in Confederation councils. At the councils, Blue Jacket, his rhetorical passions inflamed by British whiskey, became the leading proponent of war. Shawnee,

Wyandot, and Ottawa war parties ranged over southern Ohio, killing settlers and soldiers as far east as Fort Wheeling and as far west as Fort Washington. Unlike the Miami, who hit military targets and had a strategic purpose, most of these attacks were aimed at isolated farms and settlements and thus of limited military value. They did, however, increase the warriors' sense of power and purpose.

Blue Jacket prepared for another battle with the Americans by increasing Confederation ties to the British. He began working more closely with Britain's Lt. Governor for Upper Canada and British agents Elliot and McKee. Blue Jacket and his British allies agreed that the conflict in the Ohio country would develop into a full-scale war between the United States and Britain, and he applauded the British decision to built a new post, Fort Miami, along the Maumee. Whatever garment had given him his English name, Blue Jacket most often wore the red tunic of a British army officer.

The Washington administration saw a frontier war forthcoming, but it did not want a larger conflict with Great Britain. Washington made one last attempt to avert war with the Ohio tribes through negotiations, but the Confederation council held fast to its demand: no settlement north of the river. Washington also dispatched a delegation to London to try to ease relations with the British, which he met with more success. With the French Revolution in full swing, King George III thought it wise to avert a conflict with the Americans. Although the two sides would not sign Jay's Treaty (in which Britain agreed to abandon its forts on U.S. soil) until after the defeat of the Second Confederation, the fact that negotiations were underway helped cool tensions between the two nations and made the British less willing to help their Indian allies.

Washington faced the challenge of forming a new army and finding a new general. After extensive debate on militia reform and expense, the Federalist-dominated Congress accepted Knox's plea for a regular army of at least five thousand officers and men for one more Ohio campaign. Congress could (and did) find a cheaper long-term solution in militia reform, but only disciplined, trained regulars could conduct the protracted campaign in the Northwest Territory that Knox envisioned. Washington and Knox found their general in forty-seven-year-old Anthony Wayne, a Revolutionary War officer with practical soldierly skills and public appeal. A failed land speculator, Wayne desperately needed a job, and he promised Washington and Knox that he could conduct the careful conquest of Ohio they wanted without pushing the British into the war.

Wayne's plan required the restoration of the U.S. Army for offensive purposes and the security of the line of forts the Americans had established north of Fort Washington. The forts were to serve as a logistical depot system that could supply an expedition of several thousand for an extended period. Unlike Harmar and St. Clair, Wayne was not leading a raiding party but an army that would stay, if necessary, as far north as the Maumee. Wayne created his special army—the Legion of the United States—with all the panache of his idol, Julius Caesar. He began organizing the legion at an encampment south of Pittsburgh where he recruited three-quarters of his 3,500-man force with bounties of money and land. The others were survivors of the earlier campaigns. Unlike his predecessors, who took undisciplined troops into battle, Wayne spent from late 1792 until October 1793 training his troops. The army began its campaign in early October when it left its second encampment north of Fort Washington.

The Legion of the United States advanced slowly and methodically. The general took great care to keep the army well supplied. The column often stopped while waiting for adequate provisions to be brought up by pack train. These problems forced Wayne to halt his advance and go into a Roman-like fortified winter quarters, Camp Greene Ville (now Greenville). When resupplied, part of the army marched to the site of St. Clair's Defeat, some twenty-six miles to the north. The army built a small fort at the site (Fort Recovery), found three of St. Clair's cannon barrels that had been buried by the tribes, and left a one-hundred-man garrison with the three guns remounted to hold what Wayne planned to make his most northern supply depot. Heavily guarded pack trains kept the fort supplied after January 1794.

With the army at Fort Recovery awaiting supplies, Wayne sent his scouts, led by William Wells in the rank of captain, further north to take prisoners to interrogate and hold them as hostages. Dressed as warriors, the scouts wrecked havoc along the Maumee and the Auglaize Rivers. In response, Blue Jacket and the other chiefs demanded action with British support, and even Little Turtle agreed to take the field since the expedition had a real objective: eliminate Fort Recovery. Blue Jacket agreed, and the two united in command once again to defeat the Americans.

The June 1794 Fort Recovery expedition marked the high point of Second Confederation cooperation, and its failure started the intertribal disintegration that contributed to Wayne's eventual victory. The expedition began with a combined force of one thousand, made up of mostly Shawnee and Miami but also including other tribes as well as British traders. Wayne's army gained an advantage when Wells' scouts ambushed a Miami advance party and learned from a captive that Fort Recovery was the primary objective. Wayne, whose main army was at Camp Green Ville, immediately ordered the fort provisioned with enough food and ammunition to sustain a siege. In the race to get to Fort Recovery, the pack train beat the war party by one day. Little Turtle now urged the other chiefs to ignore the fort and attack the empty pack train with its three hundred valuable horses when it left the fort. It is unclear if Little Turtle just wanted the horses or if he was setting a trap. If so, the trap worked. After the Shawnee-Miami ambush began, the garrison commander opened the fort gates to send reinforcements. The gates stayed open long enough for the train guards and rescue party (minus the forty who died) to make it back to safety.

Blue Jacket allowed the opportunity to storm the gates to pass as his Shawnee were busy chasing horses, looting, and scalping soldiers. The Wyandot, Ottawa, and other tribes attempted a belated rush of the gates, but musket and cannon fire drove them back. After the initial assault, Little Turtle argued that without cannon, the fort could not be taken and would not commit his men to the sallies mounted by the Shawnee, Ottawa, and Wyandot at Blue Jacket's command. The British urged Blue Jacket and the tribes to keep the siege going until the Americans had exhausted their powder and gave up. The siege though lasted only a day as more than forty tribesmen, mostly Ottawa and Wyandot, lost their lives. This split the Confederation as most of the warriors headed home with their horses and loot.

The Second Confederation expedition to Fort Recovery proved the inability of the war chiefs to organize a campaign of strategic importance. The growing rivalry between Little Turtle and Blue Jacket exasperated the British agents, who sided with the more bellicose Blue Jacket. The British agents also encouraged the participation of the Great Lakes tribes: Chippewa, Saginaw, Ojibwa, and Mackinac. Led by veterans of Pontiac's Rebellion, the these tribes believed that European forts could be taken by guile since they had done it before, and their presence initially tilted the balance of power toward the Shawnee. Early histories of the battle of Fort Recovery, largely written by the British agents who had accompanied the war party, tended to blame Little Turtle for the defeat. They claimed that Little Turtle and his allies wanted to raid supply trains for scalps, horses, and loot rather than to disrupt Wayne's supply line. The Great Lakes tribes, however, blamed Blue Jacket for his weak leadership and shared interest in looting.

After the defeat, Little Turtle headed to Detroit where he complained to the fort's commander about the limits of British aid. He wanted to know why the British supplied so little powder and why they favored the Shawnee, Wyandot, and Ottawa over the more disciplined and effective Miami. Calling Little Turtle "the most decent, modest, sensible Indian I ever conversed with," Detroit's commander promised British support. Nonetheless, Little Turtle feared betrayal and at the next council meeting warned the other tribes of British treachery, but he was shouted down and told that negotiations with the Americans were unthinkable. The chiefs asserted that Blue Jacket was their unchallenged leader and reminded Little Turtle that his son-in-law Wells was a traitor with a price on his head.

In summer 1794, Wayne moved into the last phase of his campaign. With his supply line secure, he called in reinforcements, including two seven-hundred-man Kentucky brigades. He began moving on Miami and Shawnee villages. Wayne's army met little resistance as the tribes feared a direct confrontation with the disciplined and well-supplied army. With the deployment of scouts and constant patrolling, Wayne provided the tribes with no opportunity for an ambush. When the army reached the Shawnee heartland at the confluence of the Auglaize and Maumee Rivers on August 8, it found a series of abandoned villages and fields of unharvested corn. Wayne halted and built another post—Fort Defiance—at the site of Blue Jacket's own home and council site.

Other than the obvious fact that the Shawnee had moved down river toward the newly built Fort Miami, garrisoned by two companies of British regulars, Wayne had no clear picture of the enemy situation. Neither did the enemy since Blue Jacket could forge no consensus. Tribes with the least to lose—Ottawa and Potawatomi—wanted to attack, while others—the Shawnee, Delaware, and Wyandot—wanted to ambush the Americans near Fort Miami. Little Turtle avoided the bickering. In the end, the Confederation decided to ambush Wayne's army. In the meantime, Wayne laid waste to Shawnee villages along the Maumee, while sending Wells and his scouts to gather more information. Wells gave Wayne a better picture of the situation: the Confederation force of 1,100 to 1,300 tribesmen lay in wait fifteen miles downstream in a thick forest and maze of fallen trees called Fallen Timbers.

After one last call for peace talks on August 14, Wayne began marching downstream. An August 18 skirmish demonstrated that Confederation warriors were in strength and ready for a fight. That night Wayne halted his army once more in its standard fortified camp and spent the next day resting, preparing for battle, and building an earthworks enclosure for baggage and supplies. Wayne's caution disconcerted the warriors, who had begun fasting in preparation for an August 18 battle. Some drifted way for food on August 19, and a sudden, violent thunderstorm that day further weakened Indian morale. Advised by Wells, Wayne did not advance until the storm had passed since his scouts could see more warriors abandoning their positions. The attack finally occurred at 7:00 A.M. the next morning when the Legion of the United States divided into three columns, screened by mounted troops and dragoons, and advanced down the western bank of the Maumee.

Blue Jacket deployed his dispirited warriors in a rough L-shaped ambush with the hope that the Shawnee, Wyandot, Delaware, and Miami might fall on Wayne's left flank after the Ottawa and Potawatomi engaged his advanced guard. The battle started well for the Indians as the Ottawa and Potawatomi inflicted heavy damage on the mounted guard. Most of the Americans' fifty casualties occurred in the battle's opening minutes. Confident of victory, some Shawnee joined the fight only to find themselves in an open field facing an unbroken infantry line and more mounted troops. The Americans fired a smashing volley before setting upon the Shawnee with bayonets. The Wyandot and Delaware found themselves trapped in the woods and were only saved from annihilation by a Shawnee counterattack led by Tecumseh. The Miami made token resistance and joined the growing rout. Kentucky riflemen killed tribesmen escaping across the Maumee, but the fleeing warriors received their greatest shock when the British commander of Fort Miami would not provide them sanctuary or open fire upon their American pursuers. In less than an hour, the Battle of Fallen Timbers destroyed the Second Confederation.

Their defeat at Fallen Timbers forced Little Turtle, Blue Jacket, and their allies to face the bitter fact that British policy was now to appease the United States. During Wayne's campaign, British officials were negotiating with U.S. Ambassador John Jay, who returned from London in early 1795 with a treaty that, among other things, promised to transfer British forts on American soil to the U.S. Army. After cementing his victory by building the fort that bears his name in the heart of the Miami territory, Wayne returned to his winter encampment at Green Ville and sent scouts to summon the defeated chiefs to a council at the camp in June 1795.

Understanding the shifting balance of power, all of the Confederation's tribes sent delegations to Green Ville. With tribal retinues and families, the number of Indians ran over one thousand. Wayne listened to endless speeches, including Little Turtle's uncompromising lecture on resistance: the Miami had made no binding treaties and had surrendered no lands. In the end, Wayne dictated the terms. He asserted that as English allies during the American Revolution that the tribes had lost their rights in 1783, and he demanded a treaty that opened up 25,000 square miles to white settlement and pushed the Indians into what would become the northwest corner of Ohio. In return, the twelve tribes split $20,000 in gifts and an annuity of $9,500 in goods. In other words, the American government paid the tribes about one-sixth of a cent per acre for most of Ohio.

Although the Treaty of Greenville was the requiem for the Second Confederation, both Little Turtle and Blue Jacket lived on in eclipse. Blue Jacket never recovered the leadership position that he held in 1794. He maintained good relations with the U.S. military and civil officials near his home in Detroit, proclaiming that "I desire to live and die in peace." He returned to Ohio several times after 1795 to visit the sites of his youth in the Scioto valley, and he twice called on the governor of Ohio to protest the lax enforcement of the Treaty of Greenville's provisions for the protection of Shawnee lands. Infirm and a heavy drinker, he lapsed into greater obscurity and died in 1808 near Detroit. He was almost unknown except to a small number of Loyalist friends in Canada. Most were now interested in Tecumseh, a younger Shawnee chief who had boycotted Greenville.

Little Turtle continued to work for the survival of the Miami through the help of Indian agent William Wells, who, his critics charged, worked for Little Turtle and the Miami rather than the other tribes or the United States. With General Wayne's encouragement, Wells escorted Little Turtle to Philadelphia where he met the leaders of the young nation. George Washington welcomed him warmly and gave him a ceremonial sword, and Dr. Benjamin Rush, the distinguished patriot and medical pioneer, inoculated him against small pox. Three years later, Little Turtle called on President John Adams, who found the aging but dignified chief to be "remarkable."

The government showed Little Turtle its appreciation for his conversion to peace by awarding Wells a disability pension for a wound sustained just before Fallen Timbers and appointing him as the

deputy agent for Indian affairs at Fort Wayne. There, Wells established a prosperous farm and several business ventures with Colonel
John Hamtramck. After his wife's death in 1805, Wells remarried, but
his relationship with Little Turtle continued. Little Turtle supported
Wells in every crisis—with the Potawatomi who wanted his scalp; with
Governor William Henry Harrison; with other agents; and with
Shawnee followers of Tecumseh and the Prophet, who settled the
lower Wabash in 1808. Wells was safe enough among the Miami, who
regarded him as their only hope against white exploitation.

Little Turtle and Wells's plan for the survival of the Miami entailed
using as much money as they could accumulate from government
grants and business enterprises to finance the conversion of the next
generation of Miami into yeoman farmers. To this end, Little Turtle
tried to reduce the liquor trade between white settlers and his
tribesman, but met with only modest success. Little Turtle and
Wells's plan set them on a collision course with Harrison, who as governor of the Indiana Territory intended to drive all the tribes away
from the Wabash. Harrison worked to replace Wells by accusing him
of corruption. Wells stayed on for a short while through the intervention of powerful allies, but in 1809 other tribes engineered his firing. By this time, though, the government needed Little Turtle to
speak against the growing power of Tecumseh and his British allies.
Little Turtle even went to a hostile council to confront the Miami's
pro-Tecumseh faction. After being threatened with death for accepting American patronage, Little Turtle made his last great speech:
"Kill me as soon as you please. I cannot calculate on living many win-
ters more, but rest assured . . . I will not die alone."

With the growing crisis between Tecumseh and the Americans still
unresolved, Little Turtle died of gout and other ailments in January
1812. The Fort Wayne agent reported that Little Turtle "died with
more firm composure of mind than any other I have seen." Eight
months later the Potawatomi killed Wells, who was trying to save the
besieged Army garrison at Fort Dearborn (Chicago, Illinois). At his
death, Wells was in the death paint and war dress of a Miami chief.

Within twenty years of Blue Jacket, Little Turtle, and Wells's
deaths, almost all of the surviving Shawnee and Miami had been driven into Canada or beyond the Mississippi by white settlement. The
only Indians to remain were some 350 Miami who were not removed
because they owned land as private citizens of the state of Indiana.
There are now more Miami in that state than in their last "tribal
homeland" in Oklahoma.

Further Reading

Carter, Harvey Lewis. *The Life and Times of Little Turtle*. Urbana: University of Illinois Press, 1987.

Downes, Randolph C. *Council Fires on the Upper Ohio*. Pittsburgh: University of Pittsburgh Press, 1940.

Hintzen, William. *The Border Wars of the Upper Ohio Valley, 1769–1794*. Manchester, Conn.: Precision Shooting, 1999.

Hutton, Paul A. "William Wells: Frontier Scout and Indian Agent." *Indiana Magazine of History* (September 1978): 183–222.

Sugden, John. *Blue Jacket*. Lincoln: University of Nebraska Press, 2000.

Sword, Wiley. *President Washington's Indian War*. Norman: University of Oklahoma Press, 1985.

5

Thomas Worthington
and the Quest for Statehood and
Gentility

MARY ALICE MAIROSE

ON NOVEMBER 1, 1802, a confrontation between two groups illustrated a decade-long dispute over the future of the Ohio country. On one side, Thomas Worthington, Dr. Edward Tiffin (Worthington's brother-in-law), and other Jeffersonian Republicans wanted statehood for Ohio. Territorial status did not appeal to these rising young men. Worthington frequently claimed that having the federal government appoint a governor and judges for the territory put residents in the same position as colonists subject to European powers. On the other side, territorial governor Arthur St. Clair and the Federalists believed that the Ohioans were not ready for self-government. St. Clair feared that self-government would dissolve into anarchy.

The setting for the conflict was Ohio's Constitutional Convention, which had been brought about by the election of Thomas Jefferson to the White House two years earlier. Although Edward Tiffin had been elected president of the convention, St. Clair was determined not to relinquish his power without a fight. He entered the chamber where the delegates were gathered, appointed a secretary, and demanded the delegates' certificates of election. In the words of one of the delegates, "Col. Thomas Worthington with a manly intrepidity & his usual firmness in support of political Justice successfully interfered & we proceeded to the choice of a president and Secretary & to our own organization."

St. Clair was not easily deterred. The following day, he asked to address the convention. "Give him rope and he will hang himself," remarked one of the Republican delegates. The majority shared this

60

FIG. 3 Thomas Worthington. Courtesy of the Ohio Historical Society.

feeling and allowed him to speak but as a private citizen rather than territorial governor. The Republicans could not have wished for St. Clair to make a better speech to advance their cause.

St. Clair began by exhorting the delegates to beware of party spirit, an evil threatening the future of the nation. He then stunned the convention by announcing that the delegates need not be bound by the Enabling Act—the law recently passed by Congress giving the delegates authority to write a constitution and become a state. Congress, St. Clair declared, had no right to take such action. He argued that the Ohio country would progress better if the delegates ignored the Enabling Act and allowed the territorial government to continue uninterrupted.

St. Clair's attack on the Enabling Act finally gave the Republicans the grounds they needed to have him removed. Not content to let St. Clair's tenure in office run out, Worthington and other delegates wrote to President Jefferson and members of his administration detailing St. Clair's speech, and the Revolutionary War veteran was immediately removed from office. This episode has become the cornerstone of a popular depiction of Ohio's entrance into the Union as a struggle between Worthington, the energetic, forward-looking young Virginian, and the drunken, gouty St. Clair, an elderly tyrant who wished to subvert the will of the people.

After the American Revolution, some citizens, who eventually identified themselves as Federalists, felt that the democratic ideals for which they had fought were impractical, that the masses were not capable of governing themselves. They watched in alarm as common folks openly defied the government as had happened during the Whiskey Rebellion of 1794 when farmers in western Pennsylvania attacked the federal agent collecting a tax on whiskey and closed the courts and robbed the mail. Such incidents left them feeling that "the people" were not capable of governing themselves. The Federalists were also concerned about the wholesale slaughter of the French Revolution and believed that tighter government control was needed to insure that mass violence did not break out in America. St. Clair, a Federalist himself, described the early settlers to the Ohio country as a "multitude of indigent and ignorant people." From his years as governor, he knew that many of the area inhabitants tended to be squatters with little respect for established laws, and that people of the frontier were widely scattered and had no strong allegiance to the government. Consequently, he wanted statehood delayed until a more respectable class of men inhabited the territory.

Others of the Revolutionary generation, most notably Thomas Jefferson, believed in the importance of local autonomy. Many in the Ohio country supported Jefferson and wanted to select their own leaders rather than being subjects of a governor and judges appointed by the federal government. These settlers saw their situation as analogous to that of the American colonists before the Revolutionary War. Correspondence between Worthington and other supporters of statehood contained numerous derogatory references to Arthur [St. Clair] the First and King Arthur and his Round Table.

After years of bitter fighting, Ohio's first Constitutional Convention met in Chillicothe on November 2, 1802. Of the thirty-five delegates, twenty-six were Republicans, a reflection of how strong the statehood movement had grown all over the Ohio country.

The delegates adopted the statehood resolution almost unanimously. The new constitution provided almost universal white male suffrage and created a government, which at least in theory, would be under popular control. Still chaffing from the perceived tyranny of territorial government, the Constitutional Convention made the office of governor very weak, with no veto power and two-year terms.

Although the Federalists tried to delay approval of the constitution, the delegates almost unanimously accepted it, with only one diehard Federalist voting in opposition. The delegates, however, did not submit their handiwork to the people for approval. Rather, they simply adjourned on November 29 after deputizing Worthington to carry the constitution to Washington. He left Chillicothe on December 7 and made the twelve-day trek to the nation's capitol. Upon arrival, Worthington found Congress was "very friendly and disposed to do all they can for the state of Ohio." He dined with President Jefferson, Secretary of State James Madison, and Secretary of the Treasury Albert Gallatin and spent much time lobbying for the creation of the Michigan Territory to ensure eventual statehood for settlers in that part of the Northwest Territory.

Gaining statehood for Ohio was important to Thomas Worthington. It was part of his life-long quest for gentility and position. Although Worthington was born into a moderately wealthy family, tragic circumstances caused him to be raised in an atmosphere where a lack of discipline and drunkeness reigned. One of Worthington's enemies wrote, "He is a native of Virginia—was a deputy sheriff in that state," pointing out that Worthington could not rise in Virginia's political hierarchy. Although reasonably wealthy, Worthington was not a member of the established social and political circles of Virginia. On the frontier, Worthington could advance more rapidly, and, with Ohio on an equal footing with the original states, he could advance nationally as well. Perhaps the best reflection of Worthington's quest for gentility is the home he eventually built on a hilltop outside of Chillicothe. The limestone mansion, named Adena, a Hebrew word meaning "places remarkable for the delightfulness of their situations," was surrounded by the servant cabins, outbuildings, fields, and pastures of a Virginia plantation. It was a setting in which Worthington could entertain presidents and European nobility.

The circumstances of Worthington's early life appear to have driven his quest for position. Born in Charles Town, (West) Virginia on July 16, 1773, Worthington was the youngest child of a moderately successful planter. His father owned at least twenty slaves, was a justice of the peace, and served in the Revolutionary War before his death in 1779. When Worthington's mother died the following year, the Worthington children were placed in the care of their eldest brother. For the first two years after his parents' deaths, Worthington's sister Mary was "both mother and sister" to him. Consequently, when the elder brother asked Mary Worthington to seek new quarters, this was an even greater blow to young Thomas than the loss of his parents. "Night after night," he recalled near the end of his life, "did I wet my pillow with tears. It was then for the first time, tho my parents had been dead but 2 years that I was sensible of being an orphan and mourned the loss of my more than kind sister Mary, than whom a better woman never lived." These years were among the unhappiest of his life. His brother, whom Worthington described as a drunkard, proved to be an indifferent guardian and neglected the education of his younger siblings. Worthington stayed in the care of his eldest brother until he was fourteen.

After a brief time with another brother, Worthington selected Colonel William Darke, a friend of his father and veteran of the Revolutionary War, as his new guardian. Darke and his wife proved excellent guardians for the young man and provided young Thomas with the guidance and schooling he needed. Among the subjects Worthington studied was navigation, and when he became old enough he went to sea. It was an eventful voyage. Worthington narrowly escaped being impressed by the crew of a British ship. He remained grateful to James Taylor, the ship's captain, who saved him from this fate and even named his first-born son for the man.

Upon returning to Virginia, the twenty-year-old Worthington settled into a house he inherited from his father and assumed the management of his slaves. He worked his own property, surveyed, and speculated in western lands. Active in civic affairs, he served as a deputy sheriff and was appointed a lieutenant in the militia. He became good friends with his sister Mary's husband, Edward Tiffin. A native of England, Tiffin came to the colonies on the eve of the Revolution and studied medicine in Philadelphia. Deeply religious, he also served as a Methodist lay preacher.

Worthington courted and married Eleanor Swearingen, the daughter of a prominent Berkeley County family. She was an excellent choice as a spouse for the ambitious young man. An orphan with a sizable inheritance, she brought land, money, and slaves to the marriage. Eleanor's family helped to provide the connections and advice that Worthington needed in his quest for position. In Ohio, Eleanor proved herself to be an able businesswoman who ran the family concerns during Worthington's frequent absences.

In 1796, Worthington made his first trip to the Ohio country to locate tracts of land that he had purchased, and to make plans to move west. In Virginia, Worthington could continue to be moderately successful, but Ohio offered many more opportunities. Returning to Chillicothe with Edward Tiffin two years later, Worthington was astonished by how much the town had grown. The two men selected sites and built log cabins before returning back to Virginia.

Since the Northwest Ordinance of 1787 prohibited slavery in Ohio, the Worthingtons and the Tiffins could not bring their slaves to Ohio with them. The Tiffins were Methodists and embraced that church's opposition to slavery, and it was probably his sister Mary who influenced Worthington to oppose slavery. The two families freed their slaves and brought a number of the free blacks to Ohio with them. Although legally free, these men and women lived in a state of quasi-slavery as indentured servants. The indenture drafted for George declared that for seven years he "would serve [Worthington's] interests, keep his lawful commands[,] obey[,] and gladly do." The indenture outlined acceptable behavior on George's part in minute detail; for example, prohibiting him from playing cards or frequenting taverns.

Worthington's relationship with his slaves was clearly paternalistic. The blacks joined the family each morning for prayers, and the Worthington children referred to them by the courtesy titles of Aunt and Uncle. Each slave family was allotted a tract of land to which they could gain title when Worthington considered them capable of caring for the property. "Unfortunately," his daughter recalled, "not a single family ever secured the promised boon." In Worthington's absence, tensions over the freed slaves were often strong. Worthington's son, who frequently oversaw the property while the father was away, complained of a "determination to do mischief" on the part of the "curley heads." Although Worthington was opposed to slavery, it is clear he did not view African Americans as equals. During the Constitutional Convention of 1802, he voted against all measures that would give African Americans rights as citizens, in part because he did not want to make conditions so favorable that Ohio would become a haven for runaway slaves or free blacks.

Worthington and Tiffin soon established themselves as leading citizens of the territory. Worthington served as registrar of the Chillicothe land office, which put him in contact with many of the other settlers, while Tiffin became known as a doctor and lay preacher. The two men were obvious choices to serve in the newly created territorial assembly.

The Northwest Ordinance permitted settlers to elect an assembly when the population reached five thousand white males. The territorial governor, however, still wielded the power to veto laws passed by the assembly. Already there had been discontent among the residents with the territorial government. Governor St. Clair and the judges were trying to govern a large territory that would eventually become the states of Ohio, Indiana, Illinois, Michigan, and part of Wisconsin. Residents of the territory were concerned with establishing homes and businesses as well as conflict with Native Americans. They also wanted to select their own local government.

The ambitious Worthington was not content for Ohio to remain a territory for long and soon became involved in a bitter battle with St. Clair, who believed Ohio should grow in a slower, more organized manner. Before long, Worthington's dual purpose became statehood for Ohio and the removal of St. Clair. The two men squared off on a number of issues. St. Clair supported his son's candidacy to become the Northwest Territory's nonvoting representative to Congress, but the Republicans prevailed and elected future president William Henry Harrison instead. The establishment of county boundaries and the designation of county seats was another major source of conflict. During the settlement period, becoming a county seat gave a distinct economic advantage to a town. The Republicans accused St. Clair of showing favor to towns established by his Federalist cronies. Also outraging the Republicans, St. Clair vetoed almost one-third of the bills passed by the assembly during the session.

Worthington spent the winter of 1799 in Washington where he and William Henry Harrison worked for Ohio statehood. The Northwest Ordinance specified that the territory be divided into no fewer than three and no more than five states. The first step in the establishment of Ohio as a state was the drawing of geographic boundaries. The two men pushed for Ohio's current boundaries with the western division at the Miami River, enough land to quickly meet the population requirements for statehood. They also wanted to have St. Clair removed as governor. They were successful in terms of the division but were unable to get St. Clair removed.

The division act proved controversial in the territory. St. Clair and the Federalists feared the creation of a state with a Republican majority. Jefferson's election as president in 1800 made their position precarious, so they were in no hurry to see Ohio become a state that would send Republicans to Congress and the Electoral College and take patronage positions away from their party. As Chillicothe was most centrally located town it became the territorial capital, and it would most likely become the state capital. Federalists in Cincinnati and Marietta were especially opposed to the plan. They wanted two states carved from the same territory, but divided at the Scioto River with their towns as capitals. Also, it would take longer for two smaller states to meet the population requirement for statehood.

This issue led to one of the most dramatic confrontations of the period. Long discussions in the assembly about dividing the territory or moving the capital away from Chillicothe led to anger and threats against the Federalists. Those most vocal about their displeasure were known as the "Bloodhounds." Dismissed by the more genteel residents as "rabble," this band of artisans and laborers spent much of their time in local taverns drinking and gambling. Their acknowledged leader was Michael Baldwin, a member of a prominent New England family, a Yale graduate, and a successful lawyer with political ambitions. Yet he abandoned the social conventions of his day and gained a tremendous following among the lower classes.

On Christmas Eve 1801, the Bloodhounds were prepared to show their displeasure toward St. Clair by burning him in effigy and possibly tarring and feathering the territorial governor as well. Although Worthington viewed St. Clair as the major impediment to statehood, he was angered and humiliated by the mob's actions. Worthington caught Baldwin before he and the Bloodhounds reached the tavern where St. Clair was staying. He told Baldwin that if he tried to enter the governor's lodgings, he would kill him. Although Baldwin angrily told Worthington not to threaten him, the Bloodhounds abandoned their attempts to assault St. Clair. The following night, the mob met again, and after a brief scuffle St. Clair induced them to disperse. St. Clair tried to have Baldwin and a couple of the other mob leaders arrested, but the citizens of Chillicothe closed ranks by declaring that they had seen nothing resembling a riot.

Worthington was as eager as the Bloodhounds to express displeasure over the Federalists' plans to split the future state, but he went about it in a more lawful manner. He set out for Washington to lobby Congress to oppose St. Clair's division bill. He had long been corresponding with members of Congress about Ohio's future and knew of many in Washington who were sympathetic to his cause. Strangely enough, his traveling companion was Baldwin, whose elder half brother Abraham was a senator from Georgia.

Armed with innumerable petitions calling for statehood and the removal of St. Clair, Worthington spent two weeks lobbying. During this time he met with President Jefferson twice. Jefferson was sympathetic to the cause of impending statehood, and Congress soundly defeated the division bill. With statehood a foregone conclusion, Worthington devoted much of his energy to the removal of St. Clair, but Jefferson regarded the conflict as a personal matter. Also, the imminent coming of statehood insured that St. Clair would not be in office much longer.

The Constitutional Convention allowed Worthington to accomplish both statehood and the removal of St. Clair. Yet, statehood did not prove to be everything for which Worthington had hoped. Another generation of men with a broader definition of democracy than Worthington's own came to the forefront, preventing Worthington from reaping the fruits of his labors. Worthington lost bids for both speaker of the Ohio House and governor. In spite of his service in securing statehood, his fellow Ohioans felt no special deference to him. The political climate of Ohio was changing and leaving men like Worthington and Tiffin behind.

Worthington served two terms in the U.S. Senate. As one of Ohio's first senators, he drew the shorter term for 1803 to 1807. In 1810, he was elected to serve the final four years of the term of Samuel Huntington, who had defeated him in an election for governor. In both cases, the General Assembly elected him and not the people at large. His major contributions in the Senate involved western lands. He supported the creation of the Michigan Territory, as the residents of Detroit were not happy in being part of the Indiana Territory. He worked to establish more uniform land laws and help various parts of Ohio gain their school lands. Perhaps his greatest achievement during his first term as a senator was sponsorship of internal improvements that eventually led to the creation of the National Road. From 1810 to 1812, he served as chairman of Public Lands and proposed a bill establishing a General Land Office, which was responsible for maintaining records relating to land sales and surveys.

Western lands and internal improvements received little attention as the nation moved closer to the War of 1812. Worthington believed that the nation was not prepared for war and feared that Ohio and the western territories were vulnerable to Indian attack. He voted against the war and was greatly distressed when Congress declared war on Great Britain. "I have done my duty and satisfied my conscious," he confided to his wife. "Thousands of the innocent will suffer, but I have borne testimony against it, and, thank God, my mind is tranquil."

Once war was declared, Worthington wholeheartedly threw himself behind the effort by helping to raise the Ohio militia. He participated in conferences with Indian leaders and joined a reconnaissance mission to evaluate the Indian threat in the Indiana Territory. He was also involved in recruiting reenforcements for besieged troops at Fort Wayne.

The rest of Worthington's career was spent in Ohio. Between his two U.S. Senate terms, Worthington served in the Ohio House of

Representatives. Although he was denied the position of Speaker of the House, his accomplishments include securing arms for members of the state militia, establishing a state bank, and incorporating an academy in Chillicothe that offered a classical education to young males. These years, however, marked a shift in Ohio politics that would eventually cost Worthington the prestige that he had fought so hard to achieve. Around the state, more men were becoming interested in politics, men who did not fit into the natural aristocracy that early leaders like Worthington and Tiffin promoted.

Worthington ran unsuccessfully for governor in 1810 and was defeated in part by the furor caused by the Tammany Society. The society was a fraternal organization with secret rituals, but its main goal was to facilitate more organized cooperation among Ohio's Republicans. Worthington and Tiffin were two of the leading members of the Chillicothe wigwam. The Tammany Society supported Worthington in the 1810 gubernatorial election, which did Worthington more harm than good as the society was criticized for its aristocratic and secretive nature. Others criticized Worthington's wealth and accused him of trying to dictate the politics of the young state. Already, Worthington was finding himself edged out of power in the state he had helped to create.

Worthington was elected governor in 1814. Perhaps the greatest irony of his career is that the office he strove to make weak as a delegate to the Constitutional Convention of 1802, caused him to be little more than a figurehead a decade later. His agenda as governor was ambitious and reform-minded. He urged the legislature to establish a system of elementary schools, fearing that without them the poorer classes "will be brought up in a state of comparative ignorance, unable to manage with propriety, their public concerns, much less take part in the management of public affairs." He called for the establishment of state-regulated poor farms to end the practice of farming out paupers. He wished to regulate saloons and banks, and reform the penal system and land sales. Given the weakness of his office, few of these measures were carried out.

During Worthington's administration the state capital moved to Columbus. He personally supervised state prisoners who cleared the grounds. Perhaps the major achievement of Worthington's two terms as governor was the establishment of the Ohio State Library. He used money from a contingency fund to purchase the 509 books that served as the beginnings of the library's collection. After four frustrating years in office, Worthington recorded in his diary, "I feel truly grateful to God to have nothing to charge myself with but regret it has not been in my power to do the good I wished to the state. I feel very conscious that I have left nothing undone in my power and I am content and grateful. I feel now a freeman & released from responsibility." By the time Worthington's term as governor ended, ideas of who was qualified to govern were changing in Ohio as they were across the nation. Younger men considered him as much of a hindrance as he had thought St. Clair was two decades before. Men whom Worthington considered his inferior were being elected to office in his stead. One of his sons complained that there were members of the state legislature that "cannot say the A, B, C's." He served three terms in the state legislature but was greatly resented by younger legislators who wished to keep him in the background, while he in turn had a difficult time working with men whom he considered his inferior.

The Panic of 1819 caused great problems for Worthington. Aside from his own debts, he conscientiously attempted to pay those that he had guaranteed for relatives and friends, causing a tremendous financial burden for the land rich, cash poor Worthington. Relationships with his grown children were often difficult. Worthington's two eldest daughters married men who were unable to provide for their families, leaving Worthington to bail them out. His older sons were unable to live up to their father's expectations, leading to many stormy exchanges. By the spring of 1827, Worthington confided to his diary, "I seem to be sinking gradually & hope my suffering will soon be over." While on a trip to New York, he became ill. He languished for over a month and died on June 20 at the age of fifty-three.

Today, Worthington is hailed as the "Father of Ohio Statehood." Although Worthington was unquestionably a leading figure in Ohio becoming a state in 1803, this title is something of an exaggeration since the territory was slated for statehood under the Northwest Ordinance of 1787. Worthington's contributions involved ensuring Ohio became a state in 1803, rather than later as his Federalist adversaries wanted. He was also responsible for Ohio entering the Union with its present boundaries.

The "Father" title was never applied to Worthington in his lifetime. The Jeffersonian Republicans of Ohio were too fractionalized to convey such a title on one man. Impatient, sarcastic, and self-righteous, Worthington counted as many enemies as friends. By the 1820s, the last decade of Worthington's life, younger politicians viewed him as an impediment to their careers, much as he had viewed

St. Clair. When Worthington's own grandson wrote a history of the state in the 1880s, he did not refer to Worthington as "Father of Ohio Statehood," instead, he described his grandfather as "the most earnest and strenuous of the governor's opponents" and described the treatment of St. Clair as "unjust ingratitude."

So why is it that Worthington has received so much more attention than other proponents of statehood have? Historians in many ways are limited by the information that a historical figure leaves behind. In comparison to other leaders in the statehood movement, a far greater number of Worthington's diaries and correspondence have survived and are available in repositories around the state. This makes him the easiest and most obvious choice for historical study.

Worthington is the only one of the early proponents of statehood that is the subject of a modern biography. Most of his allies in the statehood movement had very short political careers, which makes them more difficult to study and place into a context. Adena, Worthington's home in Chillicothe, has been operated as a museum by the Ohio Historical Society since the 1950s. As Ohio's first statehouse in Chillicothe has been destroyed, as have the homes of Chillicothe's other early leading citizens, this house has become an important connection to an earlier time and has emphasized the importance of its original owner.

Still, Worthington serves as a symbol of the aspirations and optimism that moved the proponents of Ohio statehood. He shows the faith that settlers had in the future of western lands and possible advancement. Although his dominance of Ohio politics proved short lived, he provided aggressive leadership as Ohio moved from territory to state. Worthington was an important transitional figure in Ohio history.

Further Reading

Brown, Jeffrey P., and Andrew R. L. Cayton. *The Pursuit of Public Power, Political Culture in Ohio, 1787–1861*. Kent, Ohio: Kent State University Press, 1994.

Cayton, Andrew R. L. *The Frontier Republic, Ideology and Politics in The Ohio Country*. Kent, Ohio: Kent State University Press, 1986.

Ratcliffe, Donald J. *Party Spirit in a Frontier Republic Democratic Politics in Ohio 1793–1821*. Columbus: Ohio State University Press, 1998.

Sears, Alfred Byron. *Thomas Worthington, Father of Ohio Statehood*. Columbus: Ohio State University Press, 1958.

6

Philander Chase and College Building in Ohio

KENNETH H. WHEELER

T HOUGH UNIQUE in temperament and philosophy, Kenyon College founder Philander Chase (1775–1852) vividly represents the goals of early Ohio college builders and leaders. To Chase and his contemporaries, Ohio was part of the western frontier. By the 1820s, many Ohioans believed that they differed from people in other regions of the country, that Ohioans had distinctive needs and values and required institutions tailored to fit their situation. Accordingly, the colleges they built operated differently from colleges elsewhere. Philander Chase and others put the goals of Ohioans, such as preparing teachers for children and offering democratic access to education, into their calculations about how to structure their colleges. Thus these colleges became expressions of Ohio culture, a culture that over time heavily contributed to a regional culture of the Midwest.

In the 1820s and 1830s, Ohio had a rapidly expanding population of settlers from eastern and southern states. These people, once they satisfied their basic needs for survival, built societal institutions they desired, such as churches, civic organizations, and schools, including colleges. Most commonly, to meet demands from Ohio citizens, state legislators chartered colleges as private institutions. And Ohioans vigorously started colleges; in fact, by 1860, the Ohio landscape was dotted by almost two dozen colleges, more than in any other state.

In Ohio and many other states, church denominations took the lead. Typically, a religious denomination, such as the Presbyterians or Methodists, decided to begin a college for the benefit of the church. The college provided a place for young members of the denomination to learn with other students whose beliefs were similar; some graduates became pastors of the denomination's churches.

FIG. 4 Philander Chase. Courtesy of Kenyon College.

Once it became known that a denomination wished to start a college, Ohio towns competed for the privilege of having the college located in their community and offered land, money, and sometimes an existing building to house the college. Just as modern Ohio cities encourage businesses to locate nearby in order to stimulate financial prosperity, nineteenth-century Ohioans believed that a college in their town elevated both the intellectual climate and their personal wealth through greater employment opportunities and higher land prices.

Philander Chase was an instrumental figure in the development of Ohio colleges. He matured in New Hampshire and at Dartmouth College, from which he graduated in 1795. Three years later, after ordination by the Episcopal Church, Chase worked in New York, Louisiana, and Connecticut before he moved westward in 1817 to Ohio, where the Episcopal Church was tiny, represented by only eight small churches, or parishes. In 1819, Chase became the first Episcopal bishop of Ohio, overseeing the Episcopal Church within the state. Yet Chase had an interest in collegiate education before his Ohio days; in 1816 and 1817 he headed a movement to found an

Episcopalian college in Connecticut. In Ohio, Chase also joined educational ventures. He served as president of a school in Cincinnati for
a year and then ran a school for boys from his Worthington home in
central Ohio. These endeavors, however, paled in comparison to
Chase's plan to found an Episcopalian seminary that would produce
ministers for Ohio and other western churches. Given the difficulties
and demands of early Ohio, along with the small number of Episcopalians, to establish such a school would take a gigantic effort.

Above all else, Chase needed money to accomplish his goal, but
when he asked eastern Episcopalians for funds, they claimed that
western Episcopalians would be best served at eastern Episcopal sem-
inaries. Most vigorous in opposition was Bishop John Henry Hobart
of New York. Hobart and Chase already had clashed over theological
issues. Hobart identified with a less evangelical wing of Episcopalian-
ism than Chase, and Chase left his Connecticut pulpit for Ohio when
Hobart became bishop of the Connecticut diocese. By the early
1820s, Hobart was the head of the New York diocese and oversaw
Episcopalian Geneva College in New York. Hobart argued that there
was no need for a seminary in Ohio, and that if there ever were a need
that Geneva College would establish a branch there. Chase believed
that Ohio needed colleges within its bounds immediately because
travel east was quite expensive and time consuming, which made it
difficult for Ohioans with little money to receive a college education.
Just as important, though, Chase clearly wanted to run his own college. Ambitious and persistent, Chase was incredibly strong-willed.
He traveled continually, which in early Ohio was indeed, in Chase's
words, a "most painful business," visiting churches, preaching, and
meeting people. Chase was domineering, a personality trait reinforced by his thick body and large build. People did not generally
have a lukewarm reaction to Chase; he made close friends and caustic
enemies.

Undeterred by the opposition to his college plans from eastern
Episcopalians or by the lack of money in his Ohio parishes, Chase
traveled to England in 1823 in search of funds. Meanwhile, Chase's
foe, Bishop Hobart, also traveled to England. Hobart claimed that he
was traveling for his health, but the New York bishop spoke in England against Chase and tried to convince people to reject Chase's
pleas. Chase's charisma, however, persuaded two wealthy English-
men, Lord Kenyon and Lord Gambier, of the need for an Ohio Episcopal school. Kenyon and Gambier donated about $20,000, a huge
sum at the time, so that Chase could execute his vision.

Bankrolled, Chase returned to Ohio and searched for suitable land to purchase. While most colleges founded at that time appeared in small towns because of the financial support and physical infrastructure these communities provided, Chase, funded by his English donors and consequently not in need of town support, considered placing his college in the countryside. In March 1825, he was "still undecided," but he was "more & more averse to putting it in or near a village." He wanted enough land that his school would "have a power to prevent immoral practice, and things that would prove injurious to the opinions and study of youth for at least 2 miles around." Chase, who opposed tavern owners, gamblers, and other individuals he found unsavory, increasingly envisioned an institution of education absolutely removed from any outside influence that might corrupt or interfere with the workings of the college.

At the same time, Chase found himself inundated with requests from townspeople who wished to host his college. Thus, when Chase considered purchasing land in Knox County in central Ohio, he reported to his wife that two "*selfish*" men he spoke to were "dead set against the Knox County plan as such because it would (in their opinion) divert the travelling from Berkshire to Sunbury and there be no gain but rather an injury to their property!!!" Chase wearily complained that "the local interests of several little towns, and villages amongst us so far warp the judgment of many that I apprehend great difficulty" in establishing the college. Chase "feared" that "such is the overbearing influence of local interests that" all the advantages that would come from having the college in the countryside "will be overlooked and disregarded for the sole purpose of building up the importance of little towns and villages." Chase had little sympathy with the "local prejudices and sectional interests so common and so deeply rooted among us." Accordingly, in 1826 Chase purchased eight thousand acres of forested land in rural Knox County, five miles from the county seat of Mount Vernon, and founded Kenyon College in the center of the property.

Chase's decision not to place the college in a town meant that he had to build everything from scratch. Until 1828, at which point the first students arrived, Chase and scores of hired workers built roads and felled trees, quarried stone and erected college buildings, founded a tiny village named Gambier next to the college buildings, constructed a grist and saw mill, and cleared land upon which to grow crops. By 1830, Chase and his associates had planted hundreds of acres in corn, wheat, rye, and oats, and fenced hundreds of acres of clover and timothy as pasture for their oxen and cattle. "Our great object," as Chase described it, "has been to convert our fine lands into a great *stock-farm*, which, after being duly prepared, should afford us an abundance of milk, butter, and cheese and viands." Chase was not unusual in this regard; many Ohio colleges at that time had working farms, often run by student labor, that provided much of the food eaten at the college.

Here, on this land, the first Kenyon College students came to study, including a young man from England named Henry Caswall. Two years into his stay at Kenyon, in late 1830, Caswall wrote about his experiences. When he first arrived at Kenyon, "the tall trees covered the face of the ground; the students occupied temporary wooden houses." Over time, workers built the main college building, which had "massive stone walls, four feet thick, and four stories in height." Caswall counted about 170 students, including some boys who were in a grammar school connected to the college, along with Chase and three other professors, and some teachers in the grammar school. Most students were from the United States and had Episcopalian parents, but the college contained "a few Irish and Welsh, one Greek, and one native of Hindostan."

Chase intended for Kenyon College and its students to play an important role in the development of Ohio. In 1827, Chase addressed the Ohio legislature on Kenyon's centrality in the education of schoolteachers. He argued that the western population lacked sufficient schoolteachers and remained poorly educated. Chase suggested that Ohio needed more schoolteachers and that Ohioans should "educate these Teachers ourselves. Let us draw from our own soil the moral seed, by which the Western country is to be supplied with the fruits of learning." Western colleges needed adequate support "so that the expense of education will come within the reach of all." The colleges should train schoolteachers, Chase believed, "from the middle and more industrious walks of life; the sons of farmers and mechanics in our country, who have witnessed the necessity, who have felt the want, and, to the welfare of our Republic, who know the great importance of *common learning*." Chase pictured his college as a place that would serve the sons not only of the wealthy, but of the "middle walks of life."

In addition, Chase told the lawmakers, Kenyon College provided a civic function by upholding the democratic civil structure of the United States. The teachers who went forth from Kenyon College would be "the surest preservative of our constitutional liberties." Chase argued that the Constitution prohibited "privileged orders of men" and that a college education must, therefore, be accessible to all. "But experience does not justify this reasonable expectation," warned Chase. "Such is the foundation of our Colleges, especially those in the Atlantic States, that NO POOR MAN, nor even one in moderate circumstances, can give his son a collegiate education." This situation, to Chase, was "in direct hostility to the nature of a republic." Chase intended that Kenyon correct this situation, that the college be accessible to men of whatever fortune.

Subsequent events only strengthened Chase's conviction that Ohio had great need of educators and educational institutions. In late January 1828, Philander Chase journeyed from Kenyon toward Coshocton. "[D]elay & bad roads" forced him at nightfall to stop short of his destination. At the house where Chase stayed, he spoke to a woman, asking her if "the troubles and difficulties of life" ever led her to religion. She replied that she did not know what he was talking about. Chase recounted this story to his wife and wrote: "You may well suppose such a reply would [have] shocked me tho of late years somewhat accustomed to hearing & seeing strange things in the way of exemplifying the profound ignorance into which our Country is fallen." Chase asked the woman if she desired to learn about religion, and she eagerly answered affirmatively, "for she was no scholar herself and her husband *Joe* was still more ignorant than herself—She *once* could read a few easy words but had forgotten—*He* could never read . . . and the children were growing up with as little learning as herself and *man*." This experience underscored Chase's belief that Ohio was in desperate need of educated persons who could go throughout the state and improve religious and civic life.

Indeed, many Kenyon students did travel throughout the state. By 1830, Henry Caswall wrote that numerous students were "already engaged in advancing the influence of religion and the Church. They have about a dozen Sunday-schools, from two to seven miles distant from Gambier, each of which is under the care of two or three students." Caswall joined this group, and each Sunday he and a college friend walked for two and a half hours to a little village with a log schoolhouse. After Caswall and his friend arrived, children and adults from the area would come to the school, then they would all spend time singing hymns and praying. Caswall also distributed free Bibles to families in Knox County.

Caswall's experiences were hardly unusual. College students not only studied in the buildings but also involved themselves in the lives of people who lived nearby. At a time when Ohioans were overwhelmingly involved in agriculture, and most Ohio children worked on farms, winter was the season when children were most free to go to school—the fall harvest was over, and the spring planting had not yet arrived. Ohio college students frequently taught school during the winter to earn money. So common was the arrangement that the Ohio Commissioner of Common Schools reported in 1860 that a high percentage of teachers in the state were college students. Oberlin College alone, he had learned, supplied over five hundred teachers to schools in the state. Thus colleges functioned in a way that allowed their students to teach winter schools for three months each year.

Take, for example, the case of Danforth Nichols, a student at Granville College (now Denison University), who was hired in the late 1830s to teach a winter school about eight miles from campus. Nichols contracted to receive ten dollars each month and room and board in the homes of his students. On the appointed day, Nichols walked along roads and pathways until he came to the right place, only to be discouraged when he found that the schoolhouse was an incomplete log structure that "had a roof of split clapboards; but no door, no chimney, and windows were visible." Nichols had to wait a week before he could begin his school while the people who lived in the area built a chimney, installed a floor and window frames, hung a door, and built writing desks and benches. Then Nichols began teaching approximately twenty children. While the neighborhood was quite friendly and Nichols got along with his students, he concluded that the educational state of the area was "decidedly of a low order." The students brought antiquated textbooks to school and resisted Nichols' efforts to persuade them to purchase newer books. Still, Nichols did as best he could, and this illustrates how a small community wanted to educate its children but either could not or would not employ a teacher year round. The alternative to Nichols was not a professional teacher in a fine building—the alternative was no school at all.

In 1854, another college student, John F. Rogers, wrote about his experience as a schoolteacher in Preble County in western Ohio, among "setlers from Penn or Virginia[,] Dutchmen & Southerners. The most of them wealthy." The Preble County residents welcomed Rogers as the schoolteacher and took him about the village of Upshur and into the surrounding countryside to meet people. As Rogers explained, introductions began with "'This is our Master for this winter,' Then I fall to shaking hands &c, without even hearing the name of those I am speaking to When I come in the midst of a crowd I just speak & shake hands with all and enquire after their health &c not waiting for an introduction for I might wait in vain." Rogers was initially startled by these habits of exuberant friendliness. "When I call on the young Buckeyes," he wrote, "they get down a fiddle and saw away for hours." Rogers decided he "had rather listen to a mangy pig Scratching against a sliver on a fence rail." Still, he willingly allowed his students and employers to influence him. By January, he reported "I have been learning the German language some, and have got to be quite a *Dutch Yankee.*" Rogers was by no means the only "Dutch Yankee" in Ohio. This pattern of cultural hybridization occurred throughout the state, as students learned from teachers who were from elsewhere, and the teachers learned from the students and their families. Furthermore, the presence of so many of these teachers shows that the new colleges affected Ohio's development far beyond the campus. At a time when the state government offered primary education for only a tiny fraction of Ohioans, the many private colleges around the state supplied thousands of teachers for Ohio children.

Moreover, the highly informal institutional structure in which Ohioans lived may have encouraged them to throw caution to the wind and be vigorously experimental. Chase had never founded a college before, but that did not stop him from founding one. Thousands of college students who had never taught school took jobs as schoolteachers. Numerous observers commented on the Ohioan's love of action. A New Englander, Charles Peabody, visited Ohio in 1850 and wrote in his diary that he liked "the frank, wide-awake, stirring spirit" he found. The energy Peabody appreciated also, in his opinion, led to impetuousness: "But this jumping and twitching at trifles, and going off half cocked without anything in but powder, I disapprove of entirely." Peabody framed the differences between the inhabitants of the two regions as analogous to the differences between an ox and a horse. "A Yankee [New Englander]," wrote Peabody, "takes every thing coolly and sits down and calculates the exact issue of his plans and projects. . . . But the Buckeye dives into things with all his might, and begins to pull and haul, very much like a fractious horse hitched to a heavy stone." When all was said and done, according to Peabody, the Yankee was more productive, but the Buckeye made "a greater fuss and more splendid flourish of trumpets."

In his analysis, Peabody pointed to the desire of people in Ohio to be energetic, to leap into work. A decade earlier, Lewis Clarke, a student in Massachusetts at Andover Theological Seminary, wrote to his brother in Ohio that Lyman Beecher, of Lane Seminary in Cincinnati, had come to Andover for a few days. Beecher encouraged the

Andover students to serve as ministers in the West, and Clarke confessed "I have sometimes been half sorry I did not go to Lane Sem.
instead of coming here—This is the better place for study:—that for
making active, efficient men." In 1848, a college student at Oberlin
said much the same thing. "I tell you what," he told a friend, "the
Ohioans learn faster, live faster, arive faster, & die faster than Penn-
sylvanians."

This emphasis on action found expression via manual labor programs. While manual labor schools appeared many places in the
nation, Ohio and other Midwestern colleges were especially dedicated to manual labor. Touting "mental, moral, and physical education," college leaders made their schools accessible to the impecu-
nious by letting students work to defray the costs of tuition. At
numerous schools, students labored on the college farm, built barrels,
worked in the print shop, or did numerous other tasks. These duties
both paid bills and engendered good health. In 1846, Jared Baldwin
inquired about admission to Oberlin. Baldwin explained that he had
heard that Oberlin operated "on the laboring system which suits my
situation, and Inclination, for I am of an active habit and require
some active exercise each day in order that I may keep up a healthy
action both Mentally and Physicaly." Manual labor programs
appealed especially to the middle classes because manual labor was
productive, resulting in useful products, as opposed to gymnastics, a
nonproductive form of exercise favored in eastern schools. During
the late 1820s and the 1830s, numerous colleges around the nation
adopted manual labor programs, but at most schools in New England
and the South, these programs did not last long. By 1838, two young
men applied to Oberlin College "for the reason that there is no Manual Labor College in New England."

Other students also found Ohio and Midwestern colleges more
likely to accept them. In the 1830s, Oberlin College became the first
college in the world to admit women and men and had a policy of
admitting students without regard to race. In the 1850s, when coed-
ucation began at other Ohio colleges such as Mount Union, Baldwin,
Heidelberg, Muskingum, Urbana, Franklin, Otterbein, and Antioch,
there were still no coeducational schools in New England or the
South. In those regions, when women went to college, it was to all-
female institutions. Ohioans, through the creation of distinctive colleges that admitted poorer students, women, and African Americans,
repeatedly showed their willingness to innovate and experiment in
order to make a collegiate education more broadly accessible.

Sometimes, though, the best people for founding institutions are not the best people for running them. Chase presided over Kenyon for only a few years before he ran into problems. Chase's eight thousand acres not only provided sustenance but also placed Chase in a position of nearly absolute control; all who lived in the vicinity did so at Chase's pleasure. The nearest town, Mount Vernon, was five miles distant. While students sometimes traveled there, when one student became intoxicated in Mount Vernon once too often, Chase expelled him and prohibited other students from visiting the town. A student who reported that Mount Vernon was now off-limits called Chase "tyrannical."

Professors, too, found that the college president wielded firm control over their lives. John Kendrick, a Kenyon professor, wrote that he desired to leave the college and find employment elsewhere. "The chief reason . . . is the peculiar arrangement . . . by which no one can own real property." Kendrick had to live on college lands to teach at Kenyon and thus had no opportunity to purchase a home for himself and his family within a reasonable distance from the college. Kendrick feared that in the event of his untimely death his family would have to move elsewhere and be left without a home.

Chase did not deny that the vast acreage of Kenyon College granted him important power. To criticisms of his control, Chase responded that while Kenyon shared some characteristics with other colleges, in some ways Kenyon was unique. "One fundamental principle," wrote Chase, "in which [Kenyon] differs from all others is, that the whole Institution is Patriarchal. . . . This Patriarchal establishment must . . . have a Father . . . clothed with authority to seek and effect the common good." Chase was the father, and as long as college lands surrounded Kenyon College for miles, no one would or could challenge the patriarch. Chase assigned himself the duty to keep at bay the forces of immorality and to determine the common good.

Henry Caswall later described Chase's power. Chase, wrote Caswall, was not only the bishop of Ohio, but that at Kenyon College he headed the board of trustees and governed the professors. "He had the appointment of professors, tutors, headmen, and clerks. . . . He was the postmaster, and had the management of the mill, the farms, the printing office, the tailors, the shoemakers, and the laborers." Not a man to share power, Chase oversaw all aspects of the college.

Charismatic and autocratic, Chase was better at building colleges than at working within a collegiate structure. In 1831, Chase lost his position as president of Kenyon College when powerful Episcopalians, in combination with the faculty and trustees of Kenyon College, forced him to resign. Critics thought that Chase intended to rule Kenyon College as his personal possession rather than as an instrument of the Episcopal Church. Some people questioned whether the Episcopal Church or Chase owned the actual lands of the college. William Sparrow and Benjamin P. Aydelott were incensed by Chase's willingness to spend all of his time and energy at Kenyon instead of helping to build the Episcopal Church throughout Ohio. Aydelott wrote to Chase's successor at Kenyon, Charles P. McIlvaine, that "the impression in the minds of most" was that Chase "had become so absorbed in the secularities of the College as to neglect his episcopal duties."

Another Episcopalian, William King, wrote to McIlvaine that under Chase the union of the episcopacy of Ohio and the presidency of Kenyon was "seriously injurious to the best interests of the church—but B[isho]p C[hase]—from his peculiar circumstances, had become so wedded to the college that it was well understood, no entreaties could suffice to sever him from it." Yet even King willingly granted Chase his due. Benjamin Aydelott argued that Chase's flawed character brought problems upon himself. King, while agreeing with Aydelott, remarked that "those defects, however, belong to a character remarkable for untiring industry & perseverance & a sanguine & impetuous temper—without some of which qualities . . . it is not likely Kenyon ever would have existed." King's comments underscore the attributes Chase displayed as a college founder, as well as the reasons Chase was unpopular as an administrator.

When forced from Kenyon, Chase no longer wanted to be the bishop of Ohio; he moved to Michigan, where he had hopes of becoming bishop and founding another college. While he failed to receive the bishopric of Michigan, Chase succeeded in starting one more school. In 1835, the five Episcopalian clergy in Illinois called Chase to be the first bishop of that state. Without even visiting Illinois, Chase accepted and immediately went to England to secure funds for a new college. Chase again acquired money, went to Illinois, purchased two thousand acres in Peoria County, and began Jubilee College, which he oversaw until his death in 1852.

Philander Chase is important not because of what he accomplished as an individual or simply because his forceful style and maverick tendencies allow the historian to tell a colorful story. Rather, Chase's efforts in early-nineteenth-century Ohio illustrate a process of institution building that was taking place all over the state, as

Ohioans thought about the kind of society they hoped to construct, in keeping with their values and priorities. The colleges that they built show their desire for broad access to education, their insistence upon usefulness, and their penchant for active experimentation. As they erected these colleges, they also structured, in part, the Ohio of today, reminding us of the connections of the past to the present.

Further Reading

Chase, Philander. *Bishop Chase's Reminiscences: An Autobiography*. Boston: J. B. Dow, 1848.

McCormick, Virginia E., and Robert W. McCormick. *New Englanders on the Ohio Frontier: The Migration and Settlement of Worthington, Ohio*. Kent, Ohio: Kent State University Press, 1998.

Smith, Laura Chase. *The Life of Philander Chase: First Bishop of Ohio and Illinois, Founder of Kenyon & Jubilee Colleges*. New York: E. P. Dutton & Company, 1903.

Smythe, George Franklin. *Kenyon College: Its First Century*. New Haven, Conn.: Yale University Press, 1924.

7

John Campbell and the Blending of Industrial Development and Moral Uplift in Early Ohio

PHILIP PAYNE

D URING HIS lifetime John Campbell, described by historian Anne Kelly Knowles as the "premier example" of a southern Ohio ironmaster, played a significant role in guiding the state into the industrial age. Yet for Campbell producing pig iron and personal wealth were not enough, so he founded a town. Located on the Ohio River near the triangular bottom of the state, Ironton quickly became a center of pig iron production and the culmination of Campbell's work. Inspired by a social as well as an economic vision, Campbell wanted his creation to be more than just another company town.

Campbell's life and work fits the patterns of both industrial development and moral uplift that were so common during the middle years of the nineteenth century. Campbell lived during a time of rapid change. With the nation expanding westward, new towns sprang up as boosters created places to make communities and fortunes. At the same time, the Second Great Awakening spurred on reform movements. From what we know of Campbell, he seemed to have no difficulty reconciling personal gain and social reform. Campbell was a leading businessman who sought to make a profit, but he also championed temperance and abolitionism. Campbell was very much a man of his time straddling the sometimes murky lines between self-interest, reform, and social control.

. We find in the Campbell family a familiar story in the settlement of Ohio. Like so many of the settlers in the eastern part of the state, they descended from Scotch-Irish immigrants. Earlier generations of Campbells originally had settled in Augusta County, Virginia. In 1790, Campbell's grandparents moved from Virginia to Kentucky and then to Ohio in 1798. John Campbell was born in Stanton, Ohio, on January 14, 1808. Campbell came from an obscure farm family and received the "ordinary school education of those days." A contemporary biographer claimed his parents "were of little assistance, and his life exhibits what can be accomplished by industry and integrity combined with good judgment." How much of this is accurate and how much of it is a Horatio Alger–style myth is difficult to tell. Still, it is not beyond the bounds of reason to call Campbell a self-made man.

Campbell enters into the historical record as a young man working as a store clerk, so there is a good chance that that he did receive an education somewhat beyond the "ordinary." As a clerk, Campbell showed business acumen that so impressed the proprietor that they jointly opened a store in Russellville in the late 1820s. Campbell soon bored of the slow life of a village storekeeper and invested his life savings ($600) in the riverboat *Banner,* becoming its clerk in 1830. The river trade, however, also proved to be too slow, and he sold his interest in the steamer the next year. Looking for opportunity, Campbell returned to southeastern Ohio and became deeply involved in the iron industry emerging along the Ohio River.

What was it that kept Campbell in southeastern Ohio? The importance of the Ohio River as a transportation artery cannot be discounted. Campbell certainly understood this from his work on the *Banner.* Developments in agriculture, transportation, and industry continually increased the traffic on the Ohio. The natural resources of the region were also of crucial importance. Southeastern Ohio and eastern Kentucky have a rugged landscape dominated by the foothills of the Appalachian Mountains. For years, locals referred to the hills as the "little smokies." Here Campbell and others pioneer ironmasters found the raw materials needed in the form of iron ore, limestone, and lumber.

The Hanging Rock Iron Region exemplified the connection between natural resources, transportation, and early industrial development. The region straddled the Ohio River extending into Ohio and Kentucky. In Ohio, the region encompassed six counties: Adams, Lawrence, Gallia, Jackson, Scioto, and Vinton. In 1838, Professor Kaleb Briggs of Ohio University exemplified the boosterism and excitement of the area when he wrote that the "iron region from the Ohio River, near Franklin Furnace, northward by Jackson, to the Hocking river occupies an area . . . capable of yielding 3,000,000 tons of good ore to *each square mile.*" The quality of the ore was "so great that Jackson, Lawrence, and Scioto counties are capable of producing 400,000 tons of iron annually for 2,700 years," Briggs claimed. Although Briggs's prediction proved overly optimistic (the iron ore lasted less than a century) it was in this excited climate that Campbell began his climb to the top.

Ohio's iron industry began in 1804 with smelting at the Hopewell blast furnace in Mahoning County. Two decades later, iron furnaces appeared in southeastern Ohio when Virginian John Means crossed the Ohio River, freed his slaves, and began producing pig iron. Means's story of a southerner rejecting slavery and traveling north to embrace free enterprise and free labor became an important part of the local legends surrounding the ironmasters. Still, rumors persisted that slavery did not stop at the Ohio River and that some of African American workers were secretly slaves who were owned in Kentucky but lived in Ohio. Means named the iron region after a "Hanging Rock" along the Ohio River where rivermen docked their barges. Soon a company town, aptly named Hanging Rock, appeared at the site.

Fittingly, given their southern roots, Means and his fellow iron-masters created "iron plantations." Production of iron was similar to large-scale commercial agriculture in that each furnace depended on large tracts of land. At the center of an iron plantation stood a blast furnace and a company town surrounded by a vast wilderness that provided the necessary ore and wood. By 1871, the ironmasters had created a system of small towns throughout southeastern Ohio. Typically, 300 to 500 people lived in crude company housing and performed backbreaking labor. Wages ranged from fifty cents to one dollar a day paid in company scrip or with credit at the company stores. The ironmasters, who were sometimes compared to feudal lords, lived nearby while the laborers, as described by two historians, were "the state's most victimized residential wage earners." Life on an iron plantation was often hard and dirty.

Upon returning to southeastern Ohio, Campbell met Robert Hamilton, described by a chronicler of the ironmasters' exploits as "the pioneer iron man of the Hanging Rock Iron Region." At first, Campbell's relationship with Hamilton followed a familiar path as the former went to work as a clerk at Hamilton's Pinegrove Iron Furnace in 1832. But he did not remain a clerk for long, rising to a partnership in short order. In 1833, Campbell helped build the Hanging Rock Iron Forge and, with Hamilton and Andrew Ellison, the Lawrence Furnace for J. Riggs and Company. He next formed the Campbell, Ellison, & Company and built the Vesuvius Furnace, which still stands in the Wayne National Forest. Vesuvius established Campbell's reputation as a designer of quality furnaces that were technically innovative.

Again Campbell grew dissatisfied with his situation and, in particular, his association with Hamilton. He tired of the decadent life he found in Hanging Rock and held Hamilton responsible for the rowdiness. Campbell broke with his partners, who had become more interested in the railroad business than in iron, to found the Ohio Iron & Coal Company. He combined profitability with moral reform as he entered a new venture, town founding.

Campbell's relationship with Ralph Leete, a young migrant from New England, aptly demonstrates his motives as a town founder. Like Campbell, Leete had traveled to the Ohio River Valley in search of opportunity. As a young lawyer, Leete needed business. This involved him with John Campbell's plans. When Leete inquired about a position at Hanging Rock, a disgruntled Campbell complained that a few large property holders were damaging the prospects of the area. Campbell wrote that "you might do well by coming again you might not." Part of the problem, as Campbell saw it, was the roughness of life and the excessive use of alcohol. In 1847, Leete opened a law practice at Burlington, the county seat for Lawrence County, and Campbell became one of his first and best customers.

By 1849, Campbell was ready to do more than complain about the mismanagement and moral corruption of Hanging Rock, and he set forth to make his own town where good business and good people would go together. The importance of iron for the town was, of course, reflected in the name. Thomas Walton suggested "Ironton" because the town existed for the removal of a "ton of iron." Campbell began by raising $125,000 in stock from ironmasters and selling subscriptions to the future residents of Ironton. Campbell's success in generating capital for his new venture reflected his stature among the ironmasters and their dissatisfaction with Hamilton.

Campbell brought the wealth of the ironmasters to bear in creating a town that would succeed where Hanging Rock had fallen short. Money, however, was not the only thing on Campbell's mind. He wished "to get talent, industry, & *great moral worth* in the first settlement.." Campbell enthusiastically encouraged Leete to move to Ironton by promising "a lot of attorneys who will be from ordinary down to the most worthless." In an almost bizarre promise, Campbell wrote Leete that he and his fellow investors "should try and get one or more of character as well as moral worth who has more experience than you have." For Campbell, the gathering of a great number of attorneys, including those of experience, would create a climate of fair and good competition that would push Leete to fulfill his ambitions. Campbell successfully lured Leete to Ironton not with promises of easy wealth but with talk of morality, fair competition, and self-improvement.

Fair competition among the town's attorneys was but a small part of Campbell's plan. Campbell's reform impulse manifested itself in a temperance clause for the town charter. Campbell's wealth allowed him to insist on temperance despite the objections of merchants and professionals; people who might embody fair competition but were, in reality, more concerned with profit than with great moral worth. All the original deeds prohibited the sale of alcohol on the property. A violation resulted in the property being forfeited to the Ohio Iron & Coal Company with the owner receiving only one-half of the appraised value. Campbell knew the clause dampened the enthusiasm of the original purchasers of property in the town but saw his insistence as one of "the greatest acts of my life." With the passing of time, the forfeiture feature became a dead letter, but for six to eight years it created a temperate climate.

Campbell again displayed his ambition when he succeeded in getting the county seat moved from Burlington to Ironton, an important step in making the town a center of activity. Campbell did this by collaborating with fellow ironmasters George N. Kemp and William Lambert in donating land to Lawrence County and raising private funds for the new building.

Campbell was not the only ironmaster with plans, however. Robert Hamilton wanted the county seat in Hanging Rock and mounted a campaign to frustrate Campbell. Again, Campbell went to the people and waged a successful campaign. Lawrence County voters endorsed the move of the courthouse to Ironton 1,043 to 697. On March 29, 1851, the Ohio General Assembly officially made Ironton the new county seat.

As a county seat, Ironton served as a center of patronage and socioeconomic activity. The presence of a courthouse encouraged merchants to build stores and young lawyers like Ralph Leete to find opportunity. As was typical of river towns, the county courthouse stood behind the main street. Yet, it was the Ohio River, and not the courthouse, that would dominate the city's landscape and future.

Ironton was an industrial town in an era when Ohio remained predominantly agricultural. However, during the 1840s and 1850s Ohio began the transformation into an industrial state. In 1840, only 24 percent of the state's workers held nonagricultural jobs, but by 1860 a majority of workers labored outside of agriculture. The name Ironton fit; the community was part of a new industrial order. In 1876, an observer noted that the "propriety of the name becomes more and more apparent as time passes."

Campbell's success as a town founder went hand in hand with his success in business. During the decade following the establishment of Ironton, Campbell was at the height of his wealth, which soon exceeded one million dollars, with most of his fortune invested in the community. According to a biographer, Campbell invested in "every good enterprise—in the old Iron bank, in the mills and foundries, the nail and plow factories." There was "scarcely anything worthy but what received his substantial encouragement," that is, his investment. Central to Campbell's business empire were a handful of enterprises related to iron production and community building. A credit report for R. G. Dun and Company described the furnace owners as "quite wealthy," with Campbell among the "heaviest furnace owners." He was the president of the Iron Bank, the Union Iron Company, the Iron Railroad Company, and proprietor of the Hecla Furnace. Besides local real estate, Campbell owned or had shares in the following: Ironton Rolling Mill, Olive Foundry and Machine Shop, Kentucky Iron and Coal Manufactory Company (located across the river in Ashland, Kentucky), Howard Furnace, Buckhorn Furnace, Charcoal Iron Company, Washington Furnace, S. S. Stone, Madison Furnace, Star Nail Mill, Monroe Furnace, and the Union Iron Company. He also invested heavily in the first telegraph system between Ironton and Cincinnati. In 1876, a biographer wrote that he "has done more towards developing its [the region's] resources, and at present controls more real estate and iron interests, than any other one man of the region."

Campbell clearly controlled Ironton's fate. Although not strictly a company town, Ironton existed specifically to produce Campbell's iron. Campbell and the other directors of the Ohio Iron & Coal Company planned for Ironton to be the economic, political, and cultural center of the region. A booster proudly proclaimed that "Ironton is and will be the Commercial and Business [center] of the county; the chief town of the county for trade manufactures, and consequently the principal market, and as such will be the point to which the citizens of the county will resort for business."

As tensions between North and South increased during the 1850s, Campbell became a prominent abolitionist. Lawrence County bordered two slave states—Kentucky and Virginia—and

became a battleground over the enforcement of the 1850 Fugitive
Slave Law. Ralph Leete, also an abolitionist, frequently traveled to
Columbus to work for the release of African Americans. When
Republicans won the two congressional districts in southern Ohio,
Democrats charged that the "Pig-Metal Aristocracy" pressured their
employees to vote Republican. Economic issues, however, overshad-
owed sectionalism. In 1860, iron industry leaders from southern
Ohio and Kentucky petitioned Congress for a higher tariff, com-
plaining of railroad builders using English iron. As historian Eugene
H. Roseboon notes, the iron area was conservative "on the slavery
issue but the tariff made it safely Republican."

The Civil War marked the beginning of the end of southeastern
Ohio's dominance of the state's iron industry. Politically, the citizens
of Ironton struck some observers as "intensely loyal" Unionists, while
others saw the city as a "twilight zone of neutrality." Again, economic
issues dominated local politics. Initially, the war had halted traffic on
the Ohio River, but before long U.S. Navy steamboats plied the river
and made the Ohio safe once again. The iron furnaces glowed bright
with war orders. Local iron became the armor for the river gunboats
that General Ulysses S. Grant's army used in the taking of Fort Henry
and Fort Donelson and the weapons used in the siege of Charleston,
South Carolina.

Despite the war orders, Campbell's companies found the period to
be a rocky one. Workers joining the Union Army, the uncertainty of
travel on the Ohio and Mississippi Rivers, and wartime instability all
adversely affected Campbell's businesses. Campbell, of course, lost the
southern markets where much of his iron had been sold. In January
1862, rumors of his failure circulated; in February, Campbell mort-
gaged his real estate to secure a credit extension. Although the crisis of
the early 1860s was a close call for Campbell, he soon recovered, and
by the early 1870s the company was turning a nice profit.

Campbell's respite was temporary. Ironton's days as an iron-producing center were numbered. During the years that followed the Civil
War, the iron-producing regions of northern Ohio and Michigan surpassed southern Ohio. The ironmasters found their iron ore and coal
deposits depleted and their furnaces increasingly obsolete. In the early
years of statehood, southern Ohio had led the way in industrialization,
but, as the nineteenth century progressed, the rest of the state and the
Midwest surpassed the region economically. Until 1845, all iron smelting in the United States was done with wood and wood products
(chiefly charcoal). In that year, a furnace in the Shenango Valley of

Pennsylvania was fired using raw coal. The following year the Lowell Furnace in northern Ohio produced iron using the same method. By 1873, fifty furnaces in northeastern Ohio used coal. The ironmasters of the Hanging Rock Iron Region, dependent on wood for charcoal, rightly saw these developments as a challenge to their status as the state's leading iron-producing area.

Interestingly, iron made from charcoal smelting was of a superior quality, but the shortage of trees to make charcoal limited the further development of Hanging Rock Iron Region. For all of their planning, Campbell and the other ironmasters had not planted new trees as their crews cut down the forests. Although the iron deposits in the Hanging Rock iron region still appeared deep, by the 1870s the Ironton Board of Trade worried about a shortage of charcoal. In 1873, Ohio's iron industry produced 406,029 tons of pig iron, of which 100,489 tons were produced in charcoal-burning furnaces. Nearly all the charcoal iron came from the Hanging Rock Region. Each furnace in the area required between 12,000 to 15,000 cords of wood annually. The ironmasters had timbered the "little smokies" with little concern for the future.

Campbell's interest in community building ensured Ironton's future in part by helping to diversify the economy, but the troubles of the iron business endangered his empire. The ironmasters lagged behind in investing in new facilities and technologies. There was little science in iron production. "It is a remarkable fact," wrote one economic reporter, "that furnace men know less of their business, really, than any other class of manufacturers in the United States." Of the six Ohio counties comprising the region, Lawrence County had, by far, the most furnaces. These furnaces, with the exception of one, had been built during the 1820s and 1830s and were increasingly obsolete. During the 1850s and 1860s, the ironmasters had reaped the profits of these investments, but they failed to make similar investments for the future.

As Ohio became increasingly industrial, Irontonians found themselves cut off from developments in the rest of the state. In 1870, Ohio ranked fourth among industrialized states. Before the Civil War southern Ohio had led the state in manufacturing, with only one of the top six manufacturing counties located in the northern half of the state. Wartime activity gave Columbus, the state capital, a new vigor, permitting politicians and businessmen to build the Columbus and Hocking Valley Railroad from Columbus to Lancaster and, later, to Athens. The new railroad diverted business from Ironton and the

Hanging Rock Iron Region. In 1873, the Mahoning Valley of north-eastern Ohio for the first time produced more iron than the Hanging Rock Iron Region, thanks to the use of coal. In the 1880s, the Cleveland-Mahoning Valley district permanently surpassed southeastern Ohio in iron production.

These trends meant only trouble for Campbell and Ironton. Campbell had invested heavily in the iron industry, with smaller amounts invested in banks and farmland. On January 1, 1883, Campbell's Union Iron Furnace failed. Creditors hoped his good character and lack of debt meant that he would remain solvent. By August, the Union Iron Company's situation had deteriorated. With 140 of 400 shares of the company and a personal wealth of $1,200,000, Campbell could meet his obligations providing that all the liabilities were not due at one time. Unfortunately for Campbell, this was exactly what happened in October 1883. He lost almost all his property and investments, and the downfall of John Campbell rippled throughout the local iron industry.

On Sunday, August 30, 1891, John Campbell died, leaving a wife, five children, and the town he founded. On the Tuesday afternoon of his funeral, a great throng filled his house and the surrounding downtown square. The crowd included people "of all beliefs, colors, conditions, the rich and poor, the Campbells old and young," one reporter wrote. During the viewing, "many a breast heaved and many a tear was shed." Not forgetting Campbell's abolitionist past, there "were many colored people among the throng, and they seemed visibly affected by the kindly features of the good old man who had been their friend for so long."

The idea of community that Campbell had foreseen and sought to create was evident at his funeral. Campbell's wealth was an important part of Ironton's history, but Campbell's influence went beyond riches. His story did not end with the failure of the Union Iron Company. In life, he had been an industrialist and businessman. In death, Campbell shed the vestiges of capitalism.

Irontonians began to interpret Campbell's place in their community's history. "Old age and fierce competition in the iron business prevented his recovery from financial disaster, but he went down a brave and honest man," one reporter wrote. "His financial distress never affected the sincere esteem in which he was held, or abated a jot the great influence he had in the community." Eventually the ironmasters began to fade away. Their children became businessmen, owning hotels, restaurants, and rental property, or moved elsewhere to work in the iron and steel industry. In the late 1880s, one observer wrote that the "men who built Ironton were sturdy, thoughtful, common-sense men." Their purpose was to build a "great city" rather than to reap profits. A great city required schools, churches, mills, and shops—all of which Campbell had provided or aided. However, the building of a great city required money, for without such funds the combination of social control and noblesse oblige practiced by Campbell fell short. Ultimately Campbell lacked the wealth to fulfill all of his ambitions for his town.

If Campbell had left behind the world of capitalism, Ironton had not. Although Ironton never became a great city, the economy diversified somewhat and the community seemed strong. When the depression of 1893 to 1897 hit Ironton, one reporter predicted that "a revival of business will strike us just as sure as it strikes anywhere, and you will not hasten that happy period by growling. Ironton is our home. It has been a wonderful town. It is the city of John Campbell." Even when times were bad, the founders would still be there to guide the community. Ironton's natural evolution, in the hands of local journalists, was to become "Industrial, Invincible Ironton." Despite the reality that Ironton would remain small, Campbell's dream of greatness remained.

In 1949, Irontonians celebrated their town's 100th anniversary, optimistically noting the continued prosperity even if the iron deposits in the Hanging Rock Region failed to last for two millennia. An editorial writer, echoing John Campbell's dream, wrote, "Ironton is more than an average normal city—it has always been an industrial community and a leader. . . . Nothing sensational—but just steady, and its citizens have never hesitated to invest money in the town's factories." In 1949, as in 1849, Ironton was a small town whose leaders saw potential. In 1949, however, Ironton was neither the leading city of the region nor a great city. Campbell's ambition to create a town succeeded even if it did not live up to Campbell's dream. The city outlived both the ironmasters and their iron plantations but did not outlive the community that these men helped create.

Further Reading

Boryczka, Raymond, and Lorin Lee Cary. *No Strength Without Union: An Illustrated History of Ohio Workers, 1803–1980*. Columbus: Ohio Historical Society, 1982.

Collins, Horace R., and D. K. Webb, Jr. *The Hanging Rock Iron Region of Ohio.* Columbus: Ohio Historical Society, 1966.

Ingham, John N. *The Iron Barons: A Social Analysis of an American Urban Elite, 1874–1965.* Westport, Conn.: Greenwood Press, 1978.

Knowles, Anne Kelly. *Calvinist Incorporated: Welsh Immigrants on Ohio's Industrial Frontier.* Chicago: University of Chicago Press, 1997.

8

John P. Parker and the Underground Railroad

MERTON L. DILLON

S OME TWENTY years after the Civil War ended, John P. Parker, a prosperous manufacturer and inventor of Ripley, Ohio, agreed to talk with a newspaper reporter about a part of his prewar life that, at the time, he had been at pains to hide from public view. He finally admitted that between 1845 and 1861 he had helped perhaps as many as 440 slaves escape from the South—he had lost track of just how many. Like most Underground Railroad operatives, Parker had been careful to leave no incriminating paper trail. He had kept a detailed record of the slaves he helped, but he soon realized that this was a dangerous practice. After the passage of the Fugitive Slave Law of 1850 imposed harsh penalties for aiding slave escapes, such concealment became essential. Parker then retrieved his account book from its hiding place and burned it in the furnace of his iron foundry. Thus was lost the written record that would have documented the illegal and dangerous activity he finally confessed to have engaged in for so many years: assisting fugitives make their way to freedom, often venturing into Kentucky itself, mostly at night, in order to lead slaves back across the river into Ohio.

Parker must have been aware at every moment that he risked especially harsh punishment for his actions, for he was an African American and had himself once been a slave. Parker was born in Norfolk, Virginia, in 1827. His father, he had been told, was "one of the aristocrats of Virginia;" his mother was a slave and, thus, he was a slave too. At the age of eight, he was sold at Richmond and attached to a slave coffle that walked from Virginia to its destination in Alabama.

In recounting his experience in bondage, Parker had little to say about the harrowing cruelties and indignities that darken so many slave narratives. "I know slavery's curse was not the pain of the body, but the pain of the soul," was his summation of the burden of his early life. Perhaps he even would have agreed that on the whole his lot had been a fortunate one. The white companions of his childhood taught him to read, and his owner, a Mobile physician, treated him kindly and when he reached the appropriate age encouraged him to develop a skilled trade by apprenticing him, first to a plasterer and then to an iron molder.

Upon his arrival in Alabama, his life took a harsh turn. The blame, he conceded, was partly his own. He described his youthful self as "designing, hateful, and determined." He was proud and uncompliant. He resented power and rebelled at authority, two of the essential pillars of slavery. He recoiled at injustice. A ruthless beating by his first employer, the plasterer, whom he could not please, sent him to a hospital. There, when Parker witnessed a white woman attendant administer harsh punishment to another patient, he protested. In the scuffle that followed, he seized the woman's whip and used it on her.

After this potentially catastrophic act, flight seemed his only recourse, so he stowed himself on a riverboat bound for New Orleans. By skill and remarkable luck, he eluded detection and, after many perils, eventually found himself again in Mobile in the doctor's custody without having been punished for an action that the slave regime ordinarily judged among the most heinous of offenses. The doctor then apprenticed him to an iron molder, a trade that would serve Parker well throughout the rest of his life. Still, the arrangement did not work out. He had failed to internalize the servile values considered appropriate to his status. Some thought he did not behave as a slave should; his demeanor resembled that of a free man. Enthusiastic about his new craft, he antagonized the other workmen by his exceptional diligence and skill. He spent his earnings, which his owner allowed him to keep, on clothing of style and quality judged unsuited to a slave. His associates at the foundry probably did not err in finding him both arrogant and insolent. Tensions in the shop grew. He soon fell into what he described as "a regular knock-down-and-drag-out fistfight" with the foreman.

News of this dire offense led Parker's owner to hurry him out of town to work for an iron molder in New Orleans. The arrangement lasted just a week. The doctor finally gave up on him and announced that he must be sold as a field hand. Of course, the boy could not face such a prospect. The winning ways that he evidently could muster when occasion required came into play, and his owner relented. The doctor agreed to let him pass into the custody of one of his patients, a well-to-do widow who allowed him to apply his earnings at an iron foundry in Mobile to the purchase of his freedom

The opportunity drove him to new heights of industry. On Sundays, he met incoming steamboats to unload packages and trunks, which he carted all over the city. During the week, he worked long hours as a molder, and on the side he operated an impromptu pawnshop. Within three years, he had discharged his heavy obligation to his owner. At the age of eighteen, free papers in hand and charged with an everlasting hatred for slavery and oppression, he took passage on a steamboat heading up the Mississippi toward free soil—but not before stopping at the shop where he had worked, not to say good-bye to his fellow molders but to give a thrashing to the foreman who he believed had wronged him.

Parker's northern destination was Jeffersonville, Indiana, where he expected to find work in an iron foundry. His stay there, though pleasant and lucrative enough, was brief. The booming city of Cincinnati, he explained, lured him away "to other adventures."

Parker remembered that he first helped fugitive slaves shortly after he arrived in Cincinnati in 1845. It was a particularly daring effort because it did not involve the practice, fairly common, especially among African Americans, of simply befriending runaways who already had reached the city, but the far more hazardous feat of crossing into Kentucky and spiriting slaves away from their owner. At the behest of a boardinghouse acquaintance who recently had come from Kentucky as a free man, Parker agreed to accompany him upriver to the town of Ripley and from there cross over to Maysville and bring two slave women back to Ohio. Two nights passed without the conspirators finding a suitable boat on the Ohio side. The risk and delay led his companion to return to Cincinnati in frustration. Parker persisted and completed the project by himself. He landed the women at a black settlement near Ripley where they were welcomed and given shelter for the night. The next day a guide led him and the fugitives to the house of a white abolitionist in the town. From there, the women were sent on toward Canada.

Although no doubt a milestone in Parker's life and noteworthy for its unquestioned bravura, this exploit would have been regarded by others at that time and place as foolhardy perhaps but only slightly out of the ordinary. By the 1840s, in cities all along the Ohio River the extension of aid to fugitives had become routine, and, to the great alarm and indignation of slave owners, a few daring persons were entering southern states and conveying slaves to the North. In Cincinnati white philanthropists, most notably the Quaker Levi Coffin, who arrived in the city the same year that Parker did, made names for themselves by engaging in Underground Railroad activity. Members of the free black community did as much or more. This fact was common knowledge at the time, but since few of them, unlike their white contemporaries, wrote memoirs or had friends and descendants in a position to celebrate their deeds, memory of the African American contribution faded. Only occasionally did their efforts become part of the U.S. historical narrative as it was commonly constructed.

Both groups, black and white alike, had abundant opportunity to aid fugitive slaves. Even in the colonial period, runaways were commonplace, a costly and vexatious problem for their owners. During the Revolutionary era the development of free territory in the North to which southern slaves might escape compounded the problem. Not surprisingly, slave owners, long accustomed to wielding political power in their own interest, resorted to the federal government for assistance.

Delegates to the Constitutional Convention of 1787 took up the matter. Article IV, section 2 of the Constitution provided that runaways who reached a free state did not thereby become free but must be returned to their owners. In 1793, Congress implemented that provision by enacting a fugitive slave law empowering owners or their agents to enter free states and recover their property. These official acts, taken at the founding of the new nation, gave convincing evidence of the propensity of slaves to escape into the North and, more troubling to slaveholders, of the likelihood that contrary citizens would extend aid and comfort upon their arrival. Even George Washington, himself a substantial slave owner, found that exalted status supplied no protection from such loss and aggravation. In 1786, he penned a laconic formulation of the costly fact: there are "numbers who would rather facilitate the escape of slaves than apprehend them when runaways." Sixty years later, Parker was counted among those "numbers" whose propensity to ignore the law would bedevil the South in ever-growing intensity until it seceded from the Union and the ensuing war freed the slaves.

By the time Parker arrived in Ohio, the state already had achieved its beckoning reputation among would-be fugitives. Located on the northern frontier of slavery, it early became a haven, if not as a reliably safe place for permanent settlement, then as a critical section of the route that followed the more secure freedom offered by Canada.

Once in Ohio, fugitives learned, they would not find themselves friendless. At an early date, well before Parker arrived there, slaves had proved Washington's gloomy observation correct: some Ohio citizens were indeed willing to "facilitate the escape of slaves" rather than hand them over to persons who claimed them as property.

Fugitives had to be wary, however. Not all Ohioans were hospitable to runaway slaves. If they appeared at the wrong door, their flight might be immediately stopped and reversed. Residence in a free state did not automatically make white citizens friends of the slave. Not surprisingly, economic interest came into play. Some in Ohio, as elsewhere, did not want to lose the good will of Southerners with whom they enjoyed profitable commercial ties. Prejudice manifested itself too. Some shunned helping people of a race they had been taught to dislike or fear. To this primitive and tribal impulse, motives more cerebral, though not necessarily more powerful, were added to further counter philanthropy. The act of helping slaves escape subverted society. To disregard property rights, even in slaves, was a revolutionary act that shook the standing order. Further, by the 1840s, when Parker became active in the Underground Railroad, the issue of northern aid to runaways had emerged as a key part of the seething sectional controversy that threatened destruction of the Union, and few in the North wanted that.

The elements in the white population unlikely to aid the fugitive probably constituted a majority, but no one could say for sure because only a minority ever were tested. While fugitives were a common feature of life in such Ohio River cities as Cincinnati, it would be a mistake to imagine armies of runaways thronging the streets and roads of antebellum Ohio and thereby offering themselves as plentiful objects of philanthropy. To that extent, the alarm expressed by slave owners and their representatives in Congress was disproportionate to the numbers of slaves actually lost.

Just as Parker late in life could not be sure how many runaways he personally had assisted, no one can count with certainty the number who passed through the state and received aid. The fact that some white residents, even though sympathetic to the cause, reported having had few contacts with them is suggestive of sharp limits. A white Ohioan, although reputed to be an Underground Railroad operative, was frank enough to admit that he "did not have much opportunity to aid runaways as but few passed through Warren," where he lived. For Dr. Blunt, a philanthropist of Darke County, the lack of such contact was cause for regret. He appealed for help in satisfying his curiosity: "I wish that some of your Underground Railroad passengers would come along to-night. I have never had the pleasure of seeing a fugitive slave, and I would like to see one. There have been a few in our neighborhood, and I have contributed to help them on their way, but I did not see them."

Parker, unlike Dr. Blunt, lived on the banks of the Ohio River, where such opportunity abounded. Cincinnati had a black community of considerable size and venerability. Its members had been hardened by adversity. A devastating race riot in 1829 drove many away, but neither that upheaval nor a similar event in 1836 destroyed the black community or halted its growth permanently. This continued expansion, however, coupled with white citizens' concerns for African American antislavery activism, especially as expressed in covert aid to fugitives, culminated in September 1841 (only four years before Parker arrived in the city), in one of the largest and most intense race riots of the nineteenth century. Yet, such violence, destructive though it was, did not produce black demoralization nor curb antislavery activity. Nothing could more effectively assure racial solidarity among black citizens than the prejudice and hostility that they persistently experienced. Far from discouraging their assistance to fugitives, as had perhaps been anticipated, mob action steeled their determination. Fugitives arriving as stowaways or defectors from the steamboats that crowded the city's wharves continued to find sanctuary in black neighborhoods even as they shied from contact with the unpredictable white people. As early as 1837, the white abolitionist James G. Birney reported from his home in Cincinnati, "Slaves are escaping in great numbers through Ohio to Canada." But, he added, "Such matters are almost uniformly managed by the colored people. I know nothing of them generally till they are past."

The abundant opportunity to aid fugitives was not a sufficient motive to keep Parker in Cincinnati for long. He hated the injustice and cruelty intrinsic to slavery, but he did not think of himself then— or ever—as being primarily a humanitarian or a racial reformer, much less a revolutionary. He was an ambitious, self-confidant young American intent upon employing and profiting from the talents that experience already had proved were his. Such prejudice and proscription as he may have experienced as a black man neither dismayed him nor deterred him from his goal. He intended to establish himself as a successful participant in the society and economy of his time. Along the way, however, he would not hesitate to risk life and estate to help others of his race escape the bonds of slavery and achieve the same end.

In 1848, Parker married Miranda Boulden, a resident of Cincinnati, and started a short-lived general store at Beechwood Factory, Ohio. The next year the young couple moved to Ripley, the thriving river town that had been the staging point for his first slave rescue. Ripley offered him employment at his trade as an ironworker. The town's location, convenient to Maysville, a favorite embarkation point for Kentucky runaways, may have also influenced his decision to locate there.

Ripley would be Parker's home for the rest of his life, the site of his varied business enterprises, and the center of his remarkable Underground Railroad activity. As Parker's rescue of the Maysville fugitives shortly after he left the South suggests, his new status as a free man had not at all weakened his sense of brotherhood with the slaves who remained in bondage or with those who shared his desire to escape it. Nevertheless, he harbored no romantic or sentimental illusions about the objects of his aid. On occasion, he behaved toward them in the same peremptory manner he had exhibited toward his fellow workers in Mobile. On his perilous incursions into Kentucky, he easily became exasperated at what he viewed as the folly and impracticality of the people he had come to help. Fugitives whose flight originated far to the south and who had undergone perils and hardships in their northward journey struck him as being more intelligent, more courageous, and on the whole better suited to freedom than those nearer the river whose decision to flee may have sprung from mere impulse and whose mettle remained untested. Toward such "riffraff runaways," as he called them, he exhibited limited tolerance and patience. Despite his powers of command he admitted to finding some of them unruly and hard to control, scarcely worthy of his assistance.

His forbearance, always limited, had been sorely tested during his inaugural effort at rescue. To his annoyance, he found that the two women who were the objects of his first incursion into Kentucky had clothed themselves in their mistress's "tilter hoops," whose great circumference so crowded the escape boat as to make maneuver all but impossible. The fugitives were further encumbered with frying pans and, to Parker most exasperating of all, with bundles of "trinkets and slippers." These impediments, despite the women's tears, Parker unceremoniously required them to abandon.

Years later, even after he had gained much experience in rescuing slaves, a group he had ferried to Ripley and concealed in an attic gave him trouble. Their ungrateful complaints about the constricted quarters in which they found themselves annoyed him, while their commotion threatened to reveal their hiding place. "I was so mad at their stupidity, one of the men making some slighting remark," he recalled. "I gave him a sound thrashing, and after that the crowd were meek and mild." When he was on yet another mission in Kentucky and "one of the men set up a wail," he drew his pistol and gave the unfortunate slave the choice of obeying orders "or be shot down in cold blood." With that show of force, Parker remembered, "I had my charges under my control."

Command came easily to Parker, no doubt facilitated by a gift of nature: as one acquaintance reported, he "was a large and shrewd man of impressive appearance." When Parker was a young man and a slave, he maintained his autonomy and enforced his sense of justice with his fists. When he was older and free, he brooked no transgression of the rules he set and no trespass on his authority and dignity. To that end, he still did not hesitate to use his fists and, sometimes, his gun.

Parker discovered that Cincinnati, his first Ohio home, had attracted an impressive array of abolitionists, both black and white, but this group was rivaled, and proportionally outnumbered, by the antislavery activists who had congregated in the much smaller town of Ripley and surrounding Brown County. Prominent among them were the African American residents of two farming communities established in the 1820s by former slaves whose owners in Virginia had emancipated them and provided them with land. Parker did not choose to settle among his fellow ex-slaves (he had never lived on a plantation and had no experience with agriculture), but he depended on them as reliable allies. They would help him in the future as they had helped a few years earlier when he came to them with the two fugitive women he had brought from Maysville.

Dozens of antislavery white Southerners also had made Ripley and the surrounding county their home. One of the earliest and most distinguished of them was Dr. Alexander Campbell, a native of Virginia who in 1796 moved to Kentucky, where he engaged in antislavery activity, and then in 1803 moved to Ripley, where he freed his slaves, served in the state legislature and in the U.S. Senate, and became the first vice-president of the Ohio Anti-Slavery Society in 1835.

Many of Ripley's and Brown County's antislavery activists were Presbyterians, members of congregations led by the Revs. John Rankin of Ripley, James Gilliland of Red Oak, and Jesse H. Lockhart of Russelville. Several of the Brown County group were closely tied to the national antislavery movement, which, to the alarm of white Southerners, emerged as a social and political force in the early 1830s. Rankin, in particular, enjoyed high repute among abolitionists as author of "Letters on Slavery" (1826), a pamphlet whose theologically based antislavery argument had proved persuasive to several prominent reformers including William Lloyd Garrison, editor of the *Liberator*. Rankin's failure to persuade the Presbyterian Church to accept his own advanced abolitionist principles led him, together with ten other Midwestern preachers, to withdrew from the church in 1846 to form the avowedly abolitionist Free Presbytery of Ripley, later the Free Presbyterian Church. Within Ripley itself, Rankin's house, located on a hill above the town and lighted far into the night, became famous for guiding as well as sheltering fugitives who crossed the river from Kentucky.

Lending support to such dedicated abolitionists as Rankin were several of Ripley's lawyers and businessmen who could be counted on to cooperate in Underground Railroad activity, though most of them chose not to identify themselves as abolitionists. These men, like Rankin, risked attack by slave hunters and prosecution for concealing and otherwise assisting the slaves that Parker brought to them. Courageous and generous as they were, none of them ventured into Kentucky themselves to bring runaways back to Ohio. This dangerous business remained the perilous domain of Parker and of his abettors, certain unnamed members of Ripley's generally obscure African American community.

Parker worked amicably with the white abolitionists of Ripley and Brown County, but he should not be thought of as their auxiliary. Rescuing slaves from Kentucky was his idea and his project, not theirs. He did not work for them, nor did they work for him. As Wilbur H. Siebert, a historian of the Underground Railroad, explained, Parker did not "think it proper to ask white men how to abduct slaves from Kentucky." Parker was his own independent militant activist. He needed neither authorization, encouragement, nor instruction in the antislavery cause.

White abolitionists and their specialized subset, Underground Railroad operatives, typically owed their antislavery commitment to the imperatives of evangelical religion. So prevalent was the affinity that one influential historian located "the antislavery impulse," as he titled his book on the subject, in the religious revivalism of the 1820s. But for Parker, as for many other African Americans, no such connection need be sought. They were opposed to slavery as by nature, whatever their religious conviction. It does not appear that Parker, for his part, belonged to any church. On the contrary, he is reputed to have declared churches to be the "enemy of the people." The origin of his rather exceptional aversion remains obscure, although it may reflect the same displeasure with ecclesiastical delay and compromise on the slavery issue that had led Rankin to withdraw from the Presbyterian Church shortly before Parker became acquainted with him in Ripley.

Parker understood that his labors formed part of the larger antislavery enterprise, but he did not, so far as is known, affiliate with any abolitionist society. He would perhaps have dismissed such organizations, whatever their other merits, as functioning too far from the field of battle to be immediately effective. He had little interest in the theory or rhetoric of antislavery. He was an impatient man; his sphere was action, not persuasion. After the end of slavery, when his entrepreneurial skill had brought him financial success and a measure of esteem, he anticipated Booker T. Washington's later message of the efficacy of craftsmanship as a means of racial advancement. Perhaps thinking of the example of African American skill he himself provided, Parker declared in 1869 that "a plow made by a black man, tells us more than a hundred first class speeches." It is not surprising, then, that in 1850 he had believed that the rescue of one slave from Kentucky told more than a hundred antislavery exhortations.

This does not mean that he underestimated the gravity of the unfolding sectional conflict and the central role that antislavery agitation and the Underground Railroad played in it. Although as an African American he himself was barred from electoral politics, he watched approvingly as antislavery Whigs and Democrats disrupted the old party system in the mid-1850s and formed the new Republican Party. His sympathies lay with its more radical wing. Thus, he named his first-born son Hale Giddings after two prominent antislavery founders of the new party, John P. Hale of New Hampshire and Joshua Giddings of Ohio. Another son was Cassius Clay, named for Kentucky's colorful antislavery maverick politician.

With the outbreak of war in 1861, Parker's long-practiced pattern of assistance to black Southerners lost much of its urgency. No longer did it seem imperative to risk life and property by ferrying slaves across the Ohio. Parker's activism now changed direction and assumed a more encompassing purpose. He saw that wherever Union armies drove into the South, the slave system underwent change and disruption. Accordingly, he turned to aiding the Union war effort, which he likely viewed from the beginning not primarily as a campaign to preserve the Union but as a crusade to end slavery. In antebellum days, Northerners' assistance to fugitive slaves made a major contribution to the sectional discord that eventuated in secession and war. Parker's purpose now was to build on that accomplishment by hastening the military defeat of the Confederacy. As soon as the Union government authorized enlistment of black troops, Parker became a recruiter for the 27th Regiment, United States Colored Troops (Ohio). Several hundred of its members came from Kentucky as a result of his persuasion. By that means, men whom a year earlier he might have helped individually to achieve their own freedom were now enlisted to fight for the destruction of the slave system itself.

The Civil War brought expanded business opportunity for Parker as it did for many other northern entrepreneurs. When Parker moved to Ripley, he found employment in an iron foundry. By 1854, he had accumulated enough capital to establish his own foundry and machine shop and hire a white man as his helper. He specialized in turning out spiral and general castings. Army contracts swelled his business and provided the resources that allowed the firm to develop after the war, despite fires and financial panics, into the Ripley Foundry and Machine Company, which continued to operate through most of the twentieth century. In the 1880s, probably its most prosperous period, the company employed twenty-five workmen, making it one of the largest businesses in Ripley at that time. R. G. Dun, the national credit rating agency, reported Parker's worth in 1882 as between $15,000 and $20,000. His profits derived in part from his own inventions. Parker held at least three of the seventy-seven patents that were issued to African Americans before 1886. A mainstay of his business was a tobacco press, which he marketed especially in Kentucky. Of wider sale was his soil pulverizer, a device for breaking clods in plowed ground. His product line was anything but specialized. At one time or another, his factory turned out slide-valve engines and a variety of agricultural implements including reapers, mowers, sugar mills, and steel plows. The economic shortcomings of Reconstruction and the South's persistent postwar poverty thwarted Parker's ambitious plans to develop the thriving market among the freedmen that he had envisioned. He necessarily fell back for the most part on meeting more local needs.

It does not appear that Parker's business suffered substantially from prejudice that may have been directed toward him as an African American nor on account of his illicit antislavery activity. On the contrary, according to a local history, published in 1965, no one in those years "was more prominently identified with the prosperity of the town than John Parker." (One must concede, however, that it may have been easier for local historians to make that evaluation in the midst of the twentieth century's civil rights revolution than it would have been a century earlier.) Parker's success in manufacturing was duplicated in the late nineteenth century by countless others, men whose skill and drive exploited the untrammeled opportunity afforded by vast resources, a large market, and an hospitable political environment. Every northern city, every town, could provide stunning examples of such achievement, some on far grander scale than his. But few, it seems safe to say, had started from origins so unpromising and unprivileged, and few overcame such large obstacles with such apparent ease. Yet business acumen and its rewards could not altogether banish one abiding reality. Parker never forgot the hostility and danger that surrounded him in the days when slave hunters and the Fugitive Slave Law had made his a perilous avocation. Opposition from those sources was based in the law and thus was officially sanctioned. But for Parker there always was the additional possibility of violence from persons both within the town and outside it (Parker likely would have denominated some of them as "riffraff") whose antipathy had an extralegal, secret source. Within them festered resentment toward a black man whose ability and drive had reaped success greater than theirs, a black man who had defied the law and, rather than suffering for his transgression, had garnered praise and reward. While it was always fitting for a man of Parker's pursuits to be bold and to appear fearless, prudence, as he early learned, also counted for something. One aspect of his caution became legendary. In the feverish atmosphere of the 1850s, he took to avoiding sidewalks as he made his way through the town: doorways and alleys might hide assassins and be sites for ambush. To the wonderment of small boys and the amusement of others, Parker chose to walk in the middle of the street and always left home armed with knife and pistol. No white Underground Railroad operative in Ripley experienced similar compulsion or had reason to, but Parker felt more comfortable that way. Such, it was said, continued to be his habit for a while even after slavery had ended and after the need, or so his white neighbors no doubt supposed, had passed.

James P. Parker died in Ripley on January 30, 1900. No portrait or photograph of him is known to have survived.

Further Reading

Gara, Larry. *The Liberty Line: The Legend of the Underground Railroad.* Lexington: University Press of Kentucky, 1961.

Levstik, Frank R. "John P. Parker," in *American National Biography,* vol. 17. New York: Oxford University Press, 1999.

Parker, John P. *His Promised Land: The Autobiography of John P. Parker, Former Slave and Conductor on the Underground Railroad.* Edited by Stuart Seely Sprague. New York: W. W. Norton, 1996.

Seibert, Wilbur H. *The Mysteries of Ohio's Underground Railroads.* Columbus: Ohio Historical Society, 1951.

Weeks, Louis. "John P. Parker: Black Abolitionist Entrepreneur, 1827–1900." *Ohio History* 80 (Spring 1971): 155–62.

9

Frances Dana Gage and Northern Women's Reform Activities in the Nineteenth Century

BARBARA A. TERZIAN

If as a woman to take the platform amidst the hissing and scorn, and news-paper vituperations, to maintain the rights of woman to the legitimate use of all the talents God invests her with, to maintain the rights of the slave in the very ears of the masters; to hurl anathemas at intemperance in the very camps of the dram sellers; if to continue for forty years, in spite of all opposing forces, to press the triune cause persistently, consistently, and unflinchingly, entitles me to a humble place among those noble ones who have gone about doing good, you can put me in that place as it suits you.

F RANCES DANA Gage, wife, mother of eight, public speaker, poet, novelist, and newspaper columnist, wrote these words about her life's work, the "triune cause" of antislavery, women's rights, and temperance. When Gage was born in 1808, slavery, although illegal in Ohio, was legal across the Ohio River in Kentucky, throughout the South, and still existed in some northern states such as New York and New Jersey. Even in states where slavery was illegal, free blacks did not have the same rights as whites. Women, black and white, were also second-class citizens. Higher education opportuni-ties for women did not exist, and they were banned from professional occupations such as the law, the ministry, and medicine. Husbands controlled the wages, property, children, and bodies of their wives. Married women were deemed to be "dead" in the eyes of the law. Women could not vote, even single women who paid the same taxes as men. Women did not speak in public before audiences, certainly not mixed-sex audiences, no matter how moral the cause.

FIG. 5 Frances Dana Gage. From Frances Dana Gage, *Poems*
(Philadelphia: J. B. Lippincott, 1867),
frontispiece.

When Frances became a young adult, the message to middle-class women was that they should remain in their "proper sphere" within the home. The "Cult of Domesticity" taught women to be pious, pure, submissive, and domestic. Men inhabited the public world and were expected to be competitive, rational, secular, and dominant. Women should make their homes a sanctuary for their husbands—a haven from the competitive marketplace of the public sphere.

Despite women's exclusion from electoral politics, historians have found that many women in the nineteenth century, engaged in political activity nonetheless. They did so through organizations they created to generate social reform. Some women, inspired by the Second Great Awakening of the early nineteenth century, engaged in social reform as an extension of their religious beliefs—they had a moral and spiritual responsibility to perfect the world. The temperance movement attracted many women, while others, fewer in number, dedicated themselves to antislavery work or to women's rights activism. These were not mutually exclusive endeavors, and so some women, like Frances Dana Gage, devoted themselves to all three causes. Gage's lifelong commitment to social reform and her talent for using her writing skills to further those causes had their origins in her childhood in southeastern Ohio.

Frances Barker was the ninth of ten children born to Joseph Barker and Elizabeth Dana Barker. Her parents came to Ohio in 1789 from New England as part of the settlement sponsored by the Ohio Company. As a descendant of Puritans who had settled in New England in 1638, as the granddaughter of a Revolutionary War veteran, and as the daughter of settlers in what was then the American West, Gage was extremely proud of her "pioneer" ancestry. She was particularly proud of her parents' accomplishments—her father as a builder, farmer, state legislator, and judge and her mother for raising her children in a frontier community.

Frances relished her childhood on a farm where "she had ample opportunity for indulging her love of outdoor life." She preferred milking the cows, feeding the stock, and gathering garden produce to the "dull monotonies of indoor life." Although her rural childhood satisfied her love of the outdoors and taught her useful skills, it limited her formal schooling to a few weeks at a time in the local school where she learned "grammar and geography." She supplemented this through self-education, taking advantage of her father's library to read and memorize passages from Shakespeare and Pope. At twelve, she began writing poetry, starting her on a writing career she maintained throughout her life.

Her childhood influenced her later reform activities in several ways. From her mother and grandmother, she acquired early a hatred of slavery. Her maternal grandmother, Mary Bancroft Dana, lived in Belpre, Ohio, across the Ohio River from slave-owning Virginia. Mrs. Dana and Mrs. Barker actively assisted runaway slaves, and Frances helped by taking food and clothing to the fugitives as they passed through.

Frances dated her interest in women's rights to a childhood incident in which her father reprimanded her for making a barrel, an activity he deemed inappropriate for a girl. "What a pity she was not a boy," she reported her father saying. From that moment at the age of ten "sprang up my hatred to the limitations of sex," she later recalled. By young adulthood she had acquired a sense of independence, a resentment of the limitations placed on her sex, a strong anti-slavery belief, and a love for expressing her thoughts in poetry and prose.

On January 1, 1829, at the age of twenty, Frances Barker married James L. Gage, an attorney who shared her antislavery beliefs. For the next twenty-four years, they made their home in McConnelsville, Ohio, where James practiced law, built a foundry, and at various times served as the community's prosecuting attorney, judge, and mayor. By 1842, Frances was the mother of eight children. Despite the demands of a large family, she continued her self-education by reading every book and magazine she could. In the late 1840s, she found an outlet for her poetry and letter writing in newspapers. On one occasion, though, her antislavery position caused an editor to reject her piece.

By 1850, Gage was a regular contributor to an agricultural journal, the *Ohio Cultivator,* an affiliation she maintained for the next twelve years. Published twice a month in Columbus, the *Ohio Cultivator* had a circulation of 10,000, which made it one of the most widely read of the agricultural journals in the Midwest. In addition to stories about scientific farming, news of harvests, and advertisements for farm equipment of interest to its male readership, the *Ohio Cultivator* included a "Ladies Department" with articles of interest to farmers' wives. Writing as "Aunt Fanny," Gage developed a loyal following. In the pages of the *Ohio Cultivator,* Gage, Hannah Tracy Cutler, and the other women contributors provided recipes and household and gardening tips. But, as historian Frances W. Kaye has found, they also encouraged women to appreciate the value of their work as wives and mothers, advocated better education for girls, and argued for economic independence and expanded employment opportunities for women.

Importantly, Gage encouraged women to understand that the "true sphere of woman" was the "sphere of DUTY." Rejecting the notion that the home circumscribed women's sphere, Gage argued that "if God has given to woman talent to redeem a nation from sin or slavery, she has no right to roll that talent in a napkin, or bury talent by selfishly clinging to home joys and home comforts, while she might be doing a mighty good: no right to devote the energy to ten, that would redeem a thousand, if she felt it a duty to do so."

Gage took her own advice and followed her sense of duty beyond her home and the pages of the *Ohio Cultivator* when she organized a women's rights convention in May 1850 in McConnelsville following the Women's Rights Convention held in Salem, Ohio, which she could not attend. The Salem gathering held one month earlier was the first such convention in Ohio, the second in the nation after Seneca

Falls in New York in 1848, and had been called specifically to organize for the Ohio Constitutional Convention to be held later that year.

Ohio's state constitution provided suffrage for white males over the age of twenty-one. The 1850 Constitutional Convention provided an opportunity to expand suffrage to include African Americans and women. Prompted by this opportunity, the organizers of the 1850 Salem women's convention circulated a call to the women of Ohio and sent letters of invitation to prominent Ohio and national women's rights advocates. The call announced the goal "to concert measures to secure to all persons the recognition of Equal Rights, and the extension of the privileges of Government, without distinction of sex and color." The time was right for such efforts because "[t]he meeting of a Convention of men to amend the Constitution of *our* (?) State presents a most favorable opportunity for the agitation of this subject."

The first strategic decision made by the women gathered at Salem was to permit men to attend the convention but not to participate as officers, committee members, share the platform, or even address the convention. The Salem convention was the only antebellum women's rights convention that excluded men's participation. As Paulina W. Davis reported in her history of the first twenty years of the movement, "*Never did men so suffer.* They implored just to say a word; but no, the President was inflexible, no man should be heard. If one meekly rose to make a suggestion, he was at once ruled out of order." This strategy stood in contrast to the proceedings at Seneca Falls where no woman was willing to preside; instead, the women organizers recruited Lucretia Mott's husband.

Gage had been asked to speak at the Salem Convention, but, unable to attend, she sent a letter, which was published as part of the official proceedings. In her letter, she worried that both law and public opinion prevented women from recognizing their own strength and kept women in a subordinate place in the household. In particular, she cited the unfairness of the law that took from married women their legal existence. While she believed that a woman's highest duties were as a wife and a mother, she also believed a man's were as a husband and a father. If women could meet their responsibilities yet also make contributions beyond the home, they should be given the same right to do so as men.

Not content with sending a letter to the Salem Convention, Gage organized her own convention in McConnelsville a month later. She prepared a paper discussing the laws that discriminated against women, which she read to the seventy female attendees. Despite its controversial nature, she was able to obtain forty signatures from this group for the petition she had drafted for the Ohio Constitutional Convention asking that the words "white male" be removed from the constitution.

She followed the meeting with another convention in Chesterfield, Ohio. Denied the use of the churches and schoolhouse, the women convened in a barn. Gage described the audience of three to four hundred as "farmers, their wives, sons and daughters . . . nearly all Quakers and Abolitionists but then not much inclined to Woman's Rights." She gave her speech standing on a cart, calling this her "oxsled" speech. She was pleased to add many names to her petition.

Ohio women's rights activists submitted their petitions demanding "equal rights regardless of color or sex" to the Constitutional Convention. Linking rights for women with rights for African Americans generated significant controversy at the convention. One delegate questioned whether "petitions proposing to class the negro population of Ohio side by side with our wives and daughters can be altogether respectful" and urged other delegates to "suggest to their constituents the propriety of separating in their petitions, and distinguishing carefully between the two subjects." As Gage later noted, it was "perhaps the 1st petitions that ever were presented to a deliberative body of Constitution maker [*sic*] for the Equality of Women and Negroes."

The committee charged with proposing the voting provision for the new constitution recommended retaining both the words "white and male." The delegates debated separate amendments that would remove each of the words. Several delegates spoke in favor of deleting the word *male,* but the records of the convention do not refer to any delegate arguing in opposition to the amendment. Gage later recalled that a correspondent for the *Ohio State Journal* at the convention reported that the "discussion of these memorials . . . was so low and obscene and that it was voted it be 'dropped out of the record.'"

Although the proposals to delete the words *white* and *male* from the franchise clause of the Constitution failed by votes of 75 to 13 and 72 to 7, Ohio women benefitted from the experience nonetheless. The convening of the Constitutional Convention had prompted them to organize conventions of their own in which they had progressed beyond Seneca Falls by conducting them themselves. Their conventions also reflected the progression of the nascent women's rights movement in general. At Seneca Falls, demanding the right to vote had been a controversial issue, the only resolution that did not pass unanimously. At Salem, McConnelsville, and Chesterfield two years later, the demand came naturally and as a matter of course. In their petition campaign, Ohio women had raised, probably for the first time in a constitution-making forum, the connection between race and gender discrimination. White males had excluded both women and blacks from the polity, but the activists insisted that justice required the inclusion of both groups into the political community.

Encouraged by their initial women's rights conventions, Ohio women reconvened in May 1851 in Akron, Ohio. This time, Frances Dana Gage not only attended the convention but she was chosen its president. In her speech, Gage drew on her pioneer heritage. She likened women's position in the nineteenth-century United States to that of their ancestors who had struggled to create communities in the frontier. For women to receive their rights, there were "mountains of established law and custom to overcome and a wilderness of prejudice to be subdued."

Despite the favorable reaction to her own speech, Gage herself would contend that it took second place to that of Sojourner Truth. Truth, born a slave named Isabella Van Wagner, received her freedom, changed her name in 1843, and became a preacher and anti-slavery and women's rights activist. Truth's address has become known as her "Ar'n't I a Woman" speech in which she pointed out that she had worked as hard and could do as much physically as any man, yet as a woman was denied rights based on women's supposed fragility. There is no question that Truth spoke at the Akron convention, and it appears that she spoke very movingly. But whether Truth actually used the famous phrase, "Ar'n't I a woman" as a repetitive refrain has generated a controversy among scholars with Frances Dana Gage at the center. A newspaper account of Truth's speech published at the time in the Salem *Anti-Slavery Bugle,* known for its favorable and generally accurate reporting of the women's rights conventions, does not mention the phrase. The phrase first appeared in a letter Gage published during the Civil War recalling Truth's speech. Historian Nell Painter argues that Gage perhaps saw in Sojourner Truth the perfect symbol of race and gender oppression and created the phrase to match the symbol.

Gage followed the 1851 Akron convention with a trip to Chicago for an antislavery meeting. She continued to make appearances at local women's rights conventions and her reputation as "Aunt Fanny" came in handy at times. When she appeared for a meeting in

Mt. Gilead and was warned that no one might attend, she paid some boys to circulate word that Aunt Fanny would be speaking. It worked—producing an audience of fifty.

Gage also continued her work for temperance, participating in a women's petition campaign in McConnelsville asking the local judge to deny licenses to "grog-shops." The judge refused and, according to Gage, exhorted the women to maintain their place in the nursery and the parlor. In September 1852, she attended the World Temperance Convention in New York. When the credentials of women were not accepted, the delegates spent two days debating women's rights to participate and speak at the convention, with much of the opposition coming from clergy members. By the next year, attitudes had changed sufficiently that Gage was a speaker at the New York convention. In Ohio, women had been holding temperance conventions regularly and created a statewide organization, the Woman's Temperance Society of Ohio, in 1853; Gage routinely spoke at its annual conventions.

In 1853, Gage's family moved to St. Louis so that her husband could pursue business interests. The move did not slow down either her writing or her speaking engagements. In addition to her contributions to the *Ohio Cultivator,* Gage became a correspondent to several women's rights journals: Paulina Wright Davis's *Una,* Amelia Bloomer's *Lily,* and Jane Swisshelm's *Saturday Visitor.* She also found outlets for her writing in the *Missouri Republican* and the *Missouri Democrat.* But her antislavery views did not receive a hospitable reception in the slave state, and her relationships with the two newspapers ended.

During the remainder of the 1850s, Gage maintained an ambitious speaking schedule for women's rights—touring New York, Ohio, Indiana, Iowa, Illinois, and the Nebraska Territory. In addition, Gage faithfully attended and spoke at the annual conventions of the Ohio Woman's Rights Association, founded in 1852. She also attended the annual National Woman's Rights Convention, serving as president of the 1853 convention in Cleveland and as vice president of the 1854 Philadelphia convention.

The Panic of 1857 caused the failure of her husband's business, and they relocated to Carbondale, Illinois. Here he became so ill that Frances had to find a way to earn money for the family. Consequently, she joined the remunerative Lyceum lecture circuit. A trip to the West Indies with family in 1859 provided her with both a popular subject and a way to reach audiences who would not otherwise have come to hear her speak.

An offer to become the editor of the Home Department of the *Ohio Cultivator* prompted Frances and James to move to Columbus, Ohio, in 1860. Although she continued to travel throughout Ohio, her editorial responsibilities prevented extensive out-of-state lecture tours.

While living in Columbus, Gage worked with Hannah Tracy Cutler and Elizabeth Jones to expand married women's property rights. In 1857, the Ohio General assembly had responded to women activists' demands and provided some relief in this area, perhaps in part to appease the women for its rejection of a women's suffrage proposal. In 1861, the women returned to the legislature seeking a stronger property rights law. Gage, Jones, and Cutler testified before the Senate and convinced the Ohio legislature to pass a new law. Although the 1861 law did not contain all that Gage wished, it expanded the rights of married women to control their own property and wages.

The outbreak of the Civil War in 1861 changed Gage's life, professionally and personally, as it changed the lives of most Americans. For one thing, the Civil War brought the antebellum women's rights movement to a halt. Northern women, including women's rights activists, threw themselves into supporting the war. The U.S. Sanitary Commission, a private organization, coordinated the thousands of soldiers' aid societies created by Yankee women. Contributing more than $15 million worth of supplies to the Union cause, women held theatrical events, fairs, grew produce in "Sanitary Potato Patches," and made care packages for the soldiers.

Although a majority of Northerners did not initially hold emancipation as a war goal, African Americans and abolitionists did. To push for an antislavery amendment to the U.S. Constitution, women activists such as Elizabeth Cady Stanton and Susan B. Anthony created the Women's National Loyal League and organized petition campaigns. Ohio women made a significant contribution to the drive. Congressional Republican leaders would later credit the women with facilitating the passage of the Thirteenth Amendment, which banned slavery forever.

As emancipation became a reality during the war, some northern women moved to occupied areas in the South to assist the newly freed African Americans as relief workers and teachers. Southern law and custom had prohibited teaching slaves to read and write, and it was one of the first things freed blacks wanted. By 1862, the *Ohio Cultivator* had ended Gage's employment when it merged with the *Ohio Farmer*. Free to travel, Gage went to South Carolina with her daughter Mary to assist the freed slaves. During the first months in South

Carolina, the Gage women helped on an informal basis. Their work became "official" when Gage was appointed superintendent of the 4th District of the Freedmen's Bureau—a community of approximately five hundred former slaves living on Parris Island.

News of her husband's worsening health prompted Gage to leave South Carolina in June 1863, but James died before she could reach him. She remained in the North for a month lecturing in New England and Pennsylvania on her experiences in the Sea Islands and raising money for her relief work. She returned briefly to South Carolina but left again to return to the lecture circuit to generate northern support for emancipation. In December, she addressed the convention of the American Anti-Slavery Association in Philadelphia, which was celebrating its thirtieth anniversary. During the winter of 1864, she spoke throughout the Midwest, finding audiences less receptive to the rights of the African Americans and the doors of some churches still barred to her as a woman speaker. She raised money for soldiers aid societies, freed slaves, and Clara Barton whom Gage extolled to northern audiences for her battlefield nursing dedication. In April 1864, she finished her tour by working at the Freedmen's relief booth at the Mississippi Valley Sanitary Fair in St. Louis.

From St. Louis, she returned to the South, traveling down the Mississippi River as an agent of the Western Sanitary Commission and providing relief to freed slaves. She also visited wounded white soldiers in the Soldiers Home in Vicksburg, wounded African American soldiers in the General Hospital for Colored Soldiers, and injured former slaves in the Contraband Hospital—contraband being the name the U.S. government gave to runaway slaves who fled to Union lines. Earlier in the war, such runaways might have been returned to their masters. By 1864, they had become a crucial part of the Union war effort.

Gage wrote about her experiences and returned to the North to tour once again. She hoped her poignant stories about the former slaves would not only generate funding but also political and psychological support for the rights of the freed people. Unfortunately, while on tour in Illinois in September 1864, she was injured in a carriage accident that incapacitated her for months. In March 1865, she relocated to Lambertsville, New Jersey, to recuperate. While there she continued to write about temperance and women's rights.

By 1865, it became apparent to women's rights activists that suffrage for women would be inextricably intertwined with congressional plans for Reconstruction. In January, Congress sent the Thirteenth

Amendment prohibiting slavery to the states for ratification. With the ultimate goal of the antislavery movement almost accomplished, women's rights activists pushed to merge the American Anti-Slavery Society with the women's rights movement to create a national organization dedicated to universal suffrage without restriction based on race or sex. Both the antislavery and women's rights movements had allied with the Republican Party to achieve emancipation. Now the question centered on how much protection the former slaves would receive from the national government. That they would need some protection of their basic civil rights became obvious when white southern legislatures passed Black Codes restricting their rights. Although Congress passed civil rights bills while the southern states were out of the Union, it became apparent that for enduring protection the Constitution would need to be amended.

Frances Dana Gage and other women's rights activists wanted to assure that any amendment concerning voting rights would not focus solely on race but would also include women's suffrage. When rumors of a proposed Fourteenth Amendment began to circulate in the summer of 1865, Gage and other women's rights activists, particularly Susan B. Anthony and Elizabeth Cady Stanton, became concerned that their allies in the Republican Party and the antislavery movement would abandon the cause of equal rights for all.

Much of the proposed amendment greatly pleased women's rights activists. Section one provided for a national citizenship for all persons born in the United States or naturalized as a citizen. Further, it provided that U.S. citizens had "privileges and immunities" that the states could not take away. Nor could the states deprive a citizen of due process or equal protection under the law. These protections applied not only to the former male slaves but to all citizens, including women, it would seem. The problem arose with the language in section two. In an attempt to pressure the southern states to provide suffrage to black men, section two placed, for the first time, the word "male" in the U.S. Constitution. If a state denied the right to vote to any male citizens over the age of twenty-one, then the state's population, for purposes of federal apportionment of representatives, was reduced by the number of disfranchised men.

Women's rights activists complained and were frustrated by the lack of support they received from some abolitionists who before the war had supported equal rights. Gage excoriated them as fair weather friends. Had they forgotten "that when they were a weak party and needed all of the womanly help of the nation to help them on, they always united the words 'without regard to sex, race, or color'? Who ever hears of sex now from any of these champions of freedom?"

By May 1866, Gage had recovered sufficiently to travel to New York to attend, as an Ohio delegate, the first National Women's Rights Convention to be held after the Civil War. Once again she was elected vice president. During the convention, the women's rights activists put into place their plan to merge the antislavery movement with the women's rights movement to pursue universal suffrage. To lead the effort, they created a national organization, the American Equal Rights Association. Soon, however, tension between two agendas—rights for former slaves and rights for women, black or white—exploded in rancorous argument and resulted in serious divisions within the women's movement.

Gage did her best to unite the two agendas by emphasizing the need for former slave women to have the right to vote. Drawing on her experiences in the South, she argued that black women needed suffrage not only to protect themselves from white encroachment but also from potential oppression by black men. She tried to persuade abolitionists that they should join her in the "cause of woman, without regard to color."

Women's rights activists worried that if Congress proposed a voting amendment, women would be left out. They were right. The Fifteenth Amendment proposed by Congress prohibited denying the right to vote based on "race, color, or previous servitude." States would be free to continue to deny women the right to vote. Debate over support for the Fifteenth Amendment dominated the American Equal Rights Association when it met in 1869. Stanton and Anthony opposed the amendment, with Stanton's complaining that ignorant black men, "Sambos," would receive the vote while educated white women would not. This prompted an angry response from Frederick Douglass and others. The women's movement split.

Gage had been unable to attend the New York convention, having suffered a stroke in 1867 that left her an invalid. But she took up her pen once again. Although disappointed that the amendment did not provide equal rights for all, she could not join Stanton and Anthony in opposing its ratification. "Could I with breath defeat the Fifteenth Amendment I would not do it," she wrote. Since keeping black men out, "would not let me in sooner, then in God's name why stand in the way?"

The split in the movement resulted in the formation of two separate women's suffrage organizations that would not unite until 1890.

Stanton and Anthony formed the National Woman Suffrage Association, which focused on obtaining an amendment to the U.S. Constitution. Lucy Stone and her husband, Henry Blackwell, led the way in organizing the American Woman Suffrage Association, which focused on gaining women's suffrage by amending state constitutions. Frances Dana Gage added her name its list of supporters.

Gage's daughter Mary attended conventions and kept her mother well informed. Gage also corresponded with Ohio women's rights activists such as Rebecca Anne Smith Janney who led the suffrage petition campaign aimed at Ohio's 1873–74 Constitutional Convention. Although the delegates voted 49 to 41 in favor of sending a woman suffrage amendment to the voters, the proposal fell short of the fifty-three votes needed. Nonetheless, support had increased significantly since the 1850 convention. Gage would have been pleased with the temperance activities of Ohio women during the winter of 1872–73 as well. Women in Washington Courthouse and Hillsboro launched crusades to close the saloons in their towns that spread across Ohio and the Midwest, leading to the creation of the Woman's Christian Temperance Union (WCTU).

Frances Dana Gage died in 1884 in Greenwich, Connecticut, where she is buried. Although she lived to see slavery end, she did not live to see the WCTU become, by the turn of the century, the largest women's organization in the world. Nor did she live to see Ohio women receive the right to vote, which would not happen until ratification of the Nineteenth Amendment in 1920. And the words "white male," which Gage had fought so hard to remove from Ohio's constitution, were not stricken until 1923—only after Ohio women could vote.

Further Reading

DuBois, Ellen Carol. *Feminism and Suffrage: The Emergence of an Independent Women's Movement in America, 1848–1869.* Ithaca, N.Y.: Cornell University Press, 1978.

Isenberg, Nancy. *Sex and Citizenship in Antebellum America.* Chapel Hill: University of North Carolina Press, 1998.

Kayes, Frances W. "The Ladies Department of the *Ohio Cultivator,* 1845–1855: A Feminist Forum." *Agricultural History* 50 (Spring 1976): 414–23.

Mattingly, Carol. *Well-Tempered Women: Nineteenth-Century Temperance Rhetoric.* Carbondale: Southern Illinois University Press, 1998.

Steinhagen, Carol. "The Two Lives of Frances Dana Gage." *Ohio History* (Winter–Spring 1998): 22–38.

10

Clement L. Vallandigham, the Ohio Democracy, and Loyalty during the Civil War

ROBERTA SUE ALEXANDER

C LEMENT L. Vallandigham, a leader of Ohio's Democratic Party from the 1840s through the Civil War, remains as controversial a figure today as he was then. His contemporaries and historians ever since have debated his contribution to Ohio and U.S. history. They either praise or vilify him; few are neutral. Was he a patriot who fought unceasingly to protect the Constitution and preserve the Union, or was he a traitor to his region who, either naively or with intent, gave aid and comfort to the Union's enemies—the southern rebels?

Born July 29, 1820, in New Lisbon, Ohio, Vallandigham was the fifth of seven children born to Clement and Rebecca Vallandigham. The senior Vallandigham, a Presbyterian minister and school teacher, descended from Huguenots who had immigrated to Virginia in 1690. His mother's Scotch-Irish family arrived in Pennsylvania in 1766, establishing themselves as farmers and merchants. Married in 1807, Vallandigham's parents moved to Ohio to establish their new life.

After being taught at home, Clement, at age seventeen, went off to Jefferson College in Pennsylvania—his father's alma mater—to complete his education. While at college, Vallandigham distinguished himself as the school's leading debater. But in January 1841, after a disagreement with the college's president over Vallandigham's staunch states' rights interpretation of the Constitution, the young student demanded and received "an honorable dismission." Leaving without graduating, he returned home, studied law with his oldest brother, and gained admittance to the Ohio bar in 1842. He then launched his career as an attorney and an ambitious politician who would become known for his spellbinding oratorical skills.

FIG. 6 Clement L. Vallandigham. From James L. Vallandigham, *A Life of Clement L. Vallandigham* (Baltimore, Md.: Turnbull Brothers, 1872).

As a Jacksonian Democrat, Vallandigham believed that the Constitution created a permanent and more perfect Union, but a Union in which the central government's powers were limited. He adhered to the philosophy that Thomas Jefferson and James Madison had spelled out in the Kentucky and Virginia Resolutions—states had an obligation to protect the Union from any encroachments by a central government that exceeded its delegated powers. Vallandigham's other political inspiration came from Edmund Burke, whom he saw as advocating law and order, stability, and social peace.

Vallandigham's conservative, states' rights philosophy combined with his "western" outlook to produce a hatred of New Englanders and their abolitionist views. Vallandigham explained: "I am a WESTERN MAN . . . ; and although still a United States man with United States principles, yet within and subordinate to the Constitution, am wholly devoted to Western interests." He believed that New Englanders claimed a "religious and cultural superiority" that held westerners to be "outside barbarian[s]." Their dogmatic abolitionism, spurred by emotionalism, could, he feared, needlessly split the Union. Abolitionists ignored the constitutional commands of localism; slavery was a local, domestic institution protected by the Constitution.

But Vallandigham's anti-abolitionism was not merely based on his belief that antislavery agitation might break up the Union. Vallandigham, like many if not most Ohio Democrats, was a negrophobe. Like their hero Andrew Jackson, many Ohio Democrats spoke of equal rights for all; special privileges for none. But for them, equal rights were for common white folks. Vallandigham argued that African Americans, as descendants "of a servile and degraded race" cursed by God as the children of Ham, could not be made equal. Although he claimed he opposed the institution of slavery in principle, he opposed the naturalization for African American immigrants, attacked Negro suffrage, and denounced any attempt "to elevate such a race to social and political equality."

Vallandigham experienced early political success. At twenty-two, his district elected him to the state legislature as the youngest member ever. During his two terms in the Ohio House of Representatives, he opposed banking and industrial interests, capital punishment, and African American migration to Ohio. He also supported the Mexican War (which he declared to be just and constitutional) and other policies that he saw as helping the common man, such as public education.

In 1846, the twenty-six-year-old Vallandigham married Louisa A. McMahon, with whom he would eventually have five children. Friends then urged him to move to Dayton, Ohio, where the Democrats needed an editor for their newspaper, the *Dayton Western Empire*. Vallandigham agreed to purchase the paper and its print shop for $150. Moving to this growing town in August 1847, Vallandigham soon made the *Empire* "the voice of the Democracy of Montgomery County" and continued to practice law.

Selling the paper in 1849, Vallandigham devoted himself to law and politics. In 1852 and again in 1854, he won his party's nomination for the local congressional seat but lost both races to Lewis D. Campbell, an incumbent Whig/Know-Nothing. In 1856, Vallandigham again squared off against Campbell, who now ran as a Republican. Vallandigham appealed to the Irish and German Catholics of his district by attacking Campbell's Know-Nothing background. Moreover, he attacked the Republican Party, arguing that it would destroy the Union with its radical rhetoric. Campbell replied by accusing Vallandigham of being a stooge for slaveholders and slave catchers.

After election officials declared Campbell the winner by nineteen votes, Vallandigham went to Washington to contest the election, charging fraud, including the casting of illegal votes by African Americans. After a six-month battle, in May 1858, the House, by a 107 to 100 vote, declared Vallandigham duly elected. But by then the legislative session was nearly over. Vallandigham returned to Ohio, was re-nominated, and this time bested Campbell by 188 votes.

Vallandigham's activities as a lawyer enhanced his prominence among Democrats. In June 1857, U.S. marshals, enforcing the Fugitive Slave Act of 1850, took into custody several runaway slaves found in Ohio. More than fifty armed men who opposed enforcement of the Fugitive Slave Law pursued the marshals, overpowered them, and rescued their captives. The "liberators" acted under a writ of habeas corpus issued by a judge under a newly enacted Ohio law. In response, the marshals sought protection from the federal district court in Cincinnati. Governor Salmon P. Chase and his Republican Party supported the liberators, arguing for the superiority of state authority while, ironically, Vallandigham, along with two other leading Democrat lawyers, George E. Pugh and Stanley Matthews, supported federal law.

In arguing the case, Vallandigham, while applauding states' rights, insisted on federal supremacy when the national government was acting within its proper constitutional authority. So-called personal liberty laws like Ohio had just enacted, he told the court, were "madness and folly," being simply organized "resistance to the authority and process of the courts of the Union." If Ohio was going to live in peace with its neighbors, there needed to be respect for the laws of the nation and all of the states. "If any one State . . . may disregard or annul any one law . . . because in its judgment it is harsh, cruel and unjust, any other State may, in like manner . . . disobey." This is anarchy. Vallandigham also criticized the "liberators" belief that "they do God's service" in obeying a higher law.

As a member of the 36th Congress, Vallandigham continued his struggle for moderation, compromise, and respect for law and order. In December 1859, he warned both northern and southern extremists that there was a West whose interests also had to be served. Vallandigham condemned the Republicans as a sectional party and attacked northern radicals for ignoring the Constitution. The Republican Party, he argued, was dominated by fanatical puritans trying to impose their rigid views on others and New England businessmen who sought to advance their economic interests.

Throughout the congressional term, Vallandigham joined with Illinois's Stephen Douglas and other midwestern Democrats in supporting free trade and low tariffs, free farms for homesteaders, and the doctrine of popular sovereignty. This led to their split with President James Buchanan, for they opposed Congress accepting Kansas's proslavery Lecompton Constitution, which Buchanan and southern Democrats supported. Vallandigham also displayed his defense for the underdog—other than African Americans—with his resolutions declaring American Jews to be entitled to the same rights as other citizens when traveling abroad and protecting of American seamen by ending cruel practices aboard U.S. ships.

The crisis that would lead to southern secession loomed at the Democratic National Convention in Charleston in 1860. Ohio Democrats supported Douglas. Southerners rejected him and his platform of popular sovereignty, insisting on unconditional protection of slavery in the territories. Northern Democrats knew they could not win on such a platform. George E. Pugh, Vallandigham's close friend and a U.S. Senator from Ohio, told southern delegates that "Northern Democrats . . . had worn themselves out defending Southern interests. [But] neither he nor his fellow Democrats of the North would give in to the[ir] ultimatum."

When the Democratic Party split in two, Vallandigham headed Douglas's 1860 national campaign. He stumped Ohio and other northern states, praising Douglas's unionism and attacking Republican sectionalism. For the election, the Ohio Democratic Party approved a platform that reflected Vallandigham's basic beliefs. It advocated state sovereignty and attacked the Republican's appeal to a higher law doctrine which they used to justify opposition to the Fugitive Slave Law and the Supreme Court's *Dred Scott* decision. It also declared that Ohio laws were for whites only. Finally, as a carrot to southerners, it called for the acquisition of Cuba, although it refused to support attempts to reopen the African slave trade.

Although the Republicans swept the North in 1860, Vallandigham managed to retain his House seat largely because in his district a third candidate divided Republican voters. But Ohio Democrats were now clearly the state's (and the North's) minority party. Republicans controlled the governorship, legislature, and congressional delegation. Faced with the reality of war, Ohio Democrats further weakened their power by dividing into peace and war factions. The War Democrats, led by Samuel Cox, William Allen, David Tod, and John Brough, were willing to vote for men, money, and supplies.

The peace faction, led by Vallandigham, Pugh, Samuel Medary, and Edson B. Olds, hesitated to give such support.

Though divided over support for the war, Ohio Democrats agreed on a surprising number of issues. To them, the Civil War was not an "irrepressible conflict." Rather, it was started by radicals on both sides who would sacrifice the Union needlessly over the issue of slavery, which if left alone would eventually solve itself and which was, at any rate, sanctioned and protected by the Constitution. Further, they insisted that the war be fought within the bounds of the Constitution. Thus Ohio Democrats attacked the Lincoln administration's suppression of free speech and a free press and its arbitrary arrests and the suspension of the writ of habeas corpus. They opposed emancipation and the recruitment of black troops. Indeed, during the 1862 congressional campaign, the *Cincinnati Enquirer* frankly appealed to racist sentiment when it advised laboring men to vote for Vallandigham if they did "not desire their places occupied by negroes."

Ohio Democrats also generally opposed the southern blockade, oaths for civil officers, and confiscation of Confederate property. Most agreed with Vallandigham's opposition to the tariff and to all measures leading to "consolidation," like federal subsidies to build a transcontinental railroad and the National Banking Act of 1863, which they saw as an attempt to revitalize the monstrous bank Andrew Jackson had valiantly destroyed.

Still, unlike the war faction, the Peace Democrats steadfastly opposed the war. Sneeringly called Copperheads by their opponents, Peace Democrats drew their support from four major groups. The first were Irish Americans who were attracted by the call for equal opportunities for all and special privileges for none, feared that ending slavery would flood the job market with cheap African American labor, hated New England Puritans, and believed Republicans were tainted with anti-Catholic Know-Nothingism and prohibitionism.

The second group, German American Catholics, supported the Peace Democrats for many of the same reasons. Some Catholics, however, did support Republicans. The German American Catholic hierarchy in Cincinnati, led by Archbishop John Purcell and Bishop Sylvester Rosecrans, the brother of General William S. Rosecrans, spoke out against slavery and Civil War dissenters.

The third group in the peace coalition was the "Butternuts." Mainly residents of Ohio's backwoods area, they were recently emigrated from the southern uplands and were still tied to the South through blood and their views on race. They had been the backbone of Jacksonian Democracy. Belittled by their opponents as ignorant and illiterate racists, they fought against the moralistic and activist government Republicans advocated.

The final group consisted of businessmen whose prosperity was linked to the South. Trade down the Mississippi River was vital not only to Cincinnati and Dayton but for much of southern Ohio. These businessmen also feared that Republican support for industrialism and high tariffs would transform the nation from one of small farms and commerce to belching factories and large cities dominated by "slave" workers and impersonalism.

For all these groups, Vallandigham's slogan—"the Constitution as it is, the Union as it was"—summarized their beliefs and fears. The Peace Democrats blamed the Republican Party for secession and subsequent failures to achieve a compromise. They believed that a civil war would undermine the true union by leading to further consolidation. Thus Vallandigham searched for a compromise that would give the South the assurances it needed to return to the Union. In February 1861, Vallandigham introduced in Congress several constitutional amendments that would give the South and the Midwest countervailing powers to check antislavery forces and Northeast industrialists. He proposed dividing the nation into four sections for the purpose of voting in both the electoral college and in the U.S. Senate; a majority in each section would be required to elect a president and to pass major bills. His amendments went nowhere.

Republicans attacked Vallandigham and other Peace Democrats as traitors and secessionists, whose opposition to the war and attacks on administration policies gave aid and comfort to the enemy. Senator Benjamin Wade of Ohio, for example, attacked Vallandigham as being "devoted" to the "destruction" of the nation and as a "disgrace" to his state. Two Ohio Republicans petitioned Congress to expel him as a traitor. But Vallandigham never advocated treason. For example, despite the fact that he opposed conscription, and especially the $300 commutation clause, which he believed favored the rich, once it passed he urged his supporters to obey it. Indeed, he even helped raise troop quotas for Ohio.

While Republican congressional efforts did not succeed in getting rid of Vallandigham, the actions of the Republican-dominated Ohio General Assembly did. In 1862, after the state legislature added heavily Republican Warren County to Vallandigham's Third Congressional District, the voters defeated him.

Defeat, however, did not silence Vallandigham. As his chief biographer, Frank L. Klement, put it, Vallandigham was "a man of action, one who enjoyed argumentation, controversy, and challenges. He had endless confidence in his own ability. . . . He liked attention and he liked the spotlight. He gained great satisfaction in developing rapport with an audience and applause was essential to his ego. Politics enamored him, making him prisoner and patron."

Thus after his defeat, Vallandigham set his sights on the Ohio governorship. The 1863 Democratic victories, brought about, in large part, by Union military defeats, increased Vallandigham's optimism for victory. State Democratic Party leaders, however, rebuffed Vallandigham in his quest for the nomination. Fearing that his notoriety would lead to the party's defeat, they preferred a more temperate candidate.

General Ambrose Burnside unwittingly helped further Vallandigham's ambitions. Still chafing from his defeat at Fredericksburg, the new commander of the Army of the Ohio issued General Order No. 38 on April 13, 1863, to stifle what he saw as treasonous dissent by prohibiting the declaration of "sympathies for the enemy." Now Vallandigham saw his chance both to become a martyr and to gain his party's nomination by intentionally violating Burnside's order. Thus on May 1, in Mount Vernon, Ohio, Vallandigham delivered a fiery political speech. Burnside, determined to silence the Copperhead, had sent observers to Mt. Vernon. After hearing their reports, the general ordered Vallandigham's arrest, charging him with "declaring disloyal sentiments and opinions, with the object and purpose of weakening the power of the Government in its efforts to suppress an unlawful rebellion." Specifically, the indictment pointed to Vallandigham's assertion that the war was "wicked, cruel, and unnecessary," waged not to preserve the Union but rather to crush "liberty and [erect] despotism" and to achieve "the freedom of the blacks and the enslavement of the whites." Lincoln, Vallandigham maintained, could have ended the war "months ago" by guaranteeing southern "rights under the Constitution." Instead, Lincoln's representatives undermined the Constitution in the North through actions like General Order No. 38, which was "a base usurpation of arbitrary authority." True Americans had to resist such "restrictions upon their liberties" or be enslaved.

At 2:00 A.M. on May 5, soldiers arrived at Vallandigham's Dayton home, woke the politician and his family, broke down the door when he refused to open it, and escorted him to Cincinnati to await military trial. Immediately, Vallandigham used his arrest to his political advantage. Writing to the "Democracy of Ohio" from "a military bastille," he portrayed himself as a martyr fighting for his party, his country, and the Constitution. "I am a Democrat; for Constitution, for law, for Union, for liberty; this is my only crime." Never, he insisted, did he sympathize with the South nor counsel disobedience to national law. Northern abolitionists were the true traitors and disunionists; it is they, along with southern hotheads, who were responsible for the current war.

The military commission began hearing Vallandigham's case on May 6. Vallandigham refused to plead either guilty or not guilty, arguing instead that the military commission had no authority over a civilian in an area where civil courts were open and functioning. After the court entered a not guilty plea for him, the testimony began. Government witnesses simply testified about Vallandigham's Mt. Vernon address. Conducting his own defense, Vallandigham cross-examined each witness to emphasize the fact that throughout his Mt. Vernon speech he had insisted that his listeners remain loyal to the Constitution and the Union. Indeed, he urged them to use all peaceable means possible to restore that Union. Vallandigham's own witnesses, including leading Ohio Democrats such as Samuel Cox, testified that the defendants condemnation of the war was directed solely at "its perversion from its original purpose."

During closing arguments, Vallandigham explained that he was merely exercising his constitutional right to speak to the people "in an open and public political meeting, lawfully and peaceably assembled, under the Constitution and upon full notice." He spoke not treason but "words of criticism of the public policy of the public servants of the people . . . [and] an appeal to the people to change that policy . . . by free elections." Never, he insisted, did he counsel "disobedience to the Constitution, or resistance to laws and lawful authority." Such arguments proved unpersuasive to the military commission, which found Vallandigham guilty and sentenced him to confinement for the duration of the war.

Meanwhile, George E. Pugh, Vallandigham's co-counsel, was taking other measures to free his client. He filed a petition for a writ of habeas corpus in federal court. This strategy was no more successful. While Pugh argued eloquently for the protection of American liberties, the government's attorneys insisted that the country had rights, too, including the right to wage war effectively. The suspension of the writ of habeas corpus, which Lincoln had ordered, was one such right. Ignoring these issues, the presiding judge, citing precedent, wrote that civil courts had no authority to grant the writ for someone detained by "military authority." Judgment as to the necessity of such arrests, as a means for the government to protect the Union and thus the Constitution, was in the hands of Abraham Lincoln, the commander in chief of the armed forces and his appointees, including Burnside. Pugh appealed the decision to the U.S. Supreme Court, which declared that it had no authority to hear appeals from or review the decisions of military commissions.

Democrats in Ohio and throughout the North rallied around the new martyr and against the Republicans. Even those Democrats who supported the war and disapproved of Vallandigham and the Peace Democrats protested. Every Democratic newspaper published editorials attacking Burnside's order, the trial, and the Lincoln administration. In nearly every northern city, sizable crowds held protest rallies and meetings.

Riding this wave of outrage, Vallandigham's supporters gained the martyr's nomination for Ohio's governor by a landslide at the state Democratic convention. Many party leaders, including Samuel Cox, unsuccessfully tried to stop Vallandigham's grassroots movement, fearing that his rashness would destroy the party. The convention also nominated Pugh for lieutenant governor. The party platform condemned the Lincoln administration's subversion of the Constitution, denounced abolitionism and northern radicals, and criticized Ohio's Republican-Union governor, David Tod. The Peace Democrats even secured a resolution calling for "a convention of the States" to achieve peace and reunion and to recommend measures to prevent future wars.

Vallandigham's arrest, coupled with the Union army's defeat at Chancellorsville, had clearly turned public opinion against the Republicans. To help defuse the situation, Lincoln countered the military commission's sentence of imprisonment and instead ordered Vallandigham to be put "beyond our military lines." If he returned, he was to be rearrested. On May 19, the military, with their prisoner, began their trip to southern lines.

Vallandigham stayed in the South for only twenty-four days. During that time, he made it clear that he was not a Confederate. He wrote to General Braxton Bragg, commander of the Confederate army in middle Tennessee: "I came to your lines upon compulsion & against my consent, as a citizen of Ohio, & of the United States in exile banished from my country for no other offense than love of

constitutional liberty." While the Confederacy used his arrival to portray the war as one for subjugating a free people, they were ill at ease
with Vallandigham's presence. He was an alien enemy who insisted on
his loyalty to the Union.

More important, Vallandigham realized that he needed to be elsewhere to wage his campaign for governor. Therefore, after running
the Union blockade, he arrived in Canada in July 1863. From his new
base, he issued an "Address to the Democracy of Ohio," which
emphasized now-traditional themes, criticizing Lincoln and portray-
ing himself as a martyr. He assured Ohioans that, based on his con-
versations with southerners while in exile, the Confederates were
ready "to consider . . . the question of reunion" once the invading
Union troops withdrew.

Meanwhile, back in Ohio, the Republicans had nominated John
Brough to oppose Vallandigham for the governorship. In their "campaign of abuse," they attacked Vallandigham and his Copperhead
supporters as traitors, often misquoting them to portray them as
southern sympathizers. They accused Vallandigham of helping to
plan Confederate general John H. Morgan's raid into Indiana and
Ohio during July and linked the Democratic candidate to the Knights
of the Golden Circle, an organization they claimed was plotting other
treasonous activities.

Democrats countered the Republican attacks by labeling Brough
a "renegade," a "fool," and a "nigger-lover." They played the race
card by attacking the Republican Party as the "Abolition party" and
Republicans as "Black Republicans." A vote for Vallandigham, they
argued, was "a vote for Liberty," while a vote for Brough was a vote
for "despotism," emancipation, and Negro equality. Emotions ran so
high that violence and some fatalities occurred. Women "pulled each
other's hair, tore dresses, or scratched faces."

It was not words or emotionalism, but Union victories at Vicksburg and Gettysburg that turned northern public opinion once again
in favor of the Republicans. On October 13, voters defeated Vallandigham by 100,000 votes, the 61,752 "home" majority swelled by
a 40,000 majority among the soldier vote for the Republicans. Victo-
rious Republicans continued to insult Vallandigham supporters and
often destroyed Democratic property. But there was some solace for
the defeated candidate. Traditional Democrats continued to support
him. Most Irish and German Catholics along with backwoods Butternuts voted for the exile. And Vallandigham's defeat was not a personal one. Democrats suffered throughout the North.

The Democratic Party tried to regroup in 1864. In March, Ohio Democrats met in Columbus to adopt resolutions and select delegates to the presidential nominating convention to be held in Chicago. The resolutions tended to support the peace wing of the party. They praised the 1798 Kentucky and Virginia Resolutions' principles of states' rights, labeled the Lincoln administration tyrannical and an "abject failure," and called for the "immediate inauguration" of peace efforts to end the war and restore "the Union under the Constitution." Yet, while the platform supported the principles of the Peace Democrats, the convention's at-large delegation was pledged to George B. McClellan and did not include Vallandigham.

The Third Congressional District Democratic Party meeting, which convened in June, was far more radical than the earlier statewide meeting. Vallandigham's supporters continued to urge him to return illegally from exile to reassert his influence and gain a seat at the Democratic National Convention. They assured him that Lincoln would not dare arrest the popular martyr. The exile finally agreed and the day before the meeting friends secretly escorted him back to the United States. Disguised with false whiskers and a cape, the former exile hid in Hamilton, Ohio, until the convention met the next day.

The disputes at the Third Congressional District illustrate the divisions within Ohio's Democracy. Alexander Long, William M. Corry, and Samuel Medary represented the extreme peace wing. Samuel Cox and George Manypenny represented the other end of the spectrum. They urged Democrats to "put patriotism before partisanship" and to support George B. McClellan and the war until victory could be achieved. In the end, the district convention gravitated toward the position of the extreme peace wing, passing a controversial resolution demanding an "immediate cessation of hostilities" and negotiations for "a just and lasting peace." In addition, the resolutions blamed the Republicans for an unnecessary war and the Lincoln administration for unconstitutional actions in violation of basic liberties.

The radical peace plank was even extreme for Vallandigham. In an emotional speech to the convention on June 15, Vallandigham called for peace but also for law and order. The former exile's caution paid off. Not only did he gain a seat in the Ohio delegation for the Chicago convention, but he remained free. While Republican Governor Brough requested Vallandigham's arrest, military leaders stalled and Lincoln and other Republican leaders followed a policy of restraint.

In Chicago, Ohio Democrats remained divided. Vallandigham, who was introduced at the convention as "the Honorable Exile and Patriot," reiterated his peace and compromise theme. Moreover, he defended a secret organization he had agreed to head, the Sons of Liberty, as merely an organization to help elect Democrats. It was not the subversive organization Republicans tried to portray it as. Unlike the Knights of the Golden Circle or the Order of American Knights, which had been organized in the South before the war to promote expansion into Mexico, Cuba, and elsewhere, the Sons of Liberty, at least as Vallandigham saw it, insisted that nothing be done to aid the South. The Sons of Liberty was simply a mutual-protection organization to counter the Republican Party's Union Leagues and to gain Democratic political victories.

Trying to woo Vallandigham to support McClellan, the Ohio delegation named him as Ohio's representative to the Committee on Resolutions. Vallandigham's efforts to win a peace and compromise plank in the platform paid off. The convention adopted his resolution attacking the war and arguing that "justice, humanity, liberty, and public welfare" required an "immediate . . . cessation of hostilities, with a view to an ultimate convention of the States." The convention accepted this plank in part because of Vallandigham's obstinacy, in part because many agreed with its arguments, and in part because Vallandigham's resolution was more moderate than the proposed substitute, which demanded the immediate end to the war.

In return for their support for the peace plank, after the first ballot, Vallandigham and other Peace Democrats switched their votes to McClellan, who eventually became the nominee. In return, George Pendleton, an Ohio peace man, gained the vice presidential nomination. Despite McClellan's later repudiation of Vallandigham's peace resolution, the latter supported the ticket and spoke throughout the state. But the Democrats could not prevail over military victory and Republican political skill. With the help of the soldier's vote and the tactic of labeling Democrats as traitors, Lincoln won reelection.

After the war ended in April 1865, Vallandigham continued his struggle against the Republicans, denouncing their Reconstruction policies and their efforts to further consolidate federate power. He opposed confiscation of former rebel property, fought against any penalties or test oaths imposed on Confederates, and criticized any attempt to make African Americans equal. As a delegate to the Ohio Democratic Convention in August 1865, he defended President

Andrew Johnson and argued that the Democrats were the true
unionists because they urged immediate reconciliation.

However, Vallandigham's wartime notoriety caused many Ohio
Democrats to wish he would disappear. For example, they asked him
to resign as a delegate to the Philadelphia Union Convention of 1866
because they feared that his reputation would injure Johnson and his
attempt to build a Union party of Democrats and moderate Republicans to oppose Radical Republicans. Vallandigham finally did agree to
withdraw as a delegate, although he campaigned for the doomed
party during the 1866 election.

Vallandigham was again a good party stalwart in 1867, campaigning for the Democratic candidate for governor, Allen G. Thurman.
While Thurman narrowly lost, the Democrats did win control of the
Ohio legislature. Vallandigham believed that as recognition for his
martyrdom and his party loyalty he should be given a seat in the U.S.
Senate. But by a vote of 51 to 24, his party chose Thurman. Vallandigham, disappointed, sulked for months. But he could not stay
away from politics for long. In 1868, Vallandigham again ran for
Congress, but the Republican nominee, Robert C. Schenck, won by
475 votes. Democrats could not yet overcome the Republicans wav-
ing the bloody shirt.

After his 1868 defeat, Vallandigham looked for new ways to revitalize the Democratic Party. While many in his party wanted to cling to
traditional issues, Vallandigham, Pendleton, and others, called for a
"New Departure" to overcome the stigma of the party's opposition to
the Civil War. The new Democratic Party would stand for universal
manhood suffrage coupled with universal amnesty, for honest and efficient government, for civil service reform, for low tariffs and support
for the working man as opposed to the railroads and large corporations.

Just as it appeared that the "New Departure" would bring Vallandigham the success he had always longed for, he died in a freak
accident. Vallandigham had taken the case of Thomas McGehan, a
disreputable man accused of murder. At a conference with fellow
attorneys on June 16, 1871, Vallandigham rehearsed what he was
planning to demonstrate to the jury the next day—how the supposed
murder victim had, in reality, accidentally shot himself. Taking a
loaded pistol by mistake, Vallandigham fatally wounded himself.
Twelve hours later, he lay dead.

On June 20, an array of political leaders attended his funeral at
Woodland Cemetery in Dayton, Ohio, including: Salmon P. Chase,
then chief justice of the U.S. Supreme Court; Samuel Cox, now a

New York Democratic politician; and old allies including Thurman and Pugh. Pendleton delivered one of the many eulogies. In addition, thousands of commoners attended the funeral—former Butternuts from the countryside, Dayton workingmen, and others from Hamilton and other small towns. The funeral procession took over an hour to pass the courthouse steps.

Clement Vallandigham represented both radical and conservative impulses within Ohio's Democratic Party. The Democratic Party played a vital role throughout the middle years of the nineteenth century. It was the opposition party fighting to maintain a democratic government and individual liberties during crises and war. Vallandigham's part in that struggle was significant. During the Civil War, he defied General Burnside's order and fought for civil liberties. He advocated free trade, opposed capital punishment, and fought for equal rights for many groups, including Jews. For example, he fought to allow rabbis to serve as regimental chaplains during the Civil War. As an advocate of the "New Departure" of the 1870s, he looked forward to the twentieth century.

However, basically Vallandigham was a Burkean conservative. He clung to a states' rights philosophy, opposed industrialization and urbanization, and advocated white supremacy. He continually struggled to preserve the Union as it was. As his chief biographer noted: "Like Burke he believed changes should be evolutionary and not revolutionary and that the deep roots of the past should be continually cultivated."

After the dissent over the Vietnam War in the late 1960s and 1970s, Americans can better understand how millions can oppose a war that they feel is not in the national interest and still consider themselves loyal Americans. While "patriots" during the Vietnam era attacked protestors and shouted "America, love it or leave it," the opposition eventually became a majority. Similarly, during the Civil War, Vallandigham, though labeled a traitor, always considered himself more loyal than his opponents; he was fighting for the true America and for America's cherished liberties. While some Democrats might have aided the South, deserted the army, or otherwise promoted the southern cause, so did some Republicans. Vallandigham's peace efforts were the work of a loyal opposition that called on the nation to protect constitutional rights against tyranny and oppression.

Further Reading

Gray, Wood. *The Hidden Civil War.* New York: Viking Press, 1942.

Klement, Frank L. *The Limits of Dissent: Clement L. Vallandigham and the Civil War.* Lexington: University Press of Kentucky, 1970.

McPherson, James M. *Battle Cry of Freedom.* New York: Oxford University Press, 1988.

Milton, George F. *Lincoln and the Fifth Column.* New York: Vanguard Press, 1942.

Porter, George H. *Ohio Politics during the Civil War Period.* New York: Columbia University Press, 1911.

11

George H. Pendleton and the Resurrection of the Democratic Party

ROBERT SAWREY

O N JANUARY 11, 1865, as the U.S. House of Representatives debated a constitutional amendment to prohibit slavery throughout the nation, George Hunt Pendleton, a four-term Democratic Congressman from Cincinnati, rose from his chair to speak against the proposal. He argued that an amendment to the Constitution on an issue of supreme importance to southerners could not be adopted in their absence. Aware that some could interpret his position as disloyal to the United States, Pendleton felt compelled to defend his patriotism. "I love my whole country, South as well as North," he declared, "and it is because I love it that no action of mine shall retard the restoration of peace or the reconstruction of that Union which made it all my country. I am a northern man; I have their prejudices; I love my section; I love its people; I love its institutions; I am jealous of its honor; and no act of mine shall stain the luster of the fame of its good faith."

Pendleton's apparent defensiveness reflected the status of the Democratic Party throughout the Union and in Ohio. By 1865, it had suffered a serious decline due to its ambivalence and even outright opposition to the Union war effort. If the Republican/Union Party could claim to be the party of reunion and victory, the Democrats were stuck with the label of party of secession and disunion. Yet, remarkably, within three years of his comments, Pendleton had led a Democratic resurgence in Ohio. Exploiting voter frustration with Republican Reconstruction and postwar economic policies and relying heavily on racist appeals, Ohio Democrats in 1867 captured the state legislature and nearly elected a governor. Pendleton played a key

FIG. 7 George H. Pendleton.
Courtesy of the Ohio Historical Society.

role in these developments and emerged as the party's leader in Ohio and much of the Old Northwest.

George Hunt Pendleton was born in Cincinnati in 1825, and young George did not have anything quite like the typical early Ohio upbringing. His grandfather, Nathaniel Pendleton, had served as an officer in the Revolutionary War, became a close associate and supporter of Alexander Hamilton, and served as the latter's second in his deadly duel with Aaron Burr. His father, Nathaniel Greene Pendleton, moved from New York to Cincinnati in 1818 and quickly established himself as a successful and influential member of the community. By the 1830s, he had risen high enough in the Whig Party to earn three nominations for a seat in Congress, losing twice before winning in 1840.

Nathaniel Greene Pendleton had married and started a family that ultimately included ten children, who benefited from their father's wealth and prominence. Young George, for example, graduated in 1841 from Cincinnati College, received further training in classical studies, and then in 1844 embarked on a two-year tour of Europe.

While abroad, he traveled extensively and occasionally studied, including a term at the University of Heidelberg in Germany. In 1846, at the age of twenty-one he returned to Cincinnati to study law and was accepted to the bar in 1848. Thus, George Pendleton emerged as a young lawyer with extraordinary education and experiences.

Pendleton entered a law partnership in Cincinnati with George Pugh, a school classmate and future U.S. senator, but he clearly sought a career in politics. In 1853, at the age of twenty-eight, he was elected the youngest member of the Ohio Senate as a hard money, states' rights, nationalistic Jacksonian Democrat. The reasons Pendleton deviated from the political allegiance of his father remain fuzzy, but the son certainly held dearly to his positions at considerable personal cost throughout his political career.

Pendleton served in the Ohio Senate with enough distinction to earn in 1854 his party's nomination for a seat in the U.S. House of Representatives from the First District (Cincinnati). The turbulent events in the Kansas and Nebraska Territories dominated political campaigns that year and provided much of the impetus for the newly formed Republican Party's victories in many northern states, including Ohio, where Pendleton and many other Democrats lost. Two years later, however, he was renominated for Congress and won a seat he would hold for eight years, 1857–1865.

Thus began a national political career that can be divided into three distinct phases. The first was the Civil War years in which Pendleton emerged as a leading Democrat, who ultimately ran as the party's vice presidential nominee in 1864. Next, in the immediate postwar years Pendleton emerged as the leading advocate of paying portions of the federal debt with legal tender but not redeemable paper money. He used the proposal, known as the Pendleton Plan, to build a political base that almost secured him the 1868 Democratic presidential nomination. Finally, in 1878 Pendleton began the third portion of his political career, as a member of the U.S. Senate. In all these activities, Pendleton exhibited commitment to the idea of small, frugal government, to protection of the rights of white citizens, and to a strict interpretation of the Constitution. Despite his affluent background, he often spoke for the perceived interests of the laboring classes. These stands did not necessarily make him popular nor result in many political victories.

Extremely divisive sectional issues and the Civil War dominated Pendleton's time in the House. In a very real sense, he spoke for those frustrated Ohioans who could not quite accept that war was the solution to the national crisis and who refused to quietly acquiesce in the Republican programs created to fight that war. Still, they wanted to support their government and restore the Union as quickly as possible with as few changes as possible. Pendleton emerged as their strong, articulate spokesman on positions that found infrequent success.

During the secession crisis of the winter of 1861, Pendleton endorsed the Crittenden Compromise, which sought to preserve the Union by a series of constitutional amendments that would placate the slaveholding states by protecting slavery in all existing and future territories located south of 36° 30', preventing Congress from abolishing slavery in the District of Columbia, and forbidding federal interference with the interstate slave trade. These amendments would have been perpetual and not subject to repeal. In January 1861, he presented to Congress a petition signed by approximately 10,000 Cincinnatians who urged approval of the compromise. On their behalf and in line with his own views, Pendleton begged Congress to "grant all their [southerners'] reasonable demands." However, Republicans, unwilling to vote for a compromise that would undercut the essence of the mandate they had received in the 1860 elections, defeated the Crittenden Compromise.

After the attack on Fort Sumter in April 1861, the Lincoln administration embarked on a series of actions designed to facilitate federal success in the war. Although committed to national reunion and careful never to denounce the war effort, Pendleton thought the war could have been avoided by ratification of the Crittenden Compromise and invariably found fault with the precise way the Republicans went about running the country and fighting the war. One historian notes that "through these years of stress and struggle he was usually an obstructionist and much of a thorn in the side of Abraham Lincoln." Surely, at times Pendleton was an "obstructionist" but one based on principles which he voiced frequently and with determination.

Throughout the war, Pendleton found himself, along with most of his Democratic colleagues, on the losing side of many issues. For example, Pendleton refused to grant the Lincoln administration the constitutional flexibility it believed necessary to fight the war. Thus, Pendleton opposed as patently unconstitutional all attempts to confiscate the land, slaves, or other property of Confederates. He adamantly fought against all efforts to curtail civil liberties, such as the suspension of the right of the writ of habeas corpus and the utilization of military tribunals in areas of the North where civil courts remained open and functioning. In July 1861, he linked together several themes in a resolution in which he urged that Congress not harm slavery. In it, he declared that "under the Constitution, the rights, powers and duties of all the States are equal; that the Union is founded on this equality; that in order to maintain the Constitution and the Union, this equality must be preserved." To accomplish this goal, "every honest effort to perpetuate the Union must be made in accordance with the Constitution." Furthermore, any attempt to "abolish or interfere with slavery . . . would be an attempt to destroy this equality, and would, if successful, subvert the Constitution and the Union." Clearly, Pendleton believed that the essence of southern concerns revolved around slavery and that saving the Union required protection of that institution. His relative priorities were abundantly apparent. During the war, he consistently opposed efforts to free any slaves, expand the goals of the war to include emancipation, or to enlist freedmen into the military services of the United States.

Pendleton also quarreled with the Lincoln administration over financial issues. As a hard money Jacksonian, he had no sympathy for Lincoln and Secretary of the Treasury Salmon Chase's plan to finance the war partially by abandoning specie payments and expanding the money supply by issuing unbacked currency, commonly called greenbacks. He also disapproved of efforts to secure additional funds by selling hundreds of millions of dollars worth of federal bonds. Nor could he tolerate Chase's proposal to create a national banking system. Chase's scheme envisioned allowing investors to use federal bonds as capital in creating a national bank, expanding the market for these bonds. To Pendleton, all of these ideas violated sound financial principles, threatened to push the country into economic chaos, and promised to pit the wealthy, bondholding class against the working class, who presumably would be taxed to pay off the bonds. In addition, Pendleton perceived in most Republican actions that resulted in a more active federal government an insidious trend toward centralization of authority and power.

Two specific episodes provide clear indications of how Pendleton viewed the war and the issues related to it. In the spring of 1864, Alexander Long, who also represented Cincinnati in Congress, delivered a blistering attack on Lincoln, the Republicans, and their handling of the war. Long, a leading Peace Democrat, declared the war a failure and urged that the Confederacy be allowed to go in peace. The Republicans reacted with vigor and outrage to Long's congressional speech and pushed a resolution to censure him.

On April 12, 1864, Pendleton took the floor of the House to defend Long. Granting the House's right to "preserve decorum in debate" and to expel members for specific offenses, he nonetheless asserted, "[i]t is not within the constitutional power of the House to expel a member for the expression of opinion upon any political question, when such expression of opinion is pertinent to the measure before it." Thus, he once again defended his reading of the constitutional right of free speech and linked it to the concept of free debate. Pendleton also raised another interesting line of defense. He insisted that removing Long from Congress would disfranchise the voters of Ohio's Second Congressional District. After all, they had elected Long to represent them. From yet another angle, then, Pendleton had returned to the issue of defending the Constitution by insisting that the expulsion of Long was the same as the House dictating who the voters should send to Congress.

Just as Pendleton had made no attempt to defend what Long had said—he fully understood the House majority would not buy that argument—neither did Pendleton discuss the merits of slavery. Late in the war, Congress debated the future of slavery, ultimately approving what became the Thirteenth Amendment. Pendleton actively participated in those discussions, always speaking against emancipation. He did not, however, suggest that slavery was a good institution, nor did he utilize the inflamed rhetoric of some Democrats who warned that abolition would be followed by a mass migration northward and inevitably in miscegenation. He did, though, present some predictable and some not so typical, explanations for his stance.

He insisted that "three fourths of the States did not possess constitutional power to pass this amendment." He argued that amendments dealing with certain types of issues required the approval of every state. If a state considered an amendment hostile to the interest of that state, then it had the right of revolution. This position placed Pendleton very close to the concept of concurrent majority with the additional proviso that every state retained the right to decide for itself on critically important amendments, including those dealing with a state's internal institutions, such as slavery.

Pendleton also denied that the nation had the right to assume "that the seceding States have no voice on this amendment, but are absolutely bound by it." Thus he did not quite argue that the nation could not legislate on issues related to the Confederate states in their absence, but for all practical purposes he reached that conclusion. The Ohio congressman also raised the practical matter of which states would ratify the proposal. After tallying those states that might endorse it, he concluded that the amendment stood no chance of ratification "without a fraudulent use of the power to admit new States or a fraudulent use of the military power of the Federal Government in the seceded States." He reasoned that even if all nineteen free states ratified the amendment, proponents would still need approval from an additional eight states. Crucial to this analysis was his insistence that the Union contained thirty-five states, which of course included all the members of the Confederacy. He suggested that if the border states of Missouri, West Virginia, Maryland, and Delaware ratified the amendment, ratification still required another four states. Pendleton declared that the necessary votes could be found only by either admitting several new states solely because they would vote for the amendment or by manipulating the restoration of a handful of southern states and somehow finding a bogus convention or legislature there that would presume to grant the state's approval to the amendment. In either case, the Constitution and the dignity of democracy would have received a dreadful blow.

Pendleton further reminded the members of the House that the amendment was "another step toward consolidation, and consolidation is despotism." He closed what became yet another futile argument with a solemn warning that "while they [the federal government] attack the institution of slavery today you may smile, but tomorrow you will tremble when your religion, your manufactures, your capital are wrested from your control and subject to their will." Despite providing some insightful comments and even predicting with some accuracy the enlargement of federal powers during the immediate postwar period, Pendleton failed to change the votes of the Republican majority.

By early 1864, Pendleton had emerged as a leading Democratic critic of the Lincoln administration. Often labeled a Peace Democrat, he certainly had more in common with men such as Clement Vallandigham than he did the War Democrats. In fact, the Democratic Party was quite divided on war issues. The differences emerged in stark display at the party's 1864 national convention in Chicago. The leading presidential aspirant was General George B. McClellan, who, despite being removed as commander of the Army of the Potomac, had no intention of declaring the war a failure. On the other hand, the vocal and angry critics of the war had significant support to force a compromise. McClellan received the nomination but the Peace Democrats wrote the key platform plank, which demanded that, because "the experiment of war" had not reunited the country, "immediate efforts be made for a cessation of hostilities, with a view to an ultimate convention of the states, or other peaceable means, to the end that, at the earliest practicable moment, peace may be restored on the basis of the Federal Union." In addition, the convention nominated Pendleton for the vice presidency.

Although the Democrats entered the campaign with optimism, the success of the Union armies propelled Lincoln to victory. The 1864 election did provide Pendleton with his first significant national exposure, but it also cost him his seat in Congress because he logically was not renominated for that position while running for vice president. Thus the first phase of his political career ended. He had emerged as a major figure in the Democratic Party based on his defense of the Constitution, his devotion to traditional Democratic issues such as hostility to the central government, and his personality, which allowed him to press his views aggressively but not alienate his opponents.

As the war ended, Pendleton found himself a private citizen for the first time in nearly a decade, but that did not mean that he had lost interest in either state or national political developments. By 1867, he had reemerged as a significant factor within the Democratic Party and sought to rebuild it around one old and two new issues. The old issue involved race. For years Democrats, including Pendleton, had denounced their opponents as the party of "nigger equality." Before the war, the Democrats loudly argued that the Republicans would destroy the Union in their zeal to free the slaves. With slavery a war casualty, the Democrats in the postwar period insisted that the hidden Republican agenda was social, economic, and political equality for the freed people. Given the racial views of the typical American and the policies of the Republican Party in the 1860s, those charges made absolutely no sense. However, they still produced powerful political responses among voters. Pendleton never shied away from assuring audiences of his commitment to keeping the United States a "white man's country." In late 1864, arguing against any effort to end slavery, he charged that the slaves lacked the ability to care for themselves. If freed, taxpayers would need to care for them. Thus, Pendleton concluded, the country must continue slavery indefinitely. Later, in 1867, he warned that the Republicans intended to use ignorant black voters to stay in power, allowing them to impose "New England Puritanism" on the workers of the Midwest. Congressional colleagues may have called him "Gentleman George," but African Americans and their friends would surely have chosen a different nickname. In playing on Ohioans' racial prejudices and fears, Pendleton struck political gold. In fact, Ohioans either opposed or cared so little about racial justice that they did not delete color as a criterion in the state's voting requirements until 1923, over half a century after ratification of the Fifteenth Amendment.

While antiblack sentiment was an old standard for the Democrats, the two new issues which Pendleton developed concerned Reconstruction policies and economic. Pendleton was a determined foe of Congressional Reconstruction, basing much of his opposition on his perception of the Constitution and his assessment of the appropriate place African Americans should occupy. However, he directed the bulk of his energy aggressively criticizing efforts to contract the currency and resume specie payment. Styling himself as the protector of the working class, Pendleton skillfully used the issues of race, Reconstruction, and currency to revitalize the Democratic Party in Ohio and propel himself back to national political stage.

At the war's end, the country not only faced a huge national debt but also hundreds of millions of dollars of paper money, some backed by federal bonds, others backed by little more than the federal government's promise to accept them as legal tender. Secretary of Treasury Hugh McCulloch convinced Congress that specie resumption required contraction of the currency. In April 1866, Congress authorized McCulloch to withdraw $10 million in U.S. notes (greenbacks) each month for the first six months and then no more than $4 million per month thereafter until the nation had been able to reduce the premium on gold, thus allowing the resumption of specie payments. Funds to purchase the greenbacks would come from the sale of bonds, which meant that a non-interest bearing debt would be exchanged for an interest bearing one. This, of course, increased the government's expenses. Unfortunately for McCulloch and his program, the country's economy slid into a recession which many, with little real evidence, blamed on contraction. Howls of protest followed.

The critics had many arguments from which to choose. Some questioned the sanity of increasing the federal debt by more borrowing to pay a non-interest bearing debt. Many assailed the very idea of contraction, arguing that the country's currency needs would rather quickly expand to the point where gold payments could be resumed without contraction. A large number challenged the fairness of government policies that promised to enrich bondholders at the expense of common taxpayers. A few, arguing that the federal debt had been created in a tragic and evil war and that it only benefited "bloated" bondholders, advocated that the federal government simply repudiate its obligations. All of this became overtly political after the 1866 congressional elections in which the Republicans, campaigning on a platform that promised a secure reunion based on the proposed Fourteenth Amendment, swamped the Democrats and won a nearly veto-proof majority. Democrats sensed that, despite growing weariness with high taxes and continued sectional tensions, Reconstruction issues might not provide them with the opportunity to return to power. In short, they were looking for new issues and found them in contraction and payment of the federal debt.

Washington McLean, the Democratic editor of the *Cincinnati Daily Enquirer,* emerged as one of the leading proponents of financial reform, which was far more popular in the Ohio Valley than in the eastern states. In the fall elections of 1867, the Democrats rode these issues and increased northern hostility to reconstruction, that by then included a demand for enfranchisement of African American males, to a surprising resurgence. McLean apparently envisioned himself as a president maker who only needed the right candidate. Pendleton became the potential beneficiary.

Pendleton had apparently been pondering the nation's financial woes for some time before he unveiled at a speech in Milwaukee in early November 1867 his plan to deal with matters related to the federal debt and the greenbacks. The Ohioan suggested that the problems were due to "New England Puritanism," which he equated to Radical Republicanism and which "believe[d] devoutly that the earth belongs to the saints of the Lord, and that they are the saints." Having aroused regional antagonism toward New England, Pendleton proposed that the greenbacks should be used to retire a series of federal bonds called the five-twenties, bonds that were redeemable in five years and payable in twenty. Those bonds, which Pendleton and others insisted were held mainly by easterners, earned 6 percent interest that by law had to be paid in gold. However, the law that authorized the sale of these bonds did not mandate that the principal be paid in gold, only stipulating payment in lawful money, which many interpreted to mean any form of legal tender including the greenbacks. Redemption in greenbacks would save the government millions of dollars in interest compared to Treasury Secretary McCulloch's plan to sell bonds to raise the funds to retire the five-twenties. Pendleton and others thought that repayment with greenbacks was not only financial responsible but fair. After all, they argued, the bonds had originally been purchased with depreciated greenbacks. The bondholders simply did not deserve the windfall profit that would result if the bonds were repaid with gold.

Pendleton saw another advantage in his plan. As the bonds were quickly retired, they could no longer be used to back the currency issued by the national banks created during the Civil War. Pendleton had never reconciled himself to the new national banking system and relished the hope that it might be undermined by his plan. The concept had the further political attraction of finding a use for the greenbacks, which would preclude further contraction. Thus, Pendleton could present himself as a person dedicated to economic prosperity, which many people believed contraction jeopardized. Pendleton presented a series of calculations that indicated that the federal government could pay off its entire debt within fourteen years with no increase in taxation, no repudiation, and no contraction of the greenbacks. The country could also return to specie payments in 1881. And, not incidentally, the plan could lead the Democrats back into power.

Pendleton's remedy found a receptive audience among westerners who harbored suspicions of easterners and bondholders and who tended to oppose contraction. However, the proposal raised some crucial questions about its proponent. In 1862, Pendleton had voted against the creation of the greenbacks; now he advocated keeping them in circulation even if it meant delaying the resumption of specie payments. That was a curious shift for a hard money Democrat but one that can probably be explained. Pendleton was also a realist. Whether he liked the greenbacks or not, they did exist. Contraction had proved politically damaging to the Republicans and even suggested a new issue for Democrats to exploit. Pendleton had principles, but he also had ambition. His plan, soon known simply as the Pendleton Plan, held the potential to be a basis for a run for the 1868 Democratic presidential nomination.

Pendleton took great care to distinguish between types of federal debt, those whose principal had to be paid in gold and those, such as the five-twenties, that did not. He did not want to be considered a repudiator of the federal debt; nor did he want to be identified with the repudiators. In fact, the Pendleton Plan was a moderate proposal, compared with some advocated during 1867 and 1868.

As McLean and Pendleton hoped, the Pendleton Plan quickly became the base of the latter's campaign for presidential nomination, and he emerged as the favored western Democratic candidate. However, many eastern Democrats despised the plan and planned to nominate a candidate more in sympathy with their views. The two forces met at the national convention in New York City in July. Although Pendleton led on the early ballots, he could not garner the necessary two-thirds of the delegates, and on the twenty-second ballot the Democrats nominated Governor Horatio Seymour of New York, an opponent of using greenbacks to pay the debt. Following the contradictory pattern of 1864, the Democrats endorsed the Pendleton Plan in its platform.

Pendleton must have been keenly disappointed. The second phase of his national career ended with a depressing outcome. He had come closer to the Democratic presidential nomination than any previous Ohioan. McLean and the *Cincinnati Daily Enquirer* presented what in Ohio was surely a widely accepted, if somewhat flawed, analysis of the delegates' decision: "The candidate of the people has been defeated by a combination of the moneyed interest of the East with a few envious and jealous partisans of the West." Still, it may have mattered little. Ulysses S. Grant defeated Seymour that fall. The Pendleton Plan was extremely unpopular in the East among both Democrats and Republicans. Pendleton surely would have won fewer votes in the East than Seymour. In short, he had little real chance of carrying the nation.

For the next decade, Pendleton largely disappeared from politics, spending his time as an attorney. However, in 1878 he returned to Congress as a senator. His single six-year term was highlighted by the passage in 1883 of the Pendleton Act, which perhaps has become his most famous legacy. For nearly two decades, civil service reformers had attacked with marginal success two related evils. The spoils system of filling federal appointments, they believed, bred incompetence and corruption. They had also denounced the practice of assessing federal officers a percentage of their salaries for use by the political party that appointed them. By providing the party in power with massive financial resources, this practice perpetuated a system that undercut the very essence of democracy.

Only after the 1881 assassination of President James Garfield by a disappointed office seeker did members of Congress conclude that the people were demanding reform. Pendleton, who had previously shown only marginal interest in civil service reform, introduced a bill that had been drafted by Dorman Eaton, a longtime advocate of reform. Despite his late conversion to the cause, Pendleton was committed to ending political assessments and to awarding federal jobs to those who had scored the highest on required examinations. Because his bill promised to make significant steps in those directions, it would deprive congressmen of key sources of financial support and influence. Thus, many had for years opposed such legislation. However, the public outcry after Garfield's death drove Congress into action. In January 1883, both houses approved the Pendleton bill, the first meaningful attempt to assure that federal employees were chosen by a merit system based on competitive examinations, not politics, and to end political assessments. The bill was only a first step; it covered barely 10 percent of federal workers.

Still, it greatly irritated many politicians. In fact, Pendleton cast the only non-southern Democratic vote for it in the Senate. Politicians did not enjoy doing the right thing even when the public demanded it. Pendleton's courage and honesty did not go unrewarded. He had made a major contribution to the welfare of the nation, but in January 1884 Democrats in the Ohio General Assembly refused to support him for another term. However, in March 1885, President Grover Cleveland nominated him to be minister to Germany. While on that assignment he died in Brussels, Belgium, on November 24, 1889.

Thus ended the life of one of the most significant political figures from Ohio in the nineteenth century. Pendleton served the state and nation with courage, integrity, determination, and civility for over thirty-five years. As a dedicated Jacksonian Democrat, he defended his interpretation of the Constitution, hard money, states' rights, frugal government, and keeping the country under white domination with limited overall success. With his career based on these principles—which could prove malleable when necessary to satisfy his personal ambition—he rose to a prominence in national politics attained in the nineteenth century by no other Ohio Democrat. He also played a crucial role in the reemergence of the Ohio Democratic Party as a viable political force. And as a means of doing so he contributed to keeping racial issues alive in Ohio, much to the detriment of justice, into the twentieth century. His great misfortune was to be wedded to principles better suited to rural, agrarian America, at the historical moment when the country fell into civil war, which increased federal power, changed constitutional principles, and propelled America on to becoming an urban, industrial nation.

Further Reading

Hoogenboom, Ari. *Outlawing the Spoils: A History of the Civil Service Reform Movement, 1865–1883*. Urbana: University of Illinois Press, 1968.

Sawrey, Robert D. *Dubious Victory: The Reconstruction Debate in Ohio*. Lexington: University Press of Kentucky, 1992.

Sharkey, Robert P. *Money, Class, and Party: An Economic Study of the Civil War and Reconstruction*. Baltimore, Md.: Johns Hopkins University Press, 1959.

Silbey, Joel H. *A Respectable Minority: The Democratic Party in the Civil War Era, 1860–1868*. New York: Norton, 1977.

Unger, Irwin. *The Greenback Era: A Social and Political History of American Finance, 1865–1879*. Princeton, N.J.: Princeton University Press, 1964.

12

B. F. Goodrich and the Industrialization of Ohio

MANSEL G. BLACKFORD

O N JULY 11, 1888, just three weeks before he died, Dr. Benjamin
Franklin Goodrich met with the officers of the rubber company
he had founded eighteen years before. Suffering from tuberculosis,
Goodrich had moved to Manitou Springs, Colorado, earlier in the
month, with the certainty that his health was quickly failing. At this
final conference, Goodrich gave his executives advice on how to continue operations after his death, stressing the need to maintain the
high quality of his firm's products. "The only anxiety I have,"
Goodrich observed, "is whether the discipline is kept up, whether the
repairs are kept up to the mark and whether the standard of quality is
right up to the mark." When the firm's general plant superintendent
asked if his standards might not be too high, Goodrich replied, "That
is just where you are mistaken. By God, the standard can not be too
high."

Despite the firm's commitment to the production of high-quality
products, success did not come easily. B. F. Goodrich almost failed
during a depression in the mid-1870s and required refinancing before
emerging as a healthy concern in the 1880s. In establishing his company as a going concern, Dr. Goodrich helped advance industrialization in Ohio and the Midwest. Seeing the success of the B. F.
Goodrich Company, other rubber producers located in the Akron
area, making the region the leading rubber-making district in the
United States. More generally, the development of the firm signaled
the rise of the Midwest as the dominant manufacturing region of the
United States for decades to come.

Born on November 4, 1841, on a farm near the small town of Ripley in upstate New York, Benjamin Goodrich was the son of Anson

FIG. 8 B. F. Goodrich.
Courtesy of the Ohio Historical Society.

Goodrich and Susan Dinsmore Goodrich. Named after Benjamin Franklin—his mother greatly admired Franklin and often read to her son from Franklin's autobiography and *Little Richard's Almanac*—Goodrich as a boy performed chores on the farm and attended the local school. He enjoyed making maple syrup in the spring, swimming and fishing in the summer, and ice-skating in the winter. Inventive like Henry Ford, who a bit later tinkered with machinery on a midwestern farm, Goodrich even devised a wind-powered sled. Goodrich's father died in 1847, and his mother two years later. He then went to live with his mother's brother, John Dinsmore, not far from Ripley. In the Dinsmore household, Goodrich found a supportive family. Writing a cousin, he observed, "You know I love Uncle John Dinsmore as a father and I think he cares nearly as much for me as for his own boys." Educated first by a teacher tutoring Dinsmore's children at home, Goodrich went on at the age of fifteen to attend a boy's boarding school at Austinburg, Ohio, and a year later attended the Academy in Fredonia, New York, another private school.

Goodrich was attracted to the field of medicine. He studied the subject in 1858 with his cousin Dr. John Spencer in Westfield, New

York. Such personal preparation for the medical profession was common in the nineteenth century. Goodrich went farther by enrolling in the highly regarded Cleveland Medical College in 1859—this institution later became the renowned medical school of the Case Western Reserve University—from which he graduated in the following year. In 1860, he opened a medical practice in Mayville, New York, with his office and rooms in a hotel. Goodrich's initial foray in medicine proved discouraging. According to one biographer, a year after entering the field "his practice amounted to nothing and he was without both money and necessary clothing."

At this low point in his life, the Civil War intervened to change Goodrich's fortunes. He traveled to Albany, New York, where he became a hospital steward in the Ninth New York Cavalry, serving in the same company as the cousin (John Spencer) with whom he had earlier studied. Soon promoted to assistant surgeon, Goodrich was transferred to a battalion of engineers, where he would remain until the close of the conflict. During the war, Goodrich continued his medical studies at the University of Pennsylvania while on leave from the engineers in late 1862 and early 1863. After returning to duty, he served with the Army of the Potomac as a commissioned assistant surgeon, taking charge of a small hospital.

Like so many Americans, North and South, Goodrich found his life disrupted by the Civil War. David Goodrich recalled that his father was possessed by "a sort of restlessness" after the conflict. If Goodrich resembled many of his countrymen in this respect, he differed from them in others: even after the death of his parents he benefited from an upbringing in what he later described as "comfortable circumstances" and from a superior education. At a time when few Americans went beyond grammar school, Goodrich had attended college. The personal and family connections so important in providing advantages in his early life would continue to aid Goodrich in the postwar years. Although differing from most Americans in his background, Goodrich was similar to America's leading business executives of the late nineteenth and early twentieth centuries. Like Goodrich, most came from upper-class or middle-class families and were well educated. Few were the sons of immigrants, and none came from minority groups. "Rags to riches" stories were rare in American business.

After the war, Goodrich continued to try his luck as a doctor, but as before with little success. Moving first to Jamestown, New York, a commercial center not far from his hometown of Ripley, he soon went on to newly developing towns in the oil fields of Pennsylvania. E. L. Drake had sunk America's first commercial oil well there in 1859, ensuring the region's development as America's first major oil district. Tideout, Rouseville, and Pit Hole all attracted Goodrich's attention, and by the fall of 1865 he was practicing in the latter town. Conditions were primitive, but expensive. Writing a relative, Goodrich observed that "there are no women here . . . the food is so bad . . . and the life is so hard that you would not last here a month." Goodrich found it difficult to make ends meet because of the high cost of living. He and his partner paid the astronomical sum of $1,000 for one year's rent for two office rooms. Although they hoped to erect their own office building, as Goodrich lamented, "I have not the money to do it." Lacking the patience and capital to persist as a doctor, Goodrich entered the employ of Brown Brothers Oil Company—a firm with which he had become acquainted in Pit Hole—as a member of its shipping department in New York City.

Goodrich's career change and move to New York City set the stage for his entrance into the rubber industry. He boarded in the home of a Mrs. Sanderson and there became friends with a young attorney, John P. Morris. The two men became involved in real estate deals, several of which may have been quite profitable. At least one such venture was not, however. Ironically, it was this one that first involved Goodrich in the rubber industry. Goodrich had come to know Ezra Frost and others through the Hudson River Rubber Company, whose production works were at Hastings-on-the-Hudson, but whose head office was in New York City. This company produced rubber fire hose, belting and steam packing (seals and gaskets) for factory machinery, and railroad car springs. Intrigued by what he saw in the company, Goodrich persuaded Morris to join him in trading $10,000 worth of real estate in New York City for an equal value of stock in the company. Hudson River Rubber Company officers, facing intense competition and desperate for capital, eagerly accepted Goodrich's offer in 1869. Presumably, they sold the lots acquired from Goodrich and Morris to raise cash for their company.

According to Morris, Goodrich was "anxious to make this trade"; Goodrich was perhaps too eager. The Hudson River Rubber Company, burdened by rundown machinery and suffering from competition, turned out to be in bad financial shape. To protect their investment, Goodrich and Morris bought out all of the other stockholders through a further exchange of New York City real estate for shares in the rubber company. Goodrich then became president and manager of the company, while Morris served as its secretary and treasurer. As Morris later recalled, "Dr. Goodrich immediately took charge of the works at Hastings," even though he possessed no previous knowledge of how to manufacture rubber products. Problems continued to plague the company: worn out machinery, high rents, and ever-present competition. Seeking to salvage the operation and perceiving opportunities elsewhere, Goodrich closed the Hastings plant, leased a small rubber factory in Melrose, New York, and transferred all of the Hastings equipment there. The move accomplished little. "The Melrose factory did not succeed any better than the Hastings factory," Morris later remembered, "and the Doctor said we would either have to have some more money or close up and sell the business out."

Goodrich entered the rubber business just a few decades after its beginning in the United States. By the 1820s and 1830s, merchants in East Coast cities were offering rubber shoes, bottles, and syringes for sale. Made from liquid latex obtained by tapping wild rubber trees in the Amazon River basin, these goods were waterproof. Because the raw latex could not be transported very far without spoiling, American rubber makers sought chemical and mechanical means to break down the rubber shoes and other items as a first step in making new products from them. There were challenges: goods made from the reconstituted crude rubber softened in the heat of summer and grew brittle in the cold of winter. In the 1830s and 1840s, several rubber manufacturers, most notably Charles Goodyear, discovered how to solve these problems by vulcanizing the rubber. They added sulfur to cut-up rubber as it was being prepared in mixing mills and then baked the new finished rubber products in ovens. This vulcanization process ended problems with softness and brittleness, and the manufacturing of rubber goods soared.

Far from discouraged, Goodrich sought rubber manufacturing opportunities farther west. It may be, as Morris explained, that the inspiration to look beyond New York came from him. "I thought that if one was started out West where there were then no factories and he could get enough money so he would not be cramped for two or three years, that he would succeed in business." Or perhaps Goodrich's earlier experiences with education in Ohio led him to venture across the Appalachians. Goodrich was a young man on the make, only twenty-eight years old, and not easily dispirited by what he saw as temporary setbacks. He was optimistic enough to marry Mary M. Marvin of Jamestown, New York, the daughter of one of the state's leading jurists, in late 1869. The two had met in Jamestown during Goodrich's search for a place to practice medicine right after the Civil War. Before long, the couple had several children: Charles Cross, born in 1870; Isabella in 1874; and a second son, David, who arrived in 1876 (in addition, twins born in 1872 died in infancy).

Goodrich spent much of 1870 seeking a new location, eventually choosing Akron as the site for his future operations. Perhaps, as legend suggests, Goodrich was traveling by train to Cleveland when by chance an Akron business leader entered into conversation with him and convinced him to visit his city. More likely, Goodrich came to know about Akron through a broadside letter that was widely distributed in the East by the town's Board of Trade in the spring of 1870. Boosting Akron as being "at the beginning of greatness," the one-page flyer praised the town as possessing all of the prerequisites of a manufacturing center: abundant coal resources, transportation facilities, and a government responsive to the needs of industry.

Akron indeed had much to offer a budding industrialist like Goodrich. The town possessed canal and railroad connections to raw materials, such as coal, and to regional and national markets for finished goods. Sitting astride the intersection of the Ohio & Erie and the Pennsylvania & Ohio canals, Akron had grown up as the "City on the Summit," perched on the crest of Ohio's watershed and linked to the rest of the state by mule-drawn canal boats. By the early 1870s, however, the canals were falling into disuse and being replaced by railroads. The coming of the Cleveland and Pittsburgh Railroad in 1852 provided connections to regional markets, while the Atlantic and Great Western Railway offered direct links to New York eleven years later. If the canals declined in significance for transportation purposes, they remained important as sources of clean, mineral-free water drawn from reservoirs, such as Portage Lake and Long Lake. Copious supplies of pure water were needed in the making of rubber, especially in the first stage of work, when impurities such as dirt were washed out of the natural rubber gum.

Probably most important to Goodrich, Akron was emerging as an industrial town and had the people, business leaders and laborers, needed to support manufacturing. During the 1860s, Ferdinand Schumacher put up the first of the great cereal mills on South Summit Street, naming his enterprise the Empire Barley Mill. Established before the Civil War, the clay industry was expanding, making Akron one of America's centers for sewer pipe production. Several entrepreneurs opened a branch of the Aultman works of Canton under the name of Aultman, Miller & Company to produce the Buckeye Mower and Reaper. John Seiberling moved his company, another manufacturer of reapers and mowers, to Akron from Massillon. Many of the business leaders involved in these industries would soon support Goodrich in his nascent rubber manufacturing venture. With industrial development came population growth. From an overgrown village of 3,500 in 1860, Akron became a good-sized town of 10,000 a decade later. The town had a growing industrial workforce ready for employment in Goodrich's projected rubber factory.

Most appealing initially, Akron possessed a business elite eager to attract Goodrich's plant and willing to provide him with financial backing. When Goodrich visited Akron in November 1870, he sought out George Crouse on his first day in town, because, as president of the Board of Trade, Crouse had signed the board's promotional flyer. In approaching Crouse, Goodrich made a fortunate choice, for Crouse was well connected to the rest of Akron's business leaders. Born in 1832 in Summit County, Crouse had been, like Goodrich, raised on a farm. Like Goodrich and many other late-nineteenth-century Americans, however, Crouse left the farm for town life, working as a teacher, deputy treasurer, auditor, and treasurer for Summit County in the late 1850s. He soon turned most of his attention to business affairs. In 1863, he became the local agent for the Atlantic & Great Western Railroad in Akron. A few months later, he became the financial manager for the Akron Branch of Aultman, Miller & Company and was made its secretary and treasurer in 1865. Crouse's interests extended beyond manufacturing reapers. In 1863, he was elected president of the Board of Trade, and seven years later he helped organize the Bank of Akron.

After talking privately with Goodrich, Crouse called a meeting of twenty-one of Akron's business leaders at the Empire Hotel, and at the gathering Goodrich outlined his plans of constructing a two-story rubber factory to house the machinery from his closed venture in upstate New York. Something of a dreamer, Goodrich estimated that his company would soon annually be earning a gross profit of $90,000 on sales of $225,000, estimates which later events would prove wildly optimistic. After making his presentation, Goodrich called on those at the gathering for their support. Their response was favorable, but the businessmen wanted to know more about Goodrich and his previous experiences. They selected George T. Perkins, who had just replaced Crouse as president of the Board of Trade, to travel to New York to look over Goodrich's operations.

Perkins was a logical selection for the task. Like Crouse, he would be important in the first several decades of Goodrich's rubber company's evolution and would serve as the firm's second president. Grandson of the founder of Akron and son of one of Summit County's largest landowners and business leaders, Perkins understood Akron's development first-hand. Born in 1836, he was only five years older than Goodrich. After graduating from local schools and briefly attending Marietta College, Perkins went to work in 1859 in an uncle's coal company. Enlisting as a private in the Civil War, he served capably and at times heroically in the 105th Ohio Volunteer Infantry. Upon his return to Akron, Perkins solidified his family's status by marrying a daughter of Levi Rawson, a former mayor of Akron and a merchant in the shipping trade. In 1870, he became the president of the Bank of Akron, the same bank Crouse had helped start.

After inspecting Goodrich's New York plant, Perkins urged his fellow business leaders to invest in Goodrich's proposed venture. Twenty-three of them pledged $15,000 to Goodrich, the loan to be secured by a mortgage on his property ($13,600 was actually paid in, and this loan was paid off in 1875). Perkins loaned $500 of his own funds. It is high testimony to the spirit of mid-century boosterism sweeping through U.S. towns and cities, especially in the Midwest, that representatives in industry, trade, and finance all supported Goodrich's plans. Like Goodrich, Akron's business leaders were extremely optimistic about the future of their town and of the rubber industry. They had to be; after all, they were backing a man who, while successful in real estate, had failed as a doctor and had failed twice in the rubber business. No doubt working in Goodrich's favor in their eyes was the fact that he was ready to uproot himself and his family, that he was willing to invest all of his own capital in the venture, and that he had pledges of additional financial support from friends and family in New York. Still, backing Goodrich was a gamble.

Assured of the needed financing, Goodrich dismantled the New York plant and moved to Akron to begin making rubber goods anew. On the last day of 1870, Goodrich and four others set up the partnership Goodrich, Tew & Co. under Ohio law. The partnership resembled most new companies, past and present, in that personal trust was essential in providing the initial financing. Goodrich, his wife's family, and the son of his landlord in New York City accounted for three-quarters of the financing of the company. But, as a persuasive businessman, Goodrich was able to reach beyond his immediate acquaintances to tap additional capital in Akron. The key to doing so lay in his relations with Crouse and Perkins. Through their intercession Goodrich was able to win the backing of the Akron group.

Goodrich formed his company at an auspicious time, one of tremendous economic expansion in Ohio, the Midwest, and the nation. From a country based on farms and small towns, the United States was fast becoming a nation of factories and large cities. In the 1880s, for the first time, more people worked at non-farm than at agricultural jobs. Between 1870 and 1920, manufacturing output rose almost tenfold. Yet, that growth was uneven. A major depression in the 1870s and a lesser recession in the 1880s hurt the nascent rubber company by drying up markets.

Goodrich, Tew & Co. began operations in South Akron. In early 1871, the company finished construction of a two-story brick factory, moved in machinery, and began manufacturing rubber products. Goodrich purchased raw rubber from brokers in New York City, shipped it to Akron by railroad, and had it hauled from Akron's railroad station to his factory in mule-drawn wagons. Work passed through several steps. The initial processing took place on the first floor, where the crude rubber was soaked in warm water and then run through washers composed of rough rollers until all dirt had been removed. The clean raw rubber was next hung to dry for two weeks to six months over a large heater. Once dry, the rubber was ready to be made into usable items. The first step was to cut up the raw rubber, mix it with sulfur and other chemicals, and pass it through heavy rollers from which it came out in thin layers. Depending upon what the final products were, the remaining steps varied. If rubber belting or hoses were desired, the strips of rubber were fed, along with cotton duck (cloth), into calenders made up of three massive rollers kept continuously hot. These rollers pressed the rubber and cotton duck together, according to a contemporary account, "filling every fibre of the cloth with the rubber." If products not using cotton duck were being made, this step would be abbreviated or skipped altogether. Next, the rubber or rubber-impregnated duck was taken upstairs where it was made into finished products. The final step occurred when the products were taken back downstairs for curing in vulcanizers.

Two rubber goods dominated the company's product line: fire hose and industrial belting. Its thorough impregnation of the cotton duck with rubber through extensive calendering operations produced what the firm's publications correctly called "the first really serviceable conductor of fluids" made out of rubber. Earlier hoses had been made out of leather, which was subject to cracking and breakage. Labeled the "White Anchor" brand, the company's hoses quickly became well known for their high quality. It is possible, as company lore avers, that Goodrich had once watched a neighbor try in vain to extinguish a house fire with a leaky hose and, dismayed by what he saw, decided to improve the quality of the fire hoses. More likely, Goodrich simply improved upon the operations he had already supervised in New York. Similarly, Goodrich, Tew & Co. made rubber belting from its earliest days, another product inherited from the New York factories.

Hose and belting were logical items to emphasize. The Midwest was rapidly urbanizing and industrializing. Consequently, the region's burgeoning cities required fire hoses, and its factories needed miles of belting to connect steam engines to pieces of machinery. Goodrich, Tew & Co. was at the right place at the right time to reach these newly opening markets. Nonetheless, the company followed a policy of diversified production. Scrambling to survive and grow, it made whatever rubber goods its owner-managers thought they could profitably sell. Footwear was one of the few rubber items the company did not initially make. Large eastern firms produced and sold it at prices Goodrich, Tew & Co. had no hope of matching. In addition to hoses and belting, the company made wagon springs, steam packing, wringer rolls for washing machines, valves, billiard cushions, tubing, gas bags, and fruit jar rings.

The early 1870s were prosperous years for Goodrich, Tew & Co., but a severe nationwide depression in the mid-1870s temporarily shattered the company's hopes for expansion. The depression slowed the development of America's rubber industry. In 1870, the United States possessed fifty-six manufacturers of rubber and elastic goods capitalized at $7.5 million and employing 6,025 people. A decade later, despite considerable recovery in the late 1870s, little growth had occurred. Although the number of rubber companies had grown to ninety, their total capitalization had fallen to $6 million, and their employment (6,265 people) was about the same as ten years before.

For Goodrich, Tew & Co., the depression was little short of disastrous. By mid-1874, the company teetered on the brink of failure. The company's problems were not unusual. Industrialization proved to be a double-edged sword for Ohio: in prosperous times many could benefit from it, but in economic downturns just as many suffered. All of Akron's industrial establishments were hit hard by the depression. Finally, by the end of the 1875, B. F. Goodrich—as the partnership of Goodrich, Tew & Co. had been reorganized and renamed in the previous year—was once more earning profits. In large part, B. F. Goodrich's return to profitability resulted from economic recovery that occurred across the United States. With their tax bases restored, municipalities again bought fire hoses. The superiority of its fire hose continued to give B. F. Goodrich what one observer called "almost a monopoly" in that market. By 1877, cities across the United States—from Jackson, Mississippi, to Indianapolis, Indiana, and from Topeka, Kansas, to Oil City, Pennsylvania—purchased Goodrich hoses. The market for industrial belting also picked up, and the company was able to sell to such emerging industrial concerns as the Standard Oil Company of Ohio and the E. Anheuser Company Brewing Association of St. Louis, as well as to hundreds of smaller industrial ventures in the Midwest.

B. F. Goodrich expanded but remained cash-poor, leading those involved in the partnership to agree that the time had arrived to incorporate their firm. In 1880, they transformed their partnership into the Ohio-chartered corporation, the B. F. Goodrich Company. A major reason for incorporation was the chronic need for capital. The corporate form of organization, with its promise of limited liability to investors (individual investors in the corporation could not be held personally responsible for the company's debts, should the firm fall upon hard times again), offered a means to secure additional capital, which, in turn, permitted further expansion. At the close of 1881, its first full year of operations as a corporation, B. F. Goodrich possessed assets of $233,000, made sales of $319,000, and posted profits of $69,000. In 1888, the year in which Dr. Goodrich died, the company had assets of $564,000, made sales of $696,000, and earned profits of $107,000.

B. F. Goodrich's growth occurred as a part of the continuing development of industry in Ohio and, more specifically, in Akron. In 1881, the Valley Railroad (later part of the Baltimore & Ohio) provided additional transportation facilities for Akron, and by the close of the decade five lines linked the city to the outside world. New factories followed. John Seiberling put up a six-story cereal mill, later converted into an oatmeal factory; and the Enterprise Manufacturing Company began making luminous paint. The Diamond Match Company was formed in 1881 as a combine of twenty-eight formerly independent companies. Older establishments expanded. Robinson Brothers & Company, for example, operated six clay mills, making it one of the largest producers of stoneware pottery in the world. During the decade,

Akron's population rose from 16,500 to 27,600. As one booster publication noted in 1886, the city's recent growth had been "marvelous," and the "future of the city is bright with the bow of promise."

Goodrich lived to see his company benefit from several years of accelerating growth before his death in 1888, and as the major stockholder in the company he enjoyed the fruits of that growth. Some remembered Goodrich as "a gentleman of quiet dignity," but there was more to him. Goodrich was also one of the best poker players in Akron. As his prosperity increased, Goodrich enjoyed driving fast horses hitched to his buggy and, his health permitting, trips to Europe, where he bet on horse races. He was successful in at least some of his wagers, for his son David later recalled that after visiting a Parisian track in 1885 his father returned to his hotel with his "clothing completely padded out with huge French bank notes" from picking "winners in five out of six races."

However, Goodrich's health had been seriously deteriorating. Never robust, Goodrich suffered from the demands of business. "[F]ather worked like the devil," David later remembered. In the end, exhaustion and disease caught up with him. Goodrich was buried in the plot of his wife's family in Jamestown, a befitting resting place for a man who had depended so much upon his in-laws during his early years in the rubber business. Among his pallbearers were George Perkins and his old partner in real estate, John Morris. The employees of his Akron firm contributed a white anchor made of flowers for Goodrich's grave.

No single factor accounted for Dr. Goodrich's success in business. Rather, a complex array of elements led to the emergence of B. F. Goodrich as a viable manufacturing firm. Dr. Goodrich's greatest contribution was his optimism. Despite the problems he encountered in the rubber industry in New York in the 1860s and in Ohio during the 1870s, he continued to work hard to make his company a success. Goodrich proved innovative and flexible in his approach to business. He aimed at making high-quality goods through advanced production processes. He was willing—indeed eager—to take the lead in manufacturing new products. Nonetheless, other companies headed by owner-managers just as hard working and innovative as Dr. Goodrich failed. The social and economic environments within which his company operated were also crucial to Dr. Goodrich's business success. Dr. Goodrich's acceptance by the Akron business elite was especially important. Like Goodrich himself, many other Akronites were young men on the make, adventurous entrepreneurs seeking out opportunities in commerce, finance, and, increasingly, in industry. They were willing to support Goodrich's enterprise as a way of improving their own fortunes, as well as those of Akron. The national economic environment also proved favorable to the growing company. Despite periodic economic downturns, the late nineteenth century was a time of tremendous economic growth; and B. F. Goodrich's fire hoses and industrial belting served well the cities and factories that were developing as part of that growth.

B. F. Goodrich's success helped make Akron America's rubber center. Multiple factors accounted for Akron's rise as a rubber city. The availability of clean water, good transportation facilities, cheap fuel from Ohio's coal mines, and a relatively inexpensive labor supply enticed would-be rubber manufacturers to Akron. The biggest attraction was, however, B. F. Goodrich's example. Frank and Charles Seiberling—the sons of John Seiberling, one of the Akron industrialists who had loaned money to Dr. Goodrich in 1871—formed the Goodyear Rubber Company in 1898 as an Akron corporation. Henry Firestone started his Akron rubber company in 1900. Firestone Tire began business by first attaching rubber tires made by other companies, including B. F. Goodrich, to carriage wheels and then selling them. Former B. F. Goodrich employees founded Diamond Rubber in 1894, putting up a factory right across the street from the Goodrich plant. With an infusion of capital from Ohio Barber, Dr. Goodrich's poker-playing crony, the company developed into one of Akron's leading rubber companies—only to be acquired by B. F. Goodrich in 1912. Entrepreneurs were well aware of B. F. Goodrich's growth and profitability and located in Akron hoping to duplicate the firm's enviable record.

Further Reading

Blackford, Mansel G., and K. Austin Kerr. *BF Goodrich: Tradition and Transformation, 1870–1995*. Columbus: Ohio State University Press, 1996.

Jordan, Philip D. *Ohio Comes of Age, 1873–1900*. Columbus: Ohio State Archaeological and Historical Society, 1943.

Love, Steve, and David Giffels. *Wheels of Fortune: The Story of Rubber in Akron*. Akron: University of Akron Press, 1999.

Nelson, Daniel. *Farm and Factory: Workers in the Midwest, 1880–1990*. Bloomington: Indiana University Press, 1995.

13

Martin Foran and the Creation of Cleveland's Labor Movement

MICHAEL PIERCE

I n 1886, Martin Foran praised the potential of the United States. For him, the nation, guided by the hand of God, promised unbounded opportunity and the chance for men to rise and fall on their own merit. Unlike Europeans, Americans were unencumbered by restrictions of class, and Foran looked forward to the day when only "the natural differences between men" determined success and status. The only impediment to this was the "wage system," which Foran considered "a species of slavery, in some respects more galling than chattel slavery." Historically, white American men saw wage labor as a temporary condition that allowed them to save enough money to buy a farm or tools and a shop with which to support a family. They considered such economic independence to be the cornerstone of American democracy. Only those who were economically independent could be free to exercise their franchise free of coercion. But after the Civil War, wage labor and dependence became a permanent condition for an increasing number of American workingmen. Corporations, which pooled resources of investors, began replacing individual entre- preneurs and family partnerships as the primary owners of U.S. indus- try. With access to capital and labor saving machinery, corporations often drove small competitors out of business and forced wages down. Foran feared that large corporations and the wage system were creat- ing a class of workmen who did not have the opportunity to rise and fall on their own merits or achieve economic independence.

To overcome the wage system and check the increasing power of corporations, Foran proposed that businesses adopt "profit sharing" arrangements in which a portion of the profits was set aside for the workers' benefit. Such arrangements would ensure that workers

FIG. 9 Martin Foran.
Courtesy of the Ohio Historical Society.

would profit from the wealth that they had produced and provide opportunities for their families. If corporations proved reluctant to share profits with their workers, Foran called for "collective ownerships in the great engines of production and agencies of distribution." Foran was not some socialist crank who had read a few tracts by Marx when he wrote these words. He was serving the second of his three terms in the U.S. House of Representatives. His election symbolized the fear that many Cleveland workingmen had of industrial corporations during the Gilded Age and the growing power of labor organizations in Ohio politics.

Foran was born on November 11, 1844, in Choconut Township in Susquehanna County, Pennsylvania. His parents had migrated to Susquehanna County in the 1820s or 1830s from south-central New York as part of a contingent of Irish-Catholic canal laborers recruited by land speculators to settle the area. Little else is known about his father, James; his mother, Catherine O'Donnell; or his many brothers and sisters. Foran spent his first sixteen years on the family's farm where his father taught him the rudiments of coopering, or barrel

making. Like many farmers, James Foran did not rely solely on agricultural pursuits to provide for his family. During the winter and slack
times, Foran and his sons produced barrels, which area farmers used
to ship their goods to market.

In the winter, young Foran attended a county school where he
picked up basic grammar and mathematics, but most of his learning
took place outside the classroom. In the early 1870s, Foran wrote *The
Other Side,* a novel loosely based on his life, in which he suggested
that the local school was neither rigorous nor inviting for a poor, yet
talented, farm boy. Like his alter ego, Richard Arbyght, Foran was
frustrated by the slow pace of learning and "devoured all of the
books, papers and periodicals that came in his way." At sixteen, Foran
enrolled in St. Joseph's College in nearby Montrose, Pennsylvania.
Despite its name, the small Catholic school was little more than a glo-
rified high school that prepared students to become teachers. Foran
completed St. Joseph's two-year course and began teaching school in
the fall of 1862. Not much is known about his stint as a teacher, but
that he would later give up teaching for coopering suggests that he
did not consider it to be a rewarding career.

In February 1864, nineteen-year-old Foran resigned his teaching
position and enlisted in the Fourth Pennsylvania Cavalry. Arriving at
the front when Union victory seemed assured, Foran missed the
Union's major defeats but witnessed the army's most devastating
losses of men. Attached to Ulysses S. Grant's Army of the Potomac,
Foran's company spent the last twelve months of the war shadowing
Lee's Army of Northern Virginia. With the Confederates fighting
from well-defended positions, these battles proved to be especially
bloody. In one five-week period, Grant's troops suffered 18,000 casualties at the Battle of the Wilderness, 8,000 at Spotsylvania, 12,000 at
Cold Harbor, and another 20,000 in smaller skirmishes. Like many
soldiers, Foran was traumatized by the war, refusing to speak about
his experiences even as other politicians sought to turn their war
records into political capital.

After the war, Foran did not return to Susquehanna County,
which he later insisted "was not a place that offered much induce-
ment for anyone." After spending a year traveling from city to city,
Foran settled in the northwest Pennsylvania town of Meadville, which
had been booming since the 1859 discovery of oil in nearby
Titusville. He taught school for a short time but only to save enough
money to buy coopering tools, which would allow him to complete
his apprenticeship.

The discovery of oil transformed not only the region but the entire nation. Refined into kerosene, oil quickly became the illuminant of choice in U.S. households and businesses. It was cheaper and burned brighter than tallow candles and cost substantially less than whale oil. Demand pushed oil production from a mere 2,000 barrels in 1859 to over 4,500,000 barrels annually by 1869, almost all of it produced in northwestern Pennsylvania. Entrepreneurs built refineries near the wells to minimize transportation costs. To distribute the kerosene, these refineries needed huge numbers of barrels since pipelines and tankers were just being developed and only used for crude. Cooperages dotted the area, providing employment to hundreds of coopers like Foran.

The oil boom created inflation and economic uncertainty in northwestern Pennsylvania, making it difficult for local refiners to survive. By 1866, investors had poured more than $100 million into the purchase and development of the region's wells. Tales abounded of speculators paying $400 for blanket-sized plots of land. Saloon keepers increased liquor prices, boardinghouses raised room rates, and dance hall girls demanded more for their services. Inflationary pressures of the mid-1860s were so great that drillers paid teamsters over $20 a day, almost ten times the normal rate. Having to compete with drillers for labor, materials, and capital, area refiners found it difficult to compete with entrepreneurs who transported the crude out of the region to be refined using cheaper labor and less expensive materials.

Pittsburgh, Cleveland, Baltimore, Philadelphia, and New York all vied to take northwestern Pennsylvania's place as the nation's largest refining center, but by 1869 Cleveland had prevailed. In that year, the city refined about one-quarter of the 4,500,000 barrels of oil produced in the nation. Low transportation costs account for Cleveland's rise as a refining center. Two rail lines connected Cleveland with the oil fields 150 miles to the east. The competition between the lines kept transportation rates low enough to give the city a decided advantage over its rivals. Once refined, the oil could be cheaply transported over rail or the Great Lakes to markets in North America. Although fifty firms refined oil in Cleveland in 1870, John D. Rockefeller and his Standard Oil Company would soon dominate the industry. Reasoning that competition lowered prices and squeezed profit margins, Rockefeller sought to control the market by eliminating rivals. Through purchases, mergers, and predatory pricing, Standard Oil gained control of Cleveland's refining. By 1882, the company controlled all of Cleveland's refineries and 96 percent of the refining in the nation, making it the nation's largest corporation.

As oil refining shifted to Cleveland, so too did the demand for barrels, and Foran, like hundreds of other coopers, left northwestern Pennsylvania for the banks of Lake Erie. Arriving in March 1868, he found a city undergoing rapid change. In 1850, Cleveland had been primarily a commercial and banking center serving the prosperous farmers of Ohio's Western Reserve. Fewer than 1,000 of the just over 17,000 Clevelanders earned their living manufacturing or processing goods. The city's factories tended to be small, family-owned firms employing three to six hands and manufacturing for local consumption. By Foran's 1868 arrival, Cleveland bore little resemblance to the regional commercial center of 1850. Its population had more than quintupled to about 90,000, and manufacturing had replaced commerce as the city's most important economic activity. Almost 10,000 Clevelanders worked in the chemical factories, iron and steel mills, refineries, and shops that dotted the city. While most factories and shops remained small, large firms dominated the city's industrial life. In 1870, two firms, the Cleveland Rolling Mills and the Standard Oil Company, each employed over 2,500 workers. In other words, half of Cleveland's industrial workers labored for firms employing over 2,500 people.

Cleveland's workers had ambivalent feelings about the rise of large corporations. On one hand, they admired men like immigrant Harry Chisholm, who through hard work and ingenuity built the Cleveland Rolling Mills into one of the nation's largest iron producers and provided gainful employment to thousands of workingmen. As a Cleveland labor federation would declare in the early 1870s, "we believe that there should be no antagonism between capital and labor . . . in this country every workingman should consider that he has a chance to become an employer himself." On the other hand, Cleveland workingmen feared that these corporations could use their power to lower wages, drive small manufacturers out of business, and, ultimately, destroy the promise of America—the ability of individual workers to rise and fall on their own merits. Shortly after Foran's arrival, a local labor leader predicted that "the next great fight would . . . [be] between laborers and capitalists."

This ambivalence to the rise of large corporations was revealed in Foran's novel, *The Other Side*. Both the novel's antagonist, Alvan Relvason, and its protagonist, Richard Arbyght, were industrialists. The difference between them was in their treatment of employees.

Arbyght treated his workers with dignity, sharing with them the profits of the enterprise. He believed that it was both the just thing to do and in the long run more profitable, since a happy worker would be more productive. Relvason, though, was motivated by greed. He used his power to force his workers to accept poor working conditions, deprive them of a just wage, and rob them of their manhood. Relvason ended up a broken, destitute man, while Arbyght was prosperous and happy. Foran saw industrial conflict not as an inevitable outcome of the nation's economic system but as the result of greedy, shortsighted capitalists.

Not only was Cleveland in the midst of a great transformation at the time of Foran's arrival, so was the craft of coopering. Like other crafts dating to pre-industrial times, coopers had developed a system that ensured the stability of wages and promised economic independence to those who worked hard. Coopers regulated the supply and price of labor by limiting the number of apprentices. Apprentices performed drudge work in return for training. After three or four years and satisfactory progress as a cooper, the apprentice became a journeyman who traveled from shop to shop selling his labor to a master cooper, the owner of the cooperage. Journeymen sought to save enough money to establish their own shop and become a master. Like other artisans, coopers saw economic independence as the cornerstone of citizenship. Only those who were not dependent on others for their livelihood could be considered truly free.

Coopers also developed a distinctive work culture. Prizing manliness, production, and independence as much as high wages, coopers mixed work and leisure in the shop. Paid by the barrel rather than the day, journeymen saw themselves as subcontractors who controlled their own labor rather than employees whose every action was directed by a foreman. While technically working a six-day week, coopers really produced only four. Saturday was payday, and not much work was done, as historian Franklin Coyne explained: "Early on Saturday morning the big brewery wagon would drive up to the shop. Several of the coopers would club together, each paying his proper share, and one of them would call out the window to the driver, 'Bring me a Goose Egg,' meaning a half-barrel of beer. Then others would buy 'Goose Eggs,' and there would be a merry time all around. The coopers spent most of Monday recovering from their weekend festivities." Coyne continued, "Many coopers spend this day sharpening up their tools, carrying in stock, discussing current events and getting things in shape for the big workday on the morrow. Thus,

'Blue Monday' was something of a tradition with the coopers, and the day was also more or less lost as far as production was concerned."

The cooper's traditional craft culture did not mesh with the industrial economy that emerged after the Civil War. The proliferation of railroads and the lowering of transportation costs intensified competition, forcing employers to seek ways to lower expenses. Master coopers saw the traditional craft culture as an obstacle to lower costs. Shops sat idle on "Goose Egg Saturday" and "Blue Monday," and limits on the number of apprentices kept wages high. Not surprisingly, journeymen defended the traditional craft culture and resisted efforts of masters to impose new work rules. In *The Other Side*, the first sign of trouble between the master and the journeymen occurred when the master chastised the journeymen for telling stories while working. The novel's protagonist saw this as a sign that the workers were losing control of their labor and muttered that they were becoming "slaves."

A little more than a year after Foran's arrival in Cleveland, trouble erupted between the city's master coopers and the journeymen. In March 1869, the master coopers formed an employers' organization, which they hoped would end the cutthroat competition by establishing uniform wages and barrel prices. A month later, the employers' organization reduced journeymen's wages by five cents per barrel. To protest the reduction, a few hundred of the city's 2,000 coopers went on strike, proclaiming that they could not feed, house, and clothe a family at the reduced pay scale. The striking coopers visited shops in which journeymen remained working in hopes of convincing them to join the walkout. By the strike's third day every cooperage in the city was idle. The masters were unprepared for concerted action on the part of the journeymen. Their stocks were low, and the demand was high. This gave the journeymen tremendous leverage and forced the cooper bosses to capitulate after one week. Like most nineteenth-century strikes, the coopers' strike was spontaneous. There was no union, and whatever organization emerged during the course of the strike proved to be temporary. Although Foran undoubtedly participated in the strike, his exact role remains unknown.

In August 1869, the master coopers again attempted to reduce journeymen's wages by five cents per barrel. The master coopers complained that the market price had dropped by over twenty-five cents per barrel and that the journeymen should shoulder part of this reduction. Without the reduction, the coopers worried that refiners would import low cost barrels from Akron, Youngstown, or western Pennsylvania. Anticipating a strike, many stockpiled barrels, which they hoped to sell once the strike drove up the price of barrels.

The reduction set off another spontaneous strike. By the strike's second day, over 900 coopers were off the job. The strikers organized a mass rally on Public Square, but it got off to an inauspicious start. As one newspaper reported, "[I]t became painfully apparent that no business was prepared. There had been no committee appointed, no plan of arrangement laid down, no officers elected, and no one ready to recommend anything." This chaos, though, convinced the coopers in attendance of the necessity of a permanent organization.

Elected president of the newly formed union, Foran took charge of the strike. He used the newspapers to counter the master coopers' charge that a drop in the market price of barrels warranted a reduction in journeymen's wages. Citing statistics, Foran demonstrated that wages had already fallen by the same twenty-five cents that the price of barrels had fallen, and that it was the master coopers, rather than the journeymen, who had not shouldered any of the reduction. Calling the master coopers "short-sighted and unscrupulous money bags," Foran insisted that the reduction would double the employers' profits at the expense of the journeymen's ability to provide for their families. Foran's argument was so forceful that the city's newspapers backed off their earlier condemnations of the strikers as selfish malcontents.

As the strike continued into the winter of 1870, Foran and the coopers union became convinced that the masters would not capitulate and sought to establish a union-run cooperage. Not only would the cooperage provide employment to union members, it would also be owned by the workers who would receive dividends at the end of the year. Such a cooperative venture held the potential to transform industrial relations by eliminating the distinction between labor and capital and allowing workers to keep all of the profit that their labor produced. Under Foran's direction, the union's cooperage began operation on January 21, 1870, initially employing fifty journeymen. The shop was so successful that by the first week in February the union had formed two more shops, bringing total employment to 300. The city's most conservative paper, the *Cleveland Leader*, praised Foran's organization of the cooperative as bringing a "new dignity" to the workers' cause.

The establishment of the cooperative cooperages probably helped bring an end to the strike. In late February, the strikers and the master coopers reached a compromise in which the master coopers rescinded part of the wage reduction and agreed to abide by union work rules. Unlike after previous strikes, the coopers union did not disappear but continued to protect the interests of the workers. The union's cooperages, though, did not outlast the strike. The exact fate of the union-run cooperages remains unknown, but in *The Other Side* Foran suggested that barrel buyers boycotted cooperative-made barrels. More likely, the continuation of the cooperative cooperages posed a conflict of interest for union members employed by other firms.

The journeymen's coopers union was but one of a number of trade unions formed in Cleveland in the years following the Civil War. Although the city's first labor unions—printers, carpenters, and stone cutters—had been formed before 1860, the city's labor movement picked up steam at the end of the war, as blacksmiths, cigar makers, iron molders, machinists, ship caulkers, and other skilled workers formed powerful locals. The city also witnessed the formation of its first citywide labor federation in 1868, which was reformed in 1872 as the Industrial Council. Unlike individual locals which dealt mainly with economic and workplace issues, the Industrial Council's aim was to educate workingmen on political issues and to lobby for legislation in the workers' interest, such as the eight-hour day, factory and workplace inspections, currency reform, and tax equalization. Although never an officer in the Industrial Council, Foran would become the de facto leader of the city's labor movement.

At a time when many Americans viewed labor unions as sources of violence and conflict, Foran argued that trade unions were more than simply instruments to protect the interests of members. By fighting to raise wages and reduce the hours of toil, they ensured the preservation of American democracy and the nation's economy. High wages also increased productivity and gave workers a stake in the status quo. Shorter hours allowed workers the time to improve themselves and participate in civic affairs. As Foran declared, "cheap men are dangerous as well as non-productive, and intelligent labor means greater security to the state." Most importantly, high wages allowed families to send their children to schools rather than into factories. Foran argued that only universal education would ensure that all children had an opportunity to succeed and could prevent the nation from descending into an aristocracy.

The 1869–70 journeymen's strike convinced Foran that trade unions could not be effective if organized solely on a local basis. Not only had low transportation costs opened up Cleveland to barrels made in other cities with low wage, non-union labor, but master coopers could also recruit out-of-town journeymen to break strikes. To protect the gains made by the union, Foran called for journeymen throughout North America to send delegates to Cleveland for the purpose of forming a national union. Arriving in Cleveland in May 1870, delegates from seven states and Canada formed the Coopers' International Union (CIU). They elected Foran president of the new union which had thirteen locals (three of which were in Cleveland) and represented just under 1,600 journeymen. The CIU grew very rapidly; within five months, the union had forty locals representing 3,350 journeymen. A few months later, Foran reported that the CIU represented over 6,700 coopers and 142 locals.

The union sought to protect skilled coopers by regulating conditions on the shop floor and limiting the supply of coopers. The shop rules in Cleveland were probably very similar to those in New York. New York locals mandated a nine-hour day (7:00 A.M. to 5:00 P.M. with an hour for lunch), forbade workers from using materials partially processed elsewhere, set wages at $4.00 per day for steady men and $4.50 per day for transient workers, limited the number of apprentices, and prohibited union members from working with non-union coopers. The locals also collected enough dues from its members to set up a strike fund, to provide sick and death benefits, and to pay travel expenses for journeymen to leave an area with an excess supply of labor.

The rise of the CIU created difficulties for master coopers. Refiners and other consumers demanded cheaper barrels, but the CIU's policies made price reductions impossible. To combat the CIU's influence, many master coopers turned to barrel-making machinery that was perfected in the years after the Civil War and could be operated by easily replaced, low-paid unskilled laborers. The union's *Coopers' Monthly Journal* observed, "Whenever our craftsmen demanded an increase in wages and it was refused, some employers would buy barrel machinery because they [the machines] would not strike." Some barrel consumers sought to circumvent both master coopers and the CIU by building their own cooperages. The Standard Oil Company, for example, built a machine cooperage in Cleveland to provide its refineries with cheap barrels and to pressure master coopers to lower prices.

By the early 1870s, Foran and other Cleveland-area labor leaders, such as Robert Schilling of the CIU and John Fehrenbatch of the blacksmiths' union, concluded that the Industrial Council was strong enough to take a more active role in city and state politics. They realized that such action could better the lives of workingmen and their families by improving access to public education, ensuring police support during strikes, protecting unorganized workers through workplace hour and safety regulations, and enforcing charter provisions that limited the size and activities of corporations. In many cities, such as Cincinnati, workers had successfully formed workingmen's parties, but Cleveland labor leaders thought such an approach would be unwise. The Industrial Council argued that the ties that bound Cleveland workingmen to the traditional parties were too strong. For example, Foran, like most Irish Americans, was a Democrat who was drawn to the party not only by tradition but also by its strong antimonopoly views that stretched back to the days of Andrew Jackson. Other Cleveland workers voted Republican. Fehrenbatch insisted that the Republicans' high tariff policy was the best way to protect U.S. industry and workers from European imports. Rather than convincing workingmen to abandon their old parties for a new one, Cleveland labor leaders developed a nonpartisan strategy that called for workingmen to vote for trade union candidates regardless of party affiliation.

The labor leaders put the strategy into effect in 1872. The Ohio Constitution called for the state's voters to decide every twenty years if they wanted to hold a convention to either write a new constitution or propose changes to the existing one. When Ohio voters ratified the call for a new convention to meet in 1873, Foran announced his candidacy to serve as one of four Cuyahoga county delegates. Recognizing a rising star, the Democratic Party placed Foran on its slate. While most Cleveland voters were Democrats, the county as a whole tended to vote Republican, so Cleveland labor leaders called for Republican workingmen to vote for Foran instead of a certain Republican candidate. The strategy worked as Foran joined three Republicans in the county's delegation.

At the Constitutional Convention, the twenty-eight-year-old Foran, who had begun legal training a year earlier, proved to be an excellent debater, holding his own against some of the state's most accomplished political minds. As one of the youngest and, as he would boast, the poorest of the delegates, Foran fought to protect the economic opportunity of Ohio workingmen, devoting most of his energy to an amendment to prohibit child labor. "There is no greater evil, sapping the foundation of our physical, intellectual, and moral greatness as a people," he declared, "than the practice of employing young children in the factories and workshops." Not only did child labor depress the wages of factory workers, it stunted children's growth, deprived them of an education, destroyed their souls, and made many of them unfit to be citizens. If the nation was going to fulfill its promise of opportunity, Foran insisted that all children spend their days in school rather than working. Foran also lobbied for an amendment requiring the legislature to pass mine and factory safety laws and another to preserve the legislature's ability to pass usury legislation. Although Ohio voters rejected the constitution proposed by the 1873 convention, the experience enhanced Foran's reputation as the state's most articulate champion of labor.

The Industrial Council's success in electing Foran to the Constitutional Convention convinced it to find trade unionists to run as Democrats and Republicans for the General Assembly in the fall of 1873. Both parties claimed to be the party of the workingman and nominated trade unionists to burnish that image. The Democrats, who stressed their antimonopoly tradition, nominated Industrial Council officers Robert Schilling and Thomas Stow, while the Republicans emphasized their support for a high tariff and nominated blacksmiths' union president John Fehrenbatch. Foran became labor's main spokesman during the campaign. At one rally, he orated for an hour and a half, telling workers that they had to elect workingmen to the legislature if they wanted to prevent the type of legislation that had led to the "concentration of wealth into the hands of a few men" and to the impoverishment of the working class. None of labor's candidates were elected that time around, but Fehrenbatch was elected to the Ohio House two years later.

Just when it was looking as though Cleveland's labor movement was emerging as an effective force in the city's politics, the Panic of 1873 began a depression that would last until 1878 and devastate the city's labor movement. With widespread hardship and unemployment, one of the trade unionists' main weapons—the withholding of labor—became nearly useless. Trade unions had little recourse when employers cut wages, and workers saw little advantage to maintaining their memberships. Only a handful of the city's trade unions—the typographers, iron molders, and cigarmakers—were strong enough to survive. The coopers union was one of the first casualties. Barrel-making machinery allowed cooperages to replace skilled journeymen with unskilled and low paid machine operatives further aggravating the effects of the depression. Those journeymen who remained had little bargaining power in their quest for higher wages and better conditions, and for all practical purposes the union ceased to exist past 1874.

The demise of the CIU coincided with Foran's departure from an active role in the labor movement. He passed the bar in 1874 and began practicing law. His real intention, though, was to enter politics. In the spring of 1875, with the support of the Industrial Council, Foran was elected police prosecutor. Seven years later the voters of Cleveland elected him to the first of three terms in Congress where he was, according to historian David Montgomery, labor's most effective advocate. Deciding not to seek reelection in 1888, he returned to Cleveland to practice law. Just before the start of World War I, he reentered the political arena, serving as a Cuyahoga County Common Pleas Court judge until his death in 1921.

Although Cleveland's labor movement was decimated by the depression of the 1870s, Foran helped to create models that Ohio trade unionists—with a few notable exceptions—would use until the rise of industrial unionism in the 1930s. Foran organized workers to fight for what he considered to be their rights on two fronts: the economic and the political. On the economic front, he organized workers along craft lines. Not easily replaced, skilled workers used the collective threat of withholding labor to increase wages and improve working conditions. Since this tactic could not be used by easily replaced, unskilled workers, Foran spent little energy organizing the unskilled, including blacks, immigrants, and women. On the political front, though, Foran sought to protect all Ohio workingmen regardless of skill. His efforts at the 1873 Constitutional Convention to improve educational opportunities, protect borrowers from usury, and require workplace safety legislation offer a clear example of this. When mobilizing workers for political action, Foran understood the loyalty Ohio workers had to traditional parties and worked within the two-party system. Foran saw economic action and political action not as alternatives but as complements. He advised the labor movement to pursue both paths and warned of the dangers of ignoring either. This proved to be insightful advice. From the Gilded Age through the modern era, the state's labor movement flourished when it followed this course and floundered when it did not.

Further Reading

Foran, Martin. *The Other Side, A Social Study Based on Fact.* Cleveland: Ingham, Clarke & Co., 1886.

Gutman, Herbert G. *Power & Culture: Essays on the American Working Class.*
New York: New Press, 1987.

Montgomery, David. *Beyond Equality: Labor and Radical Republicans, 1862–1872.* New York: Knopf, 1967.

Tussey, Jean Y. *An Introduction to the History of the Cleveland Labor Movement, 1865–1929.* Cleveland: United Labor Agency, AFL-CIO, 1996.

14

Benjamin Arnett and the Color Line in Gilded Age Ohio

MICHAEL PIERCE

W ITH WILLIAM McKinley's 1896 election to the presidency, Bishop Benjamin Arnett became the most powerful African American in Ohio and perhaps the nation. Arnett rose from humble origins to this position by serving two constituencies, the African American community and the Republican Party. Not only did he lead two of the most important black institutions in Ohio, the African Methodist Episcopal (AME) Church and Wilberforce University, but he had spent twenty-five years organizing African Americans for the Republicans.

By mobilizing both constituencies, Arnett accomplished astonishing things. In the 1880s, for example, he won election to the Ohio General Assembly from an 85 percent white county, helped pass legislation desegregating the state's public schools, and convinced the General Assembly to provide the financial support needed to allow Wilberforce to survive. During the 1896 presidential campaign, Arnett had served McKinley and the Republicans, speaking at rallies and coordinating the campaign among African Americans. After the election, African Americans considered Arnett to be their most effective advocate with the new administration as well as the gatekeeper for blacks seeking federal appointments. Arnett looked forward to the new administration knowing that McKinley, with whom he had worked for decades, had defended African American rights at great political risk.

Arnett's high hopes gave way to disappointment. After the election, the goals of Arnett's two constituencies—the African American community and the Republican Party—began to diverge. Seeking to heal the tensions between North and South, McKinley's administration

FIG. 10 Bishop Benjamin Arnet and family.
From Lucretia Newman Coleman, *Poor Ben: A Story of Real Life* (Nashville:
Publication of the AME Sunday School Union, 1890), 132.

turned its back on the nation's blacks, ignoring some of the most outrageous violations of civil rights since Reconstruction. Arnett was
caught in the middle. Having devoted his career to both constituencies, he was not ready to abandon either. Like a tragic figure, Arnett
was unable to please either side and fell from grace in the eyes of both.
The five years of McKinley's presidency transformed Arnett from one
of the African American community's most powerful figures into one
of its most abused.

Those who knew Arnett characterized him as a man driven by
ambition. Writing in the late 1950s about events over sixty years in
the past, the scholar and activist W. E. B. DuBois still had vivid memories of Arnett and his will to power. DuBois described him as a
"ruthless politician" and a "thick-set man with a sharp, dark face, a
blazing eye, a rare smile and a will to do." Although DuBois personally disliked Arnett, who forced him to leave a teaching position at
Wilberforce, he had a grudging respect for Arnett, grouping him with

the men who "with high ideals and brute force" had transformed Wilberforce into "a force in the whole nation."

Information about Arnett's early life comes from his biographer, Lucretia Coleman, who obviously worked very closely with Arnett. Published in 1890 by the AME Church, the biography reveals as much about Arnett at that time as it does about his past. Arnett was born on March 6, 1838, in Brownsville, Pennsylvania, about fifty miles south of Pittsburgh. At the intersection of the National Road and the Monongahela River, Brownsville was an important mercantile hub for the region, and its factories built many of the keel and steamboats that worked the Ohio and Mississippi Rivers.

Coleman did not mention how Arnett's family earned a living, but this is hardly surprising. Because of limited opportunities, few African Americans defined themselves in terms of occupation, preferring instead to emphasize relationships with voluntary organizations, especially churches. Arnett's parents were devout members of the AME Church. His father provided the land for the local church, served as a trustee and steward for thirty years, and taught Sunday school for twenty-five. His father was seven-eighths African American and one-eighth Irish, while his mother was six-eighths Scottish, one-eighth African American, and one-eighth Native American. Arnett was proud of his mixed-race heritage and saw it as proof of the existence of a more harmonious time when the color line was more porous.

The oldest of eight children, Arnett began working as an eight-year-old to augment the family's income. Only when he was eleven did Arnett begin his formal education in the classroom of his uncle, Ephraim Arnett. Happy for the opportunity, Arnett excelled at school, quickly learning the rudiments of reading, math, and penmanship. Although his formal education ended after a few terms, Arnett continued to devote much of his leisure time to the study of natural science, history, and literature.

Through Coleman, Arnett presented his childhood as free of racism and Brownsville as a place where the races easily socialized. His friends and neighbors included both whites and blacks. When the family's house burned down, the entire community helped the family rebuild. Coleman and Arnett made no mention of the fact that blacks could not vote because Pennsylvania disfranchised them in 1838 or of the growing antiblack sentiment that was sweeping the North from the mid-1830s onwards. The situation was actually so grim for northern blacks that one observer noted, "they are pariahs,

debarred from every fellowship save with their own despised race . . .
all tongues have learned to turn the very name of their race into an
insult." By reconstructing his past as free of racism, Arnett was suggesting that the racism of the late nineteenth century was a social construction—that racism was not God-given or natural but was created
by humans. The implication was that if humans created racism, they
could end it.

In the early 1850s, Arnett found work on the steamboats that
plied the Monongahela River between Pittsburgh and Morgantown,
Virginia (now West Virginia). Beginning in the kitchen, one of the
few areas open to African Americans, Arnett gradually worked his way
from helper to managing the boat's commissary. Ship captains recognized his hard work and recruited him for larger boats that fre-
quented the busy ports of Louisville, Cincinnati, St. Louis, St. Paul,
and New Orleans. During the winter, when the rivers were frozen,
Arnett found work as a waiter at one of Pittsburgh's large hotels.

In the late fall of 1856, tragedy struck Arnett. He was working on
a steamboat traveling the upper reaches of the Mississippi when the
ice flows became heavy. In a rush to unload cargo and head south
before the river froze over, Arnett slipped, injuring his ankle, which
became infected, swelling to eighteen inches in diameter. Unable to
give up working, Arnett continued using the ankle until the infection
had spread throughout his lower leg, forcing him to return to
Brownsville in late 1857. Rest and his mother's care did not help the
leg, which was amputated in March 1858. The amputation brought
out the benevolence of the entire community. Coleman writes: "All
the prominent whites citizens as well as his colored friends, came with
flowers, delicacies, and warm and sympathizing hearts, to ask after
and assist in watching over Poor Ben." More importantly, the town
collected over $100 to buy him an artificial leg.

While recuperating, Arnett visited relatives and met Mary Louise
Gordon, the niece of his uncle's wife. It was love at first sight, according to Arnett: "From the first day I plainly saw that she loved me and
she plainly saw my love for her." After a brief courtship, the couple
married on May 25, 1858. By all accounts, the marriage proved to be
happy and fruitful; the couple produced seven children. A devoted
and attentive father, Arnett gave his children important advantages
that he had never known—formal education, the ability to escape the
drudgeries of child labor, and a middle-class home. The children,
however, had trouble finding their way and relied on their father for
support and jobs. Arnett's zeal to help his children and his children's

inability to take advantage of the opportunities their father provided proved to be detrimental to Arnett's career. According to DuBois, Arnett's main flaw was that he was "handicapped by his family."

Marriage forced Arnett to reevaluate his life and future. Until that time he had lived life as it had come, not looking beyond the next few weeks or months, but now he had a wife to worry about. With an artificial leg, he could not earn a living working the steamboats, waiting tables in hotels, or at any other job requiring physical labor. He needed to find an occupation where the loss of a leg would not be a handicap, so he turned to teaching, one of the few such occupations open to African Americans. Although Arnett had had little formal education, he had studied McGuffey's *Reader,* Harvey's *Grammar,* and Clark's *Analysis* in his spare time and had little difficulty convincing local school officials of his talents. Receiving his teaching certificate in December 1859, Arnett would earn his living in the classroom for the next twelve years.

Arnett's injury made military service during the Civil War impossible, but the war marked a turning point in his life as it awakened his racial consciousness and pushed him into the public arena. He joined the Equal Rights League, an early civil rights organization that was founded in 1864 to "advance the political, moral, and educational status of African Americans." As a district leader, and later national official, Arnett learned to debate and speak in public, skills that would propel his career as a preacher and politician.

Toward the end of the Civil War, Arnett moved to Washington, D.C., to become the principal at the African Civilization Society school. While there he became ordained as a minister in the AME Church. The largest of the African American denominations, the AME Church was founded in the first decades of the nineteenth century by northern blacks who felt unwelcomed and ignored within white-dominated Methodist churches. As one of the few institutions that provided blacks with the opportunity to develop leadership and organizational skills, the church and its ministers quickly became pillars within northern African American communities.

Arnett moved to Ohio in 1867 to take a pulpit and teaching position in Walnut Hills near Cincinnati. At the time of his arrival the state's African American population was booming as thousands of former slaves migrated north. Between 1850 and 1870, the state's black population more than doubled from 25,279 to 63,213 and increased from 1.3 percent of the state's population to 2.4 percent. While Ohio was much more hospitable than southern states, the state had a long history of racial intolerance. Believing African Americans to be by nature lazy, immoral, stupid, and irresponsible, most white Ohioans thought that blacks lacked the ability to become productive citizens and envisioned the state as a land for whites only. The state's constitution limited suffrage to white males, declaring "No Negro or mulatto shall ever be eligible for any office, civil or military, or give their oath in any court of justice against a white person." Later, the General Assembly required blacks moving into the state to post a $500 bond that would be used to provide support if the family became destitute. African American children were not allowed to attend public schools until 1848, and after that most attended segregated schools.

Arnett stayed at the Walnut Hills church for three years before moving to Toledo in 1870 and then to Cincinnati in 1873. In 1876, Arnett took a pulpit in Urbana where he remained until moving to Columbus in late 1878. In each city, Arnett took an active role in the community, joining fraternal organizations, helping to establish programs at YMCAs, and organizing African Americans for the Republican Party. In Toledo, he made history as the first black foreman of an otherwise all white jury. As he moved from church to church, Arnett gained contacts and allies that helped him rise in the AME hierarchy. The AME General Conference elected him assistant secretary in 1872 and secretary-in-chief in 1876.

Arnett's 1867 arrival in Ohio coincided with the state's debate over African American suffrage. That year the General Assembly submitted a constitutional amendment to the voters calling for the enfranchisement of male African Americans and the disfranchisement of those who had borne arms against the Union or had deserted the military. Republicans, led by gubernatorial nominee Rutherford B. Hayes, campaigned for the amendment, while the state's Democrats centered their platform on opposition to African American rights and Congressional Reconstruction. The campaign became quite nasty. Playing on white fears of black sexual aggression, one Democratic rally featured what observers called the parade of virgins, young white girls under a banner reading "Fathers, save us from Negro equality." The Republicans countered with slogans such as "Honest black men are preferable to white traitors" and "Democrats murdered our President."

While Hayes narrowly won the governorship, the suffrage amendment went down to defeat 216,987 to 255,340, and the Democrats took control of the General Assembly. The Democratic assembly quickly rescinded the state's ratification of the Fourteenth

Amendment to the U.S. Constitution, granting African Americans citizenship and civil rights. Congress and the secretary of state, however, ignored the action and included Ohio in the three-fourths of the states needed for approval. The Democrats also passed legislation to disfranchise mixed-race Ohioans who had been granted the right to vote by an 1860 Ohio Supreme Court decision. Universal male suffrage did not come to Ohio until after the 1869 election. Republicans regained control of the General Assembly that year and narrowly ratified the Fifteenth Amendment to the U.S. Constitution, which said that suffrage could not be denied on the basis of race or previous condition of servitude.

The debates over African American suffrage pushed Arnett into politics. By the early 1870s, Arnett had become a prominent figure in the Ohio Republican Party, traveling throughout the state, speaking to both African American and mixed audiences, and building political alliances. In 1872 alone, he gave thirty-two speeches supporting Ulysses S. Grant's presidential campaign and similar numbers for Hayes in 1876 and James A. Garfield in 1880. In nonpresidential years, he spoke on behalf of scores of Republican candidates for governor, Congress, and the General Assembly. Arnett's work for the Republicans extended outside the borders of the state. His position within the AME Church required him to travel throughout the nation, but especially the South, where he established political contacts and helped set up Republican clubs. These activities helped Ohio Republicans gain the support of African American–dominated southern delegations at Republican national conventions throughout the 1870s and 1880s.

By all accounts, Arnett was an electrifying speaker. The *Toledo Blade* praised his "wit, logic and stirring appeal," while the *Kenton Republican* credited Arnett with "the most thoroughly logical and comprehensive speech made here during the campaign." Most of Arnett's speeches centered on the Republican civil rights record. He warned a Toledo audience that if elected, the Democrats would again "rivet the chains of slavery" upon the nation's African Americans. Arnett made the goals of political action clear; he wanted members of his race to be judged by their actions rather than their skin color. He told a Columbus crowd, "What we want is that everyone stand on his merits or demerits. . . . [W]e say judge each individual of our race as is done in all other cases and to all other races."

If blacks were to be judged by their actions, Arnett sought to make sure that they measured up. He told African Americans that they had to reform themselves and take control over their own lives if they were to get ahead. Not only would self-improvement convince whites that they deserved equal opportunities, but it would make African Americans better people in the eyes of God and the nation. He simplified his message into four steps:

- **FIRST.** Get religion; that will give you communion with God.
- **SECOND.** Get knowledge or education; that will enable you to control the forces of nature.
- **THIRD.** Get money, houses, and land; that will give you power with men.
- **FOURTH.** Get integrity; this gives you power over yourselves. It will enable you to keep your religion, to use your education properly, and give your money for good objects.

In 1880, the AME's General Conference elected Arnett both secretary-in-chief and financial secretary. His duties included keeping the church's records, editing their publications, and balancing the books. With the new position, he moved his family to the center of AME activities, the town of Wilberforce, about three miles from Xenia in Greene County. The location was originally the site of a 350-room resort hotel called Tawawa Springs. In the 1820s and early 1830s, slave holders, their concubines, and their children comprised most of the hotel's guests. The growth of abolitionism in Ohio and the financial panic of 1837 conspired to drive the hotel out of business, but a group of slaveholders bought the site, transforming it into a school for their mixed-race children. In the 1850s, the school was bought by white Methodists from the area, who renamed it after British abolitionist William Wilberforce and incorporated it as a university. The AME Church bought Wilberforce in 1863 for $10,000 and transformed it into the flagship school of the nation's oldest African American denomination.

At the time of Arnett's arrival, Xenia and Greene County had the highest proportion of African Americans in the state. 1,943 (28 percent) of Xenia's 7,026 residents were African Americans, while in the county as a whole African Americans comprised 3,815 (14 percent) of the 28,014 residents. Within Xenia, African Americans attended segregated schools and churches, lived within concentrated areas, and tended to be less prosperous and less educated than their white neighbors. Nonetheless, the area offered African Americans greater opportunities than almost anywhere else in the nation. There was a substantial middle class; schools, though segregated, were well-funded; and the community voted regularly, giving it an important voice in civic affairs.

In the early 1880s, Wilberforce University, which had never been on firm financial footing, teetered on the verge of insolvency. The school's administration recognized that impoverished AME churches and their congregations did not have the resources to adequately fund the school and decided to seek state money. To gain an effective voice in the General Assembly, the school's faculty and administration called for the Republican Party to nominate Arnett for the Ohio House of Representatives. In early 1885, Arnett's supporters circulated a petition among Greene County Republicans reminding them that African Americans comprised a quarter of the party's faithful and hinting of a possible defection unless Arnett received the nomination. After what one newspaper described as a "bitter contest," Arnett received the Republican nomination, which, given the county's strong Republican majority, ensured success in the general election.

As a legislator, Arnett devoted his energies to the successful passage of two measures: approval of state funding for Wilberforce University and the repeal of a law requiring the racial segregation of public schools, a measure that came to be known as the Arnett Bill. Unlike the 1891 effort to secure Wilberforce a portion of the federal funds allocated under the second Morrill Act, the attempt to secure state monies for the school generated little controversy among African Americans. Whereas in 1891 many African Americans, led by Cleveland legislator John P. Green, argued that public funding of all-black Wilberforce perpetuated the color line, in 1887 the need to keep the school afloat and provide opportunities for African American students overrode those concerns. To secure passage, Arnett presented the legislature with a petition signed by major politicians of both parties as well as prominent business and community leaders of both races. Arnett cleverly constructed the legislation to avoid the thorny issue of state funding of a religious college. The legislation called for funding a "Combined Normal and Industrial Department at Wilberforce." The choice of "at" was deliberate. The new department was to have a separate legal existence with its own board of trustees, but function as part of Wilberforce. In the first year, the legislature provided $5,000 to Wilberforce, but that amount steadily grew, accounting for nearly two-thirds of the university's 1900 budget. State aid continued until 1942 when the state severed the Combined Normal and Industrial Department from Wilberforce, creating Central State University.

The effort to desegregate the state's public schools was already underway when Arnett entered the General Assembly. Led by Columbus city councilman James Poindexter and *Cleveland Gazette* editor Harry Smith, African Americans had been lobbying for school desegregation for over a decade and had already convinced influential politicians to join the fight. The previous governor, Democrat George Hoadly, had broken with his party's traditional opposition to civil rights legislation to call for the "repeal of all laws discriminating among citizens on account of color." Hoadly complained that not only were African American schools "often inferior" and "inconveniently remote," they stamped the children with "a badge of servitude" and made them feel "unworthy of equal privileges." While Hoadly was defeated in his 1885 reelection bid, his successor, Republican Joseph Benson Foraker, insisted that "our colored fellow-citizens must have the same rights and same opportunities for education and self-elevation that other citizens have."

The effort to desegregate Ohio's schools aroused opposition from within the African American community. A few black leaders feared (correctly as it turned out) that integration would lead to the firing of African American teachers and administrators. As one African American newspaper insisted, "We prefer separate schools with colored teachers to mixed schools without them." More importantly, opponents insisted that white teachers were more likely to ignore African American students and fail to protect black students from insults and harassment.

In the end, Arnett and his allies mustered enough support to overcome the opposition of traditional Democrats and African Americans fearful of the unintended consequences of integration. In the General Assembly, nearly one-half of the Democrats joined the entire Republican delegation in voting to repeal the segregation law. The repeal set off celebrations throughout the state. In Springfield, Arnett told a mostly African American crowd that the passage of the legislation made African Americans responsible for their own fate and that they no longer had discrimination to blame for their shortcomings: "The schools are open; the churches are open; and the penitentiary is open. What I mean my friends is this; if you do wrong they will punish you as other men; it you do right they will honor you. But the opportunities, blessings, and privileges of this day bring with them corresponding responsibilities; and to make this victory secure, our race must vindicate itself in the State and country."

The celebrations over desegregation, though, proved to be short lived. In city after city, school boards redrew district lines and school boundaries in order to maintain racial division. The *Cleveland Gazette,* the state's most influential black newspaper, reported that in Xenia, "A zig-zag line has been so skillfully run that all of the colored children are thrown into one school and all of the white children into another. . . . [T]he color line is drawn about as clearly as ever."

In March 1887, Arnett announced that he would not seek reelection to the General Assembly. AME bishop J. P. Shorter had recently died, and Arnett expected to succeed him as the presiding bishop of the church's third district, which encompassed Ohio, California, and part of Pennsylvania. He told friends that his new duties would preclude another term and returned to Wilberforce to take up his new duties. In fact, Arnett would have had a difficult time regaining the Republican nomination. His fight to end segregation violated a tacit agreement he made two years earlier with Greene County Republicans. It appears that a majority of white Greene County voters had no problem with an African American representing them in the General Assembly, but they did not want their children attending school with black children. This is not surprising. White Ohioans have generally been more supportive of African American political rights than efforts to integrate schools and job sites.

The passage of the Arnett Bill marked the high point of race relations in nineteenth-century Ohio, according to historian David Gerber. Although the state never disfranchised African Americans or enacted segregation measures, beginning in the early 1890s Ohio witnessed an increase in both violence directed toward blacks and de facto segregation of public facilities. White mobs lynched black men in Oxford, Bellefontaine, New Richmond, and Adams County in the early and mid-1890s, and many more would have met the same fate if Governor William McKinley had not dispatched state troops to protect black prisoners on several occasions. In 1894, African American legislators, supported by McKinley and the Republican Party, passed legislation making communities financially liable for lynchings. Although the law proved to be ineffective, its passage signaled the Republicans' continued support for African American rights.

McKinley's strong statements against lynching, willingness to use state troops to protect blacks, and support for civil rights legislation made him extremely popular within Ohio's African American community. During McKinley's 1896 presidential campaign, the state's black leaders, including Arnett, lined up to support him. Arnett vied with John Green and George Myers for key African American positions in McKinley's presidential campaign and a future administration.

Although Green and Myers worked tirelessly for McKinley, their net-work of African American activists was limited to Ohio and a few northern states where blacks made up a relatively small segment of the Republican Party and an even smaller part of the electorate. Arnett's ties to the AME Church gave him a much more extensive network of activists, especially in the South. Even though African American suf-frage in the South was often limited and southern states voted over-whelmingly Democratic, Arnett's southern ties were important because these states held disproportionate power at national Republi-can conventions where votes were apportioned on the basis of popu-lation rather than the number of Republican voters. Understanding Arnett's value in keeping the support of southern Republicans, Hanna and McKinley appointed Arnett associates to key campaign posts, including son Henry, who ran the black campaign in Ohio.

McKinley's landslide election made Arnett the most powerful African American in Ohio and possibly the nation, but it also con-tained the seeds of his demise. After the election, African Americans seeking federal jobs besieged Arnett reminding him of earlier promises and efforts for the party. Even though McKinley provided more posi-tions to African Americans than any previous president, the number of applicants greatly exceeded the number of posts. Those unable to secure patronage blamed Arnett, who was seen as McKinley's gate-keeper. One black paper criticized Arnett for helping a Congregation-alist when "A.M.E. brethren have not been given places," while another charged him with hypocrisy for favoring a certain candidate.

The fact that many of the choicest positions went to Arnett's fam-ily and close friends exacerbated the problem. Arnett secured a chap-laincy in the Army for his son Ben and a federal clerkship for son Henry. The latter appointment provoked a sarcastic comment from a black newspaper: "Bishop Arnett rendered the race another great ser-vice when he secured his son a clerkship." Most controversially, Arnett's friend and attorney, Campbell Maxwell, received one of the best positions reserved for African Americans, ambassador to Santa Domingo. Prominent African Americans, especially those in the Myers-Green faction of the Ohio Republican Party, complained that Maxwell and many others were not being rewarded for service to the party or race but for their service to Arnett.

More troubling for Arnett's reputation, though, was the adminis-tration's indifference to violations of African American rights. Want-ing to heal "the feeling of distrust and hostility" between North and South, McKinley remained silent as incidents of racial violence increased throughout the nation, but especially in the South. He ignored calls from the African American press to denounce civil rights violations such as the lynching of an African American postmaster and his family in South Carolina, the disfranchisement of black voters by the Louisiana legislature, and the intimidation and murder of African American voters in Wilmington, North Carolina. Black newspapers, including the *Cleveland Gazette* and the *Columbus Vindicator,* began to openly criticize the president and his closest African American adviser.

The final blow to Arnett's reputation came during McKinley's 1900 reelection campaign when the *Ohio State Journal,* whose editor was close to the administration, reported that the president had deleted a strong denunciation of lynching from a major address at Arnett's suggestion. Insisting that African American criticism of McKinley was unfair, the paper claimed that the president was simply heeding Arnett's warning that such a denunciation "would do no good and might even do harm to the Negro cause." Whether Arnett offered such advice or the administration fabricated the story to deflect criticism remains unknown, but Arnett paid the price. Throughout the nation African American newspapers excoriated Arnett, calling for him to explain his comments. He never did. To have denied making the statement would have alienated him from the president, while to have acknowledged it would have further eroded his standing in the black community.

Arnett's increasing unpopularity within the African American community undercut his usefulness to McKinley, and administration sought other African American leaders who could deliver votes and support. With McKinley's 1901 assassination, Arnett faded from the political scene altogether. He devoted his remaining years to Wilberforce and AME affairs. After a long illness, he died in October 1906. As befitting a disgraced leader, the *Cleveland Gazette's* obituary simply listed his achievements and offices. There were no testaments to his greatness and character or moving accounts of his accomplishments and service.

The failure of the type of leadership offered by Arnett prompted African American leaders of the early twentieth century to be wary of political alliances with whites. While alliances with the Republicans had enabled African Americans to gain the right to vote, elect representatives to legislative bodies, and pass civil rights legislation, they had left the black community dependent upon the actions of often-unreliable white leaders such as McKinley. Anxious not to repeat the same mistake, black leaders, such as DuBois, Booker T. Washington, and Marcus Garvey, sought to develop power from within the African American community. Although these men offered vastly different approaches, they agreed that lasting change could be achieved only when the black community was not dependent on the actions of whites.

Further Reading

Coleman, Lucretia H. Newman. *Poor Ben: A Story of Real Life*. Nashville: A.M.E. Sunday-School Union, 1890.

DuBois, W. E. B. *The Autobiography*. New York: International Publishers Co., 1968.

Gerber, David A. *Black Ohio and the Color Line, 1860–1915*. Urbana: University of Illinois Press, 1976.

Meier, August. *Negro Thought in America, 1880–1915*. Ann Arbor: University of Michigan Press, 1963.

15

Tom L. Johnson and Progressive Reform in Cleveland

ANDREW R. L. CAYTON

I N THE first decade of the twentieth century, visitors passing
through the foyer of the large house at 2343 Euclid Avenue in
Cleveland entered a great hall dominated by a massive twelve-foot
fireplace. Among the array of couches and seats surrounding the
fireplace was an armchair off to the side reserved for Tom L. Johnson, owner of the house and mayor of the city of Cleveland. From
this comfortable perch, Johnson presided over many lively conver-
sations; here the mayor and his wife, Maggie, welcomed politicians
and journalists, such as William Jennings Bryan, Lincoln Steffens,
Ida Mae Tarbell, Henry George, Samuel L. Jones, and Clarence
Darrow; and here Johnson met with his "kitchen cabinet" of advis-
ers, including Peter Witt, Newton Baker, and Frederick Howe.
Beyond the great hall, guests and their families enjoyed suppers,
picnics, masquerade balls, and skating on an ice rink. Adding to the
excitement were the Johnson children, Loftin and Bessie, who were
devoting their twenties to experimenting with a range of careers and
diversions.

Loftin and Bessie came by their enthusiasms naturally. Weighing
just under 230 pounds and standing 5' 7" tall, Tom Johnson was
incapable of restraining himself. He was perpetually busy with one
ambitious project after another. If he wasn't inventing a magnetic railway car in his basement, he was developing a trout farm in the countryside, playing golf, or following professional baseball. One of the
first people in Cleveland to own an automobile, Johnson liked to
careen around the city with more speed than caution. At the end of
the day, nothing interested the mayor more than the combination of
good food and stimulating conversation. Some people found the

FIG. 11 Tom L. Johnson.
Courtesy of the Ohio Historical Society.

mayor exhausting. But the young men who joined his administration
and visited his home admired him as much for his energetic engagement with the world around him as for his political achievements.

Johnson broke the mold of Ohio reformers. Most of the many
men and women who had advocated change in the nineteenth century were northerners; either they or their parents were from New
England. Most were devout Congregationalists, Presbyterians, and
Methodists who infused their calls for the improvement of mankind
with deep emotional fervor. Viewed from the perspective of the early
twenty-first century, Ohio's nineteenth-century reformers seem
humorless at best. Much as we admire their opposition to slavery,
their zeal sometimes resembled fanaticism and their insistence on
self-discipline a call for repression. For them, the reform of human
beings and their surroundings was a moral imperative. If only individuals would choose to control themselves, to learn through education, religion, and self-restraint to behave in a respectable fashion,
they would become model citizens interested not simply in their own
welfare but in the welfare of the larger political communities of

which they were members. Ohio's future depended on the personal morality of its citizens.

Tom Johnson also believed in the importance of creating good citizens. Like several U.S. mayors at the turn of the twentieth century, he wanted the people of Cleveland to think of themselves as participants in a larger world that extended far beyond their families and neighborhoods. Johnson worried that corruption and monopoly were destroying the promise of the American dream of a land of relatively equal opportunity for decent white men. But, unlike most nineteenth-century Ohio reformers, Johnson concentrated on economic rather than moral change as the best way to improve the world. Rather than exhort people to make themselves better citizens through self-restraint, Johnson sought to transform the environment in which they lived. The key to reform was the creation of a public world that would attract and sustain the commitment of its members. A Cleveland freed of monopoly and corruption, a Cleveland dotted with public buildings and public parks, a Cleveland famous for museums and music as well as industry and commerce, would be a Cleveland that its citizens would embrace and cherish.

While Johnson was only moderately successful in achieving his goals and died shortly after being defeated for reelection in 1907, he embodied an alternative model of reform that anticipated the popularity of less ascetic ideas of twentieth-century American life. Johnson behaved in public as he did in private. Life was about self-fulfillment, not self-sacrifice. The important thing was to engage the world in which you lived. His critics thought him hypocritical, a businessman reformer, a hedonistic politician. Yet what Johnson stood for more than anything else was the ideal of a city that encouraged its citizens to think broadly, to welcome new ideas, to treat each other with respect, and to have a good time doing all of these things.

One night, Mayor Johnson welcomed into his home William Jennings Bryan, who, as the nominee of the Democratic Party in 1896, had lost the presidency to Republican William McKinley. Many attributed the outcome of the election not only to Bryan's controversial support for free silver but to his self-righteous style. A famed orator, Bryan was a committed evangelical. He alienated some traditionally Democratic Catholic and immigrant voters, a weakness exploited by McKinley and his chief strategist Mark Hanna through their emphasis on economic rather than cultural issues. At dinner, Johnson asked Bryan what he would do about trusts and monopolies in the United States if he had absolute power. According to Johnson's associate, Frederick C. Howe, Bryan said that he would regulate business through the enforcement of laws and the appointment of good officials. "The trouble," according to Bryan, was "that government does not use its power vigorously." Howe thought this meant that Bryan intended to accomplish reform by giving power to good men and punishing evil ones.

Johnson, on the other hand, knew that corporations had the money and the legal talent to outmaneuver any legislative prohibition. The only way to change things was to take away the means by which corporations obtained privilege. Echoing his hero Henry George, Johnson explained that the solution lay in destroying monopoly through competition. If government taxed all land at its full value (including unearned income), established free trade, abolished patent rights, and controlled transportation as a public utility, monopoly would cease to exist. Instead of trying to reform people, Americans should reform institutions. Creating an environment that encouraged competition rather than monopoly would go a long way toward eliminating corruption and privilege. More democracy on the local level would float all boats.

These ideas emerged naturally out of Johnson's origins as a Southerner and a Democrat, although little in his early career as a businessman suggested that he would become famous as a reformer. Born at Blue Spring near Georgetown, Kentucky, on July 18, 1854, Tom Johnson was the son of a planter and his wife who owned more than one hundred enslaved African Americans and divided their time between Kentucky and Arkansas. His father became a colonel in the Confederate Army during the Civil War; his family accompanied him as he fought in Georgia and then in Virginia. After the war, the Johnsons settled about eighteen miles south of Louisville, Kentucky. Because the family was now relatively poor, Tom went to work in a rolling mill at the age of fourteen. Within months, relatives offered him a job in the office of the Fourth and Walnut Street Lines in Louisville, one of several enterprises using horse-drawn carriages to convey the residents of the rapidly expanding city. Not only did the young man prove adept at keeping the company's books, he invented several improvements, the most important of which was the farebox. Johnson devised a box in which deposited coins were held on a glass shelf until the conductor released them into a metal container. Eventually, Johnson made more than $20,000 from the farebox, on which he had secured a patent. In 1876, when he was twenty-two, Johnson bought the Citizens Street Railway Company in Indianapolis. While he genuinely tried to improve service, he was primarily an aggressive businessman. Johnson began to buy struggling streetcar companies, fix them up, and then sell them for more than they were worth.

By 1879, the young entrepreneur was considering the possibilities of Cleveland. With eight streetcar companies and an exploding population, the city seemed a logical place for a young man of Johnson's energy and expertise to establish himself. In 1880, Johnson paid $8,000 for the Brooklyn Street Railroad Company. Over the next several years, as he bought other companies, he battled with streetcar operators, including Mark Hanna, to create a through line from one side of Cleveland to the other. The problem was that the streetcar lines owned different parts of the city. Thus, Hanna, who owned a streetcar that ran directly into the center of the city, made it difficult for someone like Johnson to make money. All of Johnson's customers had to get off his cars, board Hanna's, and pay another fare to get downtown. In 1883, a City Council that had been pressured illegally as well as legally by all sides, granted Johnson the first through line in Cleveland. It ran from the old viaduct to the Square and out to East 55th Street. In the same year, Johnson confirmed the importance of Cleveland in his business operations by moving his family from Indianapolis.

Two years later, Johnson's acquisition of a twenty-five-year franchise renewal on one of his companies marked him as one of the most powerful men in Cleveland. He now controlled the streetcar business in the southern part of the city. Johnson rejected Hanna's offer of a partnership because he knew that he could make more money on his own. Not only was the rapid growth of Cleveland expanding the demand for streetcars, the replacement of horses with electricity and cable systems were transforming urban transportation patterns. In the 1880s and 1890s, bolder and wealthier companies began to buy out their weaker competitors; Johnson expertly played this game. While most Americans were reeling from the severe economic depression of the mid-1890s, Johnson made a huge profit when he finally sold his Cleveland streetcar companies in 1894 and 1895. By 1905, he was out of the business entirely, having divested himself of his holdings in streetcar companies in Detroit and Lorain. In a quarter of a century, Johnson had turned an investment of a few thousand dollars into a fortune worth several million dollars.

As Tom Johnson's interest in business declined, his interest in politics increased. Like many of his contemporaries, he worried about the impact of rapid, large-scale industrialization, urbanization, and immigration on the United States, especially in eating away the bonds of citizenship that he and others believed were the ligaments of democratic communities. Cleveland in 1900 was bursting with energy, a smoky and noisy conglomeration of peoples living together in a place that had sprung up almost overnight around the mouth of the Cuyahoga River.

Founded in 1796, Cleveland took off in the 1830s with the opening of the Ohio and Erie Canal. The city thrived as a crucial point in a huge commercial network that extended from the Ohio Valley to Lake Erie, east over the Erie Canal to the Hudson River, and south to New York City and the Atlantic world beyond. The construction of railroads in the 1850s and a burgeoning demand for iron and oil products during the Civil War ignited rapid industrial development. Steel mills appeared in the Flats and Clevelander John D. Rockefeller built an empire refining oil brought from western Pennsylvania.

With demand for labor high, Cleveland attracted tens of thousands of immigrants from all over Europe in the late 1800s. Like other cities, it grew at a rate far beyond the capacity of any institution, public or private, to keep up with. In the 1880s, Cleveland's population expanded by 63.2 percent and in the 1890s by 46.1 percent. A city of 92,829 in 1870 became a city of 381,768 in 1900. At the dawn of the twentieth century, Cleveland was the seventh largest city in the United States, producing roughly $140,000,000 worth of manufactured goods each year. In the wake of this growth followed a host of problems: poverty, disease, and miserable living conditions. No one was able to provide the basic services required by such a huge mass of people. Providing water, health, sanitation, and transportation was a challenge, usually haphazard at best.

Cleveland, like other cities, was a collection of neighborhoods. While the affluent northern Protestants congregated in mansions along Euclid Avenue, immigrants clustered in ethnic enclaves built around work, churches, and saloons. By 1900, more than forty languages were spoken in Cleveland. Three-quarters of the population were either first- or second-generation immigrants, mainly from southern and eastern Europe. Italians, Hungarians, Poles, Czechs, Slovenes, Greeks, Austrians, and Jews lived near each other, maintaining their own customs, languages, and beliefs. African Americans constituted a small but significant percentage (about 1.6 percent) of the total population. While many middle-class Protestants worried about the disintegration of the city into self-contained parochial communities that had little or no contact with each other, Cleveland was a remarkably diverse city with many citizens who insisted on maintaining their ways of doing things and passing them onto their children. In the early 1890s, middle- and upper-class Protestants, who tended to support Republican candidates, secured reform of the public school system in order to encourage immigrant children to assimilate into their way of life. Catholic and Jewish residents who became citizens of the United States, on the other hand, tended to support Democrats because of their commitment to local autonomy and weak government.

Although Tom Johnson took advantage of the transformation of Cleveland to build a personal fortune, he and his family remained relatively isolated in their own cultural enclave in the affluent world of Euclid Avenue. His life, with its elegant house, skating rink, and business operations throughout the country, was worlds away from that of most of his fellow citizens. Nevertheless, Johnson had the instinct of a populist. Extraordinarily gregarious, he loved talking with all kinds of people. If his solutions to Cleveland's problems were simplistic, they were rooted in his energetic commitment to making the city a better place to live.

Johnson slowly got out of business in the 1890s because he was quickly getting involved in politics. The catalyst for this major change in his life, he later recalled, was a chance encounter with the writings of Henry George. He bought a copy of George's *Social Problems* to while away a tedious train trip from Indianapolis to Cleveland in 1883. Intrigued by George's ideas, Johnson bought George's most famous book, *Progress and Poverty,* and devoured it. Two years later, on a trip to New York City, he met George, and they became good friends. The writer became a regular visitor to the Johnsons' Euclid Avenue home. Johnson's friend was one of the leading social critics of late-nineteenth-century America. Born in Philadelphia in 1839, George had worked as a printer and journalist in California before setting his sights on the problem of poverty in the industrializing United States. Years of study had persuaded George that the best way to deal with poverty and other social ills was a Single Tax on land. He believed that land essentially belonged to communities and that individuals should only benefit from what their labor created. With all other taxes abolished, a tax on the value of land minus the value of improvements would undermine monopoly and privilege while it encouraged competition and responsibility. Taxing land would prevent the concentration of wealth.

Bored with transforming companies into profit-making machines, the energetic Johnson took up the Single Tax cause with the fervor of a religious convert. He later claimed that he wanted to get out of business immediately but that George convinced him otherwise. "Stay in business," the writer urged the businessman. "Make all the money you can, even if you do not believe in the methods of getting riches: for in your case these same riches, taken from the people by the laws giving special privileges, will be used for the common good, in overthrowing those same laws." Johnson took that advice until George's death in 1897. In the meantime, he got into politics. In 1888, he ran for Congress as a Democrat and lost. Two years later, he won a seat that he held until 1895.

As influential as George was in shaping Johnson's political philosophy, he was very much a Southern Democrat in the tradition of Thomas Jefferson and Andrew Jackson; George merely focused his beliefs. Johnson fought for issues that had preoccupied Southern Democrats throughout the nineteenth century: local control, free trade, death to privilege, and equal justice for white men. When he decided to run for mayor of Cleveland in early 1901, Johnson proclaimed his commitment to "a great principle" associated with the Democratic Party, "that of equal rights and equal justice to all and special privileges to none." He pledged himself to seeing that "every privilege granted by law to an individual should be stricken from the statute books." As he wrote in his autobiography, "the greatest movement in the world" was "the struggle of the people against Privilege."

Whether in Congress or in city hall, Johnson lived by that credo. He was like a Jacksonian Democrat in his battle against the "monsters" of privilege and corruption. George's Single Tax was a way of summarizing a plan of action that called for a restoration of a world in which individuals could live together in some harmony with the fruits of their own labor. White men could work and profit from their talents without amassing so much wealth that they could hinder the careers of other men or bend governments to their will. Like George, Johnson was an idealist interested in the revival of a public world of democratic participation. Rather than insist on moral reformation, he argued that the best way to build a society of good citizens was to remove all obstacles to the fulfillment of that role. Johnson's world was that of his great hall on Euclid Avenue. It was a place where white men gathered together to engage the great issues of their times while their families enjoyed the blessings of prosperity.

Elected mayor in 1901 through a combination of Republican incompetence, his own charisma, and a recognition by leading Cleveland businessmen of the need for reform, Johnson was a dynamic leader. Perhaps his great achievement in the eight years he held office was to remake both the physical and political landscapes of his adopted city. Johnson wanted Cleveland to be the home of a great public whose interests were best represented by government staffed by well-educated, disinterested men. To realize his vision, Johnson exploited the Federal Plan of 1891 under which the mayor of Cleveland exercised strong power with the assistance of a cabinet made up of the directors of six municipal departments. Indeed, he was so effective that his opponents arranged for a special session to the Ohio General Assembly to replace the Federal Plan with a weaker system of governance by boards.

Undaunted, Johnson surrounded himself with a coterie of bright young men, eager to improve local governments. Professor Edward W. Bemis held a Ph.D. from Johns Hopkins University and was a founder of the American Economic Association. Johnson invited Bemis to Cleveland to study taxation, and he stayed on as director of waterworks. Bemis was only one of several experts recruited by Johnson. More generally, the mayor encouraged civil service reform so that political appointments, especially in the police department, would reflect merit more than corruption. Although he worked long hours, Johnson prided himself on being decisive and democratic.

Johnson and his allies wanted to transform Cleveland into a city that encouraged public participation. He saw to it that the city's filthy streets were paved and cleaned. His administration constructed public baths in poorer sections of the city so that people would have the opportunity to clean themselves. Typhoid rates fell from 114 to 12.2 per 100,000 by 1908 with the opening of a new water-intake tunnel from Lake Erie. "Keep off the grass" signs were removed from public parks, and playgrounds were built for children. In Johnson's view, these measures restored public space to the people. Parks and cleanliness were not the preserves of a privileged elite. Frederick Howe claimed that hundreds of people played baseball on weekends in a collective celebration of the realization that parks belonged to all of them.

The Johnson administration worked under the assumption that government's job was to help people become good citizens. He sought to reform the city police department under the leadership of Fred Kohler. Rather than raid brothels and gambling dens, the police wrote down the names of customers. Kohler authorized policemen to use discretion in handling misdemeanors and petty crime. If a young person or intoxicated person committed a crime without malice, the officer should consider sending them home rather than arresting them. Workhouses developed liberal parole policies. According to the Reverend Harris R. Cooley, the director of charities and corrections, "delinquent men, women, and children" were "fellow human beings who had been deprived of the opportunity to get on in the world" and should "be cared for by the society that had wronged them." Overall, Johnson's appointees were realistic about human behavior. Opposed to vice, they sympathized with people and looked to solutions other than moral crusades to improve living conditions as well as individual character.

Cleveland was not unique in the early 1900s. Cities throughout Europe and North America were reinventing themselves. London, Paris, and Chicago had merged boosterism and citizenship in the development of wide streets, impressive waterfronts, and grand buildings such as government centers and museums. Johnson's administration wholeheartedly backed a Group Plan to create an impressive array of public buildings that would create community through physical space. In 1903, a commission of three experts proposed a great mall, 560 feet wide, decorated with sculptures and fountains, around which would congregate the city hall, the county courthouse, federal building, the post office, and the public library. At the top of the mall would be a magnificent train station that would deposit travelers into the heart of the public city. While they tried to avoid monotony, the commissioners sought architectural harmony through uniform dimensions, similar materials, and a style that aped that of imperial Rome. Not only would the mall and its buildings represent the power and majesty of the city, they would develop a sense of pride in citizens, making them realize that they were members of a community whose interests transcended individual or parochial concerns.

Little of this elaborate design, part of what Howe called "a city planned, built and conducted as a community enterprise," was completed in Johnson's lifetime. Nonetheless, everything except the train station was eventually constructed. The federal building opened in 1910, the county courthouse in 1912, and the city hall in 1916. The Group Plan made Cleveland the second city in the United States to execute a downtown development plan. The grand scheme embodied the urban vision Johnson sought to implement as mayor.

More important than landscape to Johnson was the public ownership of basic services. Like other reformers of his era, the mayor and his experts sought to bring order out of what they considered to be the chaos created by the monopoly by private companies of things people in burgeoning cities had to have. Before the early 1800s,

governments granted charters to various corporations to handle essential services such as fire protection that they lacked the resources to
manage; they assumed that private and public interests overlapped.
But with the expansion of the United States in the 1800s, state legislatures and city councils had granted corporate charters to multiple
organizations that seemed intent upon asserting and protecting their
interests. Streetcar companies were a case in point. Citizens had to get
around ever-larger cities, which is why governments granted privileges
to companies in the first place. As Johnson himself attested, however,
private ownership produced a welter of competing companies, complicated fares, and disdain for consumer interests. Meanwhile, ruinous
competition tended toward consolidation, as had happened in Cleveland. "The public utility corporations are a bunch of thieves," said
Johnson in 1901. "I ought to know. I was one of them."

Just as city government ought to encourage people to take ownership of public space, it ought to encourage them to own essential
public services. Johnson and his allies worked to see that natural gas
was extended into Cleveland. They also fought to construct an electric light plant owned and operated by the city. Why should citizens
have to pay private companies for electricity any more than they
should pay them for using public parks? In Johnson's view, municipal
government embodied the will of the people. In this sense, he deviated some from Jeffersonian and Jacksonian notions of small government. But not much. Both Jefferson and Jackson had believed in the
importance of local control and in the people acting together. Johnson seemed to be doing nothing more than institutionalizing those
principles. Government was the only thing strong enough to allow
the people to fight corporate privilege.

Not surprisingly, Johnson encountered fierce resistance from
vested interests and others who disdained his style or thought he was
a socialist. They vehemently opposed municipal ownership of utilities,
and, as a consequence, the electric light plant was not constructed
until several years after his death. Most controversial was a long battle to gain public control of streetcar companies and fulfill a campaign
promise to lower the fare to three cents. Many thought Johnson a
hypocrite since he was the very model of a streetcar magnate and had
fought Detroit Mayor Hazen Pingree in the 1890s when Pingree tried
to lower street fares. Nonetheless, Johnson persisted in his crusade to
turn the basic services of municipal life over to the representatives of
the people. In 1908, he and his negotiators got the Municipal Trac-
tion Company, a holding company for most Cleveland streetcar lines,

to set a three-cent fare in return for eliminating service on unprofitable lines, establishing a one-cent fee on transfers, and charging five cents to travel outside of the city. When workers went on strike because they had received a one cent an hour raise rather than the two cents an hour they had been promised, violence ensued and service deteriorated. Forced to hold a referendum on franchise grants to three-cent companies, Johnson lost by 38,249 to 37,643. Finally, Judge Robert W. Taylor proposed letting private companies run the lines under the supervision of the municipal government. Fares would be three cents, if possible, but no more than five cents under any circumstances. With this settlement approved in 1910 by a vote of 27,270 to 19,232, Johnson's protege and successor, Mayor Newton W. Baker, was able to use the regulatory power to offer better service at a lower cost than virtually any other U.S. city.

One of the biggest frustrations of the Johnson administration was the lack of local autonomy. City governments in Ohio functioned at the mercy of the General Assembly in Columbus. Significant taxation and regulation had to win approval from legislators, the majority of whom represented small towns or rural areas and had no interest in seeing government grow in size and scope. Johnson, therefore, became a champion of home rule, or the right of cities to regulate themselves. During an unsuccessful campaign for governor of Ohio, the mayor made a traditional Democratic case for local autonomy. Once again, Johnson won only a day after he died. In 1912, an Ohio Constitutional Convention proposed an amendment creating home rule, which was approved by the voters.

The crusading mayor of Cleveland became a national figure. In 1905, leading muckraking journalist Lincoln Steffens wrote in a famous article in *McClure's Magazine* that Johnson was "the best mayor of the best-governed city in the United States." Others disagreed, dismissing Johnson as a hypocritical businessman playing political boss. Yet Johnson was nothing if not sincere. His faith in reform was genuine. More problematic than his beliefs was his relationship with the people in whose cause he fought. In the tradition of Southern Democrats, Johnson talked of the people in general terms. While he was outgoing with all individuals, he, like virtually all of his peers, largely defined "the people" as white men, people who shared his values, people who were willing to affirm his good sense and that of his experts.

There is no denying Johnson's charisma. When he was running for Congress, he had turned to holding open meetings in tents to reach voters. By the time he was mayor, he had perfected the art of speaking before public gatherings, some of which numbered close to 10,000. Johnson saw these meetings as a combination of persuasion and information. They made citizens more knowledgeable. He also liked their informality. Johnson specialized in turning the tables on hecklers by thanking them for their comments. Inviting people to ask him questions, he would answer in plain language, often laced with humor. Johnson reveled in debate. He almost never lost control of either himself or his audience. Rather than give formal speeches, Johnson created an atmosphere that mixed revivalism with town meetings by interacting with his audiences. People attended his tent meetings because they were entertaining. As always, Johnson won people over with style as much as substance. He was a likeable person who came across well in public settings and stated his case without alienating his audience.

And yet, substance mattered, too. Johnson told his audiences was that the problems they faced were not their fault and that they could be remedied through collective action. He encouraged people to imagine themselves as members of a powerful public who could defeat the forces of corruption and monopoly if they only focused on what they had in common rather than what divided them. Johnson's problem, of course, was that he was far too idealistic. In fact, he never really understood his constituents on their own terms. For the mayor, they were just mere guests in his great hall, arguing with the sharp, good-humored man who was always the center of attention. It never occurred to Johnson that the people might not be who he thought they were.

The mayor was popular with working-class Clevelanders. Although he opposed vice, his administration was not particularly aggressive in attacking saloons, a policy that won him the opposition of the Anti-Saloon League. Ethnic voters had little to fear from Johnson because he did not emphasize cultural issues; he did not threaten their religion or way of life. Rather, he focused on economic issues that cut across ethnic divisions. The mayor attempted to create a more equitable system of taxation and to provide lower costs for basic public services. No less important to Johnson's election as mayor in 1901, 1903, 1905, and 1907 was his control of the city government and the Democratic Party.

Support for Johnson tended to divide along traditional partisan lines. Republicans, who were largely native-born, Protestant, middle-class and pro-business, generally opposed him because they saw him as a radical who verged on socialism. Democrats, meanwhile, endorsed him because he stood for relative equality and local control. He did well with Austrian, German, Hungarian, and Irish voters. Indeed, in 1903, most of his voters were the children of European immigrants. Johnson also generally won wide support in suburban areas, largely because of his advocacy of low-cost transportation. When the mayor finally lost in 1909, it was largely because of the difficulties with the streetcar strike. Failing to highlight transportation issues in his campaign, he lost votes in suburban areas. To be sure, some people were just tired of Johnson's bluster. But close analysis of election returns suggests that as long as the mayor kept the focus on economic issues, he tended to best his opponents.

Johnson's health declined rapidly toward the end of his tenure. After leaving office in January 1910, he traveled and worked on his autobiography. By early 1911, his weight had dropped from 230 to 170 pounds. He was literally wasting away. The end came on April 10, 1911, but not before the once indefatigable mayor had lost the will to live. "I am so tired—so very tired. Let me sleep," he remarked before his death.

In retrospect, Johnson's focus on local transportation issues may seem less than earth shaking. Intellectually lightweight and unable to recognize let alone overcome his racism and sexism, he sometimes came across as a wealthy paternalist who dabbled in politics because he was tired of business. To be sure, his motives were complex. Johnson was never as altruistic as he presented himself. But, whatever his failings, his life was a model of civic engagement. Voters responded to him because he seemed genuinely interested in them and their futures. In many ways, Johnson's greatest achievement was to persuade tens of thousands of people that Cleveland was their community and that the primary job of politicians was to facilitate the realization of the possibilities of life within their city. Johnson envisioned a government whose responsibility was to ennoble rather than punish citizens. If his division of the world into the people and privilege seems hopelessly naive, he nevertheless won the hearts and minds of many voters with his boundless faith in their power to fashion a government that would serve the interests of the many rather than the few.

Further Reading

Campbell, Thomas F., and Edward M. Miggins, eds. *The Birth of Modern Cleveland, 1865–1930*. Cleveland: Western Reserve Historical Society, 1988.

Howe, Frederic C. *Confessions of a Reformer.* New York: Charles Scribner's Sons, 1926.

Johnson, Tom L. *My Story.* New York: B. W. Huebsch, 1911.

Rarick, Molly M. *Progressive Vision: The Planning of Downtown Cleveland, 1903–1930.* Cleveland: Cleveland Museum of Art, 1986.

Warner, Hoyt Landon. *Progressivism in Ohio, 1897–1917.* Columbus: Ohio State University Press, 1964.

Whitlock, Brand. *Forty Years of It.* New York: D. Appleton, 1914.

16

William Oxley Thompson and Popular Education, Social Justice, and Social Control in Progressive Era Ohio

AMY FANCELLI ZALIMAS

W HEN WILLIAM Oxley Thompson became president of Ohio State University on September 21, 1899, he could not have imagined what the next quarter century had in store for him and this relatively new state university. Upon arrival in Columbus from Miami University, where he had served as president since 1891, he found a relatively small campus nestled on just over 330 acres. The first class to graduate under his tenure numbered only ninety-nine. Total enrollment that year was 1,268. By the time Thompson retired in 1925, the typical graduating class outnumbered the total enrollment of his early days as president. Moreover, the annual budget of the school had skyrocketed from a little more than $300,000 in 1899 to well over $6 million, and the grounds of the university had expanded to over one thousand acres.

Thompson's importance to the history of Ohio State University cannot be denied. As its longest serving president, he presided over the most significant changes in the birth of this modern university. Throughout his presidency, he was also a prominent public figure whose influence extended far beyond the walls of the university and even the borders of his home state. As the head of a growing mid-western land-grant university, Thompson became a spokesman for expanding opportunities in higher education—the very symbol of which was the state university.

Thompson's service at Ohio State, moreover, corresponds roughly with the turn-of-the-century Progressive reform movement. Although historians have been frustrated in their attempts to advance a definitive

FIG. 12 William Oxley Thompson.
Courtesy of The Ohio State University Archives.

and coherent analysis of the Progressive movement, most agree with
Arthur S. Link and Richard L. McCormick that "for almost every
social problem of the early twentieth century, somebody offered a
solution which focused on the schools." One of the central features
of the historiographical debate over progressivism has been the extent
to which it, in its varied incarnations, represented an effort to democ-
ratize the nation's institutions, including its educational system.

The relationship between racism and Progressive reform has also
interested historians. The traditional view held that racism was out of
step with the spirit of progressivism. Cooperation, not racial conflict,
was the hallmark of the true progressive. That the South continued
to languish under the weight of Jim Crow and that many in the
North displayed a seeming lack of interest in the plight of African
Americans was explained away, as Link and McCormick put it, as "a
blind spot . . . an anomaly, a deviation from the essence of progressivism." On the other hand, historians like David W. Southern and
Jack Temple Kirby have emphasized the close relationship between
racism and Progressive reform. Kirby has argued that segregation

was itself a "progressive" reform in the South, while Southern has argued that there was little substantial difference in the North where "progressivism and racism rode in on the same horse."

For those who hold the latter view, the Progressive Era is often interpreted not as a forward-looking, inclusive movement but rather as a backward-looking attempt to maintain "traditional" American values. Social control, not democratic reform, was the hallmark of this brand of progressivism that sought to protect a white, Anglo-Saxon, Protestant society from the harmful influence of African Americans, newly arrived immigrants, and other undesirables.

The elusive, and often contradictory, nature of progressivism has been well recognized; historians have long been wary of labeling the varied reforms as any kind of unified "movement." Moreover, these inconsistencies existed not only among the various reform agendas of the time but within individuals as well. William Oxley Thompson's lifetime of public service reveals a man who struggled, often against himself, with some of the most pressing issues of his day, not the least of which was the race question. His life embodied the same inconsistencies that historians see in the Progressive movement. At times he was a racial egalitarian, while at others an ardent segregationist. He could speak of the democratizing influence of public education, yet support a two-tiered university system.

Born on November 5, 1855, in Cambridge, Ohio, to a family of Scotch-Irish descent, Thompson was reared in the Presbyterian faith. In 1878, he graduated from the Muskingum College in New Concord, Ohio, and, in the following year, he enrolled in Western Theological Seminary from which he graduated in 1882. In the meantime, he had also received a master's degree from Muskingum and had been licensed to preach by the Zanesville (Ohio) Presbytery in 1881. He earned his way through school by teaching, but initially the call to the ministry was stronger than the call to education. Thompson always considered himself a Presbyterian minister first and a university president second. Having served as pastor at churches in Longmont, Colorado, and Odebolt, Iowa, Thompson returned to Ohio in 1891 to become president of Miami University. After moving to Columbus in 1899, Thompson remained involved in the Presbyterian Church, preaching occasionally at local churches as well as serving on the General Assembly of the Presbyterian Church, U.S.A. Although he believed in the separation of church and state, Thompson always recognized the importance of religion, even at a secular school. In 1928, Thompson declared his long-held belief that "all religion is educational and education carries with it something of the idealism of religion." Thompson was as passionate about the burgeoning democracy of education as he was about the interdependence of education and spiritual development.

As head of what would become the largest state university, Thompson helped to define and defend the mission of the land-grant colleges and universities, which had their origin in the Morrill Act of 1862. These colleges opened the doors of higher education to more Americans than ever before. The rise of these institutions prompted high praise from some corners but severe criticism from others. Thus, a persistent theme of Thompson's speeches across the years was his passionate defense of the democratic mission of the public universities. He warned that those who believed that classical liberal arts should remain the cornerstone of higher education "must prepare to surrender their beliefs or accept permanent disappointment." They must come to recognize that the world is a laboratory that must be acted in and upon. He described the traditional view of education as the "vestibule theory" of education. This approach to education was perennially preparatory: teachers were always preparing students for some undesignated time in the future. Modern education, he argued, "regards the child as living—not as getting ready to live." Education should have practical application in the present, not just in the future.

Thompson's rhetoric in defense of the agricultural, industrial, and other vocational arts was often peppered with disdain for haughty professors of the older tradition. The agricultural professor, unlike the eastern liberal arts professor, was not intended to lounge in his "dressing gown, pipe in mouth, far removed from the scenes where the clanging noise of the school bell would disturb his meditations upon his favorite subject." On the contrary, the agricultural (or other vocational) professor should not be "ashamed to wear overalls or to have a little mud on his boots." Using the practical needs and daily experiences of their students as a starting points, teachers in landgrant institutions would equip their students with the tools and skills they needed to make practical and immediate changes in their daily lives. In advancing such a view, Thompson, along with the presidents of other state universities in the Midwest, often found himself at odds with the heads of eastern colleges. By 1890, according to historian Laurence Veysey, a "distinctive Mid-western educational spirit" had emerged in which a regional loyalty to the ideas of "action, practicality, realism, and progress" vied with a perceived eastern view of education as relating to "books, tradition, and culture."

Veysey suggests, however, that such a divergence between public and private universities of the era was more imagined than real. He argues that although debates over the purpose and meaning of education persisted, the overall trend of the Progressive Era was towards uniformity among the nation's various institutions of higher learning. This trend can be seen, he argues, in the accreditation movement, the establishment of the Association of American Universities (1900), and, most importantly, in the increasing bureaucratization of university administration. This form of organization, modeled after that of big business, standardized university operations, revolutionized the university presidency, and provided a framework large enough to support widely varying philosophical approaches to education and enough flexibility to sustain the American university without "recourse to specific values." In this light, the populist tone of Thompson's rhetoric conceals the extent to which his distinctively midwestern and "democratic" views on education were, in many ways, similar to the views of those he sometimes attacked.

Thompson never believed that vocational education should or would replace the liberal arts. Rather, he argued, only a small segment of society was fit for a classical, liberal arts education. His goal for Ohio State was not to purge the liberal arts from the curriculum but rather to expand the curriculum to include areas of study with both broad appeal and direct relevance to the needs of the state. Both types of education had a role to play in society and both could coexist, he argued, even on the same campus; in fact, for Thompson the coexistence of the two was essential. While vocational education was essential for the efficient operation of the U.S. economy and society, the liberal arts were indispensable both for citizenship and moral reasoning.

While Thompson believed in the importance of the "intelligent public sentiment" of the masses, he also believed in "the general principle that all the great beneficent movements have started in the upper spheres . . . some great soul must, missionary like, go to the field and reap the harvest." In private correspondence, he was adamant that the liberal arts were in no way "losing ground." Rather, he argued, "it is folly . . . to assume that the masses of the people who desire more education can conform to classical or literary requirements." For all the passion that he summoned in defense of democracy in education, at heart Thompson retained a strong sense of elitism.

Veysey has argued that the "democratization" of American higher education and the call for greater access to educational opportunity can be viewed in a conservative rather than a progressive light. He argues that rhetoric, like Thompson's, upheld the idea of a "classless system of education," which included vocational education "might be valued for keeping the nation free of radical discontent in the manner of a safety valve." Expansion of the curriculum to include technical training would allow more Americans to earn college degrees, but the segregation of students into various degree programs would help to maintain existing divisions in society.

Since Thompson stood at the helm of a state-sponsored institution, he did not have the opportunity to turn away many students. Admission standards merely required that prospective students meet only one of two conditions: either they were to have earned a high school diploma or they were to have reached the age of twenty-one. These standards did not exclude anyone from attending OSU on the basis of race, ethnicity, gender, or class. Admission requirements did not, however, keep presidents like Thompson from discouraging applications or from trying to dissuade some students from pursuing certain courses of study.

Thompson displayed a good deal of suspicion toward the new immigrants of the city. Born and raised in rural southeastern Ohio, Thompson was a product of his small town roots. Speaking in 1908, Thompson warned of the "struggle in our country between what may be called the home and foreign ideals." He feared that unassimilated immigrants were gaining access to teaching positions and thereby threatening the high ideals for which Americans had always stood. Thompson went so far as to suggest that examinations should be administered to prospective teachers not for knowledge of subject matter but rather in basic ethics and morals. When asked to supply application information about Ohio State for the international division of the American Council on Education, Thompson complied but added "I am not sure that The Ohio State University has any interest in immigrant students."

More African Americans also sought access to higher education during the Progressive Era. A young black scholar named Hartford Jennings wrote to Thompson in July 1913 to inquire about a course in electrical engineering. Thompson responded (one and a half months later), "There is no objection to your coming to the Ohio State University and entering any course for which you are qualified. Every year we have a number of young people of both sexes and of the Negro race who attend the university without any embarrassment or hindrance." Thompson went on to say that he would be glad to help him in any way possible and that the way was "entirely open" for

Jennings to attend. He added, however, "I feel constrained to say just a word. . . . [T]he sentiment north of the Ohio River seems to be so persistent against the Negro in skilled labor that I doubt very much whether an educated Negro has a fair show worth while in this part of the country." Clearly discouraged, Jennings wrote back: "only a few years ago, while still in High school, I thought if a man deserved anything, could prove himself able to fill the bill and was the possessor of a good moral character, nothing more was needed . . . it now appears that the requirements are—prove yourself worthy, fill the bill, but *do not be a Negro*." Thanking Thompson for his honesty and claiming comfort in the fact "that you [Thompson] do not approve of this condition of affairs," Jennings vowed to try elsewhere and to test the dictum "all things come to him who hustles."

This exchange was not an isolated case during the Thompson years, nor was it a subconscious act on Thompson's part. Two years earlier, Thompson had frankly stated the logic of this policy. "I am discouraging colored young men from taking courses in engineering, chiefly on the ground that social conditions will not tolerate their preference." Although Thompson professed his disapproval with the existing situation, he made it clear that "colored people should not undertake to force that issue and if it came about [at Ohio State] I should request them not to do it." He also questioned the wisdom of blacks who tried to "practically force the doctrine of social equality." Not surprisingly, in July 1915 black students numbered only thirty-five on campus, constituting less than one percent of the student population.

This is not to suggest that Thompson was opposed to educational opportunity for African Americans, nor can he fairly be charged with an utter disregard for their welfare. Several letters in his personal papers from former black students thank him for his efforts on their behalf. Nonetheless, Thompson did have a rather limited view of what kinds of opportunities African Americans should seek.

Although Thompson was clearly in favor of education for blacks, he wavered on the issue of black equality, at least in the present. Thompson believed that slavery had been a moral evil, but he also felt that blacks had benefited from the "beneficent attitude acquired by [some] people of wealth and estate . . . toward . . . those who serve[d] them." In an address timed to correspond with George Washington's birthday, Thompson discussed Washington's legacy, including the fact that he was a slaveholder. He praised Washington for his belief that slavery should be abolished and for his recognition that "no one man could abolish the institution by giving freedom to a few hundred slaves." He argued that Washington "understood also that these slaves born and reared on an estate, with neither education nor worldly preparation, were not quite able to take care of themselves."

This kind of interpretation of slavery, argues historian Jack Temple Kirby, is the root of "progressive" educational reforms in the South. Kirby argues that southern educational reformers "contended that blacks had benefited from the civilizing tutelage of slavery. . . . Reconstruction interrupted the evolutionary process of black American history, removing blacks from kindly guidance and duping them with delusions of political grandeur beyond their reach." Thompson spoke similarly in a 1917 speech: "many of our fathers in the North thought that the ballot was essential to the freedom of the colored race . . . most of their sons regard that as a mistaken theory and an unfortunate practice." He concluded that extending the vote did not necessarily result in better political conditions and that "if it could be wisely restricted and then rationally developed, we should probably reach a desired condition more promptly than by any other method."

Thompson got the opportunity to put these views into practice as a member of the Columbus Board of Education. He served as a member-at-large from 1905 to 1924 with a brief interlude as president from 1909 to 1910. Those years were filled with controversy about the legality of segregation in Columbus Public Schools. Historian Harold S. Carter has explained that although a law barring segregation in Ohio schools had been passed in 1887, a movement to establish separate schools for black and white children was well underway by the time Thompson became head of the school board. In 1904, school board president P. D. Shriner endorsed segregation ostensibly, according to Carter, as a way to win support for employing more black teachers in Columbus schools. In reality, argues historian David Gerber, the board was responding to concerns from white constituents whose children had to go to school with the growing number of black children in Columbus. Along these lines, in September 1907 Thompson publicly announced that "it is in the best interests of both that they be educated in separate schools." The headline in the *Columbus Dispatch* read: "Dr. William Oxley Thompson is not Unfriendly to Them but Thinks it is for the Best."

Although there was some division within the black community, the vast majority opposed segregation. On September 24, 1907, over eight hundred African Americans showed up at an ice rink on Mount Vernon Avenue to protest the board's plan to open an all-black school by redrawing the lines of the district. These activists sent a resolution to the school board objecting to the action and promising to register their dissent "at the polls and in the courts."

Despite the efforts of the protestors and the ruling of the city solicitor that the school board had no legal right to establish a segregated school, Champion Avenue School opened in the fall of 1910. In June, Thompson received an inquiry about possible employment at the school. His reply strikes an insincere note: "It is not true that the Board of Education is establishing a school for colored youth. It is true, however, that the Champion Avenue School will have more than 90% of colored children in it. All the teachers will be colored teachers."

Thompson knew full well that Champion was designed to be an essentially all-black school; he had been one of the architects of the policy. By the time this man had written, all the jobs had been filled. Thompson could have simply reported this fact to the potential applicant. Instead, he wanted to make it absolutely clear: the Columbus School Board was not breaking the laws of the state, this was not an officially segregated school. For Columbus-area blacks, however, it mattered not whether the policy was official or unofficial: the Progressive Era meant segregation in their public schools and in other areas of life as well. Black access to movie houses, hotels, restaurants, and other public places was restricted despite legal prohibitions to the contrary.

Thompson felt that racial change, like any change, must proceed in a controlled, orderly fashion. In a 1924 commencement address, Thompson talked about both the inevitability of change and the need to control it. He told his audience that "[t]wo things are inevitable. First the status quo cannot be maintained. We may fight for it tooth and nail but it is bound to go. . . . Second—public sentiment will be the force determining the direction of whatever change or progress the future may hold. Our chief concern . . . should not be to prevent any change but to administer [it]." In this way, Thompson could reconcile his belief in racial justice and the need for social control. The latter was a tool by which to eventually create the former.

Thompson was willing to wait longer for this evolutionary process to take place than were most African Americans. In 1921, an anonymous letter signed only "voters" was sent to Ohio governor Harry L. Davis demanding a "probe of the damable treatment . . . being accorded our colored students at the Ohio State University." The letter complained that black students were "jim crowed in everything" and were subject to racial slurs in their classes. The offending white students, they argued, were never punished or even discouraged. Even instructors, the writers asserted, treated black students "like they [were] dogs." The letter makes special mention of President Thompson who "is not a genuine northern man of the old stock." They claimed that their many attempts to approach him about these issues had produced no results. The letter also names two particularly offensive professors and warns that they "are going to die in their shoes and it [may] be that the tragedy will be polled [pulled] off in the classroom too, but we are not in the position to state just when." The authors of the letter also attempted to use their political power to influence Governor Davis. They warn him that "if you . . . whom we have help[ed] to rise to your high position don't probe the bitterness and bring an abrupt stop and very immediately to this prejudice [the] city of Columbus is more than apt to run red with blood . . . please sir do everything in your power to ward off a terrible race riot which will surely come if the proper parties don't act." There is no evidence of Thompson's response to this letter, but it was preserved in his file.

From one perspective, Thompson's reticence on racial issues can be viewed as part of an effort to avoid issues that might conflict with the democratic beliefs he so often professed in his many public addresses. Historian David Southern has argued that this tendency on the part of northern progressives was malicious and a clear sign of the lack of "insight and integrity" that characterized their attitudes on race. In contrast, historian Leon Fink offers a much more generous interpretation of Progressive Era intellectuals. He argues that even though they were flawed, they deserve credit for facing the challenging issues of their times and for "uphold[ing] the banner of universal education, and contest[ing] the political status quo even in the face of gnawing doubts." Thompson's career makes way for both of these interpretations.

While many aspects of his public service remain suspect and call into question the manner in which he dealt with issues of racial equality, many of his contemporaries were avowed racists and open segregationists. Thompson would countenance no such view. Though he supported informal segregation, his motives for doing so are not entirely clear. Given the racial attitudes of the white populace, it is plausible that one could support such a course of action as a protective measure rather than as a restrictive one. Some African Americans, after all, had come to the conclusion that segregation was preferable to integration on less than equal terms. To his credit, Thompson did speak out against the Ku Klux Klan when the group began to enjoy renewed popularity in Columbus in the early 1920s. He drew both praise and criticism for his September 1923 address before the Women's Christian Temperance Union in which he attacked the activities of the KKK. Although the text of the speech has not been preserved in his records, an address given before the Alpha Sigma Phi fraternity earlier that day provided a preview. In it, Thompson mentions his plans for the evening and criticizes the KKK calling it an "un-American thing . . . based on class prejudice and other things that cannot stand the light of day long." Although his speech to the fraternity does not focus on the racial prejudices of the KKK, he addresses the issue of struggling against your own. He said, "I have race prejudice in my mind and have had for sixty odd years. My prejudice is against the Jew, the colored man, the Japanese, the Mexican, against the Chinamen, against the Turk . . . [M]y recent prejudice is against the German . . . and my perennial prejudice is against the Englishman. I have been struggling with those prejudices just as you have, only I have done it longer . . . it is a hard process to go against your own prejudices and clean house."

That Thompson did struggle against his prejudices is laudable, and that he was sometimes unsuccessful in the struggle may be understandable given the time in which he lived. Regardless of his intentions, however, when it comes to Thompson's record on racial issues, it is clear that social justice often took a back seat to social control. For Thompson, as with many of his progressive contemporaries, the two did not always come in equal measures.

Further Reading

Fink, Leon. *Progressive Intellectuals and the Dilemmas of Democratic Commitment*. Cambridge, Mass.: Harvard University Press, 1997.

Kirby, Jack Temple. *Darkness at the Dawning: Race and Reform in the Progressive South*. Philadelphia: Lippincott, 1972.

Pollard, James E. *William Oxley Thompson*. Columbus: Ohio State University Press, 1955.

Southern, David W. *The Malignant Heritage: Yankee Progressives and the Negro Question, 1901–1914*. Chicago: Loyola University Press, 1968.

Veysey, Laurence R. *The Emergence of the American University*. Chicago: University of Chicago Press, 1965.

17

Florence E. Allen
and "great changes in the status
of women"

JOAN E. ORGAN

I N 1913, Cleveland native Florence Ellinwood Allen carried the
banner of the National American Woman Suffrage Association
(NAWSA) at the head of a national suffrage parade in New York City.
A few months later, the Cleveland *Plain Dealer* noted Allen's graduation from New York University Law School: "A boundless field for
women who are anxious to help other women get a square deal in life
is the law, and more and more every year young college women are
cultivating the acquaintance of Blackstone and fitting themselves to
win justice in 'a man's world.' Cleveland has more than one woman
lawyer. Now comes the news that a brilliant young woman who called
this city home for several years has become a modern Portia with high
honors."

Despite such praise, when Allen arrived in Cleveland ready to practice law, no firm would hire her. One male lawyer, pointing to a few
snowflakes floating past the window, declared that he would not think
of sending a woman down to the courthouse on a day like this. Undeterred, Florence Allen opened her own law office by September 1914,
and soon Cleveland woman suffragists sought her help, as did others
needing assistance in concerns about jobs, property, and wills. This
would mark the beginning of a legal career which would allow Allen
to become the first woman in Ohio to serve as assistant county prosecutor and the first woman in the nation to serve as a common pleas
judge and a state supreme court justice. She also made history again
in 1934, when President Franklin D. Roosevelt appointed her to the
U.S. Court of Appeals Sixth Circuit, making her the first woman to
reach such a position. From 1936 until her retirement from the bench

FIG. 13 Florence E. Allen.
Courtesy of The Western Reserve Historical Society, Cleveland, Ohio.

in 1959, Allen's name surfaced as a possible nominee each time a vacancy occurred on the U.S. Supreme Court.

Allen's career, though, was more than just a series of "firsts." It symbolized the transition of the women's movement from protest to participation. For suffrage activists like Allen, the franchise was not an end in itself but rather a means by which to create what they saw as a more just and equitable society.

Although Florence Allen's family was originally from northeastern Ohio, Allen was born in Salt Lake City, Utah, on March 23, 1884, the third of six children of Clarence Emir Allen and Corrine Tuckerman Allen. Her father, who had graduated from Cleveland's Western Reserve University in classics and law, had become ill soon after he married and had been advised to move to a drier climate. A friend, Cleveland *Plain Dealer* owner Liberty Holden, hired Allen to manage his salt mines in Salt Lake City, so he moved his family there in the early 1880s.

In 1895, when single-taxer Clarence E. Allen went to Washington, D.C., to represent Utah in the U.S. House of Representatives, Florence

Allen and her two older sisters, Esther and Helen, moved to Ohio to live with their Tuckerman grandparents. Here Florence attended the Grand River Institute in Lyme, Ohio, where her grandfather Jacob Tuckerman was director. In 1900, at age sixteen, Florence Allen started her studies at the Women's College of Western Reserve University. She graduated with honors in music in 1904.

In 1904, the Allen children traveled with their mother to Berlin, where they would live for the next two years. Along with studying music at a conservatory and working as a music editor for the *German Times,* Allen became deeply involved in women's rights. She already had some awareness because her mother was active in the Utah Congress of Mothers. Corrine had been invited to Berlin to address the 1904 International Council of Women (ICW) on her organization's efforts to curb polygamy, and, more generally, Utah's decision to grant women the right to vote in 1897 as a way to halt polygamy. Prior to the opening of the ICW conference, Carrie Chapman Catt, an elder stateswoman of the U.S. women's rights movement, hosted a gathering attended by suffragists from around the world. There Allen met some of the major suffrage leaders of the time—NAWSA president Dr. Anna Howard Shaw, Hungarian suffragist Rosika Schwimmer, and Dutch suffragist Aletta Jacobs. What a beginning for the young Allen who would later become a comrade of these suffrage leaders, and in fact, several years later would march with Catt, Shaw, Schwimmer, and Jacobs in a suffrage and peace parade in Cleveland.

After their stay in Berlin, the rest of the family returned to Salt Lake City, but Florence Allen settled in Cleveland. Not only did her Tuckerman cousins live there, but also several close women friends from her college years resided in Cleveland. Allen still contemplated a career in music, and from 1906 to 1909 worked as a music editor for the Cleveland *Plain Dealer* and as a music teacher at the Laurel School for Girls. In 1907, however, she began a graduate degree in political science at Western Reserve University and thoroughly enjoyed the course work. Political science professor A. R. Hatton suggested that she study law. Allen reported that "it came like a revelation from on high. That was what I wanted!" Most university law schools, including Western Reserve, refused to admit women at the time, so Allen, most likely at Hatton's suggestion, gained admission to the University of Chicago Law School.

Although she stayed in Chicago only a year before transferring to New York University, this was long enough for her to make lifelong friendships with residents of Jane Addams's Hull House, including

Sophonisba Breckinridge, Edith Abbott, and Florence Kelley, and familiarized herself with social reform work. During Allen's year in Chicago, she also developed strong bonds with other young women who wanted to become lawyers. The discrimination they encountered from those who felt that women should not practice law taught Allen and her future sisters-in-law, especially Alice Greenacre and Greta Coleman, to rely upon each other for personal and professional support.

Such mutual support was demonstrated in 1916 while Allen was in Montana campaigning for Woodrow Wilson. Allen learned that her East Cleveland Municipal Suffrage case was to be heard before the Ohio Supreme Court in Columbus in two days. She immediately wired her two former Chicago Law School friends, Greenacre and Coleman, requesting their assistance. When she stopped to change trains in Chicago, they met her with a suitcase full of relevant law books. In her diary, Allen wrote, "I grabbed the suitcase and dashed for my train. I spent the night reviewing the legal questions." In part because of their help, Allen successfully defended the East Cleveland Municipal Suffrage case the next day.

During her year studying law in Chicago, Allen also met Frances Kellor, who convinced Allen to move to New York City and work for Kellor's League for Protection of Immigrants. For much of 1910 and 1911, Allen served as a legal investigator for Kellor's organization. The next year, however, she moved to a job as assistant secretary to Maud Wood Park, vice president of the National College Equal Suffrage League, a NAWSA affiliate. Allen was responsible for the correspondence with college suffrage leagues and planned Park's schedule of speaking engagements.

From 1911 to 1913, Allen divided her time between her suffrage work and studying law at New York University. Following a short stay at the Henry Street Settlement, she lived with her close friend, former Clevelander Bertha "Bert" Miller, and Bert's sister Marie. Bert, who was already a law student at NYU, may actually have played a larger role than Kellor in inducing Allen to move to New York. To judge from Allen's diaries, Bert was one of the most important people in Allen's life. Together, Allen and Miller became friends with Mary Ware Dennett, founder of the National Birth Control League, as well as other suffragists and peace activists such as Chrystal Eastman and NYU law student and suffragist Inez Mulholland.

"To do justice bit by bit is in reality nothing else than to tolerate injustice for years," Allen wrote in her special little red book, "New

York City—Notes During Law School." Filled with verses that she
had copied from the works of Frances Bacon, Robert Louis Steven-
son, Walt Whitman, and South African writer Olive Schreiner, this little journal points to Allen's growing interest in the issues of justice
and women's freedom—most significantly the vote for women.

The campaign for women's suffrage in Ohio, as in the country at
large, during the second decade of the twentieth century awakened
from a nearly dormant state. In 1910, Elizabeth Hauser, inspired by
the possibility that Ohio's upcoming constitutional convention could
help secure women's suffrage, began mass mobilization efforts.
Hauser, a newspaperwoman, former secretary to Cleveland's progressive mayor Tom Johnson, and recent secretary of NAWSA, re-
energized the Cuyahoga County Women's Suffrage Organization,
later the Woman Suffrage Party of Greater Cleveland. Earlier in 1910,
Inez Mulholland and Maud Wood Park had arrived in Cleveland to
organize a chapter of the National College Equal Suffrage League at
Western Reserve University. The two groups worked together,
recruiting women and men to share their cause and gathering signatures on petitions in preparation for the 1912 Ohio State Constitutional Convention.

Although Florence Allen was still in law school in New York, she
too joined the suffrage effort in her home state during the summer of
1912. On several occasions, she accompanied Park on campaign trips
through Ohio. Under Park's tutelage, Allen made "ninety-two
speeches in eighty-eight counties." Allen wrote that "this work gave
me a fine acquaintance among forward-looking Ohio women."

Although male voters failed to approve a women's suffrage
amendment to the state's constitution in 1912, the campaign helped
Allen develop a network of Cleveland suffragists with whom she was
becoming close both on and behind the suffrage lines. Her decision
to return to Cleveland after her 1913 graduation from law school
resulted from "the whole experience in the suffrage movement [1912
campaign]. . . . I met such fine women in Ohio—Harriet Taylor
Upton, Elizabeth Hauser, Minerva Brooks, Rose Moriarity, Edna
Perkins and countless others—that I came to Ohio to practice law."

Over the next several years, Allen established herself as a first-rate
attorney, a fighter for social justice, and an active campaigner for the
Democratic Party (although she could not herself vote). It was fitting,
therefore, that in July 1919 she was among "the brainiest and most
interesting women in the United States" who gathered in St. Louis
for the first convention of the National Federation of Business and

Professional Women's Club. The 225 delegates to the convention represented business and professional women's clubs from thirty-five states and forty-eight different vocations, "with lawyers in the lead." The following November, Allen invited Kentucky lawyer and executive secretary of the National Federation of Business and Professional Women's Club Lena Madesin Phillips to address business and professional women who worked and lived in Cleveland about forming a branch. Over eight hundred women attended that first meeting of what would become the Cleveland Federation of Business and Women's Clubs. A few months after the establishment of the Cleveland branch, business and professional women from all over the state joined together to form the Ohio Federation of Business and Women's Clubs.

Many years later, Cleveland municipal judge Mary Grossman remembered that the Ohio Federation played a key role in securing Allen's appointment as judge in the Cuyahoga County Court of Common Pleas. A vacancy had occurred and the federation appealed to Democratic governor James M. Cox to fill that position with Allen. This initial attempt failed because suffrage had not been ratified, and a woman could therefore not be appointed to an elective position. But once suffrage was ratified in August 1920 and Allen declared her candidacy for judge of the Cuyahoga County Common Pleas Court, the Cleveland business and professional women's branch as well as other women's organizations actively supported her candidacy.

In 1922, Ohio women representing both political parties organized Florence Allen Clubs throughout the state and collected over 43,000 signatures—20,000 more than required—to get Allen's name placed on the November ballot as a candidate for the Ohio Supreme Court. Women crossed party lines to work and vote for Allen. In April 1922, at the annual convention in Baltimore of the Leagues of Women Voters, Rose Moriarity announced that "being a Republican, I am going to start out by telling you what a Democrat has done in Cleveland."

Last year our good friend Florence Allen was a candidate for judge. I was admonished by the Republican leaders who advised me THAT IT was not right to support Miss Allen. I said I felt Florence Allen could render service to the State and to the people of Ohio and Cleveland and that it was my duty to serve her.

When Florence Allen came in she was made presiding judge in the criminal bench. She put a woman in as chairman of the grand jury, and we

cleaned up the gang in Cleveland. . . . I want to confidently predict that
the Republican women and the Democratic women are going to elect her
to the Supreme Court this year.

On November 7, 1922, Allen won one of two vacancies on the Ohio
Supreme Court, leading incumbent Judge W. Hough by nearly
50,000 votes.

The first two opinions Allen wrote as an Ohio Supreme Court justice brought home rule to the cities and government to the people. In
Reutner v. City of Cleveland and *Hile v. City of Cleveland,* both delivered in January 1923, Allen affirmed the constitutionality of the city
manager plan of government. In the first opinion, Allen wrote that
"communities acting in local self-government may work out their own
political destiny, and their own political freedom, on their own initiative, and in their own way." All but one judge concurred with Allen's
opinion. Similarly, in *Hile v. Cleveland,* Allen wrote that "the state law
is still in force in Cleveland, and where legislative statues in Cleveland
give way to . . . municipal ordinances, they give way under the highest
form of state law . . . as enacted by the people [of Ohio]."

In her 1923 affirmative opinion in *Sprinkler Co. v. Fender,* Allen
articulated her commitment to protective legislation. The case
involved Hannah Fender, an operator of a punch-pressing machine
for the Ohio Automatic Sprinkler Company in Youngstown, who, in
November 1918, caught her left thumb in a machine, requiring
amputation near the first joint. Fender thereupon sued Automatic
Sprinkler, claiming that the company violated the Ohio General Code
in failing to provide a safety guard for dangerous machinery. A trial
court in Mahoning County decided in favor of the Sprinkler Company, but the court of appeals reversed that judgment and remanded
the case for further proceedings. *Sprinkler Co. v. Fender* then came to
the Ohio Supreme Court upon petition in error. In her opinion
affirming the court of appeals decision for plaintiff Fender, Allen
wrote that sections of the General Code and of the Industrial Commission Act "were enacted for the purpose, not of affording compensation, but for the purpose of requiring the employer to conserve
human life and human energy."

Upon learning of Allen's opinion, attorney and friend Rose Moriarity telephoned her approval of the decision. Moriarity, who was on
the Ohio Industrial Commission, followed up her phone message
with a letter in which she wrote: "I think your decision in the Hannah Fender case v. Ohio Automatic Sprinkler Company was right and

just and above all the proper interpretation of the law as it stands on the statute books. I am glad that you are not going to be one of the kind of judges that *makes laws* instead of interprets them. I am proud of you."

By December 1926, Allen had obtained national visibility. She became a favored candidate for various posts in both community organizations and on the bench. When Franklin D. Roosevelt ran for president in 1932, Allen's network provided him extensive support and, upon his victory, reaped benefits in appointments to federal positions essential to supporting the new president's liberal policies.

Among the women policymakers with whom Allen maintained contact was Molly Dewson, who in 1933 served as vice chair of the Democratic National Committee. Former suffrage leader Carrie Chapman Catt suggested to Dewson that she urge Roosevelt to consider Allen for "women's posts" in his administration. Catt was aware that Dewson knew Allen personally and was cognizant of "her splendid record."

In January 1934, Dewson advised Allen to have "her friends get active and send down statements from leading lawyers" in support of her nomination to the Sixth Circuit of the United States Court of Appeals. In the first months of 1934, "Friends of Florence Allen" deluged the White House with her praise. From Chicago, for example, Allen's former law school pal Alice Greenacre wrote U.S. attorney general Homer S. Cummings attesting to Allen's qualifications for the position. In addition to the testimonials from women lawyers across the country, Allen's own law partner, campaign manager, and housemate Susan Rebhan traveled to Washington to discuss the appointment with Dewson. Throughout the campaign, Dewson orchestrated the efforts in Washington, while Rebhan played a similar role for Allen in Cleveland. Rebhan sent copies of the decisions Allen had written while on the Ohio Supreme Court to individuals involved in the nomination process, and for those individuals who were not lawyers she even explained in "lay" terms the significance of the opinions. In the end, Allen's qualifications, her positions on protective labor legislation and government regulation of utilities, and her network of friends assured her success. On her fiftieth birthday, March 23, 1934, the U.S. Senate ratified her nomination to the Sixth Circuit Court of Appeals, based in Cincinnati and covering Ohio, Kentucky, and Tennessee.

In 1937, Allen was able to use her position on the court of appeals to advance the New Deal's revolution in government activity through her decision in *Tennessee Electric Power Co. v. The Tennessee Valley Authority*. Enacted shortly after FDR became president, the Tennessee Valley Authority (TVA) built a series of government-owned power plants along the Tennessee River to provide electricity to that impoverished region. The TVA's constitutionality was promptly challenged by private power companies who claimed that it constituted unfair competition. It appeared likely that the TVA case would end up in the U.S. Supreme Court, whose conservative majority had already voided many New Deal reform programs on the grounds that the federal government was too involved in regulation of the economy. It was important, therefore, that the circuit court opinion be framed in the most careful manner to sustain the law. Allen spent most of 1937 as the presiding circuit judge along with two district judges in the TVA case. On January 22, 1938, Allen read aloud her entire eight-thousand-word decision, upholding the liberal tradition of government intervention on behalf of essential services for the disadvantaged and underprivileged. The utility companies immediately appealed the decision to the U.S. Supreme Court, which in 1939 affirmed Allen's opinion. The case set a precedent for delineating the boundaries of federal action and catapulted Allen into national attention as the most qualified woman for a Supreme Court position. Yet, although Allen had given FDR a significant victory, her supporters were stymied in their efforts to gain a Supreme Court seat for her.

Allen's contributions to social policy through her work as a judge and lawyer were publicly recognized by her sisters at the bar who knew her best. Judge Marion Harron organized the ceremony held in 1959 to celebrate Allen's retirement as a federal judge. Harron also managed the "Judge Allen Portrait Fund," which tapped women lawyers across the country for donations for the painting of Florence Allen that hangs today in the Ohio Statehouse in Columbus.

Florence Allen died at the age of eighty-two on September 12, 1966. In eulogizing her friend, Harron noted:

> The unique and remarkable fact in the life and career of Judge Allen is that during her life-span she herself did and achieved outstanding things that in themselves constituted the great changes in the status of women in the U.S. and the world. . . . In her early years she worked for the attainment of those rights for women; she worked for human rights. When some of those rights had been won, Judge Allen then went to do the things which women had claimed they could and were entitled to do; she accepted the heavy responsibilities of those rights and by her hard and brilliant work, she

entered the highest judicial services as a judge . . . that she did not serve as a Justice of the Supreme Court of the US is Our Nation's loss.

Harron concluded by quoting from Allen's own work, *This Constitution of Ours* (1940): "liberty cannot be caged into a charter and handed on ready-made to the next generation. Each generation must recreate liberty for its own times." Harron added, "we honor the memory of Judge Allen with immense gratitude, and with great pride knowing that she attained the immortal stature of a great and incomparable woman of the twentieth century."

Further Reading

Allen, Florence Ellinwood. *To Do Justly.* Cleveland: Press of Western Reserve University, 1965.

Allen, Florence E., and Mary Welles. *The Ohio Woman Suffrage Movement.* Cleveland: Committee for the Preservation of Ohio Woman Suffrage Records, 1952.

Morton, Marian J. *Women in Cleveland: An Illustrated History.* Bloomington: Indiana University Press, 1995.

Tuve, Jeanette E. *First Lady of the Law: Florence Ellinwood Allen.* Lanham, Md.: University Press of America, 1984.

Van Tassel, David D., and John J. Grabowski, eds. *Cleveland—A Tradition of Reform.* Kent, Ohio: Kent State University Press, 1986.

18

Jane Edna Hunter and Black Institution Building in Ohio

VIRGINIA R. BOYNTON

ECALLING HER 1905 arrival in Cleveland, Ohio, Jane Edna Hunter
noted that "my search for lodgings gave me a keen insight into
the conditions which confront the Negro girl who, friendless and
alone, looks for a decent place to live in Cleveland." Her experience,
typical for African American women migrating from southern states
to northern cities in the early twentieth century, reflected the segregation and racial discrimination that blacks continued to encounter in
their new surroundings.

Hunter's response to her situation—to create a new and separate
institution to meet the needs of black women—grew from the commitment she shared with some, but not all, black Clevelanders in the
early twentieth century to establish separate organizations to serve
the city's rapidly growing African American community. The Phillis
Wheatley Association (PWA), which Hunter founded in 1913 and led
until her retirement in 1946, was the first social service agency established in Cleveland to meet the needs of African Americans migrating
to the city. By 1927, it had become the largest black institution in
Cleveland as well as the largest independently operated residence for
African American women in the nation.

The young mulatto woman who stepped off the train in Cleveland
in 1905 might not have seemed likely to become one of that city's
best-known black leaders. A mere twenty-two years old when she
moved north, Hunter had been born Jane Edna Harris in 1882 to
South Carolina sharecroppers. Her mother, Harriet Milliner Harris,
was the free-born daughter of recently freed slaves; her father,
Edward Harris, was born into slavery as the son of an English plantation overseer and a slave woman. His death when Jane, his oldest

FIG. 14 Jane Edna Hunter.
Courtesy of Special Collections, Cleveland State University Library.

daughter, was ten years old brought an early end to her education, forcing her to take a series of positions in domestic service in order to help with the family's finances. After several years as a maid, nanny, or waitress in various South Carolina homes and businesses where she periodically faced unwanted attention from men, fourteen-year-old Jane was invited by black Presbyterian missionaries to enroll in Ferguson Academy; after four years she graduated with the equivalent of an eighth-grade education.

With no money and no desire to continue in the only occupation for which her schooling had prepared her—domestic service—the eighteen-year-old woman found herself with limited options. She later recalled that after "the boy I really loved and with whom Mother had forbidden me to keep company" had married someone else, she "capitulated" to her mother's "urgings" and married a man she did not love, Edward Hunter, who was forty years her senior. After fifteen months, the mismatched couple separated; Jane Edna Hunter never remarried. She sought work in Charleston, South Carolina, where she enrolled at the Canon Street Hospital and Training School for Nurses. Before long, she began working as a private-duty nurse in the homes of some of Charleston's elite white families. Desiring more advanced training, she moved to the Dixie Hospital and Training School at the Hampton Institute in Virginia. There she immersed herself in the educational philosophy made famous by Booker T. Washington, which emphasized the value of vocational training and manual labor for improving the economic condition of African Americans. After one year at Hampton, Hunter was persuaded by family friends to move with them to Cleveland, Ohio, where opportunities seemed to beckon to a young woman trained in nursing and willing to work hard.

In many ways, Hunter was typical of the single black women who migrated north during the early twentieth century. As historian Darlene Clark Hine has pointed out, such women most often made the entire trip in one journey, rather than working their way north in shorter stages, doing odd jobs along the way, as their male counterparts tended to do. Hunter followed this pattern, traveling from Virginia to Cleveland in a single train trip. She also typified unmarried black female migrants in her decision to journey in the company of family friends, rather than alone. Traveling alone could put both a black woman's safety and her reputation at risk; thus, according to Hine, most chose to travel with companions. Hunter's destination was also a common one for black migrants, whether male or female. By 1920, Cleveland was among the eight northern cities (including Cincinnati and Columbus) with the largest populations of African Americans. In addition, Hunter shared in the motivations common to black women who decided to transplant themselves; she hoped not only to improve her economic position but also to escape the sexual exploitation frequently faced by employed black women in the South.

Hunter's migration differed from those of many other black women, however, in several important ways. Her move preceded the Great Migration, the period between 1914 and 1919, when unprecedented numbers of African Americans migrated from the South to the industrial North to take advantage of opportunities afforded by World War I. For this reason, she not only experienced the difficulties of migration before any institutions existed to help Cleveland's new black female residents, she was also well positioned to begin addressing that problem before the greatest influx of female migrants to the city. Because Hunter did not join relatives or family friends in Cleveland who could help her find housing and employment, she quickly became aware of the difficulties faced by single women in an unfamiliar city. This provided her primary motivation for establishing the Phillis Wheatley Association. Finally, Hunter departed from the typical pattern of black female migrants who, as Hine points out, continued to maintain close family ties to the South, often because some or all of their children remained, at least temporarily, behind. Hunter, while occasionally visiting family members in the South, had no children and became firmly rooted in Cleveland's African American community. Her life certainly supports Hine's contention that "black women played a critical role in the establishment of an array of black institutions" in the northern cities in which they made their homes.

The Cleveland to which Hunter traveled, as historian Kenneth Kusmer has documented, was on the verge of transition in terms of race relations. Originally settled largely by transplanted New Englanders, Cleveland in the nineteenth century had a small black population. In 1890, it amounted to just over three thousand people, or only slightly more than one percent of the population. Black Clevelanders had also been more likely to have been born or raised in the North than African Americans in other midwestern cities such as Chicago, Indianapolis, or St. Louis. Until the early twentieth century, Cleveland's liberal integrationist heritage, a by-product of its New England roots, tended to retard and mute the growth of racial discrimination in the city. During the early decades of the new century, however, the city's black population swelled as African Americans migrated from the South in search of a better life. By 1930, blacks comprised more than 8 percent of the city's population—almost 72,000 people. Accompanying this growth was a hardening of racial distinctions in the city, with previously integrated public facilities becoming increasingly exclusionary and segregated. In the midst of these developments, Hunter stepped off the train from Virginia seeking work as a nurse, a decent place to live, and congenial forms of recreation.

Hunter's search for employment was greatly hampered; as an African American woman, she faced even greater discrimination and had fewer opportunities than her male counterparts, as historians Darlene Clark Hine and Adrienne Lash Jones have pointed out. Nonetheless, as a black woman, she was more likely to need paid employment than were her white counterparts. When working as a black nurse in the South, Hunter had been readily accepted as a private-duty nurse in the homes of white patients, who were comfortable with (and generally preferred) African American women in positions of service. Upon seeking recommendations from Cleveland's white doctors for such positions, however, Hunter reported that she frequently "met rebuffs which seemed much more severe than those encountered" in the South. Just how severe was made clear by one physician, who "told me to go back South—that white doctors did not employ 'nigger' nurses" in Cleveland. Desperately in need of funds, she fell back on her earlier occupation and began cleaning downtown office buildings, where she finally met a doctor willing to recommend her to a patient. This allowed her to begin building a network of clients among Cleveland's white population. Nonetheless, whenever nursing opportunities grew scarce, she supplemented her income by taking cleaning jobs or doing "odd laundry jobs for women who had more laundering than they could do."

This experience played a crucial role in convincing Hunter that the only truly reliable form of employment for Cleveland's African American women was some form of domestic service. Her perception certainly reflected the reality of her times. As historian Kenneth Kusmer has shown, in the early decades of the twentieth century, between two-thirds and three-quarters of Cleveland's employed black women had jobs involving various forms of personal service, primarily household service. African American women, meanwhile, were virtually shut out of the plethora of new opportunities in the burgeoning fields of clerical, sales, and other white-collar work that were opening up for white women. As late as 1915, Hunter was one of only two professionally trained black nurses in the city.

Hunter also encountered difficulties in her search for respectable housing. She later wrote of her "despairing search for decent lodgings—up one dingy street and down another" until she finally accepted "the least disreputable room" she had encountered, although she was still not pleased with her new accommodations. Her new home was a rooming house run by a family whose daughter apparently practiced casual prostitution to supplement her family's meager income and all of whose members, to Hunter's further horror, drank beer. Hunter moved out of these lodgings as soon as she could afford more respectable housing in a quieter and safer neighborhood with a family "far superior in character." Nonetheless, she observed that her "few months on Central Avenue made me sharply aware of the great temptations that beset a young woman in a large city."

Because the Cleveland YWCA, which provided both temporary and longer-term rooms for young single white working women, did not accept black lodgers, and because no other Cleveland institutions provided the same service for African American women in the early twentieth century, Hunter and other early female migrants had no alternative but to take rooms in private homes. And because, according to Hunter, black families "who could afford better houses were above taking roomers," the newly arrived female migrants like Hunter were limited to "the unsightly, run-down sections of the city" where prostitution flourished and accommodations were dingy, crowded, and frequently unsafe.

The newly arrived Hunter likewise encountered roadblocks in her efforts to relax and enjoy her infrequent leisure hours in ways she found congenial. Her first opportunity for recreation in Cleveland came when she visited Woodluff Hall, a local dance hall for African Americans. Initially excited at the prospect of meeting other young people while enjoying the dancing and music, she found herself feeling distinctly uncomfortable with the other patrons, whom she described as "women with heavily painted faces and indecently short skirts; men slightly intoxicated and somewhat noisy." Only later did she learn that a local underworld figure used Woodluff Hall to recruit young black women as prostitutes. All in all, Hunter's early experiences seeking suitable recreation, housing, and employment in Cleveland gave her, she later observed, "a first-hand knowledge of the dangers and hardships that beset the Negro woman who is a stranger in a large city, together with an overwhelming sympathy for her defenseless condition."

To Hunter, the problems faced by what she characterized as "the young Negro girl pushed from the nest by economic pressure, alone and friendless in a northern city; reduced to squalor, starvation; helpless against temptation and degradation" demanded action. But what was the solution? In September 1911, Hunter met with seven of her closest friends, all economically struggling African American working women. They discussed their common difficulties with finding acceptable, affordable lodgings as well as decent, profitable employment. They concluded that neither city officials nor the local all-white YWCA could be expected to help. Realizing that they could not rely on others to solve these problems, they decided to form what they initially called the Working Girls' Home Association. They elected Hunter as their president, each pledged to contribute a nickel each week to the organization in order to raise funds to establish a boarding home, and agreed to recruit as many new members as possible.

By working to establish a separate boarding home for black working women, Hunter and her allies stirred up considerable opposition. This opposition came not from the white community, which was generally pleased to let African Americans deal with their own problems, but instead from older middle-class black club women who were longtime residents of Cleveland. As Hunter's biographer, Adrienne

Lash Jones, has pointed out, "supporters of the idea for a Working Girls' Home literally stumbled into the thick of a national ideological debate between those who supported [Booker T.] Washington's idea of race separation and those who were demanding integration," in the tradition of W. E. B. DuBois. In Cleveland, this philosophical conflict was further complicated by regional, class, and educational differences within the local black population. On one side was the more prosperous, well-educated, northern-born old guard, familiar with Cleveland's legacy of liberal integrationist race relations. On the other side stood the economically struggling migrants who were products of the segregated South's inferior educational system and who could not help but notice the ever-dwindling impact of Cleveland's racially liberal legacy. Familiar, as was Hunter, with black institutions and "self-help" programs in the South, the newcomers were less concerned with protecting the rapidly receding ideal of integration and more focused on coping with the growing reality of segregation and exclusion in their adopted city. Hunter resented what she perceived as the attempt by the black club women, who did not face the same dire economic realities as the new migrants, to undermine her efforts. According to her autobiography, at an early open meeting of the Working Girls' Home Association, one of Cleveland's old-guard black women leaders complained, "Now that the more intelligent of us have broken down the barriers between the races, you are trying to build them up again with your absurd Southern ideas for working girls. We shall never permit it. . . . we will not permit you, a Southerner, to start segregation in this city." These women argued instead that black women should insist upon equal access to the YWCA's facilities. Hunter, however, refused to back down in the face of this opposition from what she referred to as "the militant club women." She persisted in her belief that "the Negro must develop race pride and enterprise, and continue to make his [*sic*] own contribution to the world—as a Negro," a philosophy she explicitly acknowledged sharing with Booker T. Washington. Her persistence paid off, as many of her original opponents eventually became "staunch friends of the work," won over, no doubt, by the ever-growing reality of segregation and exclusion in the city in the years after World War I.

The local YWCA's white leadership, meanwhile, supported Hunter's efforts to establish a separate institution for black women, which would relieve pressure on the YWCA to integrate. Hunter worked with the YWCA Board of Trustees and other members of Cleveland's white elite, as well as members of the city's black community, to raise the funds to establish her organization. Finally, in 1913, the Phillis Wheatley Association (the organization was renamed to honor the Revolutionary-era slave poet) opened the doors of its leased twenty-three-room house on East 40th Street to its first residents, thus becoming the first organization in Cleveland to offer assistance to African American migrants from the South. From its founding, Jane Edna Hunter served as the chief administrator for the association.

The PWA quickly demonstrated how much it was needed. Virtually always filled to capacity, the home immediately began expanding its facilities and services. Hunter recalled that "New needs kept appearing, new opportunities kept opening up." Aware that "our girls were in need of work, and . . . many housewives . . . desired efficient maids," Hunter opened an employment office at the PWA to provide referrals for domestic service jobs. The organization also established a domestic science department to provide classes in various areas of home economics.

As the Great Migration picked up steam after World War I broke out in Europe in 1914, the housing shortage in Cleveland became even more acute. The PWA's original quarters had never been large enough to meet the demand for its rooms. Consequently, in the spring of 1917, the PWA Board of Trustees purchased a three-story apartment building at the corner of East 40th Street and Central Avenue that tripled the PWA's capacity to seventy-five boarders. Two years later, the organization purchased a two-story building located next to the boarding home in order to provide space for recreational and community activities. This expansion meshed well with another of Hunter's goals: to provide safe and respectable recreational venues for African American women.

Hunter played a vital role in raising the funds from private sources located in both the black and white communities for these major capital purchases. Having been asked by the board in 1915 to work full-time for the PWA, Hunter served the organization in a variety of capacities, including as its chief fund-raiser and liaison to the white community. As executive director, she oversaw the entire organization's daily operations, including close supervision of an increasing number of employees. The number of paid staff members grew from two in 1915 to twenty by 1922. This larger staff helped provide an ever-expanding roster of services to residents of the PWA as well as to the city's African American neighborhoods: a dining room and cafeteria (the most popular dining facility among African Americans in

Cleveland), a music department, classes in handicrafts and dancing, a gymnasium and basketball team, a summer camp on the shores of Lake Erie, and outreach activities in several other black neighborhoods. The PWA also continued to fulfill its original purpose of providing black women with clean, safe, and affordable housing as well as training for and employment referrals to household service positions.

By 1922, the PWA, still the only respectable boarding home in the city for black women, was once again bursting at the seams. Hunter spearheaded yet another fund-raising campaign to build a new facility specifically designed for the PWA. Reaching out to both the black and white communities, including nationally known white philanthropist John D. Rockefeller, Hunter raised more than $700,000 (including $169,000 from African Americans in Cleveland and $100,000 from Rockefeller). The new building's cornerstone was laid in June 1927 at Cedar Avenue and East 46th Street, and the doors of the new nine-story home (plus two basement levels) opened to one hundred young black women residents in December 1927.

While helping the PWA grow and expand, Hunter was also raising her personal profile. The Welfare Federation of Cleveland (an association of the city's private social service agencies) had accepted the PWA as a member in 1918, thereby guaranteeing it regular financial support from the Community Chest and recognizing it as a full-fledged social service agency. When the Welfare Federation acknowledged the need for better social services for the city's burgeoning African American population in the early 1920s and called for the formation of a Negro Welfare Association (NWA), Hunter was among the first invited to join the new association's board of trustees. She remained for many years on the board of the NWA, which became the Cleveland affiliate of the National Urban League and sought ways to improve the economic status of the city's impoverished black population.

While working to secure the financing to build the PWA's Cedar Avenue facility, Hunter decided to continue her education. Her meager schooling in the South was in no way comparable to the college degrees held by many in the black female elite among Cleveland's old guard, a situation that frequently had been a source of concern for her. In 1922, she began working toward a degree at the Cleveland School of Law at Baldwin Wallace College, eventually passing the Ohio Bar examination in 1925. With an advanced degree Hunter no longer felt at a disadvantage when negotiating contracts or setting budgets.

The same year that she joined the Ohio Bar, Hunter also gained access to a national network of black women leaders when the PWA affiliated with the Ohio Federation of Colored Women's Clubs and its parent organization, the prestigious National Association of Colored Women (NACW). Within three years, Hunter was serving as the head of the NACW's national Big Sister Department (which was affiliated with the National Big Brother and Big Sister Association). Within ten years, she had created and was heading the NACW's Phillis Wheatley Department, which worked with black women in cities around the nation where the local YWCA did not have a black branch, helping them to establish homes similar to Cleveland's PWA.

Thus, while Hunter knew how to cultivate friendships among Cleveland's white elite and was willing to accommodate their desire for segregation, she clearly also had goals that transcended theirs and eagerly sought opportunities to work with black women elsewhere in America to achieve them. According to her biographer, she "followed the example of thousands of black predecessors: accommodating to white perceptions of black inferiority and acting out the role, while skillfully using every opportunity to gain knowledge and information which could be helpful personally, or which could strengthen her position." She remained committed throughout her life, however, to her conservative racial philosophy of gradualism, accommodation, and self-help, believing that it was "important to squarely face conditions as they exist, while at the same time using energy and intelligence to improve them." For this reason, and because of her own personal background and Cleveland's stubbornly segregated occupational structure, she believed that training in domestic service provided the best avenue for increasing the employment prospects—and thus the economic status—of Cleveland's black women.

Because Hunter had begun her employed life as a servant and had been able to use that experience as a stepping stone to a more prestigious career, she was inclined to see household service as a reasonable and acceptable means of economic improvement for African American women. During the Great Depression, as the job market tightened even further for black women, Hunter built on the PWA's experience with employment referrals and home economics classes to establish the Sarah C. Hills Training School at the PWA in 1931. The program focused on training girls and women in such subjects as hygiene, cooking, laundry, housecleaning, and sewing, so that they might be prepared to be either better homemakers or domestic servants. The original six-week course was soon expanded to nine weeks and eventually to almost five months. In 1937, the PWA's Board purchased an older house next to the PWA residence and remodeled it into a "practice cottage" where each trainee could gain experience in "the kind of home in which the girl may be employed, and giving a good model for the arrangement and furnishings of her own home." Of the 178 young women admitted to the program from 1931 to 1938, 102 completed the full course and secured immediate employment.

Throughout the Depression, the PWA under Hunter's leadership offered a wide variety of programs and activities, including academic offerings in subjects such as black history, politics, and economics; leisure activities such as mothers' clubs and girls' clubs (including tennis, basketball, dancing, and dramatics clubs); lessons in piano, violin, and voice; as well as a pre-school program for the children of working mothers and a beauty school for young women. In addition, although the residence's occupancy rate dropped somewhat as the migration northward fell off during the 1930s, the continuing exclusion of blacks from the city's hotels provided a fairly steady stream of temporary guests at the PWA. The PWA's dining room also remained a popular destination for the city's African Americans during the 1930s, serving as a regular meeting place for blacks from all walks of life. It also provided one of the few public places in the city where whites and blacks could (and regularly did) sit down to meals together.

With the outbreak of war in 1941, Cleveland again became a destination for black workers migrating in search of better jobs. The Phillis Wheatley residence was once again filled to capacity (even though midway through World War II the Cleveland YWCA finally decided, in light of the nation's fight against racism overseas, to open its doors to black women). Frequently cooperating with the Negro Welfare Association and the all-black Cedar YMCA to meet the needs of African American war workers, the PWA offered dances and other after-hours recreational activities for war workers, clerical training programs for prospective women workers, and housing on both an emergency and a long-term basis for those moving to the city.

The end of the war coincided with Jane Edna Hunter's retirement from the position she had held since 1911. In 1947, she stepped down as the executive director of the PWA after thirty-six years of leading the organization. Hunter's many years of service and accomplishment did not go unnoticed among her peers. In 1928, she was invited to be an honorary member of Alpha Kappa Alpha, an organization of African American college-educated women dedicated to public service, and during the Depression and World War II she was repeatedly elected as state president and national vice president of the National Association of Colored Women. She also received honorary degrees from Wilberforce, Fisk, and Allen Universities and from Booker T. Washington's Tuskegee Institute.

After her retirement from the PWA, Hunter established the Phillis Wheatley Foundation, an independent organization, to raise money for scholarships for young black working women seeking a college education or training in nursing, domestic science, cosmetology, or stenography. By the mid-1950s, Hunter's health began failing and after 1960 she was confined to a rest home in Cleveland, where she lived until 1971, when she died of natural causes at the age of eighty-nine. Fittingly, she left her estate to provide scholarships for college-bound women.

Jane Edna Hunter's life touches on many important historical themes and developments. A child of the limited opportunities of the segregated South, she participated in the early stages of the Great Migration, only to discover that racial segregation and exclusion were not the sole province of the states south of the Ohio River. Persistently committed to racial uplift for African Americans, she shared with many other blacks of her generation a belief in Booker T. Washington's philosophy of self-help, vocational training, gradualism, and separate institutions for African Americans. Certainly, it was as a vital part of that tradition of black institution building that she made her greatest contribution: establishing, nurturing, and leading Cleveland's Phillis Wheatley Association for thirty-six years.

Further Reading

Hine, Darlene Clark. *Hine Sight: Black Women and the Re-construction of American History*. Brooklyn: Carlson Publishing, 1994.

Hunter, Jane Edna. *A Nickel and a Prayer*. Cleveland: Elli Kani Publishing Company, 1940.

Jones, Adrienne Lash. *Jane Edna Hunter*. Brooklyn: Carlson Publishing, 1990.

Kusmer, Kenneth L. *A Ghetto Takes Shape: Black Cleveland, 1870–1930*. Urbana: University of Illinois Press, 1976.

Phillips, Kimberley L. *Alabama North: African-American Migrants, Community, and Working-class Activism in Cleveland, 1915–45*. Urbana: University of Illinois Press, 1999.

19

Martin L. Davey: Horatio Alger in the New Worlds of Tree Care and Partisan Politics

RONALD LORA

W HILE MARTIN Davey was struggling to save the Davey Tree Expert Company during the Great Depression, James Truslow Adams published his *Epic of America* (1931) in which the Pulitzer prize–winning historian pondered the status of the American Dream. The Dream moved in the world of numbers, exploit, and money, but its more complex formulation reflected the vision of "a land in which life should be better and richer and fuller" for everyone, with "opportunity for each according to his ability or achievement." The Dream was the very soul of the nation, and it separated Americans from the nations of Europe. When the Depression lingered year after year, however, many grew bewildered over the meaning of the Dream.

Martin Davey was not among them, for he saw himself as the exemplar of the Dream. He was born on July 25, 1884, in Kent, Ohio, the third of seven children of John Davey and Bertha Reeves. In 1907, Martin married Bernice Chrisman, with whom he had four children. In his twenties, he undertook a leadership role in the family tree care business and built it into a modest-sized company. Soon thereafter he entered politics, and at age twenty-nine began the first of three terms as mayor of Kent.

After his stint as mayor, he served four nonsuccessive terms as a U.S. congressman (Democrat) from Ohio's Fourteenth District. His defeat in the Ohio gubernatorial race in 1928 laid the groundwork for two successful campaigns for governor in 1934 and 1936. As Ohio's fifty-third governor, he saw a state that was experiencing all the harsh problems of the Great Depression, including closed banks

FIG. 15 Martin L. Davey.
Courtesy of the Ohio Historical Society.

and schools, soaring unemployment, and bankrupt local governments. The stormy politics of Depression-era Ohio led to his defeat
for renomination in 1938, and two years later, after winning the
Democratic primary election in 1940, he lost heavily to incumbent
governor John Bricker. Following his defeat, Davey retired from politics to devote his energies to the Davey Tree Expert Company, which
he continued to serve as president until he died on March 31, 1941.

A Horatio Alger Story

The popular Horatio Alger books, published during the last decades
of the nineteenth century, provided a formulaic version of the American Dream: a poor boy could become a millionaire, a peddler a rich
merchant, and a farm boy a president. The Alger hero—honest,
manly, and ambitious—was on alert for his main chance in life. The
goal was to be successful.

If we make allowances for a life lived in the twentieth century, Martin Davey's life in many ways reflects the Alger version of the Dream. No evidence exists that Davey had read *Struggling Upward,* a classic Horatio Alger story of success, but his unpublished autobiography resonates with its central point: Luke Larkin (the hero) "has struggled upward from a boyhood of privation and self-denial into a youth and manhood of prosperity and honor." Luck played a role, but "he is indebted for most of his good fortune to his own good qualities." Martin Davey's father did not die while Martin was young, but the son was born poor. In his autobiography, he stated: "[Father] never knew how to handle money very well. The result was that he went deeper and deeper into debt. . . . What I can remember is the misery of my own suffering, and how I cried and cried for Mother to get me some mittens." Just as bitter was the derision it brought: "The circumstances under which I grew up—poverty, debt, and the ridicule of other children—instilled in me a feeling that I was not as good as other people. . . . It had a depressing influence on me, and could have blighted my life, if circumstances had not taken me away from home at the age of seventeen."

Like many of Alger's heroes, Martin wanted more than material success. "Ragged Dick," for example, wanted above all else to achieve respectability: "You may not become rich . . . but you can obtain a good position, and be respected." For Martin, that meant having a place of one's own (better than the "rude little two-room house" in which he grew up), education (Oberlin College), a job (worth dropping out of college for), a bank account (opened with savings from door-to-door selling), and a nice change of clothes (Governor Davey in sartorial splendor). All this meant rags to respectability, if not rags to riches. An endearing trait of the Alger heroes is their cooperative attitude. In Davey's case, family members helped each other, for the Davey Tree Expert Company was a family operation until 1979, when employees purchased the firm.

Nowhere but in the United States, Davey believed, could such success stories appear so abundantly. While a member of the U.S. Congress in 1926, he addressed a state rally of two thousand Democrats, in which he illustrated his conception of the American Dream. There was a little home in the Midwest. It had but two rooms, one a bedroom, the other a combination living and dining room. A cook stove in the living room heated the house that had little more than a table and several chairs. The floors were barren, save for several inexpensive rugs. At the windows, devoid of lace curtains, poverty looked in. To the family was born a son, who knew nothing of life's luxuries or of the advantages of social position. His early days were spent in a "rugged environment of struggle and adversity." When at last it was time to leave home, his mother made a point of telling him: "You and I both ought to thank God that you were born in America, this great land of freedom and democracy and equal opportunity, a land in which there is no social caste and where there is no barrier against the children of the most lowly. . . . Go! And may God bless you in your struggle for the rewards that America alone makes possible!"

The Davey Tree Expert Company

The Davey name was known first to Ohioans as the family that introduced tree care and tree surgery in America. In 1873 after a great deal of study and work in horticulture and landscape gardening while living in England, Martin's father, John Davey, sailed for the United States, where the wanton destruction of trees shocked him. After marrying, he moved to Kent to become caretaker of a cemetery where he could practice his skills. Within a few years, it became a "place of striking beauty with new plantings of trees, shrubs and flowers." People traveled for miles to view it. He and Martin's older brother planted hundreds of trees along the streets and around homes in Kent. Known as the "treeman of the town," John wrote pamphlets and lectured frequently on nature and conservation. His experience suggested that trees would respond to surgical treatment if the job were done properly. Eager to share his knowledge with a wider audience and to acquire clients, he discussed his methods in an eighty-seven-page book, *The Tree Doctor,* published in 1901.

When door-to-door selling of the book helped to bring more work than the Daveys could handle, John in 1902 began to train others in the "new science" of tree surgery. That led to the creation of the Davey Institute of Tree Surgery, which lives on today as the Davey Institute of Tree Sciences. At the request of his father, who was a naturalist but not a manager, Martin dropped out of Oberlin College to bring organization to the growing business. He became treasurer and general manager of the Davey Tree Expert Company when it was incorporated in 1909, and on his father's death in 1923 he became president, a position he held for the rest of his life.

Martin worked diligently to become a leader. Before the age of ten, he produced, packed, and sold horseradish house-to-house, and later in the growing season he hawked vegetables from his father's garden. After graduating from Kent High School, he sold typewriters, which earned him $150 to $200 a month, an excellent income at the turn of the century, even more so for a teenager. He also honed his salesmanship skills while a student at Oberlin College by clerking in a men's store, operating a laundry route, and, in the summer months, selling life insurance. It was a hard-knock life; but Martin discovered that he was skilled in salesmanship, so he headed east in 1908 to seek clients from among wealthy estate owners, including John D. Archbold, president of Standard Oil; Emil Berolzheimer, head of the Eagle Pencil Company; William Rockefeller, son of oil baron John D. Rockefeller; and Henry M. Flagler, a businessman who had worked in several Ohio cities, including Cleveland, where he became a partner in an oil-refining firm that would become the Standard Oil Company.

While selling "big men" on the wisdom of tree surgery, Martin developed a deep respect for those with wealth. Often "maligned, belittled, and sometimes clawed to pieces by the muck-rakers and by the angry wolves of politics," Davey later observed, most of them were "remarkably fine people . . . [who] stand out conspicuously for ability, character, and civic responsibility." It is they who "do worthwhile things" and push forward "the frontiers of our civilization." The lesson for his life was "Hard work and long tedious hours, sacrifice and worry, courage in the face of all difficulties, faith when other men falter, dogged determination—these are part of the price that every man must pay for success."

Troubled by the entry into the tree care business of ill-trained people who were interested only in a job, Martin, in the March 19, 1911, issue of the company Bulletin wrote what he was to repeat again and again through the years: "The tree butcher knows no more of trees than the eunuch knows of love." It is significant in underscoring Martin's aggressive vision that in 1911, with the Davey Company already operating in more than two dozen states and in Ontario, Canada, he sought prestige for the company by seeking a commission to work on the grounds of the U.S. Capitol and the White House. Unable at first to interest the superintendent of the Capitol grounds, Martin placed before him an insect-infested branch from a maple tree. Shocked at the sight, the superintendent placed an order for tree care, which began the Davey Tree Expert Company's long commitment to caring for trees at the White House, and later, on the Parliament Grounds in Ottawa, Canada.

In the four years after he assumed the company's presidency in 1923, Davey Tree trebled its business from approximately $800,000 in sales to $2.4 million. But the following two decades were difficult ones. During the Great Depression, tree care was a low priority. With the company suffering a sharp decline in sales, Martin bid for national attention by turning to the new medium of radio. In a prelude to Franklin Roosevelt's "Fireside Chats," the company sponsored the "Davey Radio Hour," a program of old music favorites aired from New York City and transmitted by eighteen stations of the National Broadcasting Company. In eight-minute talks to his listeners, Davey discussed his philosophy of caring for trees and his views on life in general. By 1933, the situation was desperate. Davey Company income had fallen from $3 million in 1930 to $700,000 in 1933, and the company was mired in debt. It helped when the Civil Works Administration employed Davey Tree supervisors to oversee its parks projects, but even then payrolls often could not be met, some workers took half pay, creditors extended time for repayment, and family members sacrificed their salaries and contributed personal cash to the company. Such measures enabled the company to survive the Depression years and pay off its debts.

A second crisis for the Davey Company came with World War II. The war meant gasoline rationing and shortages of tools, materials, and, most importantly, manpower. Seven hundred and twenty-five Davey men and women joined the armed forces. After three seasons of severe cutbacks in its operations, the company survived the war as it had the Depression, and then began a period of substantial growth. Each time, Martin Davey had persisted. After the bleak years of Depression and war, sales in 1946 again totaled $3 million and then tripled to nearly $10 million in 1955, not including Canada. In 1977, when the Davey family decided to sell the company to its employees, sales amounted to $42.9 million and in several years topped the $100 million mark. It remains today a fine example of workers acquiring a genuine stake in their company through employee ownership.

Embattled Politician

To Martin Davey, like so many of Horatio Alger's heroes, success in life was not identified solely with making money. Success meant respectability, but the means of achieving it was unknown to Alger heroes. Davey decided that he could win public respect and serve others best through holding political office. Besides, it offered drama as well as risk: politics "is life, action," he remarked in his last campaign. Davey's interest in politics blossomed during the election of 1912, when Woodrow Wilson bested Theodore Roosevelt and William Howard Taft. Wilson's eloquence inspired him; so did his call for a "New Freedom" that challenged Roosevelt's campaign for a federal government strong enough to collect income taxes and regulate labor. When speaking to constituents during the 1920s, Davey portrayed himself as an apostle of Thomas Jefferson. There had been a titanic struggle in the early days of the Republic between the monarchical, strong federal government position of Alexander Hamilton, he told audiences, and "the great apostle of democracy" Thomas Jefferson. In Jefferson, there "breathed the spirit of democracy." He loved the masses (in Davey's overly enthusiastic reading of the third president) and on their behalf "took up the battle for human rights and popular government."

Interestingly enough, Franklin Roosevelt also was impressed by the Jefferson-Hamilton struggle. But Roosevelt and Davey differed in important ways. Davey supported Newton Baker at the Democratic National Convention in 1932, partly for the sentimental reason that Baker had served as mayor of Cleveland, Ohio, when Davey was mayor of nearby Kent. Yet ideological issues played a role, too. Baker had entered municipal politics as a legal assistant to Tom L. Johnson, the popular and highly respected reform mayor of Cleveland, but as he aged he became more conservative and gave the New Deal only tepid support. Its extension of government powers was a victory for statism, he believed; even if constitutional, it was unwise. That was the Baker whom Davey supported: the admirer of Edmund Burke's preference for prudent change and of Jefferson's faith in individualism and local self-government. Davey soon paid for having supported Baker. In early 1933, believing that his interest in tree planting and conservation, together with his success in managing the Davey Company, was enough to warrant an appointment as U.S. secretary of agriculture, Davey wrote president-elect Franklin Roosevelt, stating his qualifications for the position. Roosevelt replied that he would "consider" him for the post but said nothing else, then or later.

Running with the Roosevelt prestige that carried so many Democrats to victory in 1934, the Kent tree surgeon was elected governor by a margin of 65,000 votes. It was a difficult decade; for many Ohioans, it was a calamity. A leading industrial state, and the nation's fourth most populous, Ohio was wracked by unemployment. In

1933, statewide unemployment was nearly 40 percent, with the industrial unemployment reaching the astonishing heights of 60 percent in Akron and, for a few months, upwards of 75 percent in Toledo. Behind the percentages lay physical and emotional deprivation. In the larger cities, doctors reported nervous disorders, skin eruptions, and malnutrition-related diseases. Newspaper headlines told the story:

From the Toledo *Blade:*
> Jobless Toledoan Dies for Family, Note Says Asking Body Be Sold and Money Sent Destitute Wife and 7 Children

From *The Lima News:*
> City Relief Agency Taxed as Cold Wave Grips Community. Homeless Beg For Shelter.

From the *Brown County News Democrat:*
> Mother with Newborn Babe Found Living in Chicken House

From the Ashtabula *Star Beacon:*
> Sheriff Halts Penny Bidding at Farm Sale

Davey began his first term doubting, he later said, "if there ever was as hard a time to be Governor of Ohio as in January, 1935." Many "local governing bodies were practically bankrupt [and] all of them were looking to the State for help in staggering amounts." One hundred sixty-eight banks were closed, "nearly one-fifth of the population . . . was on relief," and, to his annoyance, a "job-seeking army" descended on Columbus.

The largest problem awaiting Davey when he took office was unemployment relief. Of Ohio's 6,000,000 citizens, 1,200,000 were on the relief rolls. When the state agency that administered relief expired in early 1935 and federal relief administrator Harry Hopkins asked Davey to administer the funds provided by the Federal Emergency Relief Administration (FERA), Davey replied that he could not administer a program that was "cruel, inhuman and wasteful." Although evidence is hard to come by, the governor insisted that people on relief received money for dental work or beauty shop visits that working people could not afford. But it is clear that Davey, alarmed by declining state revenues, hoped to avoid having to ask for a tax increase to fund the state's share of the relief program. When he delayed and continued a drumbeat of criticism in the press, Hopkins and Roosevelt struck back, with the former releasing to the public on March 16 a letter to Davey, saying: "It has come to the attention of this administration . . . that your campaign committee, shortly after your election, proceeded to solicit money from the men and business firms who sold goods to the Ohio Relief Administration. The frank purpose of this shakedown—because it can be termed fairly by no other name—was to help pay off the deficit of your campaign and the expenses of your inaugural." Although Davey was not involved in the scheme and such practices were common enough in other states, the story made headlines in Ohio and across the nation.

The standoff ended when President Franklin Roosevelt, in a strongly worded letter suggesting that corrupt political interference threatened relief work in Ohio, directed Hopkins to assume control of the distribution of all relief funds in the state. Davey's Ohio thus became one of several states in which the federal government was forced to administer relief directly. Relieved that the federal government would assume control, Davey understood that it came with a cost, namely, adverse publicity to the effect that Ohio was obstructionist, uncooperative, and ethically suspect. (Lorena Hickok, who served as field agent for Harry Hopkins, wrote her friend Eleanor Roosevelt, "God, but that sap, [Governor] Davey, has made a mess of things!" And in a report to Hopkins she wrote, "There are of course states that openly chisel. Ohio, for instance.")

In a bizarre public relations move, the governor on March 18 charged Hopkins with libel and threatened to arrest the powerful Roosevelt adviser if he ever visited Ohio: "Come to Ohio, if you dare, and show that you are a man, or turn and run like a coward and confess your contemptible character." In the same telegram to Hopkins, whom he now saw as Roosevelt's "particular pet," Davey wrote: "You have done me a grave and unforgivable wrong, and if you have any of the instincts of manhood, you will permit this wrong to be righted." He then released the telegram to the media, again creating a national news event. He called for the Ohio legislature to meet in a joint session that night. It was a dramatic moment. To a packed House, Davey defended his integrity and, among other things, charged that Hopkins had exercised "dictatorial control" in Ohio relief, released an "unscrupulous letter" to the press, and presided over a system in which "professional relief workers" welcomed "chiselers" onto the rolls.

Although Lorena Hickock's reports on the Works Progress Administration (WPA) at times substantiated Davey's claims about earlier FERA abuse, historians on the whole have given the FERA good marks for efficiency and its humaneness in the face of so many personal tragedies. Indeed, a subsequent investigation found that there had not been undue federal control of relief funds, that the Ohio Relief Administration had established family relief budgets for each county without federal interference, that the federal government had contributed most of the relief funds, and that it was appropriate to insist that certain guidelines be met. Davey found some vindication when the federal relief agent in Ohio reduced staff to save approximately $100,000 on payrolls. Several investigations also failed to uncover anything unseemly that Davey had done personally, either in the case of relief or other alleged scandals.

Later in 1935, the federal government ended making direct relief grants to the state in lieu of a works program (WPA). With Governor Davey now in charge of the state relief program, neither he nor the legislature could agree on a permanent unemployment relief program and various stopgap measures were passed during the remainder of Davey's terms of office—for example, $6 million for 1935 and $13 million for the first half of 1936.

Relief under the FERA worked best where state leaders were cooperative and responded responsibly to the state's need to help fund relief (for example, New York and Minnesota) but others (Ohio, Louisiana, and Arkansas) were difficult in the extreme, and Davey was perhaps the most difficult of all Democratic governors in this regard. Despite entreaties from Washington, he refused to request more funds from the legislature on the grounds that the program was too wasteful and, he thought, the localities should be doing more. Davey also railed at "professional relief workers" who he charged made it too easy to get on the relief rolls, thus augmenting their own positions in what, he said, was a business in and of itself—the business of making their jobs "secure and permanent."

Despite the bickering between Washington and Columbus, the New Deal in Ohio saved hundreds of thousands from extreme suffering. From the depth of the Depression in 1933 through the end of Davey's term in January 1939, nearly $1 billion dollars was provided for recovery and relief. An additional $800 million was provided in loans.

Labor-management relations provided the second major test of Martin Davey's political leadership while governor. As a congressman during the 1920s, he had supported labor legislation, voting for a $3.00 minimum wage bill in 1919, a civil service retirement bill, and a child labor amendment to the U.S. Constitution. Despite doubts about relief programs, Davey in 1935 signed into law the Ohio act that provided death benefits, hospital services, and funeral expenses for public work-relief employees. Two years later, he signed the bill that amended the Workmen's Compensation Law to add silicosis (lung disease) to the list of occupational diseases covered. It was a record of which he was justifiably proud, and the American Federation of Labor (AFL) spoke well of him.

The emerging issues of the 1930s, however, proved more than he (or the AFL) could master. The rules of labor-management relations had changed; the Wagner Act (1935) outlawed company unions, defined all employer interference as an unfair practice, made collective bargaining enforceable by law, and demanded that companies appear at the table and bargain in good faith. The conservative AFL leaders' unwillingness to organize the industrial (as opposed to craft) workers set the stage for the rise of mass-production unionism. Spearheaded by United Mine Workers head John L. Lewis, the Committee for Industrial Organization (CIO) was at the center of the major labor conflicts of 1936 to 1937. The basic dispute was over union recognition. The Steel Workers Organizing Committee (SWOC), an affiliate of the CIO, was engaged in an intensive organizing drive, often resulting in bitter strikes, when to the surprise of most observers, including CIO leaders, in March 1937 industry giant U.S. Steel capitulated to SWOC, granting union recognition to its workers as well as a wage increase and a forty-hour week.

But with "Little Steel"—Inland, Youngstown Sheet and Tube, and Republic, with plants located in northeastern Ohio—the story was different. The independent steel producers, who employed more than 80,000 workers, refused to negotiate with SWOC. In late May, tensions rose when police fired on pickets at Republic Steel in South Chicago, killing ten—the Memorial Day Massacre, as it became known. Governor Davey's attempt at mediation in Ohio also failed, despite his pressure on Tom M. Girdler, chairman of the Board of Directors of Republic Steel. In fact, Girdler refused even to attend Davey's conference. In the midst of bombings and violence on the part of strikers, and the use of special police, deputy sheriffs, and provocative agents on the part of the steel companies, Girdler let it be known that the plants would reopen. Having collected ample stocks of tear gas, munitions, shotguns, and paid private police and professional strikebreakers, the steel companies were well prepared for industrial warfare. At that point, Secretary of Labor Frances Perkins appointed a Federal Mediation Board, and Governor Davey dispatched the Ohio National Guard to Trumbull and Mahoning Counties. The Mediation Board met, and though Girdler attended, he was unmovable, occasionally pounding the table and responding to suggestions: "God damn it, the answer is no!" Having failed, the Mediation Board reported that the steel masters had refused to meet with union representatives—a clear violation of the Wagner Act. The governor then had a choice. His troops could keep the steel mills closed, or he could order them to maintain order as the plants were permitted to reopen.

In a radio address in early June, Davey lambasted the CIO. Its tactics, he said, were "violent and un-American," and its leaders were "riding high on a wave of terrorism, intimidation, and fear." Reds, he added, were a significant part of the problem: John L. Lewis, for example, kept "an astounding number of communists" around him. When Davey heard rumors that more coordinated labor violence was in the offing, he called out the militia "to suppress insurrection, and repel invasion." Even though many strikers were ready to return to work, it was Davey's use of the National Guard that broke the 1937 strike against "Little Steel."

What made Davey's actions noteworthy is not merely that he defeated the CIO ("Collapsed in Ohio," said one opponent) or that he alienated thousands of industrial workers, but that he had joined big business in its assault on the Roosevelt administration. He had stood against the empowerment of labor, at that moment perhaps the major way a free society could transform itself into a working-class democracy, one that could increase mass purchasing power, the lack of which was one of the factors that had brought about the Great Depression. The political consequences for Davey were significant. For its gubernatorial nominee in 1938, Ohio's badly split Democratic Party chose not him but Charles Sawyer, a former lieutenant governor (and future secretary of commerce under President Truman) who enjoyed the support of the Roosevelt administration. Had the Democrats been united, it is probable that John Bricker, the two-time Republican attorney general of Ohio, would never have been elected governor and, later, become his party's vice presidential candidate. The "Roosevelt recession" of 1937 to 1938 also hurt Davey's chances by deepening the Democratic disarray. Last, Davey's decision to break the steel strike cost him significant labor support, for the CIO mounted a powerful campaign against his renomination. A Republican like Bricker could carry on a feud with the New Deal, take an anti-labor stance, oppose adequate relief for cities whose budgets had collapsed, and still win elections in Ohio; but a Democrat could not, at least not during the Roosevelt years. Although Davey was selected to oppose Bricker in the 1940 gubernatorial election, he was trounced by a margin of 365,000 votes, to that date the largest in an Ohio gubernatorial election.

Most Ohio governors in the twentieth century, whether Republican or Democrat, were conservative. Until fairly recently, rural counties dominated the state legislature, and their representatives disdained urban needs. Not only was Davey aware of that political bias, it fit well his own predilection. Near the end of his life, he still insisted that anyone who had "never smelled the odor of newly turned earth or . . . the aroma of new-mown hay, cannot understand life in its full sense." It was as a turn-of-the-century Democrat who evoked memories of Grover Cleveland that Davey governed during the troubled thirties, when the battleground was shifting from farm to city. Born in the midst of the Gilded Age, and having won success in both business and politics, he saw little need to adjust his inherited moral standards and ideology to a new era. His experience in business told him that income and employment went up and down, that business cycle fluctuations were the normal routine of life. It was not unreasonable so to believe; after all, it was the story of U.S. economic development. He had experienced the shattering depression of 1893 to 1896, the brief panic of 1907, and the deep recession of 1920 to 1921. After each came recovery. He believed that the economy would respond as it always had, but he had no theory that could explain the deeper meaning of the economic earthquake because he remained trapped by the folklore of capitalism and the simple Alger formula for success.

Martin Davey was an excellent tree surgeon and an outstanding conservationist. It had taken courage for a young man in his early twenties to head into other states, seek out the estates of the wealthy, and prepare presentations that would bring work orders. And he did his homework, gathering information about his prospects, learning what points were likely to persuade them and when they were most likely to grant him an audience. He always had a plan, and it enabled him and his family to build a company that was on the cutting edge of the new science of tree care and tree surgery. Then Davey moved into the world of politics, with all of its turmoil and partisanship. Like Horatio Alger, Davey did not become a tycoon, yet when he died in 1946, he left his family a $3 million-per-year business in tree care, had served Ohio twice as governor, and had gained respectability.

Further Reading

Braeman, John, Robert H. Bremner, and David Brody, eds. *The New Deal: The State and Local Levels.* Columbus: Ohio State University Press, 1975.

Patterson, James T. *The New Deal and the States.* Princeton, N.J.: Princeton University Press, 1969.

Vazzano, Frank P. "The Feud Renewed: Martin Davey, John Bricker and the Ohio Campaign of 1940." *Ohio History* 105 (Winter–Spring 1996): 5–24.

———. "Harry Hopkins and Martin Davey: Federal Relief and Ohio Politics during the Great Depression." *Ohio History* 96 (Summer–Autumn 1987): 124–39.

———. "Martin Davey, John Bricker and the Ohio Election of 1936." *Ohio History* 104 (Winter–Spring 1995): 5–23.

20

George DeNucci and
the Rise of Mass-Production
Unionism in Ohio

WARREN VAN TINE

D URING THE bleak depression years of the 1930s, Ohio workers took part in a national movement to gain a greater voice on the job and in society. Although the movement was centered around steel, auto, rubber and other mass-production industries, it involved all types of laborers, from retail clerks to schoolteachers and janitors. After years of resignation and apathy, working-class militancy dramatically increased in 1934, as Ohio experienced more strikes than in any year since the wave of 1919 to 1920.

In 1935, workers gained much needed government and legal support with the passage of the Wagner Act, and equally important institutional and financial support with the establishment of the Committee for Industrial Organization, changed in 1938 to the Congress of Industrial Organizations (CIO). These two developments promoted the image of President Franklin D. Roosevelt and CIO head John L. Lewis as saviors of the working class. Yet, important as national leaders and federal policies were in advancing unionism, hundreds of relatively unknown men and women played an equally critical role at the grass roots level.

In almost every manufacturing center in Ohio, a handful of individuals served as catalysts for the local labor movement's upsurge in the 1930s. Iorwith Wilber (I. W.) Abel helped organize the Timken Company's Canton plant for the United Steelworkers of America. Ray Ross brought the United Autoworkers into International Harvester in Springfield, while John House led Goodyear rubber workers in a 1936 strike that became the CIO's first significant victory. Some of these activists, such as Abel who became president of the Steel-

FIG. 16 George DeNucci.
Courtesy of the Ohio Historical Society.

workers in 1965, eventually gained major positions in the national unions they helped to build. But many did not make the adjustment to the more institutionalized labor movement of the post–World War II era. Some discovered that the skills needed for organizing a union were not the same skills needed for running one. Others lacked the proper base for attaining leadership positions as power gravitated to the representatives of those locals and national unions with the largest memberships. Such men and women spent their lives in the trenches of the labor movement, only to have history forget their names. This essay explores the life of one such activist, George DeNucci, both to reclaim his importance and to highlight some significant dynamics in Ohio labor history.

George DeNucci, whose given name was Galli, was born in the small Italian town of Capratto on February 14, 1902. Within months of his birth, George's father, Vincent, left his wife, Catherine, and their two children and, on borrowed money, sailed for the United States in search of work as a skilled tailor. George's father had difficulty establishing himself in America, but after a few months he landed a tailoring job in Baltimore. Still, he did not earn enough to pay off his debts and send for his family.

Vincent DeNucci's luck changed in 1904 when William Hersch, owner of the United Woolen Mill in Parkersburg, West Virginia, traveled east to recruit Italian tailors. Vincent was a particularly valuable catch for Hersch. Having served a five-year apprenticeship, the elder DeNucci was a "complete" tailor capable of designing and assembling a man's suit from scratch. Most of the workers at United Woolen were "partial" tailors, cutting and pressing in the factory's wholesale department where young women did most of the sewing. In addition to receiving higher pay because of his skill, Vincent earned extra money from Hersch by recruiting old friends in Italy to United Woolen. This allowed Vincent to pay off his debts and send for his family, who arrived in Parkersburg in early 1906.

Once in the United States, George enjoyed a childhood shaped by his father's status as a skilled worker. His family, the Catholic Church, the local Italian community, the public schools, and sports dominated his youth. Unlike many working-class boys, George never mentioned having to work odd jobs while young. And becoming a U.S. citizen was simply something that happened under the prevailing naturalization laws when his father declared citizenship in 1918. In 1921, George graduated from Parkersburg High School, receiving no academic honors but letters in both football and baseball.

Even though United Woolen offered jobs to all of Vincent's children, George was determined that he "wasn't ever going to work in any plant, factory, or anything no sir." He particularly disliked Hersch, who he thought took advantage of his father and the three hundred other Italians who worked for him. Consequently, shortly after graduation George journeyed to Akron to join a stable of boxers, but after a few bouts he recognized that prize fighting was not his calling. Instead, for almost a year he lived off another of his skills, pool sharking. Finally, George succumbed to family pressures, returning to Parkersburg and to work as a cloth cutter. In 1925, when a fire destroyed the factory, Hersch moved his company to Columbus with George and the rest of the work force in tow.

For his first few years in Columbus, DeNucci resided with his parents, worked at United Woolen, and lived a life lacking any clear commitment or direction. This changed when he married Lena, another Italian immigrant, in October 1929, only weeks before the great crash of the stock market. To make ends meet as times got tough, she worked at the mill as a secretary while he earned extra cash as a part-time salesman at United Woolen's downtown store.

DeNucci also became more interested in unionism. United Woolen had long recognized the United Garment Workers, primarily because Hersch faced few pressures from the organization but found the union label helpful in attracting business. DeNucci automatically became a union member upon starting work at the mill but attended very few meetings until 1930. Within short order, however, he became Local 245's president because, he later said, "no one else wanted it." Actually, DeNucci brought many assets to the job. A high school graduate when many fellow union members were not, he could efficiently perform the required administrative functions. Moreover, his athletic prowess counted for much in the masculine culture of the labor movement. From his work as a pool shark and salesman, he had learned how to deal with people and motivate them to take action. And from his experiences with Hersch, he harbored strong, antagonistic feelings toward factories and the people who owned them.

The timing of DeNucci's entrance into union affairs was also propitious. Amid the general prosperity of the 1920s, various segments of Columbus's working class had not done so well. Racial prejudice confined the city's significant African American population to marginal employment. Prohibition, too, threw out of work many of those employed at the city's breweries and bottle-making plants. Furthermore, after a building boom during the first part of the decade, the city's construction industry went bottom-up, pulling down with it various suppliers of window glass, lumber, cement, bricks, and related products. In short, even before the 1929 Wall Street crash, a sizeable pool of Columbus workers were struggling.

The subsequent depression only intensified the situation. Throughout the 1920s, manufacturing employment in Columbus had stood around 26,500. By 1935, however, the number of wage earners in manufacturing had fallen to 17,516. "Our present emergency," observed the *Ohio State Journal,* "is greater than that brought about by any cyclone, fire, flood, or other sudden catastrophe."

Rising unemployment decimated the city's labor movement. In February 1931, the Columbus Federation of Labor (CFL), a confederation of local unions, increased per capita dues, appointed special organizers to raise membership, and created a special committee to cut expenses. But nothing worked, causing the organization's president to twice try to resign, only to be turned down because no one was willing to take his place.

Such a situation encouraged two parallel developments. First, leadership positions fell to older, established, and conservative men who sought simply to preserve the CFL during hard times. Second, the general apathy created opportunities for younger, more progressive unionists to gain positions on committees and lesser offices. In 1934, these progressives gained further strength as a consequence of increased unionizing activity prompted by the National Industrial Recovery Act. And although many of the locals formed at this time quickly faded from the scene, individual progressives maintained their toeholds in the their local organizations and in the CFL.

As president of Local 245 of the United Garment Workers, George DeNucci emerged as one of the progressives. Beginning in 1931, he also served as a delegate to the CFL, which seemed to interest him more than his own union. Working for the CFL when others were indifferent, DeNucci was elected its recording secretary in 1933.

Another of the progressives and ally of DeNucci was Ted F. Silvey. Born in Manchester, New Hampshire, in 1904, Silvey spent his early childhood in Zanesville, Ohio. When Silvey's father died in an industrial accident, young Ted took numerous odd jobs after school to help support his family. The direction of Silvey's life took a turn when his mother became a Jehovah's Witness and moved the family to New York City to work for *The Watchtower,* where Ted was taken on as an apprentice printer. In the early 1930s, he moved to Columbus, became active in International Typographical Union (ITU), and was elected a delegate to the CFL.

The Italian Catholic pool shark and the Jehovah's Witness printer were joined in advancing the progressive cause in central Ohio by about twenty-five other individuals, mostly in the printing trades and the miscellaneous unions but also a few in the building trades. One or two of the more radical may have been associated with the local Communist Party, but they were not very important.

In 1934 and much of 1935, the progressives were just a collection of like minds sharing the vague goal of strengthening the local labor movement through organizing industrial workers. They avoided open challenges to the CFL's established leadership but worked away at the edges. In late 1934, the progressives gained control of the CFL's Education Committee and used it to engage rank-and-file unionists in discussions on specific labor problems and broader social and economic issues. Likewise, they convinced the CFL to publish the *Labor Tribune,* with Silvey as editor and DeNucci as one of the three members of its board. The *Labor Tribune* quickly became a major forum in disputes over how to organize workers and which political candidates to support. The progressives also gained control of the CFL's Organization Committee, which in November 1934 presented to the CFL delegates a motion calling for "a policy on organization such as putting the entire personnel of an industry under one head." As had happened to a similar motion at the recent American Federation of Labor (AFL) convention, delegates to the CFL amended it to the point it became meaningless.

Throughout the spring and summer of 1935, the progressives pressured the CFL to fully support the upsurge in working-class militancy occurring in the city. The August 16, 1935, issue of the *Labor Tribune* reported strikes at the Columbus Packing Company, then in its twenty-second week; at the Hercules Clothing Company, where eight hundred workers were resisting a 20 percent wage cut; at area Works Progress Administration projects, to increase pay for skilled workers; and at Hills Cab company, where a union man was discharged without a hearing in violation of the contract.

Capitalizing on this momentum, Lew Johnson, president of ITU #5 invited DeNucci, Silvey, and five other individuals to a dinner on September 30, 1935, out of which emerged a functioning progressive caucus. Shortly thereafter, the national AFL held its convention in Atlantic City during which resolutions endorsing industrial unionism went down in defeat, and United Mine Workers president John L. Lewis punched Carpenters' president William L. Hutcheson, a gesture that symbolized the breakup of the House of Labor. On November 9, Lewis and leaders of other disillusioned AFL unions launched the Committee for Industrial Organization (CIO) as an organized bloc inside the AFL dedicated to unionizing along industrial lines, a policy the AFL majority had just rejected.

Thus, when the Columbus progressives held a second dinner on Thanksgiving Friday, 1935, attended by twenty-five individuals, they now viewed themselves as part of a larger effort. As Johnson and Silvey wrote to John Brophy, the new director of the national CIO: "We want to lend our support to your efforts and act as a clearing house in Columbus for your promotional and educational work. . . . We want to create a ferment in the local Federation so as to educate and agitate for the new industrial set-up in the labor movement."

In the weeks that followed, the *Labor Tribune* printed letters debating whether workers should be organized by craft or industry, with the vast majority on the latter side. The progressives also pressed the case for the CIO at Columbus Federation of Labor meetings, which apparently was the only thing that enlivened these sessions. As delegate Silvey noted in December 1935, CFL president Larison "is unexcelled in conducting a dull and stupid meeting. Attendance [is] continually declining." Yet in an ironic way, Larison, an opponent of industrial unionism, aided the progressives by alienating everyone with his constant sneering. "Our fear," Silvey observed, "is that he shall not only sneer himself out of a job, but sneer the Columbus Federation of Labor out of existence at the same time."

In January 1936, Larison announced he would not seek reelection as CFL president. By then, the progressive caucus had decided to nominate DeNucci, who had given a moving pro-CIO speech at the December CFL meeting yet projected a moderate image in dealing with the building trades. Moreover, DeNucci, a garment worker, both countered the image of the progressive caucus as dominated by ITU #5, and as a member of the miscellaneous trades was able to deliver the largest block of votes in the CFL.

The election proved a landslide for DeNucci. Of the eighty-four delegates voting, seventy-one cast their ballots for him, after which his opponent gracefully moved that DeNucci's election be recorded as unanimous. Along with a lack of major division or rancor, two other aspects of the election were interesting. First, no pattern to the voting emerged, with delegates from the building trades, printing trades, and miscellaneous trades overwhelmingly going with DeNucci. Second, while eighty-four delegates voted, thirty-six did not. More than likely, these thirty-six reflected the general apathy that Silvey had noted.

Shortly after his election, DeNucci delivered a radio address that outlined the direction in which he would lead the federation: "I stand for industrial unionism, and I know that some of the craft unions are not in sympathy with the movement. Let me tell you that I will not run ahead of the American Federation of Labor, although I have the conviction that new policies and new methods are needed in the labor movement. My purpose is to be ready for those changes when they come, so that organized labor may be strengthened and go on to new victories." Like the founders of the CIO at the national level, DeNucci viewed himself and his allies as initially working within the AFL.

DeNucci lost no time invigorating the Columbus labor movement. He prodded each union in the city to increase its membership and started rebuilding the locals chartered during the NRA days. When Silvey reported back to ITU #5 on the affairs of the CFL in April 1936, he was positively aglow: "New administration at Federation changes whole complexion of labor movement in Columbus. Absence of bigotry and selfish ambition; more concern for all workers;

devotion to cause and progressive policies present. . . . Organization campaign in progress. Difference between Larison's treatment of small unions and that given by DeNucci. 100 more dues paying members in last two and one-half weeks." By July, Silvey was telling ITU #5 members:

> DeNucci's general activities producing results steadily. Work with bottle blowers, meat cutters, molders, pattern makers, upholsterers. School jani-tors increase membership from 50 to 100 since new administration. . . . Quick and intelligent action by DeNucci saved Buckeye Distributing Com-pany contract with brewery workers. . . . DeNucci protested to Governor Davey the letting of state construction contracts to non-union contractors, with result that an order was sent out of the governor's office requiring all state work to be let to union contractors. DeNucci's work with governor's office has been satisfactory. Personal connections good. . . ."

With DeNucci as attentive to the concerns of building tradesmen as he was brewery workers and school janitors, enthusiasm and unity marked the first six months of his tenure.

There were individuals, however, displeased with DeNucci, but they did not openly question the direction of the CFL until the late summer of 1936. This displeasure centered around the Buildings Trades Council (BTC) and the organization's secretary, George A. Strain. It would be wrong to conclude, however, that all building trades workers and their local leaders opposed the CFL's industrial union drift. Strain's backers tended to be the heads of the Carpen-ters', Plasterers', and a few other unions. Some building trades dele-gates to the CFL constantly supported DeNucci's actions, a fact attested to by DeNucci's reelection without opposition as CFL pres-ident in January 1937. Equally important, however, a larger group of building trades delegates did not attend CFL meetings. This lack of participation may have been a strategy to avoid being caught between two forces, but most likely it reflected the building trades' historic aloofness from other unions.

George Strain's own motives for challenging DeNucci and the CFL's industrial union drift were complex. Like many labor leaders, Strain held a strong commitment to the AFL and could not accept a divided labor movement. Moreover, like so many craft unionists, Strain felt no bonds with mass-production workers. He once observed that "one reason for the building trades supporting the American Federation of Labor . . . is the fact we must serve a four-year apprenticeship before becoming a journey man, and we are reluctant to place the fate of our wage rates and working conditions in the hands of a predominate group of unskilled laborers."

Strain's opposition to DeNucci also had a political dimension. Strain was committed to the Republican Party, and the CFL was clearly going Democratic. Autumn 1936, moreover, was election season. As the BTU's representative on the *Labor Tribune*'s board of control, Strain argued frequently with Silvey over that paper's editorial policies and whether Republican candidates could have access to its mailing list or advertise in its columns. Silvey was not impartial in these matters, since in August 1936 he had become director of the central Ohio wing of Labor's Non-Partisan League (LNPL). The LNPL and the CFL not only worked to reelect Roosevelt but campaigned against a number of local anti-union Republicans.

Everything that DeNucci did seemed to alienate Strain. In August, DeNucci participated in establishing the Columbus LNPL and presided over the city's first large CIO rally. On October 31, DeNucci gave a radio address urging local workers to reelect Roosevelt. And in November and December, he worked closely with members of UAW Local 30 in their strike against the Auld Company, converting it into a political confrontation with the Republican-controlled city hall over police anti-strike activity.

While DeNucci and others cooperated with the CIO, the AFL expelled CIO-affiliated internationals at its November 1936 convention. The CFL, however, continued to seat representatives of the ousted organizations. This was in line with AFL policy, since when asked how city and state bodies should treat locals of the expelled international unions, AFL president William Green responded that they should be permitted to remain affiliated. Thus, while the United Automobile Workers was no longer an affiliate of the AFL, UAW Local 30 was an active, militant, and growing member of the CFL.

The AFL's expulsion of the CIO unions gave Strain and other AFL stalwarts hope that something could be done about the local progressives. Yet at the same time, working-class militancy encouraged the more radical CFL delegates to push their agenda harder. Thus, by January 1937 DeNucci found himself wedged between two positions. Leaders of the BTC challenged him for being a CIO advocate, while radical delegates attacked him for not being more aggressive. Explosive arguments between the stalwarts and the radicals over aid to the Flint sit-down strikers forced DeNucci to rule clearly in favor of the progressives and led Strain and the other building trades leaders to reconsider their options.

When the BTC met on February 8, 1937, it asked the AFL executive council "to investigate CIO activities in Columbus and radical political affiliations of officers and committee men of the Columbus Federation of Labor." Whether this action was done after consultation with the AFL's headquarters is not clear. But AFL president William Green responded promptly, notifying DeNucci three days later that a representative was on his way. This was the first time that the national AFL had commenced an investigation of a central body for pro-CIO activities. Green's assigning the task to CIO-hating Francis J. Dillon, the discredited former president of the UAW, suggested that Green had already determined the outcome to the investigation.

For the next several days, Dillon met with Strain and other local labor leaders—but not DeNucci, Silvey, or other progressives. Then, on February 23, 1937, he appeared at the CFL meeting where, according to Silvey, "Dillon asked DeNucci to publicly renounce the C.I.O., apologize for having helped it, promise not to do so any more, and hand him his resignation as President of the central body." DeNucci refused.

DeNucci did agree to meet with Dillon the next day to see if the dispute could be resolved, unaware that Green had already concluded that no compromise could be tolerated. Consequently, while DeNucci was closeted with Dillon on April 24, Green called upon all state and city federations to "decide whether they will be loyal to the parent body . . . or give support to an organization which is classified as dual and rival." In line with Green's position, Dillon again demanded DeNucci's resignation, and again DeNucci refused, adding, however, that he would place his future in the hands of the CFL delegates at the regular meeting scheduled for the upcoming Wednesday. Dillon abruptly responded that there would be no meeting, as he was going to revoke the CFL's charter.

The progressive forces moved rapidly to protect their organization and its leaders. DeNucci immediately moved the CFL's scheduled Wednesday meeting up to Monday, March 1. Then, after burying the records of the CFL in his backyard in case his office was seized, he went into hiding at the Fort Hayes Hotel under an assumed name so no court order could be served. Meanwhile, the local leaders of the barbers, printing pressmen, typographers, and other unions telephoned their national officers to see what pressures they could bring to stop Green.

DeNucci's supporters also convinced Judge Cecil J. Randall to issue a temporary injunction prohibiting the national AFL from lifting the CFL's charter. That night, March 1, CFL delegates met in special session and refused to accept DeNucci's resignation by a vote of 51 to 2, with two building trades representatives not voting (and almost half of the delegates not present).

For the next three months, attorneys for both sides paraded in and out of courtrooms, filing briefs and asking for extensions. Reflecting the ideological division between the parties, the progressives were represented by two members of the Lawyer's Guild, while the AFL's attorney was Paul M. Herbert, a former state commander of the American Legion and a recent Republican candidate for lieutenant governor. Yet despite rather ingenious arguments by both sides, a resolution to the situation did not come from the slow moving judiciary system but from events on the national labor front.

On March 2, 1937, the day after the vote of confidence for DeNucci, the United States Steel Corporation signed a contract with the CIO's Steel Workers' Organizing Committee (SWOC). This development, only a few weeks after General Motors dramatic surrender to the Flint sit-down strikers, established the CIO as an unstoppable force in the labor movement. Consequently, in mid-March, Green instructed city and state bodies to "draw a line between the American Federation of Labor and the Committee for Industrial Organization." In response, on April 24 the CIO announced that it would begin chartering its own city and state bodies.

The CIO's announcement undermined the progressives' efforts to keep the Columbus labor movement united. With both the UAW and SWOC successfully organizing in the area, the establishment of a separate Columbus CIO body was inevitable. Consequently, the issue became how to keep those progressives who remained in the AFL in charge of the CFL. Clearly, to appease Green and save the charter DeNucci had to go. Consequently, on May 5, he tendered his resignation and accepted a position with the CIO.

Thus by the summer of 1937, Columbus, like the nation, had two major labor bodies. In September, DeNucci became president of a newly established Franklin Country CIO Council, made up of fourteen local unions and three thousand men and women. And in 1939, he organized a statewide CIO umbrella organization that paralleled the Ohio State Federation of Labor. Several of the progressives joined DeNucci in the CIO camp, including Silvey who became secretary-treasurer of the Ohio CIO Council. These departures gave the CFL a less militant tone, yet it by no means became conservative or abandoned the efforts to organize workers. Ironically, after forcing DeNucci's departure, various building trades unions disaffiliated from the city body. In 1938, George Strain himself redirected his energies to Republican Party, and, as a reward for working for John Bricker's election as governor, became head of the state's Department of Industrial Relations.

The creation of the Franklin County CIO allowed DeNucci to do what he did best—organize workers. "I love to organize," he told an interviewer in the 1970s, "I didn't care about negotiations, taking up grievances, and things like that." He saw his primary role as being the initiator, the person who made contacts and got things started. Once convinced that enough workers in a plant were committed to unionism, he would request the appropriate organization to send in its own staff and he would depart for another target. Following this strategy, he helped the UAW organize Columbus Auto Parts and the CIO Textile Workers' Union gain recognition at Columbus Coated Fabrics. He even assisted state employees in forming what would become the Ohio Civil Service Association.

DeNucci's efforts to organize Timken's Columbus plant were typical of his activities. Off and on during 1937 and 1938, he visited the bars surrounding the plant, engaging workers in discussions. Among them was young Harry Mayfield, who wanted to do something about conditions in the plant. Mayfield had already tried working as a member the company union's grievance committee, only to get booted out of a meeting with the plant manager for pressing a case too hard. Now spied upon and followed, Mayfield nonetheless agreed to attend a clandestine, nighttime meeting at "Red" Malone's farm, far from the eyes of Timken agents. Mayfield remembered DeNucci arriving at the gathering with I. W. Abel, who had already established a Steelworkers' local at Timken in Canton. He also brought along a pony keg of beer to promote a full discussion of the issues. When the meeting adjourned, an organizing committee had been formed under Mayfield's leadership that would challenge one the most anti-union firms in the state.

In the early 1940s, DeNucci's efforts to build support for organized labor in central Ohio received help from the Catholic Church with the arrival of Bishop Michael Joseph Ready and the establishment of a Social Action Department under Father Augustine Winkler. Previously, the local Catholic leadership had been hostile to the CIO and reportedly even prevented DeNucci's daughter from attending

Catholic school because of her father's union connections. In contrast, both Ready and Winkler sought to convince people within the diocese that organized labor was respectable. Bishop Ready appointed various labor leaders' wives, including Lena DeNucci, to important positions in the Diocesan Council of Catholic Women. He also initiated an annual Labor Day Mass, which was also broadcast over radio. For his part, Father Winkler ran a school that taught local labor leaders—many not even in possession of high school degrees—the fine points of contract negotiations and labor law so they could deal effectively with the better-educated company representatives.

The outbreak of World War II dramatically altered the labor movement in central Ohio and DeNucci's career. In August 1940, the federal government decided to build an aircraft factory on the outskirts of Columbus for the Curtiss-Wright Corporation. At the peak of wartime production in 1944, this facility employed 24,684 workers—a number roughly equal all prewar manufacturing employees in the city. Most importantly for the labor movement, Curtiss-Wright's workforce unionized shortly after it began production in 1941. DeNucci had begun organizing the facility as soon as it started hiring, identifying sympathizers in key departments. The challenge he faced was not company opposition but uniting a workforce divided by religion, ethnicity, and race. Unlike most of his organizing campaigns, DeNucci saw this one through to its successful conclusion with company recognition of the UAW.

Almost overnight power relationships in both the city and the local labor movement changed, since the UAW now represented a significant proportion of the city's workers and could mobilize voters both at the polls and at union meetings. Other CIO unions also grew dramatically, in part because government contracts could only be awarded to firms in compliance with the Wagner Act. In all, CIO membership in Columbus increased 300 percent in 1942 alone.

The rise of large-membership unions altered DeNucci's future in the labor movement. When he departed the CFL in 1937 for a position in the CIO, he also relinquished his membership in the AFL-affiliated United Garment Workers. Deeply involved in organizing Columbus Auto Parts and needing an official union affiliation, he took out a card in the UAW but had to return it when a new constitution prohibited non-autoworkers from being members. He then joined a Cincinnati local of the Amalgamated Clothing Workers, but that arrangement was unsatisfactory since he could not attend the meetings. Finally, his friend I. W. Abel helped him attain a Steelworkers card. Still, DeNucci recognized that it was a courtesy membership, one that limited him to a supportive role.

Yet even when confined to staff positions, DeNucci was dynamic. The federal government required labor representation on planning committees, commissions, and boards, and with the large number of union leaders who went off to fight, DeNucci filled many of labor's slots. Moreover, as the CIO's leader in central Ohio, he was its chief lobbyist with state officials. In addition, when the secretary-treasurer of the Ohio CIO Council was drafted, DeNucci took over the duties until the elected officer returned.

For DeNucci, the war provided unions with an opportunity to "sell ourselves to the community." He convinced local unions to become involved in the Community Chest and publicized the fact that union members were the largest class of donors to the fund. He set up a religion-labor fellowship in which leaders of various faiths met monthly with local labor representatives to discuss community issues. DeNucci also pressured his wife and the wives of other union officials to volunteer at various local charities.

The end of the war brought the demise of the committees and boards and the return of the labor-activists-turned-soldiers who were eager to regain their posts. In the postwar shuffle for position that followed, DeNucci's lack of an institutional base made him dependent on the leaders of the larger unions. He frequently undertook special assignments for Phil Murray, the president of the CIO and the Steelworkers. At the CIO conventions, for example, he mobilized votes behind the leadership's agenda. When needed, he also temporarily assumed various posts until an official replacement could be found.

Increasingly, however, DeNucci used his organizing skills in the anticommunist crusade, which would reshape the postwar labor movement. In 1946, Murray appointed him administrator of the Cleveland CIO Council with instructions to drive out Communists. Again, during the 1949 Ohio CIO convention, DeNucci rounded up the votes needed to oust left-leaning executive board members. A few months later, he managed the floor at the national CIO convention that expelled several Communist-controlled international unions. Over the next decade, the CIO dispatched DeNucci to fight Communists throughout the United States as well as in Puerto Rico and Panama Canal Zone.

Ironically, in 1954 DeNucci discovered that the federal government considered him to be a Communist. As he wrote in a letter seeking help from friends: "I, who have always despised and hated them

[Communists] and thru all my years with the CIO was given assignments to ferret out and keep such creeps from responsible positions
in CIO Unions, am now denied a passport because someone with the
philosophy of McCarthy has filed a statement that I was or am a
Communist!" Apparently, an FBI agent in Portsmouth reported that
DeNucci had twice attended meetings at a cleaning establishment at
3966 Gallia Street that fronted for the Communists. From that information and the fact that his name was on the mailing list of the *Daily
Worker*, the FBI concluded he was a Communist Party member. For
the next two years DeNucci sought affidavits regarding his anticommunist activities from a host of prominent figures in the labor movement and in public life. In the end, he was able to produce copies of
old letters showing that he had appealed to the U.S. Postal Service to
stop delivery of the unsolicited Communist publications. As for
attending Communist Party meetings, he discovered that the entire
allegation was based upon sloppy handwriting: The informant's
zeroes looked like sixes. He had attended two meetings in
Portsmouth, although not at 3966 but at the Eagles Hall at 3900
Gallia Street where the local Steelworkers gathered.

The merger of AFL and CIO in the late 1950s brought with it
another shuffle for position which resulted in DeNucci ending his
career on the staff of the Ohio AFL-CIO. Even after he retired,
DeNucci remained active, spending long days in the 1970s, for example, drawing on his vast contacts to promote the Farm Workers' grape
boycott in central Ohio. He died in 1979.

Further Reading

Boryczka, Raymond, and Loren Lee Cary. *No Strength Without Union: An Illus-
     trated History of Ohio Workers, 1803–1980*. Columbus: Ohio Historical Soci-
     ety, 1982.
Dubofsky, Melvyn, and Warren Van Tine. *John L. Lewis*. New York: Quadrangle,
     1977.
Phelan, Craig. *William Green*. Albany: State University of New York Press, 1989.
Van Tine, Warren, C. J. Slanicka, Sandra Jordan, and Michael Pierce. *In the
     Workers' Interest: A History of the Ohio AFL-CIO 1958–1998*. Columbus:
     Center for Labor Research, 1998.
Zieger, Robert H. *The CIO, 1935–1955*. Chapel Hill: University of North Car-
     olina Press, 1995.

21

John W. Bricker and the Slow Death of Old Guard Republicanism

RICHARD O. DAVIES

F ROM THE time John William Bricker first appeared on the Ohio political scene in the mid-1920s, his future seemed especially promising. He came equipped with the requisite credentials. Born and raised on a small farm in Madison County, he became a popular student leader and athlete during his undergraduate days at The Ohio State University, from which he received a baccalaureate degree in 1916. After graduating from OSU School of Law in 1920, he established himself professionally in Columbus and participated in local Republican organizations while developing a wide network of friends and supporters. Extraordinarily popular with voters, he easily led the Republican ticket in four consecutive statewide elections during the 1930s. He also looked the part of a political leader. Ruggedly handsome, he carried two hundred pounds on a solid 6'2" frame topped by a mop of prematurely gray hair that provided an aura of maturity beyond his years. When he decisively won the governorship in 1938, Bricker was widely identified as a rising political star with the potential of becoming Ohio's eighth president of the United States.

That Bricker's ascending political stardom did not propel him to the White House resulted from a rapidly changing political environment that left him stranded on the far right of the political spectrum, a problem he exacerbated with a series of strategic miscalculations. However, as Ohio's attorney general, governor, and U.S. senator he placed his conservative stamp upon Ohio at a critical juncture of its history. His political career is especially instructive because it spanned three pivotal decades that saw Ohio buffeted by the pressure of severe depression, war, and unprecedented growth.

FIG. 17 John W. Bricker.
Courtesy of The Ohio State University Archives.

At the start of Bricker's career, the political power in the state resided in the overwhelmingly Republican rural counties. However, by the time of his surprising defeat for reelection for a third term as U.S. senator in 1958, Ohio's urban areas had reached a position of dominance. The enormous expansion of heavy industry between 1940 and 1945 made Ohio a vital link in the nation's defense program, and during the postwar years those industries responded to the challenges of economic reconversion as Ohio established itself as a leading manufacturing state. As Ohio's steel mills, automobile-related manufacturers, petroleum refineries, coal mines, machine tool factories, and chemical plants expanded during World War II, they stimulated a heavy migration into Ohio's industrial centers. African Americans and white Appalachians moved out of the rural South and into the urban North in huge numbers. They were joined in the cities by hundreds of thousands of native Buckeyes who left their farms and small towns in quest of greater economic opportunity. Between 1920 and 1960,

Ohio's population increased by 80 percent, with two-thirds of Ohio's 9,700,000 residents living in the rapidly expanding metropolitan areas.

The political implications of this demographic transformation were enormous. New and complex issues defied easy resolution. Merely maintaining and expanding highways, public utilities, public school and university systems, and providing essential social services constituted a daunting challenge. Traditional ways of conducting the business of local and state government had to be revisited and new, more ambitious strategies adopted. Not surprisingly, the state's political structure found itself in a period of vast change, producing a period of political instability and intense partisanship. Statewide elections were no longer relative simple battles between urban and rural factions, as they had been during the days when James Cox and Warren Harding bestrode the state's political stage. New power blocs— in particular organized labor—emerged during this period and wielded enormous clout in statewide elections that made the fate of Republicans increasingly precarious. The two major political parties and their candidates now were faced by a much more complex set of issues and variables, including an increased racially and ethnically diverse electorate. Ohio became truly a two-party state with elections often turning on issues of the moment as well as the quality of candidates. The successful candidates were those who were capable of adapting to the new realities of Ohio.

John Bricker did not prove to be one of those flexible individuals. His political values were those of traditional Republicanism that had its roots in the late nineteenth century along the main streets of Ohio's seven hundred small towns and villages and the broad stretches of productive farmlands they serviced. Coupled with the allegiance of urban professional and business groups, this was a predominately Protestant, white, and middle-class political organization. This was the party that John Bricker had embraced as a child—his most memorable childhood memory was meeting President William McKinley—and he dedicated himself to protecting and advancing its central dogmas of limited government, fiscal prudence, and free enterprise. His inability to adapt to the realities of an increasingly diverse and urban Ohio ultimately led to a premature end to his once promising political career.

His Republicanism and conservatism came naturally. He and twin sister Ella were born on September 6, 1893, on the small family farm in Madison County, located a few miles outside of the village of Mt.

Sterling. The state's capital of Columbus, where he would live his entire adult life, lay just twenty-five miles to the northeast. He learned at an early age the harsh realities of working in the fields during the blistering hot days of summer and milking cows during the brutally cold winter mornings before the sun appeared on the bleak eastern horizon. "Brick" learned his three R's from well-thumbed McGuffey's *Readers* in a one-room rural schoolhouse, worshiped regularly at a crossroads interdenominational Protestant church, swam in the murky waters of Deer Creek, and played pickup baseball and football games with friends in the pasture. In church, at school, and at home, John readily absorbed the essential truths of the Protestant ethic: sobriety, honesty, diligence, frugality, and hard work. His parents, Lemuel and Laura (King) Bricker, conveyed to young John a value system that he would never abandon: initiative, responsibility, and patriotism. From his highly partisan Republican father, young John also learned of the virtues and verities of the Grand Old Party.

The unflinching and resolute conservatism that characterized his lengthy political career thus came naturally. Unlike his contemporary Ohio Republican (and sometimes rival) Robert A. Taft, whose cerebral brand of conservatism often left his audiences vaguely uncomfortable, Bricker's came from the heart. He never questioned the values he absorbed as a youth, and it was his fate to spend his entire political career fighting a rear guard action against the rising tide of liberalism as practiced by the New Dealers in Washington, D.C., and the labor unions in Cleveland and Toledo. The New Deal's infatuation with centralized economic and social planning jarred his unwavering faith in limited government and laissez-faire economics. He thus instinctively found the essential assumptions of the new thrust of liberalism repugnant and decried its tendency to mandate national rather than local and voluntary solutions to the problems posed by the Great Depression. The transfer of authority and power from Main Street to Pennsylvania Avenue, the proliferation of federal agencies with their irritating mandates and regulations, the unprecedented intrusion of government into the affairs of business, the effort to redistribute wealth through the power to tax, the conveying of real power to independent labor unions, even the growing tendency to alter long-established racial policies—all of these things and more ran counter to his deeply ingrained view of the world as seen from rural Ohio.

After graduation from Mt. Sterling High School in 1911, Bricker spent a year as an elementary school teacher to earn tuition money and then enrolled at The Ohio State University. He followed a pre-law curriculum in political science, played catcher on the Buckeye baseball team (good fielder, poor hitter), enjoyed the male fellowship of Delta Chi fraternity, served as an officer in the influential campus YMCA (where he led an aggressive campaign on behalf of prohibition), and graduated with a slightly above average academic record. Rejected by the military in 1917 because of an abnormally slow heart beat, he volunteered as an Army chaplain and spent much of his quasi-military experience treating victims of the influenza epidemic of 1918 in an Army hospital in New Jersey. In 1920, Bricker received his LL.B. from OSU School of Law, and that same year he married Harriet Day, an OSU honors graduate from Urbana. Bricker became an associate in a prominent Columbus law firm, joined a host of civic organizations (including Rotary, Eagles, Odd Fellows), and began a lifelong involvement in the work of the Masonic Order. More than anything else, though, his instincts pushed him toward the political arena.

Throughout the 1920s, Bricker dabbled in Young Republican activities, parlaying his connections into a position as an assistant attorney general in 1923 where he concentrated on public utilities regulations. He was a delegate to his first Republican National Convention in 1924 where he enthusiastically supported Calvin Coolidge's renomination. In 1929, Governor Meyers Y. Cooper appointed him to the state utilities commission where he demonstrated a knack for attracting positive media attention by carefully balancing the interests of private companies with those of consumers. In 1932, he won his party's nomination for attorney general without opposition, and in the fall election squeaked out a narrow 10,000-vote victory despite the overwhelming Roosevelt riptide that carried the rest of the state ticket for the Democrats. Demonstrating a facility for cutting administrative costs, Bricker established a solid reputation for his handling of the legal morass created by the collapse of hundreds of Ohio banks and savings institutions. He easily won reelection in 1934, once again bucking a powerful Democratic trend, and thereby enhancing his reputation as a rapidly rising Republican star.

In 1936, Bricker took on the unenviable task of running against Democratic incumbent governor Martin L. Davey. Although the maverick and flamboyant Davey had greatly irritated his party's president with his showboating and caustic criticism, he shrewdly attached himself to Franklin Roosevelt's coattails and won a 126,000-vote victory over Bricker in an extraordinarily acrimonious campaign. Despondent over his loss, especially to an opponent he viewed as corrupt and unscrupulous, Bricker nonetheless took satisfaction in having run

300,000 votes ahead of Republican presidential candidate Alf Landon. He returned to the private practice of law but concentrated on preparing for a rematch with Davey in 1938, knowing that the mounting charges against Davey alleging rigged highway construction bids, corruption in the state liquor department, and forced kickbacks in the form of political donations extracted from businesses receiving state contracts and state employees would serve him well. Those charges of malfeasance, however, led to Davey's defeat by Cincinnati attorney Charles Sawyer in a brutal Democrat primary. The grateful beneficiary of a fractured opposition party, Bricker easily swept to a resounding 120,000-vote victory over Sawyer.

"Of all the positions he held," his longtime personal secretary, Nell Henry, told this writer in 1967, "Mr. Bricker derived the most personal satisfaction out of being governor. In the Senate he was just one of ninety-six persons, but as governor he could get things done." Perhaps as governor he could "get things done," but his vision was such that he was not motivated to launch new initiatives. His was a minimalist agenda that sought to cut the number of state employees by 5 percent, reduce state expenditures, hold the line on new taxes, and administer the daily flow of government operations efficiently and honestly. Under "Honest John," as his detractors sardonically called him, there would be no reform initiatives. Rather, his goal was to demonstrate that he could administer the affairs of state free from the "demagogy, buffoonery and chicanery" that he believed had characterized the Davey administration.

His primary goal as governor was to eliminate the $40 million state debt he inherited from Governor Davey. "It is easy to spend money and to expand government," he said. "It is difficult to save and retrench." His budgets were models of cost cutting and restraint, much to the dismay of those who depended upon state appropriations for their livelihood.

Fortunately for Bricker, his administration benefited enormously from the wartime economic boom. By 1943, unemployment in Ohio had dipped below 3 percent. Ohio's farmers, pressed to the wall during the 1930s, now enjoyed an unprecedented prosperity as agricultural income in Ohio increased by 200 percent. Despite federal wage and price controls, industrial workers saw their wages jump 65 percent by 1945. Ohio ranked fourth among all states in the amount of federal defense expenditures—some $18 billion. The wartime boom provided Bricker with a soaring economy that increased state revenues by more than 25 percent without any increase in tax rates.

Under such fortuitous circumstances, his modest fiscal goals were easily met without undue political cost.

As the surplus in the state's treasury grew, demands for its use naturally intensified, but Bricker held true to his pledge of keeping state expenses under tight control. By the time he left office in 1945, he had not only eliminated the deficit but presented his successor, Democrat Frank Lausche, a bountiful surplus of $75 million. Although he was roundly criticized by spokespersons for influential interest groups—in particular public schools, universities, and state employees—that wanted to tap into the overflowing state treasury, his prudence provided a solid financial foundation for state government as it entered a postwar era of rapid growth. True to his pledge, Bricker also left office with his reputation for honesty intact; not even a modest scandal had besmirched him or his administration.

Bricker's steadfast dedication to what he called "stringent economies no matter how distasteful" produced the only political crisis during his administration. The issue was relatively simple. Throughout the harsh depression years, leaders of Ohio's beleaguered cities had repeatedly come to the state government in the autumn months when they had exhausted their relief funds, requesting the governor to call a special session to appropriate supplemental funds to tide them over until a new state budget kicked in on January 1. The rural-dominated legislature had been unrelenting in its parsimony when it came to urban relief appropriations, and consequently the money that was forthcoming had many strings attached. Thus over the years a profusion of different, sometimes inconsistent state laws, legislative mandates, and administrative directives had erected a rickety house of cards that reminded one contemporary scholar as being reminiscent of the "principles of the seventeenth-century Elizabethan poor laws" in which "stop gap" measures reflected "no permanent planning or no permanent administration." Essentially, the system required county and municipal governments to match in varying degrees state appropriations for direct relief. The system worked against the interests of larger cities, which were confronted by declining tax revenues, hamstrung by constitutional debt limitations, and saddled with an unprecedented number of families seeking direct relief. Planning was made even more difficult because funds provided by various New Deal relief agencies fluctuated widely from year to year.

Central to the Ohio relief situation was the fact that the Ohio legislature on this issue was controlled by a bipartisan rural-dominated coalition that took a dim view of the plight of the cities. In 1938, the legislature had increased the percentage the cities had to contribute for relief from 20 to 30 percent, and in 1939 as part of Bricker's hold-the-line budget, had appropriated only $10 million for the state's contribution to county relief coffers. This meager appropriation had ignored the important fact that the federal government, going through a budget slicing exercise of its own, had reduced Ohio's public works allocation by 39 percent. In the spring of 1939, Governor Bricker informed county and city leaders that, contrary to prior years, the state appropriation would not be supplemented later in the year. He also warned that he would not call a special session of the legislature should local relief agencies run out of money.

His predecessors, both Democrat and Republican, had made similar statements only to relent under the pressure brought by the vote-rich cities. In mid-October, a delegation representing Cleveland, Toledo, and Dayton met with Bricker requesting a special session and supplemental funding. He firmly reminded the group of his pledge to hold the line. The Republican mayor of Cleveland, Harold Burton, launched an energized public relations campaign to break Bricker's resolve. His efforts served to reinforce opposition by rural legislators: "The cities should put their own house in order before coming to the governor and Legislature for more money to handle their own problem of relief," one small-town newspaper editorialized. Bricker dueled with Burton through the media, arguing that the cities had monies they could use but preferred instead to solve their problem with state funds. For several weeks during late 1939, the "Relief Crisis" became a front-page staple of Ohio newspapers, and the story was picked up across the country. Union officials weighed in with their shrill criticisms of "Breadline Bricker," while rural legislators just as adamantly urged him to hold firm. Within weeks, Bricker had been publicly condemned for his indifference to the poor by Secretary of Interior Harold Ickes, while New York mayor Fiorello LaGuardia affirmed that he had it on good authority that "thousands are on the brink of starvation in Cleveland." President Roosevelt told a press conference that Bricker was shirking his responsibilities while his aides passed out summary sheets detailing Bricker's alleged callousness to reporters.

Bricker never wavered despite the national media scrutiny and heavy criticism he received. In early December, the mayors announced that they had found emergency funds to get through the crisis. Simultaneously, Tax Commissioner William Evatt granted the cities authorization to issue tax delinquency bonds to raise additional funds. The "relief crisis" of 1939 thus ended as quickly as it had begun. Bricker had gotten his first taste of the power of the national media, and his animosity toward the New Dealers and their labor union allies had intensified.

During the early stages of the 1940 presidential campaign, Bricker's name was casually tossed about in the press, but he devoted his energies that year to the candidacy of fellow Ohioan Robert Taft. He served as the floor manager for the Taft forces at the convention in Philadelphia where Wendell Willkie won the nomination. Prior to that convention Bricker and Taft had met with top aides and concluded a general (if oft-questioned) understanding that if Taft were unsuccessful in 1940, then he would concentrate upon getting himself reelected to the U.S. Senate, leaving open the possibility of Bricker's presidential candidacy. Bricker's reputation as a frugal governor of one of the nation's largest states naturally attracted interest among conservative Republicans, and by mid-1943 he was considered one of the leading Republican contenders. After considerable vacillation, he formed a campaign committee comprised exclusively of a small group of Ohio Republican confidants and took the plunge.

When Bricker launched his campaign, however, he discovered that the very factors that made him popular in Ohio proved to be liabilities on the national level. He was perceived by the national press as a fifty-year-old governor who offered no new ideas or programs on the domestic side, and whose knowledge of international affairs was severely limited. *Life* magazine defined him as "the walking, talking symbol of middle-of-the-road Americanism." He did not inspire or excite. He was simply "Honest John"—hardworking, cautious, sturdily competent, wary of new ideas, at times embarrassingly poorly informed about international and military issues, but most definitely outspoken in his contempt for the New Deal. "His best opportunity," *Life* explained, "will come if and when U.S. voters get tired of exciting leaders and decide they want a president who looks safe and sound and solid." His presidential candidacy never kicked into high gear. A near disastrous speaking tour of the East Coast in the spring of 1943 produced a spate of critical editorials and negative opinion columns. His vague if not vacuous comments about foreign policy gave his audiences the distinct impression that he was a throwback to the isolationism of the 1920s and 1930s. Likewise, his cliché-riddled denunciations of the New Deal did not impress. "I think Bricker is a little too average," syndicated columnist Elsa Maxwell sniffed. "He is a shade too provincial—too true to his party's worn-out mottos, in danger, indeed, of leading us back to unwanted 'normalcy.'" The *New Republic* succinctly summarized the view from the left: "He is like a country boy in a big city of forces he doesn't understand. Gifted in the art of avoiding issues and uncanny in the knack of making friends without influencing people, he spins a platform of cobwebs." The venerable Kansas journalist, William Allen White, cruelly dismissed him as "an honest Harding."

At the Republican convention in late June 1944, Bricker's faint hopes that the convention would deadlock and turn to him quickly evaporated as front-runner New York governor Thomas E. Dewey easily romped to a first ballot nomination. After California governor Earl Warren turned down an offer of the vice presidential nomination, Dewey reluctantly turned to Bricker on the advice of his aides who had their eye on Ohio's twenty-five electoral votes and hoped that he could help carry several other midwestern states. The subsequent campaign found Bricker mounting an exhaustive, nonstop two-month effort to rally voters behind Dewey. He flailed away at the Democrats, even suggesting that the Communist Party was calling the shots for the political action committee headed by union leader Sidney Hillman. "Insidious and ominous are the forces of communism that are linked with irreligion and are worming their way into our national life. These forces are attempting to take a strangle hold on our nation through control of the New Deal." Even his pointed commentary about the relationship of his Democratic counterpart, Harry S Truman, with convicted felon and former Kansas City political boss Tom Pendergast, proved ineffectual.

Frustrated at every turn by Roosevelt's ability to use his role as commander in chief to make headlines, and with the war effort now clearly on the road to victory in both Europe and the Pacific, Dewey and Bricker proved unable to turn the tide, losing by five million votes. Dewey carried only nine states, but one of those was Ohio, which went Republican for the first time in four elections—by the narrow margin of 12,000 votes out of more than three million cast. Bricker had proven to be a capable campaigner, and he emerged from the election with what most pundits considered to be a bright political future. Even the prospects of another presidential run did not seem out of the question.

That Bricker did not gain such consideration in future elections was the result of a political career turned sour in the demanding glare of the nation's capital. After a brief hiatus in private law practice, he easily won election to the U.S. Senate in the triumphal Republican year of 1946. He arrived in Washington, amidst speculation about whether he or Robert Taft would emerge as the next Buckeye to be the Republican standard bearer. It proved to be no contest, as Bricker soon found himself isolated on the far right wing of his party. Even before being sworn in as a freshman senator, he suffered a devastating setback as the featured speaker at the famed Washington Gridiron Dinner in December 1946. His clumsy and overbearing effort at political humor blew up in his face. His leaden jokes aimed at Truman, who was in attendance, and at other prominent Democrats, embarrassed many of the 650 distinguished Washingtonians in the audience. Bricker's gaffe was such that influential columnist Arthur Krock suggested that he had virtually removed himself from future leadership considerations.

During the next eighteen months, Bricker ended any further presidential speculation by closely identifying himself with his party's rapidly diminishing isolationist wing, even voting against the Truman Doctrine and Marshall Plan despite his avowed opposition to communism and the Soviet Union. His energetic defense of Senator Joseph McCarthy, his relentless efforts to cut federal spending for social programs, his continued hostility to organized labor, and his steadfast opposition to federal economic regulations further removed him from his party's evolving mainstream. Nonetheless, Bricker remained popular at home, easily winning reelection over former Toledo mayor Michael DiSalle in 1952. His large margin of victory was helped by the popularity of General Dwight Eisenhower at the head of the Republican ticket.

In 1951, Bricker had introduced the first version of his proposed amendment to the Constitution. Popularly known as the "Bricker Amendment," it sought to prevent the United Nations from asserting any authority in the "internal affairs" of the United States through treaties and international covenants such as the Genocide Convention or the draft Human Rights Covenant (which he and his supporters feared would overturn southern segregation laws or impose from outside a national system of universal medical care). His amendment also would have required Senate ratification of executive agreements concluded with other nations, such as the controversial Yalta Agreements of 1945. The amendment soon became a magnet for isolationist and militant conservative groups caught up in the uncertainty and unease produced by the standoff between the United States and the Soviet Union during the early years of the Cold War.

By mid-1953, Bricker seemingly had commitments for the two-thirds votes necessary for passage in the Senate. But those commitments proved to be less than firm, as the Eisenhower administration, galvanized by fears that the Bricker Amendment would severely hamstring the president's conduct of foreign policy, mounted a clever if subtle opposition. Ultimately, in February 1954, the Bricker Amendment went down to defeat in the Senate by one vote, its demise orchestrated behind the scenes by the White House and Democratic minority leader Lyndon Johnson who put together a shaky coalition of liberal Democrats and moderate Republicans. Bricker remained undaunted, however, and resolutely introduced the amendment each year until he departed the Senate, but the intense fears that had enabled Bricker initially to assemble conservative bipartisan support steadily dwindled under Dwight Eisenhower's reassuring stewardship of U.S. foreign policy. Years later Bricker angrily, but accurately, told this author, "Ike did it! He killed my amendment!"

By the mid-1950s, Bricker had become alienated from the mainstream of his own party. Eisenhower's insistence upon compromise with the Democrats who controlled Congress during his final six years in the White House, his support for social and economic policies that veered toward the "middle-of-the-road," and, especially, his undercutting of the Bricker Amendment had left Bricker fulminating on the far right of the political spectrum. Whatever influence he might have enjoyed when he first entered the Senate had been squandered, but he resolutely announced for a third term in 1958. With a recession underway and the coattails of Dwight Eisenhower unavailable, 1958 proved to be a difficult year for Republican congressional candidates. In what proved an ignominious ending to a once highly promising political career that spanned three decades, John Bricker was soundly defeated by perennial office seeker Stephen Young of Cleveland. Bricker probably could have overcome the national Democratic trend, but a powerful group of Ohio corporate leaders placed a "Right-To-Work" initiative on the state ballot that stimulated a massive union turnout on election day.

Bricker had feared such a possibility and was angered and hurt by the insistence of many of his longtime friends and supporters to forge ahead with the anti-union measure. "You can take care of enemies but not your friends who turn on you," he wrote to one confidant when the wounds of betrayal were still raw. "Had I known the people for whom I had done the most would turn on me that way, I would not have been a candidate," he told sympathetic columnist Raymond Moley.

After his wife Harriet had disabused of attempting a political comeback, Bricker concentrated his efforts on his role as senior partner of the law firm he helped form in 1945. The firm, now named Bricker and Eckler, would grow by the time of his death to be the second largest in Ohio, with offices located in downtown Columbus as well as in Washington, D.C. He focused his energies on public relations, general administration, and in-house consulting. He contributed greatly to the firm's growth by using his political contacts to attract new business. "I read everything that goes through the office, and I keep an eye on fees," he laconically told a magazine writer in 1976.

Bricker's major interest outside the law firm was his beloved Ohio State University. A proud member of the Varsity "O" Club, he had long held season tickets for Buckeye football games. In 1948, Governor Thomas Herbert had appointed him to the university's Board of Trustees, and had been reappointed by Governors William O'Neill and James A. Rhodes. Altogether he served twenty-one consecutive years on the board. After his defeat for reelection, he became essentially a full-time trustee, regularly attending meetings, campus symposia, receptions, athletic events, and graduation exercises. He lectured frequently in political science classes. He remarked more than once that the university was outranked in his priorities only by his dedication to his family and country.

It was in his role as protective trustee that he became embroiled in his last public controversy, which proved to be a big one. In 1965, the normally quiet campus on High Street was roiled by angry protests over a policy that was used by cautious administrators to prevent controversial speakers from appearing on campus. As OSU students mimicked the "free speech" protests that had convulsed the University of California campus at Berkeley the previous year, the restrictive speaker rule that had been in effect since the Red Scare of 1919 came under attack. In May, a group of faculty and students invited the prominent Marxist historian Herbert Aptheker to present a lecture on campus. His appearance was then summarily canceled—apparently reluctantly—by President Novice Fawcett, who indicated he had no alternative but to invoke the policy. When students mounted an angry protest, Fawcett promised to ask the Board of Trustees to liberalize the speaker's policy.

Fawcett faced a divided campus and a divided state, as well as an unsympathetic board. The *Columbus Dispatch* joined the acrimonious debate, opposing Fawcett's liberalization request because the campus protestors were being "manipulated by a subversion from outside the campus." The issue to the *Dispatch* was simply "whether Ohio State

University, an institution maintained by public money, must continue to defend its regulations and purposes from the onslaught of a handful of puppets of subversion in the faculty and student body." Fawcett gave it his best effort, arguing to the board that the university's students were capable of independent judgment and would not be easily misled by radical speakers.

But Trustee John Bricker, previously a predictable strong supporter of the recommendations put forward by the university's presidents, was not persuaded. The former senator, who had denounced the "treason" of the Yalta Conference, who had resolutely fulminated about the "insidiousness of the Communist conspiracy," and who had even seen subversive intent in the U.S. labor union movement, could not support President Fawcett's request. To do so would have constituted a renunciation for much of what he championed throughout his political career: "Communists, Nazis and Fascists and members of other subversive organizations and their supporters have no right to speak at a tax-supported state university for they are not free men and hence, are incapable of the objectivity which must attach itself to all speakers at a state university." The board subsequently voted by a 5-to-3 margin to reject Fawcett's recommendation that the speaker policy be liberalized. Later that warm July day, a group of protestors hung a crude effigy of Trustee Bricker from the flagpole of the administration building.

Thus what had begun as an exceptionally promising political career ended in an acrimonious and divisive battle over the issue of freedom of speech on a college campus; that he provided the leadership on the negative side of this important issue was duly noted by his many critics. During the early 1970s, after Bricker had left the board, the speaker policy was quietly modified to encourage a wide range of outside speakers on campus, and in 1982 the administration building, where his effigy had once swayed in the evening breeze, was renamed the John W. Bricker Administration Building.

As the speaker issue faded from public view, Bricker slowly retreated from the public eye. He spent most weekdays at his office but increasingly withdrew from active practice. He welcomed visiting political dignitaries to Columbus, closely followed state and national political news, enjoyed leisurely luncheons with friends and associates, and faithfully cheered the OSU football team. It was not until after his ninetieth birthday that the ravages of old age caught up with him in the form a series of small strokes. His wife, Harriet, died in 1985 after a long and painful battle with rheumatoid arthritis, and her death seemed to destroy his spirit. He was admitted to a nursing home in January 1986, and he died there on March 22. The slow heartbeat that had kept him out of the trenches of France had finally stilled.

Further Reading

Davies, Richard O. *Defender of the Old Guard: John Bricker and American Politics.* Columbus: Ohio State University Press, 1993.

Patterson, James T. *Mr. Republican: A Biography of Robert A. Taft.* Boston: Houghton Mifflin, 1972.

Reinhard, David W. *The Republican Right since 1945.* Lexington: University Press of Kentucky, 1983.

Tananbaum, Duane. *The Bricker Amendment Controversy.* Ithaca, N.Y.: Cornell University Press, 1988.

Vazzano, Frank P. "The Feud Renewed: Martin Davey, John Bricker and the Ohio Campaign of 1940." *Ohio History* 105 (Winter–Spring 1996): 5–24.

———. "Martin Davey, John Bricker and the Ohio Election of 1936." *Ohio History* 104 (Winter–Spring 1995): 5–23.

22

James A. Rhodes and the 1960s Origin of Contemporary Ohio

WILLIAM RUSSELL COIL

A STATUE OF Governor James A. Rhodes (1909–2001) stands in front of the Columbus, Ohio, government building that also bears his name. Assuming that no one else would erect a monument for him, Rhodes had the state legislature authorize the statue while he was still in office. One journalist cleverly remarked that the statue was "a tribute in bronze to his brass." That writer nailed Rhodes's penchant for self-promotion. Yet Rhodes, and not the reporter, has managed to define the meaning of the statue. When asked once what people should remember about him, Rhodes answered with a reflective wisdom: "Nothing," he said. "Why should anyone push anything upon themselves? Ten years from now they'll look at that statue and say, 'When was he governor?'" Rhodes was right, but not because he fails to merit our retrospection. Rather, citizens of Ohio have forgotten Rhodes because his ideas, once innovative, have become the conventional wisdom.

When Ohioans do remember Rhodes, they usually recall specific, unrelated actions rather than the complex patterns and long-term consequences of his policies. Positive stories, for example, include his crisis leadership during the blizzard of 1978 and Rhodes's Raiders, the development team he sent to other states and nations to attract business to Ohio. In contrast, the most important negative event was the May 4, 1970, tragedy at Kent State University. Rhodes sent the Ohio National Guard there to quell campus unrest. His attempt to restore order resulted in four deaths when guardsmen fired on antiwar protestors and bystanders.

As even May 4, 1970, recedes in the memories of Ohioans, however, Rhodes becomes less than real, distorted even, much like his

FIG. 18 James A. Rhodes.
Courtesy of The Ohio State University Archives.

statue. Affecting a too-trim physique, a button-down business suit, and an ever-present briefcase, the "tribute in bronze to his brass" subdues his spontaneous, earthy vitality and his forceful, constant motion. Just as the statue hides the real Rhodes, the most commonly repeated anecdotes fail to suggest his subtle legacy.

Rhodes oversaw a crucial change in Ohio's political economy. Often dismissed as a quaintly entertaining relic of Ohio's rust belt past, in reality Rhodes changed long-standing political and economic relationships, those intangibles that shaped the civic priorities of Ohio voters. In four terms under Rhodes, from 1963 to 1971 and 1975 to 1983, Ohioans linked freedom and progress to material abundance and consumer choice. To achieve these goals, Rhodes created a strong, centralized administrative apparatus. In building this new state, Rhodes redefined how federalism worked in Ohio, reshaped the priorities of the public and private sector, and redesigned social policy to fit within the narrow parameters of economic growth. Rhodes was certainly a bricks and mortar, pork barrel politician, a politician

whose tangible achievements—highways, parks, and buildings—
Ohioans use everyday. Rhodes remains significant, however, because
the way he exercised state power in the 1960s still limits public policy choices today.

Three factors shaped the childhood and subsequent political
career of James Rhodes. First, his working-class parents searched for
middle-class economic stability, modeling ambition for the young
Rhodes. Second, his father died when Rhodes was nine, introducing
instability into this search. Third, and finally, his youth consisted of
small-town, working-class, coal-mining culture, steeping Rhodes in
the disposition, desires, and demands of the common man. Rhodes
began political life in 1934 with a successful run for ward committeeman in Columbus, Ohio, and finished active politics in 1986 with
an ill-advised attempt to win a fifth term as governor. Through six
extraordinary decades, Rhodes campaigned and governed in ways
that proceeded from these three factors.

James Rhodes Sr., the father of the future governor, strove to
improve his status in life and the lot of his family. When the younger
James was born on September 13, 1909, the elder Rhodes worked as
a coal miner in the southern Ohio town of Coalton, in Jackson
County. The son, later in life, recalled that his father also participated
in local politics. The coal-mining industry, however, declined. In
1910, Rhodes Sr., in search of better economic opportunities, moved
his family to the small town of Jasonville, Indiana. Located in Greene
County, a hilly, ethnically Welsh, coal-mining boom region in the
southwestern part of the Hoosier State, Jasonville offered vibrant
economics and politics. Remarkably similar topographically, demo-
graphically, and culturally to Jackson County, Ohio, Greene County,
Indiana, replicated for the Rhodes family a familiar living environment but added the chance for at least modest upward mobility.
Rhodes's father worked his way out of the mine into management
and earned a mayoral appointment to the Jasonville school board.

Governor Rhodes's fabled political instincts owed much to the
Jasonville experience. The Jasonville political scene reflected the fluid
character of the growing town. Residents broadly defined legitimate
political activity. Partisanship certainly existed, but outside the con-
fines of a two-party system. In the 1910s and early 1920s, local voters sought political leaders who reached beyond party labels and
offered nonpartisan programs for progress. In the 1913 election, for
example, four candidates from four different parties vied for mayor.
In addition to the Democratic and Republican candidates, the Union

Party and the Citizen's Party also entered the race. Renegade Democrat S. D. Dempsey headed the Citizen's Party. Dempsey won and appointed his neighbor, the elder Rhodes, to the school board. The Union Party won the rest of the offices, shutting out the Democrats and Republicans. In the early 1920s, moreover, Jasonville voters elected Socialists to power, a victory based largely on their promise to build a new high school gymnasium. Jasonville voters cared little that candidates adhered to established party doctrine as long as they promised to deliver what the common man said he wanted, foreshadowing the essence of Governor Rhodes's campaigns.

In this Hoosier environment, the younger Rhodes learned to walk, talk, and think, all the while watching his father strive for a better life. This tutelage came to an end, however, with the flu epidemic of 1918. In November 1918, James Sr., an otherwise healthy thirty-eight-year-old man, contracted the virus and died. In December, Mrs. Rhodes moved young James, then nine years old, and his two sisters back to Jackson County, Ohio, ending the Indiana education of the boy who later became Ohio's most powerful governor.

Though never well-off while James Sr. was alive, the Rhodes family at least experienced the stability and security of a regular paycheck. Now the family struggled to meet even the barest of necessities. As the governor remembered, "We had a different status in life. We were on the giving end before, helping a lot of people, and then we were on the receiving end." His mother, Susan Howe Rhodes, worked in a cigar factory and ran a boarding house that catered to workers on the Detroit, Toledo, and Ironton railroad. To help support the family, Rhodes worked a series of odd jobs, from delivering newspapers and groceries, collecting and selling scrap junk, to hunting muskrats and selling the pelts for forty cents apiece. Around 1923, the family moved to Springfield, Ohio. There Rhodes struggled to complete high school, finishing only at his mother's insistence. He spent most of his teen years playing sports, working different jobs, and promoting one scheme or another in order to contribute money to the family.

An academic education was the least of Rhodes's priorities. Yet he left Springfield in 1932 to attend The Ohio State University. Rhodes fared poorly scholastically, mainly because he spent his ample store of energy in a whirlwind of business and political ventures. One successful operation was Jim's Place. Located across the street from the university, Jim's Place was a social spot where college students could listen to music while eating hamburgers and doughnuts. When Rhodes campaigned for governor in 1962, his opponent, incumbent

Democrat Michael DiSalle, spread unverified rumors to reporters that patrons of Jim's Place could also gamble and buy pornography. In any case, Rhodes left school after one quarter and never returned. However, he stayed in the university district. The neighborhood just east of the university was his first political base, but the entire state of Ohio was his goal.

Two people helped him realize his ambitions. His tough, forceful mother taught him to pray, "Oh God, please help me be somebody," focusing the capacious but erratic vitality of the young Rhodes. His mentor, Grant P. Ward, a Jackson County native and Republican state legislator, financed Jim's Place and secured patronage jobs. With their guidance and discipline, Rhodes began his slow, steady, ambitious rise to power. In the thirties, Rhodes served successively as a Republican ward committeeman, as a school board member (like his father), and Columbus' auditor. In 1943, Rhodes, then only thirty-four years old, won the first of three terms as mayor of Columbus. In 1952, Ohio voters elected him state auditor. He served there until 1962 when he won his first term as governor.

Throughout this activity, three factors from his childhood shaped how Rhodes campaigned and governed. As a boy, he watched as his father toiled to rise above his roots. Then, after his father's untimely death, Rhodes hustled from one odd job or another to secure family stability. Finally, he absorbed the language and deportment of ordinary people. As a candidate, Rhodes was unbeatable when he relied on these three elements to guide his actions. When he avoided the lessons of his youth, he struggled.

In the late 1950s and early 1960s, as Rhodes emerged as a leading politician in the state, some Republicans expressed their displeasure that the uncultured Rhodes might soon head the ticket. One Columbus woman, for example, angrily wrote to Ray Bliss, then the state party chairman, demanding that he "please use care—get a man with education." Avoid "the rough politician. This is describing Rhodes— He has no education." Rhodes, concerned that he was too rough-hewn for many Republican voters, co-wrote with his friend and political associate, Dean Jauchius, several pieces of literature designed to show that Rhodes was cultured and literary. Two historical novels, *The Trial of Mary Todd Lincoln* (1959) and *The Court-Martial of Commodore Perry* (1961), attempted to redeem the tarnished reputations of public figures, showing how connivers had hurled false accusations that slandered the two wrongly. A third historical novel, *Johnny Shiloh* (1959), traced the life of a responsible, heroic, duty-minded nine-year-old boy who, during the Civil War, joined the Union army. A work of nonfiction, *Teenage Hall of Fame* (1960) described the lives of hard-working Ohioans who began their climb to fame and fortune before age twenty. Rhodes and Jauchius concocted, as well, a play, set in 1959 and titled "Cloakroom." The main character was a Democratic U.S. senator from the South who, when confronted with a key civil rights vote, rejected party discipline, voted his conscience, and supported the just cause. Taken together, these works cautioned against judging a person simply by his reputation, celebrated dedicated and determined youths, and lionized independent-minded politicians who, in pursuit of the common good, transcended party labels. These portraits, in retrospect, indicated how Rhodes wished voters would view him.

On the stump, too, Rhodes changed who he was. Rhodes at times aped the manners of the most popular Republicans in the state, Robert Taft, an upper-class Ivy League educated lawyer, and John Bricker, a lawyer from the respectable middle class. But this ploy failed miserably. A Republican from northwestern Ohio complained to Bliss that Rhodes in one speech "was about as warm as a cold mackerel." His subject "would have been fine for a group of professors." Rhodes was, in fact, "cultured and urbane." Nevertheless, the writer concluded, "it is too good for the public." Rhodes "has got to become a little more common" and learn how "to mispronounce an occasional word" for effect. In his effort to appear intellectual, Rhodes simply came off as stiff and disconnected.

Evidently, Bliss or someone else spoke to Rhodes, as Rhodes's southern Ohio accent, unrefined manner, and often profane vocabulary are now the stuff of journalistic legend. Before the simplicity of legend replaced the complexity of truth, however, Rhodes had to learn the value of his working-class brand of Republicanism, a brand different than the smooth, lawyerly one Ohioans had grown to expect. Ironically, only after Rhodes honestly embraced his hill country origins and trusted his natural charisma could the legend grow.

Still, the mere mechanics of his presentation fail to explain his importance. What Rhodes said and why differentiated him from his predecessors, differences that make him relevant today. Rhodes, in those early years of stability with his father and of struggle after his death, discerned what to say to people face-to-face. In Indiana and Ohio, Rhodes studied how to smile and flatter, wheedle and cajole, distract and tempt, appease and please, influence and coerce. From his father, who often talked politics at the dinner table, from his mentor

Grant P. Ward, who tutored the young man in practical politics, and from his customers, who required Rhodes to peddle, promote, and persuade, Rhodes discovered how to read people, when to push and when to pull, when to nudge and when to elbow. In *The Last Hurrah*, a novel of urban politics, Edwin O'Connor wrote that politics is promising people what they say they want but delivering what they will really settle for. Rhodes mastered that art.

During the 1930s and 1940s, when Rhodes first plied his trade, what politicians promised and what voters really settled for changed. The New Deal and Democratic President Franklin D. Roosevelt caused the transformation. As the Democratic New Deal emerged from World War II, national policy makers tried to master the business cycle, encourage economic growth, and achieve full employment. New Dealers no longer railed against greedy, unprincipled big businesses, nor even contemplated structural reform of the economy. Roosevelt and his advisors changed the New Deal because they had changed the goal of government. In the 1944 State of the Union Address, Roosevelt announced that "true individual freedom cannot exist without economic security and independence." He continued, "People who are hungry and out of a job are the stuff of which dictatorships are made." He issued, therefore, an "Economic Bill of Rights," a new list of rights "to assure us equality in the pursuit of happiness." The rights included the "right to a useful and remunerative job" and the "right to earn enough to provide adequate housing and clothing and recreation." New Deal politicians now promised an unprecedented material abundance that would form the basis of "true individual freedom." Voters settled for the highest American standard of living ever and, some critics charged, for a restricted definition of freedom. Learning his political craft "in the shadow of FDR," Rhodes became a "New Deal Republican," a Republican who adopted New Deal assumptions about economics and politics.

In the 1930s and 1940s, leaders of both Ohio parties rejected the New Deal political economy. Republican Robert Taft, a U.S. senator from 1939 to his death in 1953, certainly supported a climate favorable to business. His philosophy, however, led him to advocate a strong state and local presence within the federal system, to defend the individual from the regimentation of mass materialism, and to define freedom so that it transcended possession of material goods. With the onset of mass society, Americans, Taft observed, received their news and entertainment uniformly across the country. Mass culture, which celebrated the mass consumption of mass produced goods, challenged the peculiarity of cities and towns and sapped America of its pluralistic variety, a critical element of democracy. The national government affected local government the same way. A strong state government, Taft concluded, served as a bulwark against mass society, protecting distinctive local ways from homogenizing federal power. Taft argued, too, that the New Deal focused too narrowly on material issues. An ideal citizen understood that standardized material wealth substituted poorly for liberty. Taft criticized the crassness of the New Deal political economy, a system, he claimed, that debased both citizenship and freedom in exchange for material security.

Taft was no agrarian rebel protesting the ill effects of industrialization and economic competition. Material progress mattered to Taft more than tradition and religion. Yet, even as he celebrated the individual who strove and competed for a better life, he objected to a society that turned its citizens into consumers. In three tries, Taft sought but failed to receive the Republican nomination for the presidency, suggesting that he had failed at the national level to promise people what they said they wanted. Nor had he adequately considered what people would really settle for.

Well into the 1950s in Ohio, however, Taft's vision of government prevailed even as Ohioans began to reject his definitions of citizenship and democracy. Ohio voters consistently reelected politicians who promised to perpetuate a state government incapable of delivering FDR's promise of material security. Low taxes, minimal state services, and employer-friendly regulations characterized Ohio government. In this political economy, no successful Ohio politician advocated a policy agenda that melded the interests of the state, business, labor, and education in order to create widespread access to abundance.

Unsurprisingly, then, in the 1940s Ohio policy makers neglected an opportunity to design a technology policy that would wed government, business, labor, and education. The state legislature had recruited distinguished Ohio native, scientist, and General Motors executive Charles Kettering to advise the state on technology policy. Kettering argued that scientific research during World War II "brought out the relationship between what can be done by government, what can be done by universities, and what can be done by industries, and the fundamental correlation between those things." Kettering contended that Ohio's economy would be stronger tomorrow if the state encouraged technological development today, and that this process necessarily would blur lines separating public and private organizations.

Ohio policy makers throughout the 1940s and 1950s ignored Kettering's advice. In 1947, Republican governor Thomas Herbert, for example, acknowledged that the new science had wrought economic changes. But Herbert was uncertain as to the appropriate role of a state government in science policy. He committed to "an open minded approach" and the "trial and error method" only, claiming that "we will ultimately strike a new balance between federal and state functions." Herbert's platitude led to inaction. Throughout the 1940s and 1950s, Democratic and Republican state officials willingly ceded research and development policy to the federal government because Ohioans opposed the kind of state government that Kettering described.

By 1962, though, the political climate in Ohio had changed. A national recession that started in the late 1950s continued to hurt Ohio in the early 1960s. Michael DiSalle, the Democratic incumbent governor, devised plans to improve Ohio and raised taxes to do it, but, in the process, lost Democratic control of the legislature in 1960, antagonized his labor base, and, at least to Ohio voters, seemed incapable of leading Ohio back to prosperity. In 1962, Rhodes capitalized on the perceived weaknesses of DiSalle, promising austerity in state government and focusing intently on economic growth. One reporter quipped that "an inventor has produced the Rhodes doll. You wind it up and it goes out and finds a job for you." With a potent combination of skill, experience, and timing, Rhodes defeated DiSalle. Blurring party lines, Rhodes appealed to the non-Republican union rank and file as well as the party's base in boardrooms and rural areas. As a result, Rhodes captured a political moment when voters willingly embraced the promise of a new Ohio.

What did Rhodes promise in this new climate and what did Ohioans settle for? As governor in the 1960s, Rhodes articulated the promise in his ever-present campaign slogan "Jobs and Progress." Drawing on his personal experience, Rhodes connected social instability to poverty and unemployment. To Rhodes, a job for an individual translated into family stability. In turn, jobs for masses of people translated into social stability. Social harmony, therefore, required full employment. Rhodes recognized, though, that rather than vigor and strength, corrosion and rust characterized Ohio industry in the early 1960s. So to achieve growth, and thus social progress, Rhodes pledged to modernize Ohio's economy. Ohio voters, in turn, settled for a political economy that created new economic opportunities, built transportation networks, expanded public universities and technical schools, and developed state parks—all tangible hallmarks of the Rhodes legacy. Yet citizens of Ohio also settled for a definition of freedom as access to material abundance and for a war on poverty narrowly waged as a problem of economic development. Rhodes and the voters complicity pursued the "Jobs and Progress" agenda, Rhodes pitching his plan as a nonpartisan program for progress, the voters embracing a candidate who talked about what they wanted in a language they understood.

Rhodes developed his prose during a lifetime of talking with people in retail situations. Pursuing the nonpartisan goal of the common good, Rhodes philosophized plainly that "I'm not one of those people that likes to take my Bible and say it's the Republican platform. I'm for the people. As governor, we didn't follow every elephant that went by. You can't follow every donkey either. You get close enough to 'em and you smell like 'em."

What, then, did it mean to be "for the people"? Connecting poverty to instability, Rhodes barked repeatedly that "What people really want is security through a job. That's what this civil rights agitation, crime, and social problems all stem from—lack of jobs." Combining the two previous sentiments, Rhodes castigated his party bluntly, remarking that "Democrats every Labor Day stand and say we'll get you jobs and the Republicans, like damn fools, stand up the next day and say 'It can't be done.'" Rhodes came to "Jobs and Progress" sincerely, reflecting on the lessons of his life and drawing conclusions about the dignity of work, the necessity of material abundance, and the stability of society when policy makers created both.

During the 1962 campaign, Rhodes ceaselessly spoke of "Jobs and Progress," but offered few specifics. No one knew what the program entailed, except that it involved miles of expedited highway projects. Rhodes certainly delivered that staple of politics but also offered an unconventional plan for public investment. As governor, he expanded the authority and scope of state government, changing Ohio's place within the federal system and challenging Old Guard Republicans.

The transformation of Ohio began with its economic base. Before Rhodes took office, he and his advisors outlined their goals. His team reported that "the health of the economic base of the state needs and deserves major attention." To combat the effects of an aging industrial plant and make good on his "Jobs and Progress" pledge, Rhodes argued for the necessity of putting "into the hands of state government, and thereby the citizens of Ohio, a necessary and timely fair share of the responsibility for" Ohio's industrial growth. State leaders should not only recruit manufacturing jobs for short-term growth but also foster "the activity necessary to attract and produce the scientific and engineering research, development and training now to create and ensure new jobs in the future!" This activity, Rhodes hoped, would "capture the nation's imagination," changing the image of Ohio from an aging industrial power to an agile, vibrant economy of the future. Rhodes advocated what Kettering advised nearly two decades earlier: links between government, education, and industry, links that remade the political economy of Ohio.

The transformation of Ohio continued its place within the federal system. In the 1960s, Rhodes, like his predecessors, aggressively asserted Ohio's primacy. Unlike politicians of the past, however, Rhodes carved out a niche within the parameters of federally designed programs. In a debate with Michigan's Republican governor George Romney, Rhodes outlined his philosophy of federalism. Romney complained about the inability of governors to shape federally funded poverty programs, highway projects, and educational measures. Romney also naively suggested that the states quit competing for federal funds. Rhodes scoffed at Romney's hand wringing. "Any new programs they devise," Rhodes boasted, "we'll take it and master it and get every cent we can out of it. This pattern has been set and there's no escape." In the 1940s, Taft had envisioned a strong state government that could protect distinct local institutions. In the 1960s, Rhodes envisioned a strong state government that could exploit federal largess.

Rhodes swaggered his way through the maze of federal-state relations to create Ohio's first coherent, state-directed technology policy. The State Technical Services Act (STSA), a 1965 federal law, pleased Rhodes. Under the STSA, federal and state officials created a partnership among government, business, and higher education in order to disseminate technical information to the private sector. Before doling out matching funds, federal administrators required state policy makers to write a five-year plan in which they described the economic problems of their area, designed solutions, and explained the strategy to execute their plans. In Ohio, these conditions forced officials to inch toward a mixed economy in which government bureaucrats helped set priorities for the private sector.

Federal administrators cast the STSA as part of Democratic President Lyndon Johnson's War on Poverty. Part of this war focused "on the need to develop new industries and new firms in order to revitalize regions of the country dependent upon a healthy industrial economy."

That argument especially appealed to Rhodes, the governor of a rusting, industrial, midwestern state. Rhodes hailed the STSA as one of the best laws ever passed by Congress, excited rhetoric he normally saved for highway appropriation bills. Anxious to expedite activity, Rhodes announced in September 1965 that Ohio had asked for nearly $500,000. A U.S. Commerce Department spokesman praised Ohio's eagerness but said the federal government was not yet ready to accept applications.

Even before the STSA, however, Rhodes turned the power of state institutions toward technology policy. Only three months into the Rhodes era, one state bureaucrat remarked that Rhodes had pushed "the state of Ohio to assume an aggressive role in stimulating" science instead of "the passive role that probably would be more palatable to those who are more traditionally minded." Rhodes in the 1960s successfully constructed new state institutions and reinvigorated old ones to revive Ohio's private sector.

To provide a skilled work force to staff Ohio's proposed new economy, Rhodes expanded the public university and technical education system. To manage education policy, Rhodes assembled the Ohio Board of Regents, an agency that centralized decision making about budget requests, curriculum standards, and spending priorities. Rhodes also authorized the Regents to coordinate research and development programs with the federal government and private sector.

Elsewhere in state government, Rhodes transformed the Department of Industrial and Economic Development, the agency Rhodes's Democratic predecessor created to stimulate growth. Renamed the Department of Development (DOD), this agency prepared plans to develop the state's natural resources, cooperated with federal and local governments to coordinate growth, encouraged research and development, and collected economic information to determine when, where, and how businesses could expand. At its peak, the DOD's precursor had forty-two employees. In contrast, less than two years into its existence, Rhodes's DOD had seventy-four employees and a budget of $1.8 million, a budget three times the size of the previous agency's fund.

To help the state analyze economic information, Rhodes invented the Economic Research Council (ERC), charged with "clearly defining our economic assets and problems" so as to "bring state policy to bear effectively in these areas." Rhodes instructed the ERC to assist state officials "in designing the framework for growth." A DOD worker concluded that Rhodes had the "organization, the program, and the personnel to do the very necessary and very involved job of coordinating economic and industrial development in Ohio." Previous governors lacked either the inclination or the ability to engage in such a sweeping project.

Rhodes anticipated opposition to his flurry of activity that drastically changed the role of the state in Ohio's economy. Yet, assuming an economic crisis, he discounted any objections, claiming that he did not care "whether or not our plans are in the American tradition." The Republican-dominated Ohio Supreme Court, however, did care. Having sailed through the legislature in 1963, Rhodes's economic growth policies hit a legal barrier.

In 1964, the court ruled unconstitutional the bond program to finance the rebuilding of Ohio. Rhodes had created the Ohio Development Financing Commission to sell bonds and make loans to businesses that failed to receive money from "ordinary financial channels," effectively redirecting the investment decisions of the private sector. The state, according to the court's ruling, unconstitutionally loaned its credit to private corporations. In private, several judges attacked their fellow Republican, with one exclaiming that Rhodes's plan sounded the "death knell to private enterprise." C. William O'Neill, a former Republican governor of Ohio who then served on the court, concluded that the "state should stay out of private enterprise."

Undaunted, Rhodes bypassed the court, persuading Ohio voters to amend the state constitution. In May 1965, Ohioans voted to add section thirteen to Article 8 of the Ohio Constitution. Anyone who had ever heard a Rhodes speech was familiar with the amendment's first words: "To create or preserve jobs." The Ohio Constitution now allowed the state to borrow money, make and guarantee loans, and issue bonds in order to fund economic development projects that specifically related to "industry, commerce, distribution," and, significantly "research." Rhodes now had the constitutional authority to make the priorities of the private sector the state's "proper public purpose."

Rhodes remained a state-level politician, but his program found a receptive audience in Washington. Ray Bliss, the Republican state party chair from 1949 to 1965, took over the national Republican organization in 1965. Under Bliss, the Republicans issued a position paper on solutions to poverty. The authors concluded that the "most powerful weapon against poverty" is economic growth. "Leadership in innovation and the systematic use of science and technology to serve ordinary people is the *sine qua non* in our anti-poverty efforts."

Republicans in the 1960s, then, found useful a poverty and employment policy that originated philosophically in the New Deal and received funding from Lyndon Johnson's Great Society.

Beyond that irony, even though Rhodes died on March 4, 2001, and his last full year in office was in 1982, his legacy still shapes policy in three significant ways. First, Rhodes convinced Ohioans that government should organize around the principle of creating and spreading abundance. Michael DiSalle had approached governing with a similar goal. Because he raised taxes and because of a national recession, Ohio voters fired him. Rhodes, in contrast, promised voters what they said they wanted—fiscal restraint and expansion of state services—but delivered what they really would settle for—economic growth, an enlarged state government, and Democratic tax hikes and Republican bond debt to pay for both.

Second, Rhodes persuaded Republicans of the desirability, and even the necessity, of widely spread access to ever-increasing material wealth. This idea eliminated from the Grand Old Party Robert Taft's dour if prophetic criticism of a homogeneous, materialistic modern America. Ohioans readily embraced Rhodes's philosophy because, increasingly over the twentieth century, Americans have defined their own progress, and indeed their own freedom, in terms of their ability to choose and then consume material goods. This process has limited the use of abundance solely to providing leisure and reflecting social status. Of course, even if Rhodes had been aware of these cultural changes, he could not have controlled them. Nevertheless, his impressive political success helped to muffle contradictory views within the party.

Third, and finally, Rhodes bestowed on policy makers a tricky legacy. Republicans under Rhodes devised a poverty policy that focused not so much on the poor as on institutional partnerships between public and private entities, creating in the process a new level of power in state government. Rhodes hardly eliminated poverty. At the very least, however, his approach authentically accorded with his biography and with then-prevailing theories on poverty, social instability, and economic growth. For the most part, his Republican and Democratic successors have operated within the framework of "Jobs and Progress." Lacking Rhodes's authenticity but using his vocabulary, Ohio politicians deftly espouse their concern for the poor but actually spend valuable resources on business.

The legacy, however, has also imposed constrictive boundaries on decision makers, limiting their imaginations and stunting their abilities to ask new questions appropriate to a different time. At the beginning of the twenty-first century, Ohio's leaders have focused on declining industry, lagging technological development, and persistent pockets of poverty and unemployment. They have noisily publicized their solution: foster high-tech industry by spending massive community resources and by creating public and private alliances. Though Rhodes's heirs possess the power to distribute wealth selectively in the name of state-sponsored economic dynamism, they lack the creativity to redefine social progress.

Further Reading

Curtin, Mike. "The Old School." *Columbus Dispatch,* October 12, 1986.

Leonard, Lee. "Rhodes's Second Eight Years, 1975–1983." In *Ohio Politics,* edited by Alexander P. Lamis, 101–35. Kent, Ohio: Kent State University Press, 1994.

Zimmerman, Richard. "Rhodes's First Eight Years, 1963–1971." In *Ohio Politics,* edited by Alexander P. Lamis, 59–83. Kent, Ohio: Kent State University Press, 1994.

23

Carl B. Stokes, Cleveland, and the Limits of Black Political Power

LEONARD N. MOORE

C ARL STOKES'S election as mayor of Cleveland in November
1967 marked a watershed in African American history. Not only
did Stokes become the first African American mayor of a major city,
but his election began the transformation of the black freedom struggle from protest to politics. During his four years in office
(1967–1971), Stokes wrestled to put into effect the policies that civil
rights activists had demanded for a generation. He fought to improve
the lives of the black urban poor, to give blacks a voice in municipal
government, to raise awareness about the urban crisis, and to prove
to the nation that an African American could govern a major city.
Stokes was successful in achieving the latter three goals, but he
encountered serious resistance to his attempts to enhance the socioeconomic status of the city's black poor. As the first black mayor of a
major U.S. city, Stokes was also the first to experience the limits of
black power.

Carl Burton Stokes was born in obscurity on June 21, 1927, in
Cleveland, Ohio, to Charles and Louise Stokes, both Georgia natives.
The Stokes family already included one boy, two-year-old Louis. After
Carl's father died suddenly in 1928, mother Louise and grandmother
Fannie Stone struggled to raised the children. Although Louise
worked tirelessly as a domestic, she often found it hard to provide for
her two boys. When old enough, Carl and his brother supplemented
the family's small income by selling newspapers and running errands.
But times were still hard for the Stokes family. Despite the family's
poverty, Carl excelled in school, first at Giddings Elementary and
then at Central Junior High. He lost interest, however, in education
while attending East Tech High School, dropping out at the age of

FIG. 18 Carl B. Stokes.
Courtesy of Special Collections, Cleveland State University Library.

sixteen. Realizing that opportunities for black high school dropouts were slim, he joined the army in July 1945. "This was not a moral decision," he recalled, "the war was over. I just wanted to get the hell out of a world I had had enough of."

When his tour of duty expired eighteen months later, Stokes returned to Cleveland. "Almost immediately on arriving home," he later recalled, "I was enveloped in everything oppressive about being poor and black and uneducated." He quickly concluded that without a high school diploma he was going "nowhere." This was the turning point in his life: "My attitudes had been changed. The contact with educated black men in the Army had made me see a new value in going to school." Consequently, in 1947 he re-enrolled in school and earned his diploma. After brief stints at West Virginia State College and Western Reserve University, he worked as a state liquor agent before receiving his bachelor of law degree from the University of Minnesota in 1954, and his law degree from Cleveland-Marshall Law School in 1956.

While in law school, Stokes worked as a probation officer. His job brought him into direct contact with the black urban poor. Late one evening, the wife of one of his parolees called and told him that rats had attacked their baby. When Stokes arrived at the filthy apartment, he noticed that the child's nose and upper lip had been completely mutilated. This incident convinced him that the black poor needed more than social workers, "they needed advocates at the highest levels of government." After passing the bar exam, he went into private practice with his brother, but he increasingly desired a career in politics.

To increase his visibility in both Cleveland's black community and the city's Democratic Party, Stokes joined the local chapters of the Urban League, the NAACP, the County Federated Democrats of Ohio, and the mostly white Young Democrats. Seeking wider exposure, Stokes also volunteered at numerous community events. "Whenever some small church group needed a speaker, I would accept without question," he recalled. Stokes made his entrée into politics as a successful campaign manager in the 1957 Cleveland City Council elections. One year later, he entered the state senate race to gauge his chances in future elections. He received only 5,000 votes in the countywide contest. In 1960, he made a bid for the Ohio House of Representatives but lost after a lengthy and controversial recount. Two years later, however, he won the seat, becoming the first black Democrat to sit in the Ohio General Assembly. The young representative quickly earned the admiration of his constituents by fighting for the urban poor. He sponsored legislation concerning fair housing, prisoner's rights, and social welfare programs. But while Stokes was getting adjusted to full-time political life, Cleveland was confronted with its first serious racial confrontation.

In the fall of 1963, the United Freedom Movement (UFM), a local civil rights coalition, launched an all-out protest against de facto segregation in the Cleveland Public Schools. The nine-month campaign was filled with marches, rallies, sit-ins, riots, boycotts, and even one tragic death. Although the UFM failed to desegregate the schools, the protest served as a catalyst for greater unity and helped black Clevelanders understand the limits of mass protest. Black Clevelanders then looked to the political arena where the possibilities of black political power appeared limitless.

Changing racial dynamics within the city convinced Stokes and others that African Americans could capture city hall. Although African Americans in Cleveland had participated in city politics since the nineteenth century, they had little power. White politicians ignored them after election day, and black elected officials often placed self-interest in front of the welfare of their constituents. The lack of power was evident in the reality of black life in Cleveland: poor housing, high unemployment, segregated schools, and unfair police protection. After World War II, changes were underway, which Stokes hoped would increase the power of the black community.

The second great migration of African Americans from the South to the North transformed the city's complexion. Between 1950 and 1965, Cleveland's black population grew from 147,847 to 279,352, while the overall population shrank from 914,808 to 810,858. Whereas in 1950 black residents accounted for only 16.2 percent of the population, by 1965 they represented 34.4 percent of the city's inhabitants. In sum, Cleveland lost approximately 242,000 white people, while gaining roughly 128,000 African Americans in just a fifteen-year period.

Since the early twentieth century an uneasy alliance of ethnic working-class whites and industrial leaders had dominated the city's public life. Drawn by jobs in the city's iron and steel industries, immigrants from eastern and southern Europe began arriving in the late nineteenth century. As white ethnics collectively became a larger part of the city population, they quickly took control of the city's political structure with little interference from the industrial capitalists who dominated the city's economic life. In many ways, it was a forced compromise since the economic elite was largely unable to exercise any influence over the new arrivals. By the 1930s, Cleveland was a city that clearly had separate spheres of influence. The industrialists let working-class immigrants run local government as long as taxes remained low enough to attract investment, the requisite services were maintained, and all economic decisions were delegated to the business elite. In return, the working-class immigrant was allowed the prestige and patronage of municipal government. The city's business community accepted this arrangement because of their conservative orientation. Unlike industrial capitalists from the East Coast, Cleveland's economic elite occupied the right wing of the Republican Party. They neither looked to the public sector for long-term solutions nor needed any new infrastructure initiatives from city hall because those had been made in the early twentieth century. This "conservative social contract" between white ethnics and local industrialists would not be broken until Stokes entered city hall.

Although white ethnics were active in local politics, they did not capture the mayor's office until the 1941 election of Slovenian Frank

J. Lausche. Once in the mayor's seat, ethnic Democrats would control city politics for nearly three decades. Their rise ushered in a period of governance that catered to white ethnic mistrust of politics: limited government, low taxes, and minimal city services. White ethnic domination of city hall and city council continued under Lausche's successors. Thomas Burke, an Irish Catholic, served as mayor from 1945 to 1951, and Anthony J. Celebreeze, an Italian American, governed the city from 1953 until he joined the cabinet of John F. Kennedy in 1961. Ralph Locher, the son of Lithuanian immigrants, succeeded Celebreeze, serving until 1967. Although black Clevelanders had benefited from earlier Republican mayors, the wave of Democratic mayors launched by Lausche produced city administrations characterized by low taxes and low service levels and neglected the concerns of black Clevelanders. In sum, throughout the 1940s, 1950s, and 1960s, Cleveland had a caretaker type of government that ignored the tremendous changes taking place in the city. African Americans, more than any other group, were hurt by this political inaction.

Since African Americans made up one-third of the city's population, Stokes believed that if he entered the 1965 mayoral contest as an independent and forced a three-way contest he could win. On a shoestring budget of $44,000, the Stokes-for-Mayor campaign conducted a grassroots, community-wide effort. On election day, however, incumbent Locher defeated Stokes by the thin margin of 2,142 votes. Nonetheless, the campaign was a moral victory. "As far as I was concerned," Stokes later recalled, "we had beaten not only Locher, but the whole traditional establishment of political power, in two years we would take it for good."

Black frustration in Cleveland made national headlines in July 1966 when five days of rioting erupted in the all-black enclave of Hough, leaving four dead, hundreds wounded, and over $2 million in property damage. Both the black and white communities scapegoated Mayor Locher, and the city's business community openly supported Stokes's 1967 mayoral bid, largely because they felt that he represented the best safeguard against future black unrest. Although Stokes accepted their support, he made it clear that he was not going to be anyone's "house nigga." After a rigorous and emotional campaign, Stokes defeated Seth Taft, grandson of a U.S. president, and became the first black mayor of a major urban city. Stokes's election also signaled the transformation from protest to politics across black America.

Mayor Stokes's first nine months in office was akin to a honeymoon. He restored funding from the federal housing agency; he recruited a top-flight urban renewal director; he kept the peace in Cleveland after the assassination of Martin Luther King Jr.; and he launched a $1.5 billion urban redevelopment package called "Cleveland Now!" that focused on housing and job creation over a ten-year period. The short-range goals of "Cleveland Now!" called for spending $177 million in the first year to attack the major problems in six areas: employment, economic revitalization, youth resources, health and welfare, neighborhood rehabilitation, and city planning. Two weeks after the program was launched, Stokes had raised more than $11 million in private donations, which triggered the immediate release of $74.8 million in federal funds.

The honeymoon came to an abrupt end on July 23, 1968, when Ahmed Evans and the Republic of New Libya, a local black nationalist group, engaged in a shootout with members of the Cleveland Police Department (CPD). Within minutes after the first shots, three white policeman and three New Libya members were dead. Black youths responded by attacking police personnel. By midnight, a full-scale riot had erupted in the Glenville neighborhood. To prevent further loss of life, Stokes pulled out all white law enforcement officers, replacing them with an all-black peace patrol, which included fire and police personnel, black nationalists, ministers, politicians, and professional athletes. Although the all-black peace patrol prevented further bloodshed, white residents and white police officers complained that Stokes was protecting looters and police killers. Stokes's credibility suffered a major blow when it was revealed that Ahmed Evans had been given a "Cleveland Now!" grant to open up a African cultural center. Instead, Evans had used the money to purchase weapons used in the riot. After the shootout, Stokes encountered an onslaught of challenges for the remainder of his tenure.

Stokes's initial challenge came from the virtually all-white CPD. Although the relationship between the CPD and the black community had historically been tenuous, tensions increased during the second great migration. Complaints of brutality, insufficient police protection, harassment, unequal law enforcement, the lack of black officers, and discriminatory police personnel assignments were heard throughout black Cleveland. While most of these concerns stemmed from the overall antiblack nature of the department, many were directly related to the small percentage of black officers on the force. In 1965, only 133 of Cleveland's 2,021 officers were African American, despite the fact that African Americans made up 35 percent of the city's population. Further, only two of these black officers held any significant rank.

Days after he entered city hall, Stokes began reorganizing the CPD. He placed black officers in white areas, integrated select units, and ordered police to discontinue wearing their traditional white helmets. The personnel reassignment ignited a wave of controversy from the rank-and-file of the CPD. White officers responded to Stokes's efforts with the "blue-flu" before accepting the mayor's orders. This set the stage for a rocky relationship between Stokes and the CPD, but the Glenville pullout took police frustration to a new level.

White officers were outraged over the mayor's decision to pull out all white law enforcement, particularly when three white officers had been killed. At the largest Fraternal Order of Police meeting in local history, officers called for Stokes's resignation and asked Governor James Rhodes to remove the mayor for neglect of duty. White police officers would never let Stokes forget about Glenville.

Stokes understood that the best way to reform the CPD was to secure promotions for existing black officers and to get more blacks in uniform. In an effort to bolster his recruitment efforts in the black community, Stokes approved a "Cleveland Now!" grant to the local NAACP so that it could help potential patrolmen prepare for the police examinations. Stokes also changed the personnel of the Civil Service Commission (CSC), the city agency in charge of personnel testing, and instructed his appointees to change the nature of patrolman exams by adding an interview phase. Similarly, the police promotional exam was given a complete overhaul. Officers would now be tested on the role of the police in the community. As expected, white officers were incensed. "Our men are virtually in a state of shock due to city hall intervention with the civil service examinations," declared one officer. Despite Stokes's efforts, his own appointees to the CSC botched the situation by releasing a copy of the test to potential recruits prior to the examination date. After an investigation, a grand jury called the testing scandal the "greatest tragedy and misuse of manpower and public funds and misapplication of both that any Grand Jury could ever expect to find." Although Stokes did not excuse his appointees' actions, he believed that the scandal involved more than their failures. "White policemen had been cheating," he recalled. Nonetheless, the police testing scandal further convinced white officers that Stokes would resort to any method in order to get more blacks on the force.

On Election Day 1969, white police officers organized a mass campaign against Stokes's reelection. They arrived that morning at polling places and proceeded to intimidate black voters. "I talked to the polling officials, the presiding judge and other ladies who were there, and they were frightened, just totally intimidated," reported a member of Stokes's security detail. "They said that these policemen had been interrogating the citizens who came in to vote and just brow beat them. And they were handling the books, the polling books, which is against the law." The presence of white police officers in all-black precincts undermined black turnout. In the words of one observer, "you have to live in the ghetto to understand the effect of anybody saying there is a policeman in any place with a gun on him." Yet, despite the efforts of rogue policemen, Stokes was reelected.

Stokes continued to reform the CPD during his second term by appointing General Benjamin O. Davis Jr. as safety director. Stokes was euphoric after the air force general accepted his offer. Stokes recalled, "A military man! A General! Black or not the people would have to respect him. And, being black, he would have to be the kind of man who would agree with what I wanted to do." The mayor was wrong. The general's determination to maintain the status quo was evident when many of his administrative decisions showed a complete disregard for the black community. For example, he failed to investigate the vicious beating of an African student in Little Italy; he requested permission to purchase 30,000 dum-dum bullets and an armored tank for police; he allowed officers to carry personal weapons while on duty; and he refused to meet with the city's black police organization, the Black Shield. But the worst was yet to come. In July 1970, Davis abruptly resigned after publicly accusing Stokes of opposing strong law enforcement. As expected, the local media had a field day with the allegations, which suggested that Stokes protected criminals. Distraught over his efforts to reform the insular CPD, Stokes would not attempt any other major changes during the remainder of his tenure.

Cleveland City Council represented another obstacle for Carl Stokes in the form of bureaucratic or legislative resistance. Although Stokes was mayor, he did not control Cleveland's thirty-three-member city council, eleven of whom were African Americans. The city council was the domain of its president, James Stanton, a Stokes rival, who controlled approximately twenty votes on council. Stanton was also the de facto head of the Cuyahoga County Democratic Party. Tensions between Stokes and Stanton originated during Stokes's years as a state legislator, when he had supported two Republican-sponsored redistricting plans in an effort to boost black political power in Cleveland and across the state. The feud naturally intensified once Stokes was elected mayor.

The first clash between Stokes and city council came in the early months of his administration when the mayor campaigned to raise the city income tax from 0.5 to 1.0 percent to pay for salary increases and social welfare programs. The Stanton bloc immediately objected to the increase. Stokes countered by publishing the home phone numbers of all council members in a full-page newspaper ad. Next, Stokes engineered a walkout of sanitation workers that left a thousand tons of garbage uncollected each day. Stokes's tactics worked, and the Stanton bloc reluctantly approved the tax increase—but vowed to get revenge.

The next phase of city council hostility came during Stokes's second term, after he failed in an attempt to oust Stanton from the council presidency. Stanton retaliated by blocking Stokes's plans for two public housing projects in white areas. The council president exploited racial fears by telling area homeowners that the developments would lower their property values and eventually turn their communities into slums. Stanton did not end there. Weeks later, he refused to secure passage of an agreement between city council and the Cuyahoga County Metropolitan Housing Authority (CMHA), which jeopardized over $72 million in federal funds. Finally, Stanton engineered the ouster of CMHA executive director Irving Kriegsfeld, a Stokes appointee who had attempted to place public housing all across the county rather than just in the inner city.

The Stokes-Stanton feud again escalated in late 1970 when the Stanton bloc, now controlled by Anthony Garofoli (Stanton went to Congress), blocked another Stokes-sponsored income tax increase. "The Stokes Tax," as its critics labeled it, called for suburbanites who worked in the city to pay more city taxes. In an effort to force Stokes into governing a bankrupt city, the Stanton bloc refused support. The tax plan failed miserably, forcing Stokes to lay off 1,725 employees and close three public health centers.

After the failure of the tax increase proposal, weekly council meetings turned ugly. Customarily, Stokes and his cabinet members attended all council meetings. In early 1971, Thomas Stallworth, one of Stokes's cabinet members, came under an all-out attack when Councilman Francis Gaul accused him of "malfeasance, misfeasance, and nonfeasance" in duty. Stokes became livid. "That kind of language is uncalled for," he shouted. Stokes then had his microphone unplugged while arguing that the attack was a violation of council's courtesy rule. The mayor was told that courtesy rules only applied to council members. In response, he instructed his cabinet members to leave council floor: "What you have said is that the same standard will not be afforded to the administration. I must insist that the privileges and protections be equal. You have made it quite clear, and I am going to instruct my cabinet members to remove themselves from council chambers, and we will not return until the same standards are extended to both branches of government." Stokes and his cabinet did not attend another council session. Instead, he launched his own weekly, televised news conference. As he explained, "In a half-hour of television, I could get out what I wanted in my own words."

Although Stokes expected opposition and hostility from the CPD and city council, he did not expect it from the black middle class. In the summer of 1968, Stokes announced plans for an ambitious public housing development in the black middle-income community of Lee-Seville, on the city's southeast side. Lee-Seville validated black upward mobility. The purchase of a home there signaled one's arrival into the black middle class. Its 2,500 spacious homes had manicured lawns, sitting on wide streets, facing broad sidewalks. It was arguably unlike any other area of black Cleveland. Stokes proposed 277 new single-family homes, comparable in size and style to the existing homes in the neighborhood. The development excited Stokes for several reasons: it would shorten the housing authority's 1,700-family waiting list; it would encourage private developers to build housing for low-income residents; and it would illustrate that public housing could work outside of the ghetto.

Although the project was to be built on fifty-one acres of CMHA-owned land, the housing authority needed city council to make infrastructural improvements. At a council meeting, Stokes encountered an immediate roadblock. Councilmen Clarence Thompson and George White, both African Americans, objected to the proposed development on the grounds that city services could not handle the increased population. Stokes reminded them, however, that the city had already made commitments to increase municipal services in Lee-Seville. Thompson and White then changed their argument to reveal their true objection: class bias. "We learned that it takes a lot of struggle to get the finer things in life. You don't get it by thinking that the federal government is going to make everything right," said White. Stokes responded by labeling the two councilmen bigots. "If you permit bigoted black middle-class persons with a bigoted black public official representing them to stop the utilization of unused land in Lee-Seville for housing . . . you will have failed to support everything we want to do with housing in this city."

While Stokes and the two councilmen sparred in council sessions, Lee-Seville residents split into factions. Those in favor of the development formed the Lee-Seville Development Corporation (LSDC), while those in opposition established the Lee-Seville Homeowner's Improvement Association (LSHIA). The LSHIA contingent was much larger than the LSDC, and its members quickly mobilized against Stokes.

In hopes of generating enough public pressure to force council to pass the necessary legislation, Stokes wrote op-ed letters, staged a "Citizens Rally for Lee-Seville Housing," and held a town hall meeting. Still, the last city council session of the season recessed without a hearing on his housing proposal. Stokes was disheartened: "We have to give the poor people a chance to be part of an affluent society. We have to give poor people a chance to have their own piece of property." He had wanted to demonstrate that public housing outside of the ghetto was one solution to urban housing problems. The black middle-class opposition to Lee-Seville came as a surprise to Stokes, particularly since they had supported him throughout his political career.

Structural forces also hindered Stokes in his efforts to improve the lives of the black poor. Like other industrial cities, Cleveland experienced white residential and commercial flight. As white homeowners flocked to the suburbs after World War II, industry either went with them, migrated to the Sunbelt, or simply closed down. Between 1953 and 1964, roughly 80,000 blue-collar positions left Cleveland as urban America began its shift from an industrial-based economy to a service-based economy. Cleveland proper also experienced massive disinvestment. Of the approximately $1.7 billion spent on postwar industrial expansion, $1 billion was spent in the suburbs. Likewise, the inner city only received 70,000 of the 170,000 jobs created in that same period. The problems of deindustrialization and disinvestment were further magnified with the dramatic influx of black southerners and white Appalachians during the second great migration. Stokes found himself trying to govern a city with declining tax revenues, more unskilled and poor people, growing welfare rolls, and a massive loss of jobs.

Last, Stokes had to confront the reality of race. Although Cleveland had a reputation for being the "best location in the nation" for

African Americans, that slogan was more perception than reality. Stokes inherited a city that was polarized by decades of below-the-surface racial conflict. Further, when Stokes took office in 1967, a conservative backlash against the civil rights movement was gaining momentum as white northerners began to express openly how they felt about blacks. As the first black mayor of a major city, Stokes was always under the microscope, and he had little margin for error. "That meant I had to be more creative, more honest, more intelligent, more available, more witty, more thorough, than any other mayor in the country," Stokes wrote in his memoirs.

Despite the limits that were placed upon him, Stokes nonetheless did have some success. In the area of public housing, Stokes built more than four thousand units, which represented more than 60 percent of the units built in the previous three decades. Stokes also implemented an aggressive affirmative action program that increased contracting and employment opportunities for African Americans, and he used the leverage of city hall to force local banks to underwrite aspiring black business owners through favorable loan policies. Another major accomplishment of the Stokes administration was that he brought African Americans and women into management and supervisory positions with the city. But Stokes's greatest political success was that he served as a symbol of pride to African Americans who found inspiration in the color of his skin.

Further Reading

Moore, Leonard N. *Carl B. Stokes and the Rise of Black Political Power.* Urbana: University of Illinois Press, 2002.

Nelson, William E., and Philip J. Meranto. *Electing Black Mayors.* Columbus: Ohio State University Press, 1977.

Porter, Philip W. *Cleveland: Confused City on a Seesaw.* Columbus: Ohio State University Press, 1976.

Stokes, Carl B. *Promises of Power: A Political Autobiography.* New York: Simon and Schuster, 1973.

Zannes, Estelle. *Checkmate in Cleveland: The Rhetoric of Confrontation during the Stokes Years.* Cleveland: Press of Case Western Reserve University, 1972.

24

Dave Thomas, Fast Food, and Continued Opportunity in Ohio

H. G. PARSA AND DAVID GERALD HOGAN

O HIO IS famed for its many great industries, ranging from air-planes to automobiles to hamburgers. Yes, hamburgers. In the Buckeye State, White Castle staked its claim in the early 1930s, when founder Billy Ingram moved his chain's headquarters to Columbus. Many years later, Wendy's R. David Thomas built the world's third largest fast food hamburger chain, starting with his first restaurant on Broad Street in Columbus. A transplant to Ohio, Thomas boldly defied pessimistic analysts who predicted failure in 1969 when Thomas entered the already saturated quick service restaurant arena. Believing that consumers would pay a premium price for higher quality food, Thomas shocked industry experts by soon outpacing most of his competitors. With a simple plan offering superior quality food and service, within a decade Wendy's International successfully expanded to include thousands of franchised outlets across the country and around the world. By keeping his corporate headquarters in the Columbus area, Thomas solidified that city's reputation as the nation's "First City of Fast Food."

Dave Thomas began life in an unlikely position to ever achieve wealth and prestige. Born to a woman living in a home for unwed mothers in Atlantic City in 1932, he was adopted six months later by Auleva and Rex Thomas, a working-class couple of modest means. Hardship continued for young Dave, with Auleva dying when he was five and then living a transient, often hardscrabble life with his adoptive father. For a few years after Auleva's death from rheumatic fever, her mother, Minnie Sinclair, lovingly nurtured young Dave in her Kalamazoo, Michigan, home, providing him with stability and a sense

311

FIG. 20 Dave Thomas.
Courtesy of The Ohio State University Archives.

of security. A strong-willed and devout woman raised in the Kentucky hills, Minnie taught Dave that "if you worked hard, you made things happen." Though of modest means, every Saturday she drove her adoptive grandson to downtown Kalamazoo, eating together at the five-and-dime store lunch counter, munching on candy, and buying him a small but cherished toy. Minnie also introduced Dave to restaurant life, sometimes taking him with her to the establishment where she worked as a cook and dishwasher.

This joy and stability proved to be short-lived, however, when Rex, discontented with his job as a mechanic, sought employment as a laborer in Indiana. The Thomases moved to a new town, away from Minnie. A stern, authoritarian parent, Rex provided Dave with food and shelter but demonstrated little love or affection. He soon remarried, this time to a woman named Marie, who proved to be a cold stepmother, always ready to discipline young Dave. Rex and Marie divorced after two and a half years of marriage, once again leaving Rex and Dave alone. Now living together in a Detroit rooming house, they ate daily at local restaurants and small neighborhood bars. One of their favorite stops was a hamburger stand that fried heaping mounds of onions on top of the burgers and served rich milk shakes that were too thick to drink with a straw. Years later, Thomas credited his early exposure to so many restaurants as his motivation for entering the business, and his love for those burgers and shakes as the inspiration for Wendy's menu staples.

Living a transient existence, the Thomases moved to Evansville, Indiana, at the start of World War II, where Rex found work in a shipyard and remarried. Rex's third wife, Viola, had two daughters from a previous marriage. Though he never grew very close to his new stepmother and stepsisters, Dave found this new family environment preferable to life with Marie or living in a rooming house with Rex. Nevertheless, Dave felt that he held a second-class position behind Viola's daughters. As a way to avoid being at home and as a means of earning money, he began working at age ten at a gasoline station in Princeton, Indiana. Tiring of this job, Dave then worked as a newspaper boy, a golf caddy, and a bowling alley pin setter. Wanting a job working in a restaurant, Dave applied to several local ones who all told him that he was far too young.

Just as Dave made new friends in town and settled into a routine of family life, Rex took yet another job. Uprooting Dave for the fourth time in six years, the family moved to Knoxville, Tennessee, in 1944, so Rex could work as a construction foreman. At age twelve and depressed about moving again, Dave moped around the house until his father told him to get a job. Still too young to secure legal employment, but big for his age, Dave fibbed that he was fifteen when he applied for and was hired to work at a grocery store. After working at the grocery for a month, the owner informed Dave that the store would close for a two-week vacation. Pleased for this break in the summer heat, Dave spent the first week off frolicking at the recreation center swimming pool. Much to his surprise, the grocer returned early from vacation and phoned Dave to return to work. Enjoying his free time at the pool, Dave told his employer that he already made plans for the following week, so he would be unable to work. Displeased, the grocer put a help wanted sign in his front window. Dave clearly understood the meaning of the sign: he was fired. Stunned, but undeterred, the next week he applied for work at Walgreens, once again lying about his age, and once again was hired. Dave worked the soda fountain, making and serving ice cream sundaes, wearing a white uniform and black bow tie. Three weeks later, however, this job ended when the manager learned about Dave's actual age. Rex reacted angrily, screaming, "You'll never keep a job! I'll be supporting you for the rest of your life!" Thomas credits that moment as pivotal in his life, vowing to himself then that he would never lose another job again.

Undeterred by losing these jobs, Thomas once again set out to find work. In downtown Knoxville, he noticed a sign advertising available employment in the front window of the Regas Restaurant. Impressed by the restaurant's highly polished interior and its prominently displayed National Restaurant Association membership sign, Thomas applied for work, telling the manager that he was sixteen, rather than his actual age of twelve. Once hired, his new post was serving at the lunch counter, working alongside sixteen-year-old Bill Regas, the owner's son. Clad in a gray smock coat, white apron, white shirt, and bow tie, Thomas learned the fine points of the restaurant business under the strict tutelage of Frank Regas, perfecting the balancing of heavily loaded plates, taking orders by memory, and keeping the counter spotless. Working twelve-hour shifts, he cleaned the restaurant, made hundreds of sandwiches for the following day, and served hundreds of breakfasts, beginning at 4 A.M. every day. Frank Regas insisted on extreme cleanliness and flawless service, constantly reminding all his employees, "Work as if your job depends on every single customer, every day, because it does." Thomas admired Regas and loved working at the restaurant.

Six months into his employment, Thomas learned that his father had accepted a new job sixty miles away. Not wanting to leave the Regas Restaurant, Dave rode the bus to Knoxville every weekend and rented a sleeping room close to the restaurant. Having no hobbies, special interests, or passion for school, he was consumed by his work.

Thomas's satisfying employment at Regas finally ended in 1947 when Rex once again found a new job and moved the family back to Fort Wayne, Indiana. Leaving Knoxville was painful for Dave, as was his new life in Fort Wayne. The Thomases lived in a small house trailer, with little privacy and no indoor plumbing. Voila soon had a new baby, which meant even more crowding for the family. Having experienced limited independence during the weekends and summer in his rented Knoxville sleeping room, Dave became increasing discontented with this new living arrangement. His discontent motivated him to quickly go job hunting, applying for a busboy position at the Hobby House Restaurant. Impressed with his appearance and attitude, the manager immediately hired Dave to clean tables for fifty cents per hour. Within a month, Dave was promoted to a counter serving position. Basically a quick-service restaurant selling burgers, coffee, ice cream, and milkshakes, the Hobby House was a popular spot in downtown Fort Wayne. Seating over 150 customers with a fast turnover rate meant a hectic pace behind the counter. An efficient and hard worker in this frenzied atmosphere, the manager recognized Dave's talents and motivation, soon promoting him to cook in the front kitchen. Now making thirty-five dollars a week for fifty hours of work, Dave began to feel increasingly self-sufficient. In the meantime, he also learned from his grandmother that he had been adopted. When his dad informed him of another impending family move, Dave decided to remain in Fort Wayne with his job and friends. Renting a room at the nearby YMCA, Dave Thomas was now on his own in the world.

Balancing high school and a busy work schedule proved to be too exhausting for Dave. Believing that school was not teaching him what he needed to know for his future restaurant career, he decided to drop out after the tenth grade. Work became the single focus of his life, and Phil Clauss, the Hobby House's owner, became his new mentor. Clauss taught Dave much about the restaurant business, becoming a protective father figure, and suggesting to Dave that he move out of the YMCA and instead board with his sister, Esther Marquart, and her family. Though technically a boarder in the house, in a sense, the Marquarts became Dave's second adoptive family, providing him with both comfortable accommodations and a sense of belonging that he never before had felt. This was a time of life remembered fondly by Thomas, enjoying his dear friends at work, learning the restaurant trade from Clauss, and finding a warm family life with the Marquarts. His ambitions to manage the Hobby House and to eventually own his own restaurant, however, were put on hold.

The Korean War erupted in 1950, and seventeen-year-old Dave Thomas knew he would soon be drafted. Realizing that enlistees had a better chance of choosing their job specialties than draftees, Dave joined the army in hopes of becoming a cook. With Clauss's promise of a job when he returned, Dave headed off to basic training at Fort Benning, Georgia.

Soon after arriving at Fort Benning, bad fortune befell Dave. Tooth pain led him to the company dentist, who performed a root canal operation. Infection set in, causing pain and swelling, and an inability to talk or eat. The dentist gave Dave a medical release from training for ten days. Bored staying in bed, he volunteered at the mess

hall, clearing tables, sweeping, and cooking. Back in his favorite element, Dave displayed such talent and competence that the mess
sergeant offered him an immediate assignment to cook and baker's
school. This eight-week school superseded his obligation to complete
combat basic training, excusing Dave from carrying fifty-pound back-
packs through the swamps of Georgia. What he learned from this
favorable reassignment was contrary to army conventional wisdom—
always volunteer! The school itself also taught Dave two important
lessons: that he was a lousy baker and how to feed large numbers.

During the last week of training, eighteen-year-old Thomas
learned that his division would soon ship out to Germany and that he
had been promoted to sergeant. Once again, he credited his rapid rise
in rank to his habit of volunteering. He later discovered a more plausible explanation; organizationally, all ranks had to be sufficiently
staffed before being deployed overseas, and someone *had* to be promoted to sergeant. Nevertheless, Thomas was thrilled to ship out as
an eighteen-year-old staff sergeant.

Upon arriving in Germany, Thomas was assigned to cook at the
mess hall for division headquarters, feeding over a thousand soldiers
each day. In addition to cooking, Dave began regularly scavenging
scarce and expensive items such as dented cookware and bent silver-
ware from the dumpsters of the air force and other army units. Grateful for what Dave's salvage efforts saved his budget, the mess officer
routinely sent him around to "scrounge" for needed items and to
trade with other units for supplies. As his company's unofficial pro-
curement officer, he gained popularity in his unit, especially when he
worked tirelessly to refurbish shabby division barracks and mess facilities.

Thomas's ingenuity and hard work further paid off by his reassignment to assistant manager of the enlisted men's club, a coveted
and lucrative job usually reserved for senior career soldiers. Once
again, a new position brought new challenges. His enlisted men's
club was popular among the soldiers as a beer hall but sold little food.
To improve its food sales, Dave changed the menu from just cold
sandwiches to a broad array of items, including chicken, shrimp cock-
tail, and hamburgers. Soon sales soared from a paltry $40 each day to
over $700. His superiors marveled at how a teenager could turn
around a faltering operation and assigned him more responsibility
and authority.

Thomas's two and a half years in Germany was all work, with very
little play. Working six long days every week throughout his tour, he

never traveled to see other parts of Europe nor did he make any meaningful friendships. This prioritization of work, at the expense of life's other pleasures, would become the central theme of Thomas's life for decades to come.

Discharged in October 1953, Sergeant Dave Thomas returned to Fort Wayne and to his old cooking job at the Hobby House. Greeted at the door by Phil Clauss, who was holding out an apron, Dave was pleased to be back with his dear friends. In addition, Dave met Lorraine Buskirk, a recently hired eighteen-year-old waitress. Their relationship soon blossomed into a serious romance. Marrying after less than six months of courtship, Dave and Lorraine briefly lived with the Marquarts before buying a house with a $7,500 loan from Clauss. In January 1955, the Thomases welcomed a new daughter, Pam, to the family.

At the same time, Dave's work life flourished. Intrigued by the new trend in barbecue restaurants, Phil Clauss decided to open a second restaurant, the Hobby Ranch House. Naming Dave as its assistant manager at $75 per week, Clauss started the Hobby Ranch House with a limited menu, featuring barbecued chicken and ribs served on paper plates, potato salad, baked beans, rye bread, and sliced onions. The barbecue craze was already popular in other Indiana cities, where profitable barbecue restaurants successfully used paper products instead of china and maintained very streamlined menus. Though the Hobby Ranch House's food was quite good, its Fort Wayne customers disliked the paper plates and cups and requested several other menu items. Customer oriented, possibly to a fault, Clauss relented, changing the paper flatware and cups to china and greatly expanding the menu items. Both moves disturbed Dave, who now had a son and was frustrated by his unchanged salary.

Just as Thomas's dissatisfaction grew, however, Phil Clauss discovered a new direction for the Hobby Ranch House. While attending a National Restaurant Association convention, Clauss met Harlan Sanders, a sixty-five-year-old restaurateur from Kentucky. Using the title "Colonel," goateed, and dressed all in black, Sanders offered Clauss a fried chicken franchise featuring a new cooking technique and a unique recipe. Clauss was thrilled with the idea, but Thomas questioned the necessity of changing how they cooked chicken, especially when having to pay Sanders handsomely for the right to do so. Thomas changed his position two months later when Colonel Sanders appeared at the Hobby Ranch House wearing black tails and carrying a gold-tipped cane. They sat down together over a cup of coffee, and impressed by Sanders's smooth salesmanship, Thomas was a believer in the idea by the time he departed.

Actually tasting the chicken soon afterward at one of Sanders's franchisees in another town, Dave and Clauss became convinced that Kentucky Fried Chicken would be a hit in Fort Wayne. Clauss immediately bought a franchise and began serving the new chicken in both of his restaurants. Chicken sales boomed from the start, soon prompting the introduction of takeout service, in part to relieve the crush on their dining room. Before long, Clauss's two Fort Wayne Hobby Houses were among the biggest volume sellers of carryout chicken in the nation. To better accommodate larger orders, Clauss designed a cardboard bucket that held considerably more chicken than the existing rectangular dinner boxes. To decorate these new buckets, he also commissioned his brother-in-law to design a logo featuring the image of Colonel Sanders. (Now over forty years later, both the bucket and the logo remain prominent symbols of Kentucky Fried Chicken.)

In addition to designing this container and image, Clauss and Dave became active partners in selling both new franchises for Sanders and the concept of Kentucky Fried Chicken to the American public. Dave even went on the road with Sanders, making sales calls together on potential franchisees and accompanying him to television and radio interviews—learning firsthand the value of having a recognizable company host or hostess for marketing purposes. Traveling with the volatile Sanders, who routinely cussed in public and engaged in arguments and even fistfights, was sometimes difficult for Dave. Despite these pitfalls, however, Thomas later cited this experience as a great education in both how to sell and how to deal with people. In return, Sanders gained a great disciple. He often sent prospective franchisees to Fort Wayne to see the success of his fried chicken, with Dave always there as an enthusiastic advocate. Though still just the assistant manager of Clauss's Hobby Ranch House, he was perhaps the Colonel's greatest salesman.

One group of potential investors, visiting from Columbus, Ohio, forever changed Thomas's life. Interested in opening Hobby Ranch House/Kentucky Fried Chicken franchises in their hometown, they asked Phil Clauss for both advice and investment capital. Clauss decided to invest in their project, but because these men were not experienced restauranteurs, he insisted that they take on Dave Thomas as their "operations advisor." This role entailed a monthly trip to Columbus, consulting on all aspects of the business. The

Columbus entrepreneurs quickly opened four new Hobby Ranch Houses but soon ran into difficulties. Largely ignoring Thomas's suggestions, and always attempting to cut corners, they blundered in almost every facet of the business.

Alarmed at possibly losing his $250,000 investment, Clauss asked Thomas to move to Columbus to manage the restaurants. Friends in the industry, including Sanders, cautioned Dave against this move. Seeing the Columbus operation as an impending disaster, the blunt Sanders told him, "You're stupid if you go there!" Clauss, however, dangled before Thomas a sweet deal: a relatively low salary but a five-cent bonus for every chicken sold, a percentage of the annual net profits, and the opportunity to buy a share of the company. Intensely loyal to Clauss and in need of greater income to support Lorraine and their now four children, Thomas set out for Columbus with forty dollars in his pocket.

Thomas faced a daunting challenge, with all four Columbus Hobby Houses on the verge of collapse. Immediately he took decisive action, firing all four of his managers, repainting the dining rooms, scrutinizing costs and revenues, and advertising aggressively. The operation's dismal credit and no cash reserves forced Thomas to pay for deliveries with cash and to swap buckets of chicken for ads with the local radio stations.

Most significantly, Thomas streamlined the menu from over one hundred items to just chicken, salads, desserts, and beverages, and changing the restaurant names to Colonel Sanders Kentucky Fried Chicken Take-Home. Focusing on just chicken, Dave ran pricing specials with coupons and even designed the rotating bucket-shaped sign that would later be the standard for all Kentucky Fried Chicken franchises.

Thomas's decision to specialize in just chicken brought great success. By 1967, his hard work paid off handsomely, with a fifth store opening in Columbus and a 40 percent ownership stake in the business. The following year, the new corporate owners of Kentucky Fried Chicken decided to buy back some of their more profitable franchises, approaching Clauss and Thomas with a lucrative offer. When the deal was done, Thomas walked away with over $1 million in Kentucky Fried Chicken stock. In six years, he had gone from assistant manager and fry cook at the Fort Wayne Hobby House to a "paper" millionaire, with his riches held in company stock. To celebrate his good fortune and "early retirement," he took Lorraine out for a nice dinner and built a swimming pool—in the shape of a chicken—for their children in their backyard. Soon however, Thomas was back in the chicken business, accepting an offer from Kentucky Fried Chicken to become its regional head of operations for a salary of $50,000 per year. Pleased with having both a sizable nestegg and this ample salary, Thomas worked for Kentucky Fried Chicken for the next two years, until his relationship with the company soured over a stock dispute. Feeling cheated, he quit and then successfully sued to recover the value of his stock.

Though suddenly a true millionaire, Thomas felt uneasy being without work. He was always mindful of his adoptive father's pessimistic predictions that he would never keep a job. Just thirty-seven, he was nervous without earning regular wages, relying solely on his accumulated wealth for income. Memories of the poverty of his youth haunted him, so he hesitantly accepted National Fast Food's offer to supervise the operations of its Arthur Treacher's Fish & Chips chain. Paying only $20,000 a year, the Arthur Treacher's position was not what Dave truly wanted to do, but he decided to work at it until he settled on his next business move.

A lifelong fan of hamburgers, Thomas pondered the possibility of opening a new hamburger restaurant. He shared his ideas with a friend, Columbus car dealer Len Immke, while the two men exercised together at the Columbus Athletic Club. Primary among Thomas's ideas was his commitment to offering consumers a superior product, which would feature fresh ground beef and a larger patty. Although the fast food hamburger market appeared saturated, Thomas believed that much of the buying public wanted higher quality burgers, nicer surroundings, and more attentive service than what was offered at McDonald's, Burger King, or similar chains.

Growing increasingly bored at Arthur Treacher's and primed by Immke's encouragement, Dave made his move. From Immke, he rented a property on Broad Street across from Columbus's highly popular Center of Science and Industry museum. Next, he searched for a company name. Remembering everything that Colonel Sanders had taught him about the value of using image as a marketing device, he chose the image of a smiling little girl eating a hamburger as his logo. Dave first pondered using one of his own daughters' names for his new restaurant, but none of these seemed to fit with the logo. Finally, he settled on using his daughter Melinda's nickname as a small child, which was Wendy. Adding on the phrase "Old Fashioned Hamburgers," Thomas named his new restaurant.

Set on location, name, and image, Thomas next adopted an upscale decor for his dining room, replete with hanging Tiffany lamps, carpeting, and bentwood chairs. He envisioned that his counter workers would wear clean white uniforms, women in skirts and aprons, and men with bow ties and chef's hats. Thomas strictly limited his menu to hamburgers, offering either single, double, or triple patties, chili, thick chocolate milkshake-like Frostys, french fries, and an assortment of soft drinks.

This fare of burgers, fries, and drinks differed little from virtually every other fast food chain of this era. What made Dave's operation unique was truly the "old-fashioned" approach to the food preparation and service. Rather than preparing large quantities of identical burgers, which spent hours baking under heat lamps until sold, the Wendy's system cooked and prepared each burger especially for each customer's tastes. Not grilled until ordered, each sandwich contained the exact amount of beef and combination of condiments chosen by the customer. Though seemingly a drastic departure from common fast food practices in 1969, Dave's approach of offering higher quality food, cooked to individual taste, was certainly not new. In fact, he was only harkening back to the basic lessons he learned about the restaurant business years earlier from Frank Regas and Phil Clauss: customers will happily pay for quality food and service.

Opening day on November 15, 1969, confirmed this truth, with enthusiastic customers lined up down the street. Eight-year-old Melinda appeared at the opening as the image of Wendy, with her red-painted hair in pigtails tied with blue ribbons and wearing a blue-and-white striped dress. Business remained brisk, with Wendy's Old Fashioned Hamburgers soon becoming a popular fixture in downtown Columbus. Even surprising Dave, the restaurant began making money in less than six weeks.

When he first launched Wendy's, Dave had no intention of beginning a huge fast food chain. Downtown Columbus had few casual eating spots before Wendy's opening, so competition was light. In suburbs coast to coast, however, the fast food competition was intense, with several once-prosperous chains beginning to fail. Industry analysts prophesied that any newcomers to the field were only destined for financial disaster. Logically, with prices at least twice as high as those of the major chains, Wendy's should have been especially unsuccessful. Yet as Wendy's continued to flourish on Broad Street, Dave began to consider expansion to a second location on land he had already purchased on the outskirts of Columbus. Curious as to whether or not his first restaurant's success was a fluke, he built and opened his second Wendy's a year after the first, this time partnering with old friends. Featuring an automobile pickup window to enhance customer convenience and sales volume, this new suburban Wendy's prospered far beyond expectations. Buoyed by this repeated success, in 1971 Thomas and his partners opened two new locations in lower income areas, testing if Wendy's higher prices would succeed in such a market. Once again, these newer stores exceeded all expectations by becoming the company's most profitable.

More Wendy's appeared in the surrounding areas, even expanding out of state in 1972 when the partners built a company-owned Wendy's in Indianapolis. Expansion continued, but Dave and his partners switched their primary focus from building stores to selling franchises for $200,000 per unit. The first franchised Wendy's opened in Marion, Ohio, in March 1972. From that point the franchise business became hectic, with four to five new franchisees signing contracts each day. Dave recalls that "on any given day, you could walk into our offices and see twenty to thirty men with briefcases waiting to see us." Unlike many franchise situations, the Wendy's partners only sold franchisees the rights to their company name and trademarks, without forcing contractual purchases of food products or restaurant equipment. The only requirement was that franchisees had to make purchases and operate within Wendy's uniform specifications. Wendy's franchising terms were so agreeable that even restaurateurs affiliated with other chains began to purchase franchises. In a further departure from the norm, Wendy's began selling blanket franchises for entire cities and territories covering large parts of states. The partners realized a net profit of over $1 million in 1974. Sales continued to boom, with a thousand new Wendy's built in their first hundred months in business.

In 1976, Wendy's went from Broad Street to Wall Street, offering the public one million shares of company stock for twenty-eight dollars each. This public offering brought great wealth to the partners and most of all to Dave Thomas. Still the majority stockholder, Thomas remained with the company as its chairman, overseeing its continued growth and innovation. Under his direction, Wendy's soon began a salad bar and rapidly diversified its menu offerings. Though hamburgers remained the centerpiece of the menu, the company's franchisees wanted more options, such as chicken sandwiches and other specialty items, in order to match industry trends and changing customer demands. An increasingly health-conscious buying public preferred leaner, healthier foods, and Wendy's accommodated them. Eventually stuffed pitas, Caesar salads, and baked potatoes became popular items at Wendy's. With all this change, however, Thomas was quick to warn managers at a national meeting in 1980 that "salad bars won't wash your windows," reminding them that new products are far less important than still providing the basics of good customer service.

During the 1980s, Thomas transferred more day-to-day control of Wendy's to competent executives. In 1986, James Near, a former Borden president and Wendy's franchisee for the entire state of West Virginia, assumed the positions of president and chief operating officer, allowing Thomas the free time to pursue other activities. Already active in the community, he threw himself into philanthropy, raising funds for St. Jude's Children's Research, the Ohio State University Cancer Research Institute, and Wendy's High School Heisman program. Sensitive to the topic of adoption ever since learning of his own from Grandma Minnie, Thomas worked passionately on national adoption issues. President George H. W. Bush recognized his efforts in 1990, naming him chairman and spokesman for the White House Initiative on Adoption. He further supported this cause by starting the Dave Thomas Foundation for Adoption, for the purposes of raising public awareness and making the adoption process more affordable for many prospective parents. Thomas earmarked all the profits from his two books, *Dave's Way* (1991) and *Well Done!* (1994), to go directly to his foundation. As a result of his good works, he won countless entrepreneur and man-of-the-year titles, received honorary doctorates from prestigious universities, and earned the Horatio Alger Award for his spectacular rags-to-riches success. In 1994, Thomas returned to the White House for a reception held in his honor, with President Bill Clinton lauding his contributions to the cause of adoption and also announcing that November would be celebrated as National Adoption Month. On a later trip to Washington, Thomas testified before Congress on adoption issues, urging legislators to support tax credits for parents adopting special needs children.

Charitable work, however, did not consume all of Thomas's time. Though now more distant from daily company operations, he assumed a very central marketing role in 1989. In essence, he became the recognizable face of Wendy's, just as Colonel Sanders became the personification of Kentucky Fried Chicken. Always a firm believer in the power of advertising, but never before a company pitchman, Thomas hesitated when marketing vice president Charlie Rath suggested that he should appear in commercials as the company spokesman. Thomas replied, "I'll try, but if it doesn't work now, or ever stops working, I'm history." The ads proved to be a phenomenal success. Projecting a folksy, sincere persona, Dave Thomas became a household name and a popular public figure. Beginning with simple sales pitches, the ads eventually grew to be more elaborate, featuring the ambling Dave either in different situations or teamed up with celebrities. In all, he filmed over five hundred different Wendy's ads, proving to be an effective voice for the company.

Living much of the year in Florida by the early 1990s, Thomas finally took time to rectify a longstanding mistake in his life. Despite founding a major company, being awarded honorary degrees from universities, becoming a thirty-third-degree Mason, raising millions of dollars for charity, and achieving international celebrity status, he still was not a high school graduate. Wanting to set an example for a younger generation, Thomas earned his General Education Degree from Fort Lauderdale's Coconut Creek High School in 1993. Attending Coconut Creek's senior prom, he and Lorraine were named prom king and queen. At the Coconut Creek graduation ceremony, his classmates named him the "Most Likely to Succeed."

Succeed he did. His life of hard work, tenacity, and shrewd decisions made Dave Thomas wealthy, popular, and respected throughout the world. Right up until his death from liver cancer on January 8, 2002, he continued to use his money, good name, and boundless energy for the benefit of people in need. Even more important, his life, values, and unlikely success serve as a testament to the American dream, as phrased in the Ohio motto "that all things are possible."

Further Reading

Boas, Max, and Steve Chain. *Big Mac: The Unauthorized Story of McDonald's.* New York: New American Library, 1976.

Hogan, David Gerard. *Selling 'Em by the Sack: White Castle and the Creation of American Food.* New York: New York University Press, 1997.

Parsa, H. G., and Francis A. Kwansa, eds. *Quick Service Restaurants, Franchising, and Multi-Unit Chain Management.* New York: Haworth Hospitality Press, 2001.

Schlosser, Eric. *Fast Food Nation: The Dark Side of the All-American Meal.* Boston: Houghton Mifflin, 2001.

Thomas, R. David. *Dave's Way: A New Approach to Old-Fashioned Success.* New York: G. P. Putnam's Sons, 1991.

List of Contributors

Roberta Sue Alexander, Distinguished Professor of History at the University of Dayton, received her B.A. from UCLA, her M.A. and Ph.D. from the University of Chicago, and her J.D. from the University of Dayton. Her publications include *North Carolina Faces the Freedmen: Race Relations during Presidential Reconstruction, 1865–67,* several articles on the Reconstruction era, as well as law review articles on the Constitution and jurisprudence. She is currently completing a manuscript on the history of the federal district court for the Southern District of Ohio.

Mansel G. Blackford received his B.A. from Stanford University, his M.A. from the University of Washington, and his Ph.D. from the University of California, Berkeley. He works in the field of business history at The Ohio State University and has authored, coauthored, or edited eleven books, including *BFGoodrich: Traditions and Transformations, 1870–1920,* with K. Austin Kerr.

Virginia R. Boynton received her Ph.D. in history from The Ohio State University. Currently, she is an Associate Professor of History at Western Illinois University. Her articles have appeared in *Mid-America: An Historical Review; Ohio History; Journal of the Illinois Historical Society;* and *Chicago History.* Her current research focuses on the roles of Illinois women on the home front during World War I.

Jeffrey P. Brown earned a Ph.D. in U.S. history from the University of Illinois at Urbana. He is currently interim dean for the College of Arts and Sciences at New Mexico State University, where he has served as director of the public history program and associate dean for the College of Arts and Sciences. Additionally, he has served as president of the National Council on Public History. His publications include six articles about politics in the Northwest Territory and early Ohio, and, with Andrew R. L. Cayton, he coedited *The Pursuit of Public Power: Political Culture in Ohio, 1787–1861.*

Alfred A. Cave, Ph.D., is professor emeritus of history and former dean of the College of Arts and Sciences at The University of Toledo. He is author of *Jacksonian Democracy and the Historians; American Civilization: A Documentary History* (with James L. Clayton); *An American Conservative in the Age of Jackson: The Political and Social Thought of Calvin Colton; The Pequot War;* and the forthcoming *The French and Indian War.* He is currently researching prophetic movements among Native Americans.

Andrew R. L. Cayton is Distinguished Professor of History at Miami University. He received his Ph.D. in U.S. history from Brown University and has authored several volumes, including *The Frontier Republic: Ideology and Politics in the Ohio Country, 1780–1825; The Midwest and the Nation: Rethinking the History of an American Region; Frontier Indiana;* and most recently, *Ohio: The History of a People.*

William Russell Coil received his B.A. in history from Ball State University. He earned his M.A. in U.S. history from The Ohio State University, where he is currently writing a dissertation on James Rhodes, Ray Bliss, and the transformation of the Republican Party since the New Deal.

Richard O. Davies is University Foundation Professor of History at the University of Nevada, Reno. He is the author or editor of fourteen books, including *Defender of the Old Guard: John Bricker and American Politics; Main Street Blues: The Decline of Small Town America; The Maverick Spirit: Building the New Nevada; Betting the Line: Sports Wagering in American Life;* and *A Place Called Home: Writings on the Midwestern Small Town.* His doctorate is in U.S. history from the University of Missouri (1963).

Merton L. Dillon is Emeritus Professor of History at The Ohio State University. He is the author of several books including *Elijah P. Lovejoy, Abolitionist Editor; Benjamin Lundy and the Struggle for Negro Freedom; The Abolitionists: The Growth of a Dissenting Minority;* and *Ulrich Bonnell Phillips: Historian of the Old South.*

David Gerald Hogan writes about the history of American food and is the author of *Selling 'Em by the Sack: White Castle and the Creation of American Food.* He teaches at Heidelberg College in Tiffin, Ohio.

R. Douglas Hurt is professor and director of the Graduate Program in Agricultural History and Rural Studies at Iowa State University. He has served as the editor of *Agricultural History,* is a past president of the Agricultural History Society, and is the author of several books, including *The Ohio Frontier: Crucible of the Old Northwest, 1720–1830.*

Ronald Lora is a professor of history at The University of Toledo. He earned his Ph.D. from The Ohio State University, with specializations in U.S. intellectual history and recent political and cultural history. He is the author of *Conservative Minds in America,* editor of *America in the 1960's: Cultural Authorities in Transition* and *The American West,* and coeditor of *The Conservative Press in Eighteenth- and Nineteenth-Century America* and *The Conservative Press in Twentieth-Century America.* Lora has received teaching awards from both The University of Toledo and Ohio Academy of History.

Mary Alice Mairose is an independent historian residing in Columbus, Ohio. She received a master's degree in history from The Ohio State University. Formerly, she has worked for the National Park Service and the Ohio Historical Society. While working at OHS, she researched Thomas Worthington and his home Adena. Her other research interests include nativism in the Ohio Valley and antebellum reform movements.

Allan R. Millett is the Maj. Gen. Raymond E. Mason Jr. Professor of Military History and Mershon Center faculty research fellow at The Ohio State University, where he received a doctorate and has been a faculty member since 1969. Although he is a specialist on World War II and the Korean War, he has written about Ohio frontier conflicts in *Timeline.* Millet is a former president of the Society for Military History and the U.S. Commission of Military History. He is author or coauthor of seven books on U.S. military history.

Leonard N. Moore is an associate professor of history and director of African and African-American Studies at Louisiana State University. Moore received his doctorate from The Ohio State University and is the author of *Carl B. Stokes and the Rise of Black Political Power.* He is currently working on a project that examines police-community relations in black America.

Joan E. Organ received her Ph.D. in social policy history in 1998 from Case Western Reserve University, where she wrote a dissertation on Florence Allen. She also has earned master's degrees in English and education from Youngstown State University. Organ currently works as a counselor for the Cleveland Heights–University Heights School District and as an adjunct faculty member at Cleveland State University.

H. G. Parsa is currently an associate professor in hospitality management at The Ohio State University. He holds a Ph.D. in hospitality management from Virginia Tech and is the author of *Quick Service Restaurants, Franchising and Multiunit Management* as well as several scholarly articles. Dr. Parsa also serves on the executive board of the Ohio Restaurant Association and has received several awards for teaching and research.

Philip Payne is currently teaching U.S. and public history at St. Bonaventure University. The John Campbell essay comes from his Ohio State University doctoral dissertation, which focuses on industrial development in Ironton. After receiving his Ph.D., he served as director of the Warren G. Harding Home and Museum in Marion, Ohio, and has written extensively about the last Ohioan to occupy the White House.

Michael Pierce received his A.B. from Kenyon College and Ph.D. in U.S. history from The Ohio State University. He currently teaches at the University of Arkansas, where he also serves as associate director of the Arkansas Center for Oral and Visual History and assistant editor of the *Arkansas Historical Quarterly.*

Robert Sawrey is professor of history at Marshall University, where he specializes in the Civil War and Reconstruction eras. He received his Ph.D. from the University of Cincinnati, and has authored *Dubious Victory: The Reconstruction Debate in Ohio* and several articles on reconstruction.

Barbara A. Terzian received her J.D. and Ph.D. from The Ohio State University. She is currently an assistant professor at Ohio Wesleyan University. She is contributing a chapter on Ohio's constitutions to *The History of Ohio Law,* forthcoming from Ohio University Press, which is also publishing her book, *"Effusions of Folly and Fanaticism": Race, Gender, and State Constitution-Making in Ohio, 1802–1923.*

Warren Van Tine received his Ph.D. from the University of Massachusetts and has been on the faculty of The Ohio State University since 1970. He has authored or coauthored several books on U.S. labor history, the most recent of which is a collaborative history of the Ohio AFL-CIO.

Kenneth H. Wheeler received his Ph.D. in history from The Ohio State University. He is an assistant professor of history at Reinhardt College.

Amy Fancelli Zalimas holds master's degrees in both history and education from The Ohio State University. She currently lives in South Carolina, where she teaches both high school English and U.S. history through the University of South Carolina.

Index